Communications in Computer and Information Science 1396

More information about this series at http://www.springer.com/series/7899

Pradeep Kumar Singh · Gennady Veselov ·
Anton Pljonkin · Yugal Kumar ·
Marcin Paprzycki · Yuri Zachinyaev (Eds.)

Futuristic Trends in Network and Communication Technologies

Third International Conference, FTNCT 2020
Taganrog, Russia, October 14–16, 2020
Revised Selected Papers, Part II

Springer

Editors
Pradeep Kumar Singh ⓘ
ABES Engineering College
Ghaziabad, India

Anton Pljonkin ⓘ
Southern Federal University
Rostov-on-Don, Russia

Marcin Paprzycki ⓘ
Systems Research Institute
Warszawa, Poland

Gennady Veselov ⓘ
Southern Federal University
Rostov-on-Don, Russia

Yugal Kumar ⓘ
Jaypee Institute of Information Technology
Waknaghat, India

Yuri Zachinyaev ⓘ
Southern Federal University
Rostov-on-Don, Russia

ISSN 1865-0929   ISSN 1865-0937 (electronic)
Communications in Computer and Information Science
ISBN 978-981-16-1482-8   ISBN 978-981-16-1483-5 (eBook)
https://doi.org/10.1007/978-981-16-1483-5

This Springer imprint is published by the registered company Springer Nature Singapore Pte Ltd.
The registered company address is: 152 Beach Road, #21-01/04 Gateway East, Singapore 189721, Singapore

Preface

The Third International Conference on Futuristic Trends in Networks and Computing Technologies (FTNCT 2020) provided a single platform for researchers from different domains of Networks and Computing Technologies to showcase their research ideas. The four main technical tracks of the conference were: Network and Computing Technologies, Wireless Networks and Internet of Things (IoT), Futuristic Computing Technologies and Communication Technologies, and Security and Privacy. The conference was planned as an annual ongoing event. We are sure about its growth and quality year after year. The 3rd International Conference on Futuristic Trends in Networks and Computing Technologies (FTNCT 2020) was hosted by Southern Federal University, Russia, during October 14–16, 2020. The conference had several academic partners such as: Jaypee University of Information Technology, Waknaghat, India, University of Buenos Aires, Argentina, University of Cádiz, Spain, Manipal University Jaipur, India, University of Informatics Sciences, Cuba, Luleå University of Technology, Sweden, Institute of Control Sciences of Russian Academy of Sciences, Russia, University of Málaga, Spain, Technical University of Košice, Slovakia, University of Havana, Cuba, IAC Education, India, and SETIT, University of Sfax, Tunisia. These 12 organizations were the academic collaborators for FTNCT 2020.

We are highly thankful to our valuable authors for their contributions and to our Technical Program Committee for their immense support and motivation towards making the third version of FTNCT a grand success. We are also grateful to our keynote speakers: Dr. Valeriy Vyatkin, Aalto University, Helsinki, Finland; Dr. Sheng-Lung Peng, National Dong Hwa University, Taiwan; Dr. Arpan Kumar Kar, IIT Delhi, India; Dr. Sanjay Sood, Assoc. Director, C-DAC Mohali, India; Dr. Maheshkumar Kolekar, IIT Patna, India; Dr. Sergei Kulik, Lomonosov Moscow State University, Moscow, Russia; Dr. Sudeep Tanwar, Nirma University, India; Dr. Pradeep Kumar, University of KwaZulu-Natal, South Africa; Dr. Vivek Sehgal, Jaypee University of Information Technology, Waknaghat, Solan, HP, India; and Dr. Yugal Kumar from Jaypee University of Information Technology, Waknaghat, Solan, HP, India. We thank them for sharing their technical talks and enlightening the delegates of the conference.

The Conference Inauguration took place in the presence of the Rector, Southern Federal University, the Director of the Institute of Computer Technologies and Information Security, and the Head of the Department of Information Security of Telecommunication Systems from SFU, Russia, other guests, and media persons. We are thankful to Dr. Yuriy Zachinyaev for organizing the conference in such a nice way.

The organizing committee would like to express their special thanks to Prof. Konstantin Rumyantsev for his guidance and support from time to time.

We express our sincere gratitude to our publication partner, Springer CCIS Series, for believing in us. We are thankful to Ms. Kamiya Khatter, Associate Editor, and Mr. Amin Mobasheri, Editor, Springer CCIS Series, for extending their help from time to time in the preparation of these proceedings.

October 2020

Pradeep Kumar Singh
Gennady Veselov
Anton Pljonkin
Yugal Kumar
Marcin Paprzycki
Yuri Zachinyaev

Organization

Honorary Chairs

Gennady Veselov	Southern Federal University, Russia
Juan Manuel Dodero	University of Cádiz, Spain
Valeriy Vyatkin	Luleå University of Technology, Sweden
Sandeep Joshi	Manipal University Jaipur, India
Juan José Domínguez Jiménez	University of Cádiz, Spain
Hernán D. Merlino	University of Buenos Aires, Argentina
Bharat Bhargava	Purdue University, USA
Pao-Ann Hsiung	National Chung Cheng University, Taiwan
Wei-Chiang Hong	Oriental Institute of Technology, Taipei, Taiwan
Raúl Saroka	University of Buenos Aires, Argentina
Roman Meshcheryakov	Institute of Control Sciences of Russian Academy of Sciences, Russia
Miriam Nicado García	University of Havana, Cuba
Walter Baluja García	University of Informatics Sciences, Cuba
Iakov Korovin	Southern Federal University, Russia
Vladimir Kureychik	Southern Federal University, Russia
Konstantin Rumyantsev	Southern Federal University, Russia
Mikhail Karyakin	Southern Federal University, Russia
Evgeny Abramov	Southern Federal University, Russia
Ján Labun	Technical University of Košice, Slovakia
Pavol Kurdel	Technical University of Košice, Slovakia
José Francisco Chicano García	University of Málaga, Spain

Principal General Chairs

Yuriy Zachinyaev	Southern Federal University, Russia
Konstantin Rumyantsev	Southern Federal University, Russia

Executive General Chairs

Anton Pljonkin	Southern Federal University, Russia
Pradeep Kumar Singh	Jaypee University of Information Technology, India

Organizing Chairs

Alexey Samoilov   Southern Federal University, Russia
Abhijit Sen   Computer Science and Information Technology,
                            Kwantlen Polytechnic University, Canada
Maria Ganzha   Warsaw University of Technology, Poland
Marcin Paprzycki   Systems Research Institute, Polish Academy
                            of Sciences, Warsaw, Poland

Publication Chairs

Jitender Kumar Chhabra   Department of Computer Engineering,
                            NIT Kurukshetra, India
Narottam Chand Kaushal   NIT Hamirpur, India
Sanjay Sood   C-DAC Mohali, India

Publicity Chairs

Ioan-Cosmin Mihai   "Alexandru Ioan Cuza" Police Academy, Romania
Pelin Angin   Purdue University, USA
Sudeep Tanwar   Nirma University, India

Organizing Secretaries

Yugal Kumar   Jaypee University of Information Technology, India
Sudhanshu Tyagi   Thapar Institute of Engg. & Technology, Patiala, India

Academic Collaborators

University of Buenos Aires, Argentina

University of Cádiz, Spain

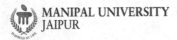

MANIPAL UNIVERSITY
JAIPUR

Manipal University Jaipur, India

University of Informatics Sciences, Cuba

Luleå University of Technology, Sweden

Institute of Control Sciences of Russian Academy of Sciences, Russia

UNIVERSIDAD DE MÁLAGA

University of Málaga, Spain

TECHNICKÁ
UNIVERZITA
V KOŠICIACH

Technical University of Košice, Slovakia

University of Havana, Cuba

JUIT, Waknaghat, India   SETIT, Tunisia

Organized By

Southern Federal University, Russia

Other Supporters of FTNCT 2020: Conference Alerts as technical promoters, IAC Education, India, Easy Chair, and many more.

Contents – Part II

Contents – Part I

Futuristic Computing Technologies

Network and Computing Technologies

Development Quantum Algorithms, Systems and Prevention or Elimination Quantum Types of Errors

Sergey Gushanskiy, Alexander Gorbunov, and Viktor Potapov$^{(\boxtimes)}$

Department of Computer Engineering, Southern Federal University, Taganrog, Russia
{smgushanskiy,avgorbunov,vpotapov}@sfedu.ru

Abstract. The article proposes the structure of operators of quantum algorithms, its mathematical and schematic representation. The procedure for developing a quantum computing system or algorithm involves the presence of interference, quantum entanglement, and superposition. In a classical computer, the amount of data is measured in bits, and in a quantum computer, in qubits. A qubit is a quantum discharge or the smallest element for storing information in a quantum computer, as well as a quantum object that can be in a superposition of two states, that is, encode both a logical unit and zero at the same time. The general structure of the universal quantum algorithm is implemented as diagrams that reveal the basic elements, their properties, functions and place in the work of the quantum algorithm. The input value for the quantum algorithm is a binary function. A detailed decomposition of each block of the schematic diagram for the description of sequential processes and stages of quantum algorithms has been performed. A quantum block that runs n times is necessary for the sequential use of quantum operators and the subsequent measurement of the result of the entire computing process. Due to the probabilistic nature of quantum computing, the obtained basis vectors will contain some of the information necessary to solve a particular computational problem. Classical and quantum types of errors and methods for their elimination are described and developed. The main obstacles to protecting the channel from noise are the inability to copy data and information, the continuity of error and the destruction of quantum information during measurement (according to the principles of quantum computing, measuring a set of qubits without destroying the information encoded there is impossible). The bit and phase types of errors were corrected by modeling quantum circuits, three-qubit coding, and a set of quantum gates.

Keywords: Qubit · Entanglement · Quantum scheme · Wave function · Quantum gate

1 Introduction

Currently, the world is actively working on the study and physical implementation of the quantum computer. Prototypes of computing devices have already been built in different parts of the world at different times, but not yet created a full-fledged quantum

© Springer Nature Singapore Pte Ltd. 2021
P. K. Singh et al. (Eds.): FTNCT 2020, CCIS 1396, pp. 3–13, 2021.
https://doi.org/10.1007/978-981-16-1483-5_1

computer makes sense to perform simulation calculations on a computer with a classical architecture in order to study and further build a quantum computer. The field of quantum algorithms is constantly updated and supplemented. However, for a long time there were no quantum programming languages for practical purposes and tasks. The result of the quantum algorithm [1] is probabilistic in nature. Due to a small increase in the number of operations in the algorithm and maximizing the entanglement of qubits, one can arbitrarily bring the probability of getting the correct result to unity. Today, there are modern quantum technologies that are capable of supporting fundamentally new computational algorithms (quantum algorithms) based on the principles of quantum mechanics. Practical development of quantum algorithms for solving not only classical, but also quantum problems is one of the main areas of activity of quantum computing.

The logic and mathematical apparatus of quantum computing devices differs significantly from the logic and mathematics of classical computing technology due to the nature and specific properties of quantum particles (qubits), which allow such calculations to be carried out.

The quantum computer operates, as described above, with quantum bits, which have two basic states $|0\rangle$ and $|1\rangle$. Qubit state $|0\rangle$ corresponds to the state of the electron spin in the atom "spin up", the state "spin down" corresponds to $|1\rangle$, and the mixed state (superposition of states) corresponds to the intermediate position of the spin. Spin is the proper angular momentum of elementary particles, but the spin is not associated with motion in space, it is the eigenvalue of a quantum particle, which cannot be explained from the standpoint of classical mechanics.

In the general case, the state of a qubit is described by a wave function (or a state vector) $|\psi\rangle = \alpha0 * |0\rangle + \alpha1 * |1\rangle$, where $\alpha0, \alpha1 \in C$, $\alpha0$ and $\alpha1$ are the complex amplitudes of the reading probability $|0\rangle$ or $|1\rangle$. In this case, the qubit will go into a state of quantum zero or one. The effect of a quantum mixed state exists only until the moment the qubit is measured, that is, when reading, we bring the qubit into one of the basic states, and which one depends on the probability obtained in the calculations.

2   The Structure of Operators of Quantum Algorithms

The design process of a quantum algorithm consists of the matrix form of representation of three operators [2]: superposition (S), quantum entanglement [3] (entangled states) (U) and interference (Int). In general, the structure of a quantum algorithm, as the basis of quantum computing, can be represented as:

$$C = [(Int \otimes^n Id) * U_F]^{h+1} * [^nH \otimes^m S], \tag{1}$$

where Id is the identical operator; symbol $\otimes$ – tensor product; S is the superposition operator, H is the Hadamard operator [4].

Operations on qubits can be mapped using a quantum schema. A quantum scheme is a sequence of physical transformations from a finite set of basic elementary transformations – gates [11]. Quantum bits are fed to the input of a quantum circuit, and its probabilistic result is obtained at the output. Due to the fact that when measuring quantum bits, they go to the state "0" or "1", then to obtain an accurate result, you can use the quantum circuit several times for the same input data.

Physically, it is possible to implement only those operations that keep the sum of the squares of the coefficient's constant over a small group of qubits. As already described above, the process of measuring the values of qubits destroys all probabilities and converts the qubits to the base states of zero and one, that is, upon completion of the algorithm, the programmer receives the classical answer, but the values of the probabilities of the states of the system or the probability of states of qubits in the process of calculations on a quantum computer are not available to the programmer.

Since in the process of modeling all transformations are performed on the probabilities of states, then, consequently, their receipt is not difficult; to obtain the probability of a qubit state, some transformations must be performed. So, in order to obtain the probability with which a particular qubit when reading will go to the zero state, it is necessary to sum the probabilities of those states in which the given qubit is at zero.

The state of one qubit of a quantum computer is a normalized vector of the complex space of two-dimensional size C^2, where the basis vectors of this space are denoted by the corresponding cat vectors |0> and |1>. The state is not static, since at each moment of time it changes under the influence of some unitary transformation.

These transformations usually affect a small number of qubits. Unitary transformations are:

$$S = U \otimes I, \tag{2}$$

where U is the matrix acting on a certain number of qubits or one, and I is the identity matrix acting on the remaining qubits.

Another visual option for representing the qubit state vector is the so-called Bloch sphere (Fig. 1). It is a mapping of the complex plane of psi-function values onto a sphere, in fact, on it you can visually see "spin up", "spin down". However, this is the space of values of the qubit state, while the spin pseudovector itself cannot be negative.

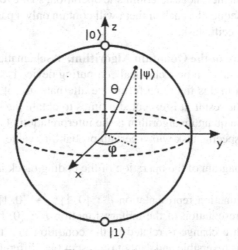

Fig. 1. Bloch's sphere

The structure of quantum algorithms operators equivalent to the expression (1) is shown in Fig. 2. The binary function f is always applied to the input of the quantum algorithm. This function is represented as a mapping that defines the image of each input binary string. First, the function f is encoded as a unitary matrix operator U depending on its properties. The resulting matrix operator U is included in the structure of a quantum cell, a unitary matrix, whose structure depends on the matrix U and on the task that the algorithm has to solve.

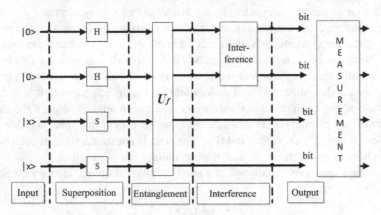

Fig. 2. The structure of operators of quantum algorithms

The superposition contains all the information needed to solve a specific task/problem. As a result of creating a superposition, a measurement operation is performed to extract information. Sequential use of a quantum operator and measurement of the result characterizes a quantum block. It is executed k times to derive a set of basis vectors. This measurement is not a deterministic operation, so the resulting basis vectors will be different. Consequently, each of them will contain only a part of the information necessary to solve a specific task.

The General Structure of the Quantum Algorithm. Aschematic diagram of the quantum algorithm simulation on a classical computing device is shown in Fig. 3. The quantum block shown in this figure performs the alternate use of a quantum operator and measurement of the result. It is executed n times to obtain the set of basis vectors.

The final phase of a quantum algorithm is the interpretation of a basis vectors set to obtain a solution to a specific task with a certain probability value.

Coding block. The diagram of the operation of the coding block is shown in Fig. 4.

1. The table of the function representation $f : \{0, 1\}^n \rightarrow \{0, 1\}^m$ is converted into a table of the representation of the unitary function $F : \{0, 1\}^{n+m} \rightarrow \{0, 1\}^{n+m}$. The need for such a change is related to the condition that the operator F(U) is unitary. Operator is reversible and cannot represent two different inputs to the same output values. Since this operator is the matrix mapping of the F function, it must be invertible. The reversibility is done by increasing the number of bits and describing the F instead of f function.

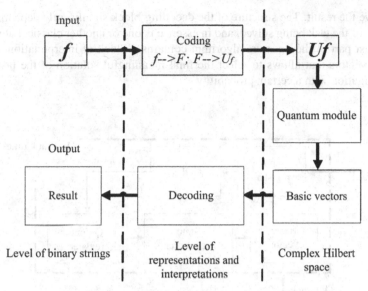

Fig. 3. Schematic diagram of a quantum algorithm

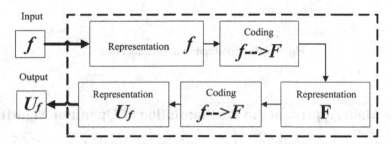

Fig. 4. Decomposition of the coding block

2. The representation of the function F is converted into a representation U. The coding table $\tau : \{0, 1\}^{n+m} \rightarrow C^{2n+m}$, where C^{2n+m} is a resulting Hilbert space.

3. The representation U is converted to a matrix operator U by the following rule:
   This rule is easy to understand if we consider i and j as the columns of a vector. Distributing these columns over the canonical basis, F determines the permutation of the rows of the identity matrix. In general, the row j is mapping to a row i. The main element of a quantum block is a quantum cell. Its form depends on the properties of the matrix operator U [5]. The matrix operator F(U) is the output of the coding block, and in this structure, it is the input of the quantum block. The unitary matrix is applied k times to the initial canonical vector of dimension mn + 2. The resulting complex linear combination of basis vectors i is measured and is produced one basis vector ix as a result. All measured base vectors are collected together. The resulting set is the output of a quantum block (Fig. 5). The decoding unit includes the interpretation of a set of basis vectors. Decoding basic vectors is to convert them into binary strings. Further, they are used as coefficients of some equation or to

retrieve the result. The structure of the decoding block significantly depends on the nature of the task being solved, and in essence is one or another classical algorithm. The last part of the quantum algorithm contains a block of interpretation, a set of basic vectors that allows to select the final meaningful solution of the task under investigation with a certain probability.

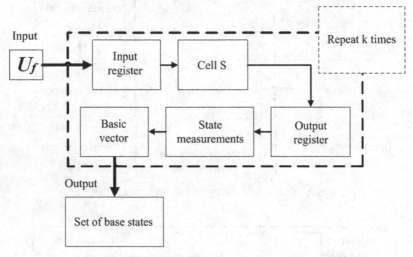

Fig. 5. Decomposition of a quantum block

3   The Main Approaches to the Simulation of Quantum Algorithms

The complexity of a quantum algorithm simulation on a classical computing device is that the core of a quantum algorithm is a set of quantum cells and unitary operators. A quantum cell is a unitary matrix with a special structure. The following approaches are known to effectively simulate quantum algorithms [6]: matrix approach; algorithmic approach, when matrix elements are calculated "on demand"; problem-oriented approach; an approach using simplified quantum operators.

The first approach (matrix) is based on the mapping of matrix operators of quantum nature. This approach is more stable and accurate, but requires a lot of computer memory for locating matrix operators. The second approach eliminate the significant disadvantage of the first approach and does not require a computer memory for quantum operators.

The approach calculates each component when it is required. This approach allows to use a slightly larger input data. But it has own drawbacks. First, since the number of necessary elements and operations increases with an increase in the number of qubits exponentially, which in turn leads to an increase in computation time. Not to mention the constant allocation of memory for the state vector. Secondly, it requires additional study of the structure of operators. The third approach is problem-oriented. The approach is based on a deep study of the structure of a specific quantum algorithm, the nature of the behavior of the state vector. For example, it is characteristic of Grover's algorithm that the state vector has only two different values (corresponding to different amplitudes of probabilities).

The fourth approach is applicable only to certain quantum algorithms that allow one to obtain a solution to the original problem using its reduced version, in which one or two basic quantum operators are missing. Each of the approaches discussed above takes place, but the applicability of most of them is based more on a specific algorithm and its features, and, therefore, does not claim to be universal. A set of qubits for the state of normalization control signals at a particular point in time.

4 Development of Approaches to the Prevention and Elimination of Quantum Errors

Classical and quantum types of errors and methods of their elimination. Suppose it is necessary to transmit a bit of information using a classical communication channel with the presence of noise. The probability of a bit changing in such a channel is $p > 0$, with a probability of a bit transmission without error is $1-p$. Such a channel is called a symmetric binary channel [7], its scheme is shown in Fig. 6.

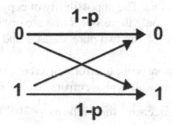

Fig. 6. Symmetric binary channel

The error of a classical nature can be corrected using three-qubit coding $0 \rightarrow (000)$, $1 \rightarrow (111)$. Let p be the error probability in one of the qubits. In other words, noise. This parameter is defined as a coefficient for operators in the Kraus decomposition [8]. If an error occurs, for example, in the first qubit, we get the new states $(000) \rightarrow (100)$ and $(111) \rightarrow (011)$. You can fix this error with decoding. This procedure is to find the final value by selecting the majority. But we should not exclude the possibility of errors in two or more qubits at the same time.

In these cases, the choice of the majority becomes unsuitable. Since the probability of an error in one qubit is p, the probability of an error in two qubits is $3p^2(1 - p)$. The dependence $\Phi(p)$ is shown in Fig. 7, where the red dotted line represents the channel without an error correction procedure, and the blue one - with a correction. The main difference between the concept of distortion and the concept of noise is on the scale of errors. Noisiness describes errors in a particular qubit, and information distortion describes errors in the entire quantum system.

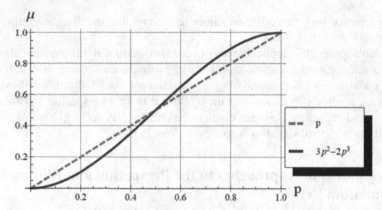

Fig. 7. The dependence of data distortion from noise

Obstacles to channel noise protection. Consider the main difficulties in securing a quantum channel:

1. Inability to copy information. It is impossible to clone/duplicate a quantum bit by analogy with the classical one. The impossibility of copying theorem [9] states that a copying device can copy only those states that are orthogonal to each other. This follows from the fact that for any two pure states ϕ and χ, the unitary operator U and the initial state |i>.
2. Quantum information is more prone to errors. Invert errors can be added to the list of errors, considered earlier, as well as phase errors: $|0> \rightarrow |0>$, $|1> \rightarrow -|1>$. A phase error entails serious consequences, since it turns $\frac{1}{\sqrt{2}}*(|0>+|1>)$ into an orthogonal state $\frac{1}{\sqrt{2}}*(|0>-|1>)$.
3. Continuity error. The set of possible errors of one qubit is continuous. Determining which error occurred will require infinite accuracy and, therefore, infinite resources.
4. The destruction of quantum information in the measurement. According to the method of counting the majority of votes to detect and correct errors, it is necessary to measure the bits in the code. However, qubits cannot be measured without destroying the information encoded there.

Implementation of Error Correction Schemes. Correction of bit errors. In the scheme implemented below, an error check and its correction are performed on the first qubit. In the proposed scheme, the correction will occur not in the CNOT basis, but in the original one. Consider the influence of the environment at the exit from the CNOT gate basis: when inverting the first qubit, all qubits are inverted, and when inverting each of the other two qubits, only they are inverted. To fix the first qubit it is necessary to invert it only in the case when both others are |1). This adjustment is performed by the circuit shown in Fig. 8.

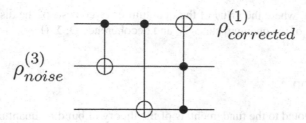

Fig. 8. The scheme of correction/correction of bit errors

Simulation of this scheme and the proposed assessment of the quality of the algorithm give the results are shown in Fig. 9. Twenty random states were taken from the Bloch sphere [10] and fifty points on the noisiness axis.

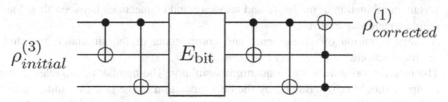

Fig. 9. The scheme of the classic error correction

The graph of the dependence of the decoherence on noise in one qubit corresponds to Fig. 7, where the dependence $\Phi(p)$ is displayed.

Phase Error Correction. There is no classical analogue of the phase error; however, it is possible to transform the phase error into the classical one. Consider a basis $.|+> = \frac{1}{\sqrt{2}}(|0> +|1>).$, $|+> = \frac{1}{\sqrt{2}}(|0> -|1>)$. The operator acts similarly in the basis $|0>, |1>$. Using this fact, it is possible to correct or correct this type of error using three-qubit encoding: $|0> \rightarrow |+++>$, $|1> \rightarrow |--->$. Using the correction circuit, it is easy to draw up a scheme for correcting the phase error (Fig. 10).

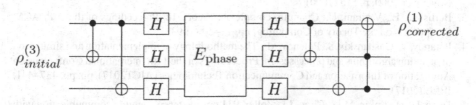

Fig. 10. The dependence of data distortion from noise

The dependence of the decoherence measure on noise in a single qubit in the case of a phase error will coincide with the case of a classical error. In accordance with the above analysis, we obtain the dependence of the error E on the measure and the purity of entanglement, where the value of the quantum error consists of the distortion of the data I, the noise of the quantum states Z, and decoherence D: Σ $(I + Z + D) = E$.

5 Conclusion

The work is devoted to the fundamentals of the theory of building quantum computers. The developed open architecture of the quantum computer model is described. A set of requirements has been developed for constructing quantum simulators based on the following principles and components.

1. The principle of open architecture of the simulator, which allowed to develop and modernize the simulator in the most economical way. Only the description of the principle of operation of the model of the quantum computer and its configuration (a certain combination of hardware and software and connections between them) are regulated and standardized.
2. A clear definition of all elements and components of the simulator and their interconnections.
3. The modular organization of a quantum simulator. The number of modules in the complex should be determined by the decomposition of the task into independent sub-tasks.

Acknowledgments. The reported study was funded by RFBR according to the research project № 20-07-00368.

References

1. Nielsen, M., Chuang, I.: Quantum Computation and Quantum Information. Cambridge University Press, Cambridge (2000). OCLC 174527496. ISBN 978-0-521-63503-5
2. Hales, L., Hallgren, S.: An improved quantum Fourier transform algorithm and applications. In: Proceedings of the 41st Annual Symposium on Foundations of Computer Science, 12–14 November 2000, p. 515 (2000)
3. Bernstein, E., Vazirani, U.: Quantum complexity theory. In: Proceedings of the 25th ACM Symposium on the Theory of Computing, pp. 11–20 (1993)
4. Potapov, V., Gushanskiy, S., Polenov, M.: The methodology of implementation and simulation of quantum algorithms and processes. In: Proceedings of the 11th International Conference on Application of Information and Communication Technologies (AICT2017), pp. pp. 437–441. IEEE (2017)
5. Duan, L.-M., Lukin, M.D., Cirac, J.I., Zoller, P.: Long-distance quantum communication with atomic ensembles and linear optics. Nature **414**, 413–418 (2001)
6. Maurer, P.C., et al.: Room-temperature quantum bit memory exceeding one second. Science **336**, 1283–1286 (2012)
7. Boneh, D., Lipton, R.J.: Quantum cryptanalysis of hidden linear functions. In: Coppersmith, D. (ed.) CRYPTO 1995. LNCS, vol. 963, pp. 424–437. Springer, Heidelberg (1995). https://doi.org/10.1007/3-540-44750-4_34

8. Rieffel, E., Polak, W.: An introduction to quantum computing nonphysicists. ACM Comput. Surv. **32**(3), 300–335 (2000)
9. Werner, R.F.: Quantum states with Einstein – Podolsky – Rosen correlations admitting a hidden-variable model. Phys. Rev. A. **40**, 4277 (1989)
10. Eckert, A., Jozsa, R.: Quantum computation and Shor's factoring algorithm. Rev. Mod. Phys. **68**(3), 733–753 (1996)

Representing a Quantum Fourier Transform, Based on a Discrete Model of a Quantum-Mechanical System

Sergei Shalagin[✉] [iD]

Computer Systems Department, Kazan National Research Technical University named after A.N. Tupolev – KAI, Karl Marks Street, 10., Kazan 420111, Russia

Abstract. This paper presents a discrete model of the quantum fast Fourier transform (QFFT) defined over a quantum mechanical system that includes N basis states (QMS(N)). In this case, the QMS(N) is defined based on a known discrete model described using 2(N − 1) parameters, of which (N − 1) parameter describes the amplitude components of the basic states of the QMS(N), and (N − 1) parameter describes the phase components. QFFT is modelled discretely by specifying the same type of operations, which are described as the known quantum gates: A single-qubit Hadamard gate and a two-qubit gate with a controlled phase. Each of these valves affects the specified parameters of the QMS(N) N/2 times. This representation allows you to display the impact of the QFFT on the QMS(N) by varying only N of 2(N − 1) of its parameters. In addition, simulation of the effects of N/2 Hadamard gates and N/2 controlled-phase gates on the specified parameters of the discrete QMS(N) model can be performed in parallel. This circumstance allows us to perform distributed modeling of the impact of QFFT on the QMS(N) when using multiprocessor computing systems, both existing and prospective, both specialized and general-purpose.

Keywords: Quantum Fourier transform · Discrete model · Representation

1 Introduction

Quantum processing research is a relevant and promising scientific area [1–8]. At the same time, there are physical barriers related to implementing quantum-mechanical systems (QMS) that include multiple basis states [4, 7]. In this context, not without interest are problems related to the mathematical modelling of QMS [6, 9–12].

When solving problems related to cryptoanalysis, of interest is the problem of factorization, i.e., factorizing an integer, for solving which the fast quantum Fourier transform algorithm is a promising method [3, 4]. Due to the quantum register being in the superposition state, there is a significant gain in the execution rate of quantum algorithms, as compared to classical ones [6]. These regularities are also true for the fast Fourier transform algorithm. This circumstance actualizes research aimed at implementing fast quantum Fourier transform. Along with that, IBM, Inc. Have currently implemented a quantum computer, in which the number of interrelated quantum bits does not exceed

© Springer Nature Singapore Pte Ltd. 2021
P. K. Singh et al. (Eds.): FTNCT 2020, CCIS 1396, pp. 14–22, 2021.
https://doi.org/10.1007/978-981-16-1483-5_2

50. Further increase in the number of qubits is technically an extremely complicated task. For the quantum algorithm of fast Fourier transform, which solves problems useful in practical cryptoanalysis, at least 1,000 interrelated qubits are required. A way out could be the computer-based modelling of QMS using models and algorithms that allow distributed computation. For instance, work [13] proposes a discrete model (DM) of QMS, which includes N basis states and which we denote as QMS(N). State of the QMS(N) can be represented based on $2(N-1)$ parameters, while changing its state can be represented based on concurrently executed multiplication operations over the elements of Galois field [14]. Work [15] shows that the DM of QMS(N) can be represented based on a system of the non-linear polynomial functions of one type [16–20], executed on distributed computer systems with programmable architecture (DCS PA) [21], the elements of which are field-programmable gate arrays (FPGA) [22].

This paper proposes representing quantum Fourier transform (QFT) [23], based on defining a quantum algorithm within the DM of a QMS(N), where $N = 2^n$, which algorithm includes the known quantum gates: Single-qubit Hadamard gate and a controlled phase two-qubit gate. The said representation allows displaying how QFT affects the QMS(N), the state of which is defined by $2(N-1)$ elements of a given DM, using the distributed variation of the elements of a given DM QMS(N) at the given value of $N = 2^n$.

2 Discrete Model of a Quantum-Mechanical System with N Basis States

A general QMS(N) is described by the finite dimensional Hilbert (unitary) space, H, $|H| = N < \infty$ [1, 2]. State of the QMS(N) with basis states $|j\rangle, j = \overline{0, N-1}$, is defined as a column-vector (ket vector) [2, 3].

$$|\psi\rangle = \left(r_0 e^{i\varphi_0} \quad \ldots \quad r_{N-1} e^{i\varphi_{N-1}} \right)^T, \tag{1}$$

where $\sum_{j=0}^{N-1} r_j^2 = 1$. A system with a finite number of basis states (levels, H dimensions) is interesting in terms of quantum processing. Changes in the states of a QMS represented as (1) are defined by a quantum gate (QG), i.e., an $N \times N$ matrix G [4].

DM QMS(N) is defined when using a graph model, i.e., binary tree T [13] (Fig. 1). Number of its points, i.e., its leaves, equals to that of the basis states of QMS(N), while that of its branch nodes, $(N-1)$, defines the number of parameters defining amplitude- and phase-based components of this model, $2(N-1)$ [15]. For binary tree T shown in Fig. 1, let us define the following properties of [15]:

$1°$ top points of T, which are its leaves, have the level of at least $h-1$, the $(h-1)$-level top points either being leaves or containing both a right and a left son;

$2°$ top points of T, which are not the leaves, are numbered as follows: Zero-level top point is defined as v_0, first-level top points – as v_1, v_2, etc., k-level top points – as v_d, ..., v_{2d}, where $d = 2^k - 1$, $k = \overline{0, h-2}$, while the $(h-1)$-level top points are numbered from v_D through v_{N-2}, $D = 2^{h-1} - 1$.

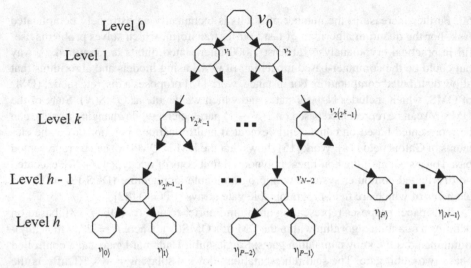

Fig. 1. Binary tree T that describes QMS(N).

Varying the states of DM QMS(N), described by system (1), is defined by a quantum gate, a unitary $N \times N$ matrix represented as $G = G_\varphi G_A$, where $N \times N$ matrices G_φ and G_A determine the variation of the phase- and amplitude-based components of DM QMS(N), respectively. Two theorems are formulated in [13, 15].

Theorem 1. A quantum-mechanical system having N basis states and defined in accordance with (1) can be represented as a vector including $2(N-1)$ parameters.

$$(\theta_0, \ldots, \theta_{N-2}, t_0, \ldots, t_{N-2}), \tag{2}$$

where $(\theta, \ldots, \theta_{N-2})$ define the amplitude-based elements of vector (1), while $(t_0, \ldots, t_{N-2})$ define the phase-based components of (1).

Theorem 2. Operation aimed at varying the state of a quantum-mechanical system having N basis states and defined based on (1) is represented by a vector including $2(N-1)$ parameters,

$$(\Delta\theta_0, \ldots, \Delta\theta_{N-2}, \Delta t_0, \ldots \Delta t_{N-2}), \tag{3}$$

which unambiguously defines quantum gate $G = G_\varphi G_A$, where G_φ and G_A have the dimension of $N \times N$. G_φ is defined by parameters $(\Delta t_0, \ldots \Delta t_{N-2})$ and describes the variation of phase-based components, while G_A is defined by parameters $(\Delta\theta_0, \ldots, \Delta\theta_{N-2})$ and describes the changes in the amplitude-based components of vector (1) elements.

Let us define a quantum gate describing the variations of the phase terms of vector (2) elements, using formula (3) [13]:

$$G_\varphi = \|\exp\{i(\Delta t_0(j \bmod 2) + \Delta P)\}\|_j I_{N \times N}, \tag{4}$$

where $j = \overline{0,\ N-1}$, $I_{N\times N}$, is the unity matrix sized $N \times N$, $\Delta P = \Delta \tilde{t} + \sum\limits_{l=1}^{h-1-c} \Delta t_{f(l,j)}$,

$f(l,j) = 2^l - 1 + \left[j2^{l-h}\right]$, $c = \begin{cases} 0 : j < |N_h| \\ 1 : j \geq |N_h| \end{cases}$, $N_h = 2N - 2^h$, and $h = \,]\log_2 N\,[$ is

the height of T. Thus, the variation of the QMS(N) phase term is only defined by the $(\Delta t_0,\ \dots,\ \Delta t_{N-2})$ parameters of vector (3).

Note 1. $\Delta \tilde{t}$ takes any value within the range of $[0,\ 360°)$.

For the QMS(N) states, St_1 and St_2, defined according to (1), the relevant ket vectors, $|\psi\rangle$ and $|\psi'\rangle$, can be obtained. Then the truth of expression $|\psi'\rangle = G_\varphi|\psi\rangle$ is immediate from formula (4) [13].

Varying the amplitude component of vector (2) is described as follows. Let us consider parameters $(\Delta\theta_0,\ \dots,\ \Delta\theta_{N-2})$. For each of these parameters, quantum gates are defined based on T as follows [13].

$$G_0 = G(\Delta\theta_0) = \begin{pmatrix} \cos \Delta\theta_0 I_{m\times m} & -\sin \Delta\theta_0 C_{m\times n} \\ \sin \Delta\theta_0 D_{n\times m} & \cos \Delta\theta_0 I_{n\times n} \end{pmatrix}_{N\times N}, \tag{5}$$

where $m = \left|L(\alpha_j) \in Left(v_0)\right|$, $n = \left|L(\alpha_j) \in Right(v_0)\right|$ is the number of T leaves belonging to the sets of the right and left children of v_0, $I_{m\times m}$ and $I_{n\times n}$ are unity matrices, $D_{n\times m} = \frac{\cos\theta_0}{m\sin\theta_0}\left(r_m \dots r_{N-1}\right)^T\left((r_0)^{-1} \dots (r_{m-1})^{-1}\right)$.

Let us put parameters θ_1 and θ_2 into correspondence with the first-level top points of B. Then $G_1 = \begin{pmatrix} G(\Delta\theta_1)_{m\times m} & \varnothing_{m\times n} \\ \varnothing_{n\times m} & G(\Delta\theta_2)_{n\times n} \end{pmatrix}_{N\times N}$, where submatrices $G(\Delta\theta_1)_{m\times m}$ and $G(\Delta\theta_2)_{n\times n}$ are defined similarly as G_0, according to (5).

In general case, for $q = \overline{0,\ h-1}$

$$G_q = \begin{pmatrix} G(\Delta\theta_d)_{m_d \times m_d} & \cdots & \varnothing_{m_d \times m_f} \\ \cdots & & \cdots \\ \varnothing_{m_f \times m_d} & \cdots & G(\Delta\theta_f)_{m_f \times m_f} \end{pmatrix}_{N\times N}, \tag{6}$$

где $d = 2^k - 1, f = 2(2^k - 1)$, $m_d = \left|L(\alpha_j) \in Left(v_x)\right|$, $m_{d+1} = \left|L(\alpha_j) \in Right(v_x)\right|$, $\dots$, $m_{d+2a} = \left|L(\alpha_j) \in Left(v_{x+a})\right|$, $m_{d+2a+1} = \left|L(\alpha_j) \in Right(v_{x+a})\right|$, $\dots$, $m_f = \left|L(\alpha_j) \in Right(v_{d-1})\right|$, $x = 2^{k-1} - 1$, $a = 0,\ 1,\ 2,\ \dots$ [13].

Note 2 [13]. For $q = h - 1$, value $G(\Delta\theta_w) = 1$, where $w = \overline{N-1,\ 2^h - 2}$.

Thus, according to (5)–(6), varying the amplitude components of vector (2) is defined by the quantum gate sized $N \times N$, represented as [13].

$$G_A = \prod_{q=0}^{h-1} G_q. \tag{7}$$

If states St_1 and St_2 are defined by ket vectors $|\psi\rangle$ and $|\psi'\rangle$, respectively, based on (1) and (2), then the truth of expression $|\psi'\rangle = G_A|\psi'\rangle$ is immediate from formulas (6) and (7) for each of parameters $(\Delta\theta_0,\ \dots,\ \Delta\theta_{N-2})$.

As a result, varying the QMS(N) state described by the elements of vector (3) is defined by the quantum gate represented as [13]

$$G = G_\varphi G_A. \tag{8}$$

At the same time, G_φ was obtained according to (4) and describes the variation of the QMS(N) state defined by parameters $(\Delta\theta_0, \ldots, \Delta\theta_{N-2})$, while G_A was obtained based on (7) and defines the change described by parameters $(\Delta t_0, \ldots, \Delta t_{N-2})$ of vector (8).

Example 1. For a QMS(4) defined according to (2), $(\theta_0, \ldots, \theta_2, t_0, \ldots, t_2)$, elements of ket vector represented as (1) can be represented, according to [13], by formulas $r_0 = \cos(\theta_0)\cos(\theta_1)$, $r_1 = \cos(\theta_0)\sin(\theta_1)$, $r_2 = \sin(\theta_0)\cos(\theta_2)$, $r_3 = \sin(\theta_0)\sin(\theta_2)$, $\varphi_0 = \tilde{t}$, $\varphi_1 = \tilde{t} + t_1$, $\varphi_2 = \tilde{t} + t_0$, and $\varphi_3 = \tilde{t} + t_0 + t_2$.

Example 2. For QMS(4) defined as $(\theta_0, \ldots, \theta_2, t_0, \ldots, t_2,)$ according to (2), quantum gate G that performs the variation of the specified parameters by the values of $(\Delta\theta_0, \ldots, \Delta\theta_2, \Delta t_0, \ldots, \Delta t_2,)$, according to Theorem 2 is represented as:

$$G = G_\varphi G_A,$$

where

$G_\varphi = \big(\exp(i\Delta\tilde{t})\exp(i(\Delta\tilde{t} + \Delta t_1))\exp(i(\Delta\tilde{t} + \Delta t_0))\exp(i(\Delta\tilde{t} + \Delta t_0 + \Delta t_2))\big)I_{4\times4}$,

$G_A = G_0 G_1$, $G_0 = G(\Delta\theta_0) = \begin{pmatrix} \cos\Delta\theta_0 I_{2\times2} & -\sin\Delta\theta_0 C_{2\times2} \\ \sin\Delta\theta_0 D_{2\times2} & \cos\Delta\theta_0 I_{2\times2} \end{pmatrix}_{N\times N}$, $C_{2\times2} =$

$\frac{\sin\theta_0}{2\cos\theta_0}(r_0\ r_1)^T\big((r_2)^{-1}\ (r_3)^{-1}\big)$, $D_{2\times2} = \frac{\cos\theta_0}{2\sin\theta_0}(r_2\ r_3)^T\big((r_0)^{-1}\ (r_1)^{-1}\big)$, $r_0 = \cos(\theta_0)\cos(\theta_1)$, $r_1 = \cos(\theta_0)\sin(\theta_1)$, $r_2 = \sin(\theta_0)\cos(\theta_2)$, $r_3 = \sin(\theta_0)\sin(\theta_2)$,

$$G_1 = \begin{pmatrix} \cos\Delta\theta_1 & -\sin\Delta\theta_1 & 0 & 0 \\ \sin\Delta\theta_1 & \cos\Delta\theta_1 & 0 & 0 \\ 0 & 0 & \cos\Delta\theta_2 & -\sin\Delta\theta_2 \\ 0 & 0 & \sin\Delta\theta_2 & \cos\Delta\theta_2 \end{pmatrix}_{4\times4}.$$

It is shown that, based on Theorem 1, the one-to-one interrelation is established between different representations of the state of a quantum-mechanical system with N basis states: As ket vector (1) and as a vector represented as (2), respectively. Theorem 2 establishes a one-to-one interrelation between the quantum gate represented as G and the vector represented as (3).

3   Quantum Gate Modelling Based on the Discrete Model of a Quantum-Mechanical System

QFT is based on two operations of one type, defined by Hadamard operator over one qubit (or two basis states of QMS(N)) and by a controlled-phase gate (CPG) over two qubits (or four basis states of QMS(N)), $N = 2^n$. Let us consider the representation of the above operations over the DM QMS(N) represented as (1).

Hadamard operator affecting two basis states of QMS(N), $|2j\rangle$ and $|2j + 1\rangle$, can be represented as: $A_j = \frac{1}{\sqrt{2}}\begin{pmatrix} 1 & 1 \\ 1 & -1 \end{pmatrix}$, $j = \overline{0, N/2 - 1}$. Let us consider parameters θ_{j+b} and

$\Delta\theta_{j+b}, j = \overline{0, N/2 - 1}, b = N/2 - 1$, of vectors represented as (2) and (3), respectively. For the model presented, there is

Statement 1. Effect provided by Hadamard operator A_j upon the basis states of QMS(N), $N = 2^n$, $|2j\rangle$, $|2j + 1\rangle$ is described by element $\Delta\theta_{j+b}$ of vector (3) computed based on element θ_{j+b} of vector (2)

$$\Delta\theta_{j+b} = \pi/4 - \theta_{j+b} \tag{4}$$

where $j = \overline{0, N/2 - 1}$, $b = N/2 - 1$, and by element Δt_{j+b} of vector (3) $\Delta t_{j+b} = \pi$.

CPG affecting on four basis states of QMS(N) – $|2j\rangle$, $|2j + 1\rangle$, $|2k\rangle$, and $|2k + 1\rangle$,

$(N/2 - 1) \geq k > j \geq 0$, can be represented as matrix: $S_{j,k} = \begin{pmatrix} 1 & 0 & 0 & 0 \\ 0 & 1 & 0 & 0 \\ 0 & 0 & 1 & 0 \\ 0 & 0 & 0 & D \end{pmatrix}$, $D = \exp(i \cdot 2^{-(k-j)}\pi)$, $0 \leq j < k \leq (N/2 - 1)$. Let us consider elements t_{j+b}, t_{k+b}, Δt_{j+b}, $\Delta t_{k+b}, j < k, j, k = \overline{0, N/2 - 1}, b = N/2 - 1$, of vectors represented as (2) and (3), respectively. True is

Statement 2. Applying the controlled-phase gate, $S_{j,k}$, to the basis states of QMS(N), $N = 2^n$, $|2j\rangle$, $|2j + 1\rangle$, $|2k\rangle$, and $|2k + 1\rangle$, is described by element $\Delta t_{k+b} = 2^{-(k-j)}\pi$ of vector (3) on element t_{k+b} of vector (2), $b = N/2 - 1$, $k = \overline{j+1, N/2 - 1}$ at pre-defined $j = \overline{0, N/2 - 2}$.

Implementing a QFT over QMS(N), $N = 2^n$, suggests executing a quantum algorithm as a certain sequence of effects provided on its pre-defined basis states defined by quantum gates represented as A_j and $S_{j,k}$, $k = \overline{j+1, N/2 - 1}$, $j = \overline{0, N/2 - 2}$. This sequence is represented as [22]: $A_{N/2-1}$, $S_{N/2-2,\,N/2-1}$, $A_{N/2-2}$, $S_{N/2-3,\,N/2-1}$, $S_{N/2-3,\,N/2-2}$, ..., A_1, $S_{0,\,N/2-1}$, ..., $S_{0,\,1}$, and A_0. That is, Hadamard gates are applied in a reverse order to the pairs of the basis states of QMS(N), numbered from $N/2 - 1$ through 0. In the intervals between Hadamard gates A_{j+1} and A_j, gates $S_{j,k}$ are applied to $k = \overline{N/2 - 1,\, j+1}$, at pre-defined $j = \overline{N/2 - 2, 0}$. According to Statements 1 and 2, the above effects provided on QMS(N), $N = 2^n$, can be represented within the DM proposed [13, 15] and computed in a distributed manner by varying different elements of vector (2) in compliance with quantum gates that are defined by the relevant elements of vector (3). Different Hadamard gates provide effects $\Delta\theta_{j+b}$ defined in accordance with (4), upon the relevant elements θ_{j+b} of vector (2), $j = \overline{0, N/2 - 2}, b = N/2 - 1$. Complex of effects defined by Hadamard gates and provided on elements t_{j+b} of vector (2), $j = \overline{0, N/2 - 2}, b = N/2 - 1$, and by controlled-phase gates $S_{j,k}, k = \overline{j+1, N/2 - 1}$, $j = \overline{0, N/2 - 2}$, within the QFT are represented as effects as follows:

$$\Delta t_{N/2-1} = \pi, \ \Delta t_v = \pi\left(1 + \sum_{l=1}^{v-b} 2^{-l}\right), \tag{5}$$

where $v = \overline{N/2,\ N - 2}, b = N/2 - 1$. At the same time, effects provided by Hadamard gates and controlled-phase gates affect different parameters independently on each other, and the order of their effect does not matter within DM QMS(N). There is

Note. When defining the QFT based on DM QMS(N), $N = 2^n$, parameters θ_a, t_a of vector (2) and parameters $\Delta\theta_a$, Δt_a of vector (3), $a = \overline{0, b-1}$, $b = N/2 - 1$, are not involved.

In view of the above said, true is

Statement 3. QFT effect provided on QMS(N), $N = 2^n$, is represented as distributed effects defined in accordance with (4) upon parameters θ_{j+b}, $j = \overline{0, N/2 - 2}$, and in accordance with (5) upon parameters t_v, $v = \overline{N/2 - 1,~N - 2}$, $b = N/2 - 1$.

According to Statement 3 and the Note, let us compute the complexity of modelling the QFT of QMS(N), $N = 2^n$, based on the DM, the state of which is represented according to (2), while varying its state is represented according to (3).To represent DM QMS(N), $N = 2^n$, $2(N-1)$ elements are required, of which only N varies: $N/2$ elements change their value in accordance with formula (4), while the other ones vary according to formula (5). Computation of $\Delta\theta_{j+b} = \pi/4 - \theta_{j+b}$, $j = \overline{0, N/2 - 1}$, $b = N/2 - 1$, according to (4), requires $N/2$ operations of deducting from constant $\pi/4$. For computing $\Delta t_v = \pi\left(1 + \sum_{l=1}^{v-b} 2^{-l}\right)$, $v = \overline{N/2,~N-2}$, $b = N/2 - 1$, according to (5), $N/2 - 1$ operations of multiplying by constant π are required, while the adding operations represented as $1 + \sum_{l=1}^{v-b} 2^{-l}$ can be performed by manipulations with the binary bits of the future sum, since the addends are the integer powers of two. At the same time, each of the values $\Delta\theta_{j+b}$ and Δt_v, $j = \overline{0, N/2 - 1}$, $b = N/2 - 1$, $v = \overline{N/2,~N-2}$, can be computed in parallel, as well as the values $\theta_{j+b} + \Delta\theta_{j+b}$ and $t_v + \Delta t_v$ additionally requiring N adding operations allowing the parallel implementation upon computing $\Delta\theta_{j+b}$ and Δt_v, respectively.

Assume that we have a distributed computing system that allows computing C different operations simultaneously: Deducting from the constant, multiplying by the constant, adding by manipulating with binary bits, and adding over the time of t_{s-}, t_{ms}, t_{sb}, and t_{sum}. Based on the above, the following statements are true:

Statement 4. Modelling a QFT based on DM QMS(N), $N = 2^n$, is performed in a distributed manner, in two stages; in the first stage, $N/2$ operations of deducting from the constant, $N/2 - 1$ operations by the constant, and $N/2 - 1$ adding operations of manipulating with binary bits of the future sum are required; while in the second stage, N adding operations are required.

Statement 5. Time of the distributed modelling of QFT, based on DM QMS (N), $N = 2^n$, on a distributed computing system including C universal computational cores, is estimated for $C \ll N$ as

$$T = T_1 + T_2,$$

where $T_1 = \left]\frac{N/2 - 1}{C}\right[(t_{sb} + t_{ms}) + \left]\frac{N}{2C}\right[t_{s-}$, $T_2 = \left]\frac{N}{C}\right[t_{sum}$.

4 Conclusion

This paper proposes to represent quantum Fourier transform when using DM QMS(N), $N = 2^n$, by using the distributed variation of N from $2(N - 1)$ elements of the said DM. Mathematical model is defined for the distributed computation of the values of quantities, on which the DM elements of a given QMS(N) are varied. This allows modelling the said quantum algorithm when using distributed computations. It is shown that the number of the parameters to be varied in the discrete model proposed increases linearly with the growing number of basis states of QMS(N).

The paper also proposes a distributed model of how the distributed model of quantum Fourier transform affects QMS(N), $N = 2^n$, defined based on the known discrete model. Findings of this study open the prospects for theoretical and applied research in the matters of using the new, distributed discrete model of quantum Fourier transform, implemented on general- and special-purpose multiprocessor computing systems.

References

1. Dirak, P.: Lekcii po kvantovoj mexanike [The Quantum Mechanics Lectures], 148 p. Izhevskaya respublikanskaya tipografiya, Izhevsk (1998). (in Russian)
2. Kholevo, A.S.: Veroyatnostny'e i statisticheskie aspekty' kvantovoj teorii [Probabilistic and Statistical Aspects of Quantum Theory], 320 p. Nauka, Moscow (1980). (in Russian)
3. Kholevo, A.S.: Vvedenie v kvantovuyu teoriyu informacii [Introduction to Quantum Information Theory], 228 p. MCzNMO, Moscow (2002). (in Russian)
4. Valiev, K.A., Kokin, A.A.: Kvantovy'e komp'yutery': nadezhdy' i real'nost' [Quantum Computers: Hopes and Reality], 351 p. Izhevsk: R&C Dynamics, Moscow (2001). (in Russian)
5. Tarasov, S.O., Arslanov, N.M., Moiseev, S.A., Andrianov, S.N.: A quantum transistor based on an atom–photon molecule. Bull. Russ. Acad. Sci. Phys. **82**(8), 1042–1046 (2018)
6. Ablaev, F.M.: On the complexity of classical and quantum models of computations. In: Matematicheskie voprosy' kibernetiki [Mathematical Questions of Cybernetics] #13, pp. 137–146 (2004). (in Russian)
7. Bogdanov, Yu.I., Valiev, K.A., Kokin, A.A.: Kvantovy'e komp'yutery': dostizheniya, trudnosti realizacii i perspektivy'. In: Mikroe'lektronika [Microelectronics] #4(40), pp. 243–255 (2011). (in Russian)
8. Childs, A.M., van Dam, W.: Quantum algorithms for algebraic problems. Rev. Mod. Phys. **82**(1) (2010). https://journals.aps.org/rmp/abstract/10.1103/RevModPhys.82.1
9. Richter, M., Arnold, G., Trieu, B., Lippert, T.: Massively parallel quantum computer simulations: towards realistic systems. In: NIC Series, vol. 38, pp. 61–68. John von Neumann Institute for Computing (2007)
10. Bogdanov, Yu.I., Bogdanova, N.A., Lukichev, V.F., et al.: Computational problems of modeling the element base of quantum computers. In: Informacionny'e texnologii i vy'chislitel'ny'e sistemy' [Information Technologies and Computer Systems] #3, pp. 3–14 (2013). (in Russian)
11. Zuev, S.V.: Modeling of quantum computing on a classical computer. In: Vestnik BelGTU [Herald of BelGTU] #2, p. 135–139 (2013). (in Russian)
12. Bogdanov, Y., Bogdanova, N.A., Belinsky, L.V., Lukichev, V.F.: Statistical models and adequacy validation for optical quantum state tomography with quadrature measurements. Russ. Microelectron. **46**(6), 371–378 (2017). https://doi.org/10.1134/S1063739717060038

13. Shalagin, S.V.: Discrete model of a quantum information processing system. Vestnik KGTU im. A.N. Tupoleva [Herald of KGTU named after A.N. Tupolev]. # 4, pp. 22–27 (2007). (in Russian)
14. Lidl, R., Niederreiter, H.: Finite Fields (Encyclopedia of Mathematics and its Applications), 2nd edn, 772 p. Cambridge University Press, Cambridge (2008). ISBN 10: 0521065674; ISBN-13: 978-0521065672
15. Shalagin, S.V.: Polinomialnaya model sistemy kvantovoy obrabotki informatsii [Polynomial model of quantum processing]. In: Fundamentalnyye i prikladnyye problemy matematiki i informatiki: Materialy XII Mtzhdunar.konf., priurochennoy k 55-letiyu fakulteta matematiki i kompyuternykh nauk [Fundamental and Applied Problems of Mathematics and Information Science: Proceedings of the 13th International Conference Timed to the 55th Anniversary of the Faculty of Mathematics and Computer Sciences, Makhachkala, 16–20 September 2019, pp. 180–185. Publishing House of DGU, Makhachkala (2019). (in Russian)
16. Zakharov, V.M.: Vychisleniye nelineynykh polinomialnykh funktsiy na mnogoprotsessornoy sisteme s programmiruyemoy arkhitekturoy [Computing non-linear polynomial functions on a multiprocessor system with a programmable architecture]. In: Zakharov, V.M., Shalagin, S.V. (eds.) Informatsionnyye tekhnologii [Information Technologies], no. 5. pp. 6–11 (2012). (in Russian)
17. Zakharov, V.M.: O razvitii apparatnykh sredstv statisticheskogo modelirovaniya [On developing hardware tools of statistical modelling]. In: Zakharov, V.M., Shalagin, S.V. (eds.) Razvitiye vychislitelnoy tekhniki i ee programmnogo obespecheniya v Rossii i stranakh byvshego SSSR: istoriya i perspekivy: sb. Trudov Tretyey Mezhdunar.konf. Sorucom-2014 [Development of Computing Machines and Their Software Tools in Russia and in the Former USSR-Countries: History and Prospects: Proceedings of the Third International conference Sorucom-2014], pp. 109–114 (2014). (in Russian)
18. Shalagin, S.V.: Predstavleniye nelineynykh polinomov nad konechnym polem raspredelennoy vychislitelnoy sistemoy [Representing non-linear polynomials over a finite field by a computational system]. In: Nelineynyy mir [Non-Linear World], no. 5, pp. 376–379 (2009). (in Russian)
19. Shalagin, S.V.: Slozhnost vychisleniya nelineynykh polinomialnykh funktsiy nad polem GF(2^2) na PLIS/FPGA [Complexity of computing non-linear polynomial functions over field GF(2^2) on FPGA]. In: Poisk effektivnykh resheniy v protsesse sozdaniya i realizatsii nauchnykh razrabotok v rossiyskoy aviatsionnoy i raketno-kosmicheskoy promyshlennosti: sb. trudov Mezhdunar. nauchno-praktich. konf. [Searching for Efficient Solutions in Creating and Implementing Scientific Developments in the Russian Aircraft and Space Industry: Proceedings of the International Scientific and Practical Conference], pp. 661–664 (2014). (in Russian)
20. Shalagin, S.V.: Realizatsiya tsifrovykh ustroystv v arkhitekture PLIS/FPGA pri ispolzovanii raspredelennykh vychisleniy v polyakh Galua. Monografiya [Implementing Digital Devices in the FPGA Architecture in Using Distributed Computations in Galois Fields], 228 p. KNITU-KAI University Press, Kazan (2016). (in Russian)
21. Dordopulo, A.I.: Vysokoproizvoditelnyye rekonfiguriruemyye vychislitelnyye sistemy [High-performance reconfigurable computing systems]. In: Dordopulo, A.I., Kalyaev, I.A., Levin, I.I., et al. (eds.) Superkompyutery [Supercomputers], vol. 3, no. 3, pp. 44–48 (2010). (in Russian)
22. Kuzelin, M.O.: Sovremennyye semeystva PLIS firmy Xilinx: spravochnoye posobiye [Modern FPGA families manufactured by Xilinx: a reference book]. In: Kuzelin, M.O., Knyshev, D.A., Zotov, V.Yu. (eds.) Goryachaya liniya – Telecom, Moscow, 440 p. (2004). (in Russian)
23. Coppersmith, D.: An approximate Fourier transform useful in quantum factoring. IBM research report RC19642 «R. Cle.» (1994)

Design of U-Shaped Multiline Microstrip Patch Antenna for Advanced Wireless Applications

Kanakavalli Harsha Sri[1], P. Vinod Babu[2], and V. A. Sankar Ponnapalli[3(✉)]

[1] Department of Electronics and Communication Engineering, National Institute of Technology Tiruchirapalli, Tiruchirapalli 620015, India

[2] Department of Electronics and Communication Engineering, Rajiv Gandhi University of Knowledge Technologies, Nuzvid 521202, India
vinod@rguktn.ac.in

[3] Department of Electronics and Communication Engineering, Sreyas Institute of Engineering and Technology, Hyderabad 500068, India

Abstract. A compact feed poly line slotted rectangular microstrip patch antenna with defected ground surface has been proposed in this paper for the wireless LANs, Bluetooth, and WiFi applications. The patch is designed based on a poly-line slot and with defected ground structure. The simulated and fabricated models of demonstrated antenna exhibit better return loss, bandwidth, acceptable gain, and other antenna parameters over the required frequency range and the central frequency of 2.4 GHz is a worldwide free spectrum ISM band. The proposed antenna is fabricated using a highly sensitive PCB technique, and fabricated antenna parameters have been achieved compared to simulated results. The simulated and fabricated results conclude less than 3% error among them and owing to the proposed method, miniaturization of antenna achieved with a gain of 5 dB.

Keywords: Microstrip patch antenna · Defected ground · Gain · Substrate · Multiline · ISM band

1 Introduction

The electronic devices with compact in size draw a lot of attention in the past few decades due to the mobile industry's high-speed development. Recently, global mobile market is pushing the technological needs beyond its expectations. There is limited use for huge/bulk components in size with excellent performance in recent portable products due to the frequency limitations. Out of these devices, microstrip patch antenna (MPA) is an ultimate solution for wireless local area networks (WLANs) and personal wireless devices like a wireless printer, mobile handsets, and wireless personal digital assistants (PDA) which utilizes the 2.4 GHz frequency band [1]. These types of MPA's have received more attention owing to their frequency of operation, but on the other side, these MPA's have the design challenges to improve the gain and bandwidth simultaneously. One of the most popular types of MPA with compact nature and design challenges are discussed in [2]. The MPA can be fabricated using printed circuit technology, which is of less price, less weight, and simple to integrate into any conformal surfaces. But narrow

© Springer Nature Singapore Pte Ltd. 2021
P. K. Singh et al. (Eds.): FTNCT 2020, CCIS 1396, pp. 23–32, 2021.
https://doi.org/10.1007/978-981-16-1483-5_3

bandwidth and the power handling capability are the designing challenges of these antennas along with less weight. The researchers have proposed different techniques to overcome these challenges and several methods. For example, cutting slots on the patch with different shapes [3–7], dielectric substrate management [8], and the most recent proposes is defected ground structure (DGS). DGS is simply etching of the ground plane, or sometimes by applying a complicated shape for better performance over the antenna's design challenges [9, 10].

The feeding technique is also determines the performance of an MPA [11–13]. There are multiple feeding techniques available for the MPA like micro strip line feeding, aperture coupling, coaxial feed, and proximity coupling and out of which micro strip line feeding is the most straight forward feed design. It provides suitable probable input impedance matching for the designed MPA [14–19]. The proposed polyline slotted patch antenna using DGS is designed and simulated in full wave electromagnetic solver high frequency structure simulator using the HFSS 18.0v software [20] that uses the finite element method (FEM) to simulate the MPA. The subsequent chapters explain the general antenna design procedure, configuration of the proposed antenna, and its fabrication with DGS is presented in Sect. 2. Simulated and fabricated results of the proposed antenna are discussed in Sect. 3, and conclusions are explained in Sect. 4.

2   Proposed Antenna Design Considerations

A U-shaped polyline slot microstrip patch antenna with a rectangular piece of metal is etched on the ground plane is proposed to achieve miniaturization of MPA, as shown in Fig. 1. The geometrical and material specifications of the proposed MPA are exemplified in Table 1.

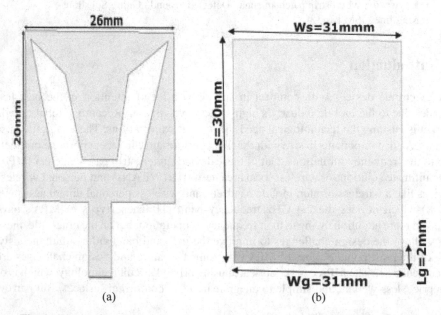

(a)   (b)

Fig. 1. Demonstrated antenna geometrical configuration (a) front and (b) back view

Table 1. Selection of specifications of the proposed antenna

Specifications	Selection
Center frequency (fc)	2.4 GHz
Substrate material	Rodger RO4232
Dielectric constant (ϵr)	3.2
Substrate height (h)	0.78 mm
Loss tangent (δ)	0.0018
Patch dimensions	20 mm × 26 mm
Substrate dimensions	

The slotting technique has applied to the basic rectangular patch to increase the radiation, and the proposed slot dimensions, which are mounted on the substrate material, are shown in Fig. 2. The corresponding dimensions of Fig. 2 are exemplified in Table 2.

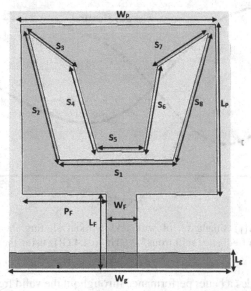

Fig. 2 Proposed antenna's geometry with dimensions marked in the symbols that illustrates the size of our proposed antenna size is 31 × 30 mm.

Owing to the application of the poly line slot to the MPA and keeping the other parameters fixed it results in a change in the resonance frequency from 3.2 GHz to 2.4 GHz. As shown in Fig. 3, this behavior can be observed where the return loss (S_{11}) is minimum at the center frequency of 2.4 GHz with the slotting method compared to 3.2 GHz without using the slotting method.

The slotting technique leads to a reduction in the patch antenna size to 20 mm × 26 mm. It is identified that the ground width (W_g) of 2 mm covers a broad frequency

Table 2. Dimensions of the polyline slots.

Slot lengths	Dimensions in mm
S1	15
S2	15
S3	06
S4	10
S5	06
S6	10
S7	06
S8	15

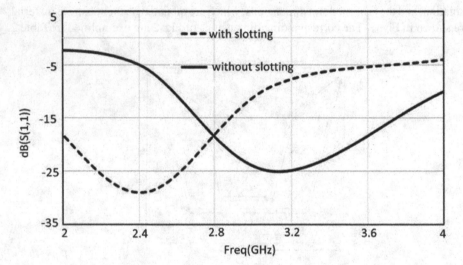

Fig. 3. Return loss (S_{11}) simulation of with and without slotting in our proposed model demonstrates the center frequency shift from 3.2 GHz to 2.4 GHz using the slotting.

range, and that provides a better performance throughout the valid frequency range. The design equations of the proposed MPA design are presented in Eq. (1) to Eq. (5).

$$Width(w) = \frac{C}{2f_0\sqrt{\varepsilon_r}} \tag{1}$$

The microstrip line looks wider electrically than the physical dimensions because a portion of the waves traveling in the air and remaining part of the waves travels in the substrate, which is due to the fringing effect. These results the MPA's dimensions are not small, but it is slightly extended by Δl. An effective dielectric constant (ϵ_{reff}) is introduced due to the fringing effects and keeps the wave propagation in the line, with reference to width to height ratio (w/h) or length to height ratio(l/h). The effective relative dielectric constant(ϵ_{reff}) is obtained with reference to the dielectric constant of the substrate, as shown in Eq. 2 (when the w/h > 1).

$$\varepsilon_{reff} = \frac{\varepsilon_r + 1}{2} + \frac{\varepsilon_r - 1}{2}\left[1 + 12\frac{h}{w}\right]^{-1/2} \tag{2}$$

Due to the fringing field effects, length has been extended on each side of the patch by a small amount Δl, the expression for extended length by taking effective dielectric constant (ϵ_{reff}) into consideration is in Eq. 3.

$$\frac{\Delta l}{h} = 0.412\frac{(\varepsilon_{reff} + 0.3)(\frac{w}{h} + 0.264)}{(\varepsilon_{reff} - 0.258)(\frac{w}{h} + 0.8)} \tag{3}$$

The antenna performance is function of its electrical length, which is taken in case of dominant TM_{010} mode at the center frequency. It is denoted by its effective length l_{eff} using Eq. 4, where it is a function of center frequency and patch antenna medium effective permittivity.

$$l_{eff} = \frac{c}{2f_0\sqrt{\varepsilon_{reff}}} \tag{4}$$

Based on the patch antenna's effective length and extended distance, the actual patch length can be calculated. The actual length of the patch is given in Eq. 5.

$$l = l_{eff} - 2\Delta l \tag{5}$$

A microstrip line feeding technique feeds the proposed antenna. Here the impedance matching among the input source, feed line, and the antennais a main hurdle for the MPA design. Impedance matching can be achieved by varying the feed position (P_F) or feed width (W_F). Feed position is varied from the origin to 20 mm by keeping all other parameters constant, and the optimized feed position for the impedance of 50 Ω is obtained at 11 mm from the origin, and feed width is varied from 1 mm to 9 mm by using parameter optometric in the design, and it is observed that feed width of 4 mm achieved the impedance matching of 50 Ω with feed length (LF) of 9 mm. A prototype of the proposed antenna has fabricated with highly sensitive PCB technology, as shown in Fig. 4 and Fig. 5 that shows the designed model's front and ground plane views. It is also marked that the slotting and the DGS according to the aforementioned dimensional values. To understand the fabricated antenna's physical size, the image was compared with the standard Indian one-rupee coin, which is in a circular shape with a diameter of 21.93 mm (0.863 in.).

Fig. 4. Fabricated antenna front view in comparison with an Indian rupee diameter of 21.93 mm (0.863 in.).

Fig. 5. Fabricated antenna back views in comparison with an Indian rupee diameter of 21.93 mm (0.863 in.).

3   Results and Discussions

The proposed antenna is designed and simulated using ANSYS HFSS 18.0v, and simultaneously antenna is fabricated using highly sensitive PCB technology. A fabricated antenna is tested using R&S ZVH cable and antenna analyzer in free space.In general, for any practical antenna analysis, 10 dB return loss gives 10% reflection, 90% of power to the antenna, whereas return loss of 20 dB gives 1% reflection, 99% power to the antenna. Any real-time application needs a minimum of 10 dB return loss. Here our demonstrated antenna achieved return loss (S_{11}) of 37 dB and 34 dB for simulated and fabricated models respectively, as exemplified in Fig. 6(a) and (b). The bandwidth of

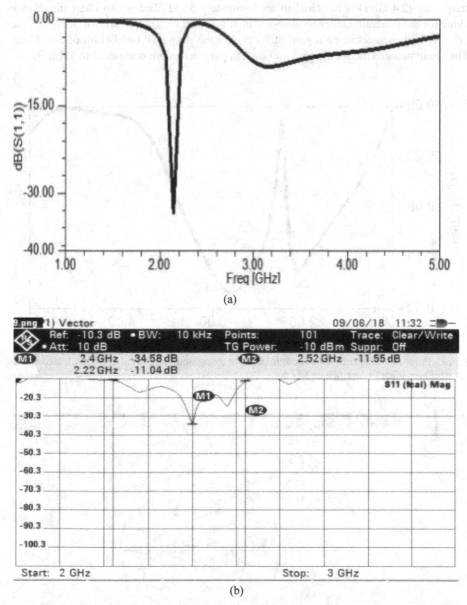

(a)

(b)

Fig. 6. Return loss (S_{11}) of the demonstrated MPA. (a) Simulated and (b) Measured values indicates the return loss is more than 37 dB and 23 dB, respectively.

the antenna defines the range of frequencies over which the antenna gain is remains constant. Here 300 MHz bandwidth has achieved for the designed antenna. Better transmission and reception of the signal will be achieved when the antenna provides a better input source impedance matching. Figure 7 exemplifies the impedance at the resonance frequency (2.4 GHz) is matched to approximately 50 Ω. The Smith chart impedance value for the fabricated antenna is approximately equal to 50 Ω, as shown in Fig. 8. The proposed antenna achieved a gain of 5 dB over the proposed bandwidth of 300 MHz. The simulated and measured gain, bandwidth parameters are compared in Table 3.

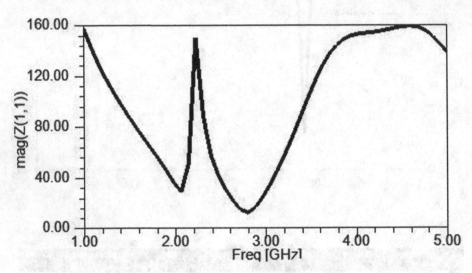

Fig. 7. Proposed MPA simulated input impedance (magnitude of Z_{11}) at 2.4 GHz, which shows the matching input impedance of 50 Ohms.

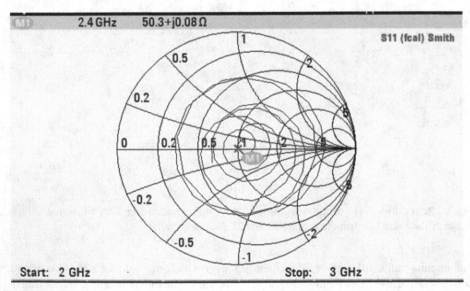

Fig. 8. Proposed MPA antenna measured input impedance at 2.4 GHz, which shows the matching input impedance (the real value of Z11) of 50 Ohms.

Table 3. Comparison of proposed simulated and fabricated/measured patch antenna results.

Parameters	Simulation	Fabrication
S11	−37.4253 dB	−34.5800 dB
Bandwidth	298.9 MHz	300 MHz
VSWR	1.2833	1.1400
Impedance	51.2850 Ω	50.3000 Ω

4 Conclusions

In this paper, a compact polyline slot antenna with DGS has been designed and fabricated to validate our novel design concept. The polyline slotting on the conducting patch reduces the antenna size, and the DGS improves the antenna performance with a loss tangent of 0.0018. The proposed MPA has achieved a simulated return loss of 37 dB, the fabricated return loss of 34 dB, a wide bandwidth of 300 MHz, a gain of 5 dB over the bandwidth of 300 MHz, and standing wave ratio, which is the measure of impedance matching between the input source and antenna feed, has achieved a value of 1.12 with 50 Ω impedance matching. The error between the simulated and measured antenna model is only less than 3%. Due to the above advantages, the proposed MPA is most suitable for the WLAN/wifi and satellite applications in ISM band with a center frequency of 2.4 GHz. The proposed design also makes sure that the complete MPA is in a compact size that can fit with any mobile systems that are using wifi or Bluetooth application modules at the ISM band.

References

1. Skrivervik, A.K., Zurcher, J.F., Staub, O., Mosig, J.R.: PCS antenna design: the challenge of miniaturization. IEEE Antennas Propag. Mag. **43**(4), 12–27 (2001)
2. Balanis, C.A.: Antenna Theory: Analysis and Design. Wiley, New York (2016)
3. Wang, Q.: Electromagnetically coupled patch antenna for phased array applications for mobile satellite communications. Microwave Opt. Technol. Lett. **48**(7), 1279–1282 (2006)
4. Sankar Ponnapalli, V.A., Jayasree, P.V.Y.: Design of multi-beam rhombus fractal array antenna using new geometric design methodology. Progress Electromagnet. Res. **64**, 151–158 (2016)
5. Yang, F., Zhang, X.X., Ye, X., Rahmat-Samii, Y.: Wide-band E-shaped patch antennas for wireless communications. IEEE Trans. Antennas Propag. **49**(7), 1094–1100 (2001)
6. Rajagopalan, H., Kovitz, J.M., Rahmat-Samii, Y.: MEMS reconfigurable optimized E-shaped patch antenna design for cognitive radio. IEEE Trans. Antennas Propag. **62**(3), 1056–1064 (2013)
7. Latif, S.I., Shafai, L., Sharma, S.K.: Bandwidth enhancement and size reduction of microstrip slot antennas. IEEE Transa. Antennas Propag. **53**(3), 994–1003 (2005)
8. Khan, A., Nema, R.: Analysis of five different dielectric substrates on the microstrip patch antenna. Int. J. Comput. Appl. **55**(14), 40–47 (2012)
9. Chiang, K.H., Tam, K.W.: Microstrip monopole antenna with enhanced bandwidth using defected ground structure. IEEE Antennas Wirel. Propag. Lett. **7**, 532–535 (2008)

10. Aravindraj, E., Ayyappan, K.: Design of slotted H-shaped patch antenna for 2.4 GHz WLAN applications. In: 2017 International Conference on Computer Communication and Informatics (ICCCI), pp. 1–5, India. IEEE (2017)
11. Waterhouse, R.B.: Microstrip Patch Antennas: Designer Guide. Kluwer Academic Publishers, New York (2003)
12. Harshasri, K., Babu, P.V., Rao, P.N.: Design of compact C-Band concave patch antenna for radar altimeter applications. In: 2018 International Conference on Communication and Signal Processing (ICCSP), India, pp. 0542–0546. IEEE, (2018)
13. Katehi, P.B., Alexopoulos, N.G.: On the modeling of electromagnetically coupled microstrip antennas-the printed strip dipole. IEEE Trans. Antennas Propagation, AP **32**(11), pp. 1179–1186 (1984)
14. James, J.R., Hall, P.S.: Handbook of Microstrip Antennas, vols.1 and 2. Peter Peregrinus, London (1989)
15. Collin, R.E.: Foundations for Microwave Engineering, chapter 6. McGraw-Hills Book Co., New York (1992)
16. Chakraborty, S., Mukherjee, U.: Comparative study of microstrip patch line feed and coaxial feed antenna design using genetic algorithms. In: 2011 2nd International Conference on Computer and Communication Technology (ICCCT-2011), India, pp. 203–208. IEEE (2011)
17. Mannam, A.V.V., Yedukondala Rao Veeranki, B.: Design of narrowband bandpass filter using open-loop square resonators with loading element. Indian J. Sci. Technol **9**(47), 1–9 (2016)
18. Hong, J.-S.G., Lancaster, M.J.: Microstrip Filters for RF/Microwave Applications, vol. 167. Wiley, New York (2004)
19. Pozar, David M.: Microwave Engineering. Wiley, New York (2011)
20. Ansys HFSS Version 18.0v.: 3D Electromagnetic Field Simulator for RF and Wireless Design, ANSYS, Inc. Southpointe, PA, USA (2020)

Problem Formulation for Multi-area Economic Load Dispatch Problem Considering Real Power and Tie-Line Constraints

Ch. Leela Kumari[1,2](✉), Vikram Kumar Kamboj[3], and S. K. Bath[4]

[1] Lovely Professional University, Phagwara, Punjab, India
[2] Department of Electrical and Electronics Engineering, Bandari Srinivas Institute of Technology, Chevella, Telangana, India
[3] Domain of Power System, School of Electronics and Electrical Engineering, Lovely Professional University, Phagwara, Punjab, India
`leela.41800411@lpu.in`
[4] Department of Electrical Engineering, MRSPTU, Bathinda, Punjab, India

Abstract. The authors in this paper formulated mathematical equations of Multi-area Economic load dispatch in conventional approach. Multi-area Economic load dispatch problem is a vital issue in power system scheduling, processing, organizing and managing. MAELD issue in power system is explored with the combination of electric utilities of various different regions. The mathematical formulation of multi area dynamic dispatch problem in view of real power and tie-line limits have been explained in this paper. This work of mathematical formulation will be useful for the research work on multi-area economic load dispatch problems with electric vehicles (EVs) and Renewable Energy Sources (RES).

Keywords: Tie-line constraint · Economic load dispatch · Active power

Abbreviations

P_{mn}^{G}	Power of nth generating units
$P_{mn(min)}^{G}$	Smallest amount of power of nth generating units
$P_{mn(max)}^{G}$	Highest amount power of nth generating units
NG	Overall number of generating units
NA	Overall number of regions
n	Index for power generating units
P_{mn}^{Loss}	Coefficient of power loss
$F(P_{mn}^{G})$	Overall fuel price of entire power generating units
a_{mn}	Fuel price Coefficient of power generating units
b_{mn}	Fuel price Coefficient of power generating units
c_{mn}	Fuel price Coefficient of power generating units

© Springer Nature Singapore Pte Ltd. 2021
P. K. Singh et al. (Eds.): FTNCT 2020, CCIS 1396, pp. 33–44, 2021.
https://doi.org/10.1007/978-981-16-1483-5_4

1 Introduction

To achieve the high reliability, economical power generation and best working performance in terms of stability, reserve power sharing and operation under critical situations requires the interconnection of electric utility systems. The power producing units can be divided into number of groups and tied up by transmission lines. MAELD determines the economical power generation in one region and interexchange of power to another region which reduces the fuel cost in all regions by meeting operational and network imperatives.

Multi-area economic load dispatch gives an optimized plan for dispatching the real power and swaps the same among multiple regions by contemplating the boundaries of operations like transmission losses, generator output imperatives, tie-line capacity limitation and balance between generation and consumption. At the outset, a two-area multi-source power system interconnected is considered as well as employed to optimize for a modified objective function. The resultant is compared with other performances. Fluctuations in power in distributed regions are often, and therefore a coordinated multi-area dynamic economic dispatch may enable. High variability of generations poses puzzle to secure cost-effective operation of power systems, especially in terms of scarcity.

2 Literature Review

Doty and McIntyre et al. [1] discussed about the power brokerage system and in detail about the different power pools and methods to minimize the generation price and finally allocate savings.

Desell A. L. et al. [2] proposed a programming method called linear programming for power system planning. This programming creates its own database based existing programs and monitors the power flow hourly and adjusts the same if any transmissions line carries overload within the imperatives of maximum and minimum power.

Hemick et al. [3] solved the region control error in multi region economic dispatch, which is the difference between desired generation level and actual generation level.

S. O. Orero et al. [4] used the Genetic Algorithm for Economic Dispatch problem in two different modes. Deterministic Crowding Genetic algorithm and Standard Genetic Algorithm are the methods in which the population multiplicity is maintained during search process. The parents that are most similar to their child are replaced with this child population. This method is so attractive as it requires only few parameters to be set compared to other methods.

Yuhui Shi and Russell C. Eberhart [5] studied the performance of PSO under linearly decreasing inertia weight and found that PSO can converge quickly irrespective of population size but suffering with the ability of global search at the end of iteration process due inertia weight decrement as search process progresses. This can be overcome by automatic updation of inertia weight strategy.

Song, C. S. Chou et al. [6] proposed an Artificial Ant Colony Search Algorithm (ACSA) to resolve ELD issue with shared heat and power. The three basic characteristics of ACSA provide the accelerating results and avoidance of premature convergence.

Jayabharathi et al. [7] developed an evolution programming based algorithm to resolve multi region economic load dispatch problems including tie lines imperatives as well as tested the results with other programming methods and proved that the developed method has excellent convergence pattern. The authors concluded that to implement the existing method to complex or large size systems the convergence pattern will occur for less number of iterations and it is to be explored.

Chun-Lung Chen and Nanming Chen [8] handled the economic dispatch problems effectively with direct search model along with transmission capacity imperatives. The multi convergence technique is integrated in DSM to reduce the multiplicity of iterations during exploration progression.

J. Z. Zhu [9] discussed a new model of approach for MAED including transmission line as well as capacity imperatives using non linear neural network approach.

Jong-Bae Park et al. [10] introduced the customized (MPSO) particle swarm optimization for ED including nonsmooth price functions. The proposed method reduces the search space if the solution is not obtained in a pre-specified time and it is terminated as soon as the iterations match to the predefined maximum number of iterations.

Cai Jiejin et al. [11], introduced an innovative strategy called chaotic used particle swarm optimization (CPSO) on the way to solve convergence of particles prematurely. The proposed technique is the combination of (CLS) chaotic local search and (AIWF) adaptive inertia weight factor. It is a two stage iterative method that performs global exploration and local exploitation.

Leandro dos Santos Coelho et al, [12] developed a new method of approach by combining the different algorithms including valve point effects. The combination of differential evolution and sequential programming gives us the global and optimal solution.

A. Immanuel Selvakumar et al. [13] discussed a novel particle swarm optimization (NPSO) along by means of local random investigation algorithm. In classical PSO cognitive component is used to remember the best previous position whereas in NPSO-LRS cognitive component is split into two, one is to remember previous best position and the other is to remember the worst position also. The balanced condition can be achieved among local and global search is possible by using hybrid heuristic algorithm.

Binghui Yu et al. [14] applied a method based on particle swarm optimization approach to resolve the short term hydrothermal scheduling by incorporating different operational imperatives to achieve nearly global solutions.

K. T. Chaturvedi, Manjaree Pandit et al. [15] applied a technique for non convex ED called a self organizing hierarchical particle swarm optimization (SOH-PSO). In this method of approach velocities of all particles are reinitialized in the event of stagnation of particles at local optima all through explore procedure. The authors also claimed that when it is operated along by way of time varying acceleration coefficients (TVAC) gives the good balancing condition between acceleration factors of PSO.

Manoharan et al. [16] explored different evolution algorithms among which covariance matrix adaptive evolution algorithm (CMAES) provides best results in terms of economic generation and stability of operation compared to other algorithms. To claim the optimality for obtained results Karush-Khun-Tucker (KKT) conditions are applied.

Lingfeng Wang and Chanan Singh [17] studied environment and economic issues in dispatching power economically by using multi objective particle swarm optimization along with local investigation algorithm, which will improve the efficiency of search ability.

Krishna Teerth Chaturvedi et al. [18] investigated that to obtain the best solution for non convex economic dispatch, the particle swarm optimization happens to operate along in the company of time altering acceleration coefficients (TVAC). Because the traditional PSO is able to give the better solutions for generator fuel cost curves are linear otherwise premature convergence occurs. This can be solved with the proposed method and gives the better global solutions with the automotive strategy of time varying acceleration coefficients.

S. M. A. Bulbul et al. [19] implemented a novel optimization technique to unravel economic dispatch problem including operational imperatives. Bacterial foraging (BF) algorithm with Nelder -Mead is used to investigate the local minima in search space.

John G. Vlachogiannis et al. [20] applied (ICA-PSO) an Improved Coordinated Aggregation-Based particle swarm optimization and compared this method with different heuristic optimization techniques for ELD issues. In this method the movement of the particles are updated as per the finest positions of remaining particles excluding the best particles, which update their positions randomly.

E. Nasr Azadani et al. [21] introduced a new constrained particle swarm optimization (CPSO) to unravel issues of constrained reserve power and generation dispatching by incorporating the different imperatives to ensure the power system stability and safety. The authors concluded that for equality imperatives the CPSO algorithms gas more advantageous compared to the other exhaustive methods.

M. R. AlRashidi et al. [22] applied a hybrid particle swarm optimization (HPSO) which is used to unravel the optimal power flow troubles under different conditions. This method is also combined with Newton-Rapson method to solve the equality imperatives. Inequality imperatives also well handled by this method.

A. Safari et al. [23] employed repetition based particle swarm optimization (IPSO) scheme to study ED with different generator imperatives. Compared to the classical PSO method the control equation in IPSO includes iteration best component to avoid the trapping of particles into local optima.

Ying Wang et al. [24] introduced a better technique for short-term hydrothermal scheduling called self-adaptive PSO, in which the acceleration factors are continuously updated so as to adjust the position of particle in the search process thereby the entire population.

Behnam M. et al. [25] implemented particle swarm optimization by means of time varying acceleration coefficients (TVAC-PSO) to deal combine power economic dispatch problem with heat. This method differs from conventional PSO in which acceleration factors are fixed but in TVAC-PSO acceleration factors are updated as the search process progress. The solution quality and convergence is improved by choosing the cognitive coefficient (C1) reduced and social coefficient (C2) increased during the progress of search process.

Neil J. Vickers [26] described the animal communication with different experiments and concluded that they will release some chemicals so as to attract the species of the same family.

Basu [27] implemented artificial bee colony algorithm for MAED problems including operational and network imperatives. The test results were give better cost convergence characteristics compared to DE, EP and GA methods.

Thabo G. Hlalelea et al. [28] introduced a proposal to increase the use of renewable energy by stochastic economic dispatch i.e., it focuses on renewable energy which is a part of optimal energy that minimizes the emissions. To obtain this a reduction algorithm is utilized to schedule an optimal dispatch energy.

Manzoor Ellahi et al. [29] explored a meta-heuristic algorithm to discover the solution for economic dispatch problem by using PSO and BA algorithms. "α" a new parameter was introduced which is a multiplier of velocity equation of PSO, and experimentally tested on the power systems based on RES.

Farzad Habibi et al. [30] implemented a novel MOPSO algorithm to obtain best results in solving ELD problem in multi area power system with different imperatives by considering pollution function and as such resulted minimum operating costs.

Ali Azizivahed et al. [31] employed HGWO-PSO algorithm in handling different optimization issues considering benchmark functions and economic dispatch problems for solving MAED problems. And the biggest achievement is the total operational cost is reduced by implementing this algorithm and proved by testing on 10 & 40 unit multi-area test systems.

Jian Lin et al. [32] discussed a new algorithm named improved stochastic fractal search to solve MAED issues when subjected to practical imperatives of a power system continuing with tie-line capacity, generator limits, ramp–rate limits and POZs. This algorithm resulted good in handling equality imperatives, improved searching ability and is tested on three test system and proved efficient.

F. Nazari-Heris et al. [33] studied economic dispatch of CHP based micro-grid in which the test system is categorized into different regions & it says every region is either grid connected or islanded mode. When comparisons are done among these then it resulted that the total operation costs are minimized in islanded mode.

Mohammad Jafar Mokarram et al. [34] introduced JAYA-TLBO algorithm to deal complicated problems. This method does not need any controlling parameters. This identifies the MAED problems in power system of every unit and interchanges power by tie-lines connecting number of areas.

M. Basu et al. [35] introduced a new algorithm named Squirrel search algorithm in solving heat and power economic dispatch issue in multi-region with assimilation of renewable powers(solar and wind).

3   Multi-area Economic Load Dispatch

The Multi-Area Economic Load Dispatch (MAELD) problem can be affirmed in brief by determining the loads of the various thermal generators available in power system for which the entire price of generation is reduced, maintaining power balance equality imperative and the generation capacity inequality imperatives. The complete mathematical formulation of Classical Dynamic Economic Load dispatch has been formulated.

3.1 Mathematical Formulation

The key idea of multi area dynamic dispatch is to have large decrease on fuel price in power generating units subjected to fulfill the various imperatives. This overall objective function of MAELD issue is categorized as the following sub-sections [1–5]:

3.1.1 Multi Area Dynamic Load Dispatch-Conventional Approach

The mathematical formulation of conventional multi area dynamic dispatch for one hour is represented as:

$$F(P_{mn}^G) = \sum_{m=1}^{NA} (\sum_{n=1}^{NG} [a_{mn}(P_{mn}^G)^2 + b_{mn}P_{mn}^G + c_{mn}]) \tag{1}$$

where m = 1, 2, 3,…..NA; n = 1, 2 ,3,…..NG.
For 'H' Hours the dispatch of power generating units may be represented as:

$$F(P_{mn}^G) = \sum_{h=1}^{H} \left(\sum_{m=1}^{NA} \sum_{n=1}^{NG} [a_{mn}(P_{mn}^G)^2 + b_{mn}P_{mn}^G + c_{mn})] \right) \tag{2}$$

where m = 1, 2, 3,…..NA; n = 1, 2, 3,…..NG; h ∈ H.

This Eq. (2) represents the exact mathematical formulation for Dynamic Dispatch. The hour 'h' may be varied for 1 to H-th Hour for time varying load demand.

3.1.2 Cubical ELD

To establish the output power of an online generating units the ELD problem aims to congregate system load at least price whilst fulfilling the system imperatives. So as to attain correct dispatch outcomes, a cubical function is used for modeling the unit cost.

$$F(P_{mn}^G) = \sum_{m=1}^{NA} (\sum_{n=1}^{NG} [a_{mn}(P_{mn}^G)^3 + b_{mn}(P_{mn}^G)^2 + c_{mn}P_{mn}^G + d_{mn})] \tag{3a}$$

Where (n ∈ NG).
The Cubical ELD by means of valve point effect is given by:

$$F(P_{mn}^G) = \sum_{m=1}^{NA} \sum_{n=1}^{NG} [a_{mn}(P_{mn}^G)^3 + b_{mn}(P_{mn}^G)^2 + c_{mn}P_{mn}^G + d_{mn})] + \left| e_{mn} \sin(f_{mn}(P_{mn(min)}^G - P_{mn}^G)) \right| \tag{3b}$$

here a_{mn}, b_{mn} & c_{mn} are the cost coefficients,
e_{mn} and f_{mn} = n^{th} generator valve point effect coefficients in m^{th} region,
$P_{mn}{}^G$ = active power generated by the nth generator in m^{th} region,
NA = number of regions and
NG = number of generators in m^{th} region.

3.1.3 Heat and Power ELD

The solution for the product of power and unit heat in a system is done by heat and power ELD. The heat as well as power ELD may be mathematically formulated as:

$$F_{Power}(P_{mn}^G) = \sum_{m=1}^{NA} \sum_{n=1}^{NG} \left(c_{mn} + b_{mn} \times P_{mn}^G + a_{mn} \times (P_{mn}^G)^2 \right) \tag{4a}$$

$$F_{Heat}(P_{mn}^G) = \sum_{m=1}^{NA} \sum_{n=1}^{NG} \left(g_{mn} + h_{mn} \times P_{mn}^G + q_{mn} \times (P_{mn}^G)^2 \right) \tag{4b}$$

$$F_{Overall}(P_{mn}^G) = \sum_{m=1}^{NA} \sum_{n=1}^{NG} \left(c_{mn} + b_{mn} \times P_{mn}^G + a_{mn} \times (P_{mn}^G)^2 + g_{mn} \times P_{mn}^G + h_{mn} \times (P_{mn}^G)^2 + q_{mn} \times (P_{mn}^G)^2 \right)$$
$$\tag{4c}$$

and the objective function for heat and power ELD in view of valve point loading effects is reframed as:

$$F_{Power}(P_{mn}^G) = \sum_{m=1}^{NA} (\sum_{n=1}^{NG} \left(c_{mn} + b_{mn} \times P_{mn}^G + a_{mn} \times (P_{mn}^G)^2 + \left| e_{mn} \sin(f_{mn}(P_{mn(min)}^G - P_{mn}^G)) \right| \right)$$
$$\tag{5a}$$

$$F_{Heat}(P_{mn}^G) = \sum_{m=1}^{NA} (\sum_{n=1}^{NG} \left(g_{mn} + h_{mn} \times P_{mn}^G + q_{mn} \times (P_{mn}^G)^2 + \left| e_{mn} \sin(f_{mn}(P_{mn(min)}^G - P_{mn}^G)) \right| \right)$$
$$\tag{5b}$$

$$F_{Overall}(P_{mn}^G) = \sum_{m=1}^{NA} (\sum_{n=1}^{NG} \left(c_{mn} + b_{mn} \times P_{mn}^G + a_{mn} \times (P_{mn}^G)^2 + g_{mn} \times P_{mn}^G \right.$$
$$\left. + h_{mn} \times (P_{mn}^G)^2 + q_{mn} \times (P_{mn}^G)^2 + \left| e_{mn} \sin(f_{mn}(P_{mn(min)}^G - P_{mn}^G)) \right| \right) \tag{5c}$$

All the above mentioned objective functions imply to both equality and inequality imperatives:

1) Power balance constraint

The below equation represents the power system balance equation without losses

$$\sum_{n=1}^{NG} P_{mn}^G = P_m^D + \sum_{k,k \neq m} P_{Tmk}; \ n \in NG \tag{6}$$

here, P_{mn}^D = power demand of mth region;
P_{Tmk} = tie line power passes through m^{th} region to k^{th} region;
P_{Tmk} = +ve while power passes through m^{th} region to k^{th} region;
P_{Tmk} = −ve while power passes through k^{th} region to m^{th} region.

The overall power demand and losses in a system must be equal to the generated power.

$$\sum_{n=1}^{NG} P_{mn}^G = P_{mn}^D + P_{mn}^{Loss} \sum_{k,k\neq m} P_{Tmk}; \ n \in NG \tag{7}$$

Where, P^{Loss} (the Power Loss), may be represented as:

$$P_{mn}^{Loss} = \sum_{m=1}^{NA} \sum_{n=1}^{NG} P_{mn}^G B_{mn} P_{mn}^G \tag{8}$$

if B_0 and B_{00} matrices for loss coefficients are given, then the above equation can be modified as:

$$P_{mn}^{Loss} = \sum_{m=1}^{NA} \sum_{n=1}^{NG} P_{mn}^G B_{mn} P_{mn}^G + \sum_{n=1}^{NA} B_{0mn} P_{mn}^G + B_{00m} \tag{9}$$

The expanded version of the above equation may be represented as:

$$P_{mn}^{Loss} = \begin{bmatrix} P_1 & P_2 & \cdots & P_{NG} \end{bmatrix} + \begin{bmatrix} B_{11} & B_{12} & \ldots & B_{1n} \\ B_{21} & B_{22} & \ldots & B_{2n} \\ \vdots & \vdots & \ddots & \vdots \\ B_{n1} & B_{n2} & \ldots & B_{nn} \end{bmatrix} \begin{bmatrix} P_1 \\ P_2 \\ \vdots \\ P_{NG} \end{bmatrix} + \begin{bmatrix} P_1 & P_2 & \cdots & P_{NG} \end{bmatrix} \begin{bmatrix} B_{01} \\ B_{02} \\ \vdots \\ B_{0NG} \end{bmatrix} + B_{00} \tag{10}$$

2) Generator limit constraint

By the upper and down limits, each and every generator's real power generation can be restricted.

$$P_{mn(min)}^G \leq P_{mn}^G \leq P_{mn(max)}^G \quad m = 1, 2, 3, ..., NA; n \in NG \tag{11}$$

3) Ramp rate limits

It is necessary to make the output power of a generating unit within the down and higher bounds of active power generation.

$$P_{mn}^G - P_0^{G_o} \leq UR_{mn} \quad m = 1, 2, 3, ..., NA; n \in NG \tag{12}$$

$$P_{mn}^{G_o} - P_{mn}^G \leq DR_{mn} \quad m = 1, 2, 3, ..., NA; n \in NG \tag{13}$$

The ramp rate limit is represented as follows:

$$\max[P_{mn(max)}^G, (UR_{mn} - P_{mn}^G)] \leq P_{mn}^G \leq \min[P_{mn(max)}^G, (P_{mn}^{G_o} - DR_{mn})] \quad m = 1, 2, 3..., NA; n \in NG \tag{14}$$

Where P_{mn}^G represents earlier output of active power in the nth generation unit and. UR_{mn}, DR_{mn} presents the ramp rate of down and higher bounds of the nth generation unit.

4) Prohibited Operating Zones

The resultant generation graph of input as well as output powers in a generating unit has prohibited operating zones (POZ) which may be discrete because of its functional limitations of the generator caused by the malfunction error in the machine itself or within the parts of the machine. This will create difficulty in determining the actual performance curve, but by not considering the performance curves in these areas, the efficient economy is achieved. These discrete input-output power bounded ranges are represented as follows:

$$\begin{cases} P_{mn(min)} \leq P_{mn} \leq P_{mn(min),1}^{POZ} \\ P_{mn(max),M-1}^{POZ} \leq P_{mn} \leq P_{mn,M}^{POZ}; \quad m = 2, 3, \ldots . N_{mn} \\ P_{mn,N_{mn}}^{POZ} \leq P_{mn} \leq P_{mn(max)}; \quad m = N_{mn} \end{cases} \quad (15)$$

Where, M = overall numerical figures of operating zones of nth generator in region m.

$P_{mn(max),M-1}^{POZ}$ = higher boundary of $(M-1)^{th}$ POZ of nth generator in region m.
$P_{mn,M}^{POZ}$ = the minimum boundary of Mth POZ of nth generator in region m.
N_{mn} = the overall numerical figures of POZ of nth generator in region m.

5) Tie line capacity imperatives

This tie line power passes through region m to region n and lies among the highest and smallest capacity limits.

$$-P_{Tmn}^{max} \leq P_{Tmn} \leq P_{Tmn}^{max} \quad (16)$$

Where $-P_{Tmn}^{max}$ and P_{Tmn}^{max} indicates smallest and highest tie-line power from region m to region n.

4 Conclusion

In this research paper, the mathematical formulation of MAELD problem in conventional approach considering real power and tie-line limits has been presented successfully by the authors. This is very important task to satisfy in power system scheduling, processing, organizing and managing. MAELD problem of electric power system is explored with electric power generating units of various different regions. This mathematical formulation of MAELD problem will be helpful in future for further research works.

References

1. Doty, K.W., McEntire, P.L.: An analysis of electric power brokerage systems. IEEE Trans. Power Appar. Syst. PAS **101**(2), 389–396 (1982). https://doi.org/10.1109/TPAS.1982. 317119.
2. Desell, A.L., McClelland, E.C., Tammar, K., Van Horne, P.R.: Transmission constrained production cost analysis in power system planning. IEEE Power Eng. Rev. PER **4**(8), 57 (1984). https://doi.org/10.1109/MPER.1984.5525972
3. Helmick, S.D., Shoults, R.R.: A practical approach to an interim multi-area economic dispatch using limited computer resources. IEEE Power Eng. Rev. PER **5**(6), 46–47 (1985). https:// doi.org/10.1109/MPER.1985.5526642
4. Orero, S.O., Irving, M.R.: Economic dispatch of generators with prohibited operating zones: A genetic algorithm approach. IEE Proc. Gener. Transm. Distrib. **143**(6), 533–534 (1996). https://doi.org/10.1049/ip-gtd:19960626
5. Shi, Y., Eberhart, R.C.: Empirical study of particle swarm optimization. In: Proceedings of 1999 Congress on Evolutionary Computation CEC 1999, vol. 3, pp. 1945–1950 (1999). https://doi.org/10.1109/CEC.1999.785511
6. Song, Y.H., Chou, C.S., Stonham, T.J.: Combined heat and power economic dispatch by improved ant colony search algorithm. Electr. Power Syst. Res. **52**(2), 115–121 (1999). https:// doi.org/10.1016/S0378-7796(99)00011-5
7. Jayabarathi, T., Sadasivam, G., Ramachandran, V.: Evolutionary programming-based multi-area economic dispatch with tie line constraints. Electr. Mach. Power Syst. **28**(12), 1165–1176 (2000). https://doi.org/10.1080/073135600449044
8. Chen, C., Chen, N.: Direct search method for solving economic dispatch problem considering transmission capacity constraints. IEEE Trans. Power Syst. **16**(4), 764–769 (2001)
9. Zhu, J.Z.: Multiarea power systems economic power dispatch using a nonlinear optimization neural network approach. Electr. Power Compon. Syst. **31**(6), 553–563 (2003). https://doi. org/10.1080/15325000390208101
10. Park, J.B., Lee, K.S., Shin, J.R., Lee, K.Y.: A particle swarm optimization for economic dispatch with nonsmooth cost functions. IEEE Trans. Power Syst. **20**(1), 34–42 (2005). https:// doi.org/10.1109/TPWRS.2004.831275
11. Cai, J., Ma, X., Li, L., Haipeng, P.: Chaotic particle swarm optimization for economic dispatch considering the generator constraints. Energy Convers. Manag. **48**(2), 645–653 (2007). https:// doi.org/10.1016/j.enconman.2006.05.020
12. dos Santos Coelho, L., Mariani, V.C.: Combining of chaotic differential evolution and quadratic programming for economic dispatch optimization with valve-point effect. IEEE Trans. Power Syst. **21**(2), 989–996 (2006). https://doi.org/10.1109/TPWRS.2006.873410
13. Selvakumar, A.I., Thanushkodi, K.: Optimization using civilized swarm: solution to economic dispatch with multiple minima. Electr. Power Syst. Res. **79**(1), 8–16 (2009). https://doi.org/ 10.1016/J.EPSR.2008.05.001
14. Yu, B., Yuan, X., Wang, J.: Short-term hydro-thermal scheduling using particle swarm optimization method. Energy Convers. Manag. **48**(7), 1902–1908 (2007). https://doi.org/10.1016/ j.enconman.2007.01.034
15. Chaturvedi, K.T., Pandit, M., Srivastava, L.: Self-organizing hierarchical particle swarm optimization for nonconvex economic dispatch. IEEE Trans. Power Syst. **23**(3), 1079–1087 (2008). https://doi.org/10.1109/TPWRS.2008.926455
16. Manoharan, P.S., Kannan, P.S., Baskar, S., Willjuice Iruthayarajan, M.: Evolutionary algorithm solution and KKT based optimality verification to multi-area economic dispatch. Int. J. Electr. Power Energy Syst **31**(7–8), 365–373 (2009). https://doi.org/10.1016/j.ijepes.2009. 03.010

17. Wang, L., Singh, C.: Reserve-constrained multiarea environmental/economic dispatch based on particle swarm optimization with local search. Eng. Appl. Artif. Intell. **22**(2), 298–307 (2009). https://doi.org/10.1016/j.engappai.2008.07.007

18. Chaturvedi, K.T., Pandit, M., Srivastava, L.: Particle swarm optimization with time varying acceleration coefficients for non-convex economic power dispatch. Int. J. Electr. Power Energy Syst. **31**(6), 249–257 (2009). https://doi.org/10.1016/j.ijepes.2009.01.010

19. Bulbul, S.M.A., Pradhan, M., Roy, P.K., Pal, T.: Opposition-based krill herd algorithm applied to economic load dispatch problem. Ain Shams Eng. J. **9**(3), 423–440 (2018). https://doi.org/10.1016/j.asej.2016.02.003

20. Vlachogiannis, J.G., Lee, K.Y.: Closure to discussion on 'economic load dispatch - a comparative study on heuristic optimization techniques with an improved coordinated aggregation-based PSO.' IEEE Trans. Power Syst. **25**(1), 591–592 (2010). https://doi.org/10.1109/TPWRS.2009.2037534

21. Azadani, E.N., Hosseinian, S.H., Moradzadeh, B.: Generation and reserve dispatch in a competitive market using constrained particle swarm optimization. Int. J. Electr. Power Energy Syst. **32**(1), 79–86 (2010). https://doi.org/10.1016/j.ijepes.2009.06.009

22. AlRashidi, M.R., El-Hawary, M.E.: Hybrid particle swarm optimization approach for solving the discrete OPF problem considering the valve loading effects. IEEE Trans. Power Syst. **22**(4), 2030–2038 (2007). https://doi.org/10.1109/TPWRS.2007.907375

23. Safari, A., Shayeghi, H.: Iteration particle swarm optimization procedure for economic load dispatch with generator constraints. Expert Syst. Appl. **38**(5), 6043–6048 (2011). https://doi.org/10.1016/j.eswa.2010.11.015

24. Wang, Y., Zhou, J., Zhou, C., Wang, Y., Qin, H., Lu, Y.: An improved self-adaptive PSO technique for short-term hydrothermal scheduling. Expert Syst. Appl. **39**(3), 2288–2295 (2012). https://doi.org/10.1016/j.eswa.2011.08.007

25. Mohammadi-Ivatloo, B., Moradi-Dalvand, M., Rabiee, A.: Combined heat and power economic dispatch problem solution using particle swarm optimization with time varying acceleration coefficients. Electr. Power Syst. Res. **95**, 9–18 (2013). https://doi.org/10.1016/j.epsr.2012.08.005

26. Vickers, N.J.: Animal communication: when i'm calling you, will you answer too? Curr. Biol. **27**(14), R713–R715 (2017). https://doi.org/10.1016/j.cub.2017.05.064

27. Basu, M.: Artificial bee colony optimization for multi-area economic dispatch. Int. J. Electr. Power Energy Syst. **49**(1), 181–187 (2013). https://doi.org/10.1016/j.ijepes.2013.01.004

28. Hlalele, T.G., Naidoo, R.M., Bansal, R.C., Zhang, J.: Multi-objective stochastic economic dispatch with maximal renewable penetration under renewable obligation. Appl. Energy **270**, 115120 (2020). https://doi.org/10.1016/j.apenergy.2020.115120

29. Ellahi, M., Abbas, G.: A hybrid metaheuristic approach for the solution of renewables-incorporated economic dispatch problems. IEEE Access **8**, 127608–127621 (2020). https://doi.org/10.1109/ACCESS.2020.3008570

30. Habibi, F., Khosravi, F., Kharrati, S., Karimi, S.: Simultaneous multi-area economic-environmental load dispatch modeling in presence of wind turbines by MOPSO. J. Electr. Eng. Technol. **15**(3), 1059–1072 (2020). https://doi.org/10.1007/s42835-020-00388-8

31. Azizivahed, A., Arefi, A., Naderi, E., Narimani, H., Fathi, M., Narimani, M.R.: An efficient hybrid approach to solve bi-objective multi-area dynamic economic emission dispatch problem. Electr. Power Compon. Syst. **48**(4–5), 485–500 (2020). https://doi.org/10.1080/15325008.2020.1793830

32. Lin, J., Wang, Z.J.: Multi-area economic dispatch using an improved stochastic fractal search algorithm. Energy 47–58 (2019). https://doi.org/10.1016/j.energy.2018.10.065

33. Nazari-Heris, F., Mohammadi-Ivatloo, B., Nazarpour, D.: Economic dispatch of renewable energy and CHP-based multi-zone microgrids under limitations of electrical network. Iran. J. Sci. Technol. Trans. Electr. Eng. **44**(1), 155–168 (2019). https://doi.org/10.1007/s40998-019-00208-4
34. Mokarram, M.J., Niknam, T., Aghaei, J., Shafie-Khah, M., Catalão, J.P.S.: Hybrid optimization algorithm to solve the nonconvex multiarea economic dispatch problem. IEEE Syst. J. **13**(3), 3400–3409 (2019). https://doi.org/10.1109/JSYST.2018.2889988
35. Basu, M.: Squirrel search algorithm for multi-region combined heat and power economic dispatch incorporating renewable energy sources. Energy **182**, 296–305 (2019). https://doi.org/10.1016/j.energy.2019.06.087

A Cost Effective Memetic Optimal Approach for Solution of Economic Load Dispatch Problem in Realistic Power System

Shivani Sehgal[✉], Aman Ganesh, and Vikram Kumar Kamboj

Lovely Professional University, Phagwara, Punjab, India
{aman.23332,vikram.23687}@lpu.co.in

Abstract. Electric power system problems are amongst the most complex and challenging problems of electric industry market. The main aim of economic load dispatch in power system operation control and planning is to satisfy the energy demand at the least cost while fulfilling all the equality and inequality constraints. This paper presents the mathematical formulation of optimal load dispatch problem by considering the sources of energy generation from conventional power plants and all the important constraints of the realistic power system. In the proposed research the memetic optimizer is developed by hybridizing slime mould algorithm with pattern search algorithm. The proposed hSMA-PS has been tested to obtain the solution of economic load dispatch problem and experimentally it has been observed that the proposed memetic optimizer is providing cost effective solution to complex economic load dispatch problem of electric power system.

Keywords: Economic load dispatch · Optimization · Transmission losses

1 Introduction

Nowadays, the electric power industry is considered to be the most challenging and complex due to the increasing demand of electric energy and lack of availability of energy resources thus necessitates the load dispatch of power generated at the most economic rates. With the development of electrification in transport industry the growth in energy demand is also increased, thus forces the use of renewable energy sources along with the conventional energy sources. In near future, use of electric vehicles is encouraged and so the energy demand. To use the generated energy effectively there should be proper use of energy during charging and discharging process and the energy available from the standalone vehicles can be used as BESS - battery energy storage system for ancillary services. The main purpose of the optimal/economic load dispatch (ELD) problem of an electric power generating system is to attain the system load requirement at the most reduced (minimum) fuel operating cost by scheduling the committed generating units, while satisfying the system constraints i.e. equality and inequality constraints [1, 2]. Electrification of vehicles also helps to eradicate the greenhouse gas emissions and air pollutants with decreased dependency on fossil fuels. Electric vehicles (EVs) are popularized in motor vehicle market universally and will prove to be a promising

© Springer Nature Singapore Pte Ltd. 2021
P. K. Singh et al. (Eds.): FTNCT 2020, CCIS 1396, pp. 45–56, 2021.
https://doi.org/10.1007/978-981-16-1483-5_5

approach to reduce the pollution in a short time, but also cause a new challenge to electric energy industry in regard to power system operation and control. To properly access the use of EVs, electricity charging facilities are being provide to plugged the vehicle into the power system and directly charge their batteries. An increased number of these vehicles will cause considerable uncertainties in the operation of power system and hence increase the load demand due to the haphazard charging of vehicles [3]. So, the continuously growing demand for energy has encouraged the researchers to consider the load dispatch problem economically. The current scenario in optimization and computing [4, 5] is to efficiently use the modern algorithms to obtain the most optimum solutions.

The remaining paper is structured as follows. Section 2 introduces the economic load dispatch (ELD) problem with its mathematical modelling. Section 3 describes the proposed methodology for solving the ELD problem. The results are presented in Sect. 4 considering different test systems and Sect. 5 concludes this paper.

2   Optimal/Economic Load Dispatch Problem

The Optimal/Economic Load Dispatch Problem stated as ELD problem in power systems is defined as the load division among the various thermal generators of an existing power system such that the total operational cost of energy generation is reduced to a minimum value while considering the power balance and power generation capacity constraints also known as equality and inequality constraints respectively [1]. The ELD Problem is classified as convex and non-convex problem where linear constraints contribute to convex problem and non-linear constraints along with the linear constraints develops the non-convex nature of the ELDP. The generation capacity and power balance constraints are categorized as linear constraints and provides the simplified approximate results and a more specific and accurate problem is modelled by considering the impact of non-linear constraints like valve point loading effects (VPLE), boundary restrictions known as RRL - ramp rate limits and non-operational regions known as prohibited operating zones (POZs) [6]. This paper includes the complete mathematical formulation of classical Economic load dispatch problem and has been tested using a newly developed hSMA-PS optimizer to enhance the efficacy and novelty of the system.

2.1   Problem Formulation

The key purpose of the load dispatch problem in conventional fossil-based plants is to minimize the total operational fuel cost of the power generating units whilst fulfilling the different equality/inequality restrictions. This can be considered by neglecting the transmission losses or by taking the transmission losses. Also, the different non-linear constraints like VPLE, RRL and POZs can be considered for a realistic power system. The mathematical modelling of ELD problem [7] has been framed with the following notations:

NG=Total number of generating units	$P^G_{n(min)}$, $P^G_{n(max)}$ = Minimum and Maximum power
$P_n{}^G$=Power of the nth generating unit	of the nth generating units
n = index for power generating units	$F(P^G)$ =Total Fuel cost of power generating units.
P^{Loss} =Coefficient of power loss	a_n, b_n and c_n = Coefficient of nth power generating units

Classical ELD Problem. The mathematical formulation of classical economic load dispatch problem for an hour is characterized as:

$$F(P^G) = \sum_{n=1}^{NG} [a_n(P_n^G)^2 + b_n P_n^G + c_n)]$$
(1)

The equation of economic load dispatch for NG number of thermal generating units for H number of hours is characterized as:

$$F(P^G) = \sum_{h=1}^{H} \left(\sum_{n=1}^{NG} [a_n(P_n^G)^2 + b_n P_n^G + c_n)] \right)$$
(2)

Cubical ELD Problem. To establish the output power of online generating units the ELD problem intends to congregate the system load at least cost whilst fulfilling the system constraints. So, as to attain correct dispatch outcomes, a cubical function is used for modeling the unit cost.

$$F(P^G) = \sum_{n=1}^{NG} [a_n(P_n^G)^3 + b_n(P_n^G)^2 + c_n P_n^G + d_n)]$$
(3a)

The Cubical ELD with Valve Point effect can be represented as:

$$F(P^G) = \sum_{n=1}^{NG} [a_n(P_n^G)^3 + b_n(P_n^G)^2 + c_n P_n^G + d_n)] + \left| \varphi_n \sin(\gamma_n(P_{n(min)}^G - P_n^G)) \right|$$
(3b)

Heat and Power ELD Problem. The heat and power ELD problem of a system aims to resolve the unit heat and power production of the generating units [8]. The mathematical formulation for heat and power ELD may be described as:

$$F_{Power}(P_n^G) = \sum_{n=1}^{NG} \left(c_n + b_n \times P_n^G + a_n \times (P_n^G)^2 \right)$$
(4a)

$$F_{Heat}(P_n^G) = \sum_{n=1}^{NG} \left(g_n + h_n \times P_n^G + q_n \times (P_n^G)^2 \right)$$
(4b)

$$F_{Overall}(P_n^G) = \sum_{n=1}^{NG} \left(c_n + b_n \times P_n^G + a_n \times (P_n^G)^2 + g_n \times P_n^G + h_n \times (P_n^G)^2 + q_n \times (P_n^G)^2 \right)$$
(4c)

The objective function for heat and power ELD considering valve point loading effects can be reframed as:

$$F_{Power}(P_n^G) = \sum_{n=1}^{NG} \left(c_n + b_n \times P_n^G + a_n \times (P_n^G)^2 + \left| \varphi_n \sin(\gamma_n(P_{n(min)}^G - P_n^G)) \right| \right)$$
(5a)

$$F_{Heat}(P_n^G) = \sum_{n=1}^{NG} \left(g_n + h_n \times P_n^G + q_n \times (P_n^G)^2 + \left| \varphi_n \sin(\gamma_n (P_{n(\min)}^G - P_n^G)) \right| \right) \quad (5b)$$

$$F_{Overall}(P_n^G) = \sum_{n=1}^{NG} \left(c_n + b_n \times P_n^G + a_n \times (P_n^G)^2 + g_n \times P_n^G + h_n \times (P_n^G)^2 + q_n \times (P_n^G)^2 + \left| \varphi_n \sin(\gamma_n (P_{n(\min)}^G - P_n^G)) \right| \right)$$

$$(6)$$

All the objective functions of ELD problem as mentioned above are subjected to equality and inequality constraints as follows:

Power Balance Constraints/Equality Constraints. The overall power produced by all the power generating units in a power plant must be equal to the total load requirement and real power loss. Mathematically it is represented as

$$\sum_{n=1}^{NG} P_n^G = P^{Demand} + P^{Loss} \quad (7)$$

Where, P^{Loss} is the power transmission loss and may be represented as:

$$P^{Loss} = \sum_{n=1}^{NG} \sum_{m=1}^{NG} P_n^G B_{nm} P_m^G \quad (8)$$

and if B_{i0}, B_{00} are loss coefficients, then the loss equation can be changed as:

$$P^{Loss} = P_n^G B_{nm} P_m^G + \sum_{n=1}^{NG} P_n^G \times B_{i0} + B_{00} \quad (9)$$

The expanded version of the above equation may be represented as:

$$P^{Loss} = \begin{bmatrix} P_1 & P_2 & \cdots & P_{NG} \end{bmatrix} \begin{bmatrix} B_{11} & B_{12} & \dots & B_{1n} \\ B_{21} & B_{22} & \dots & B_{2n} \\ \vdots & \vdots & \ddots & \vdots \\ B_{n1} & B_{n2} & \dots & B_{nn} \end{bmatrix} \begin{bmatrix} P_1 \\ P_2 \\ \vdots \\ P_{NG} \end{bmatrix} + \begin{bmatrix} P_1 & P_2 & \cdots & P_{NG} \end{bmatrix} \begin{bmatrix} B_{01} \\ B_{02} \\ \vdots \\ B_{0NG} \end{bmatrix} + B00$$

$$(10)$$

Generator Limit Constraints (Inequality Constraints). The power produced by each generating unit must lie within the maximum and minimum values of operating power.

$$P_{n(\min)}^G \leq P_n^G \leq P_{n(\max)}^G \quad n = 1, 2, 3, \dots, NG \quad (11)$$

Ramp Rate Limits. In order to maintain the rate of change of output power within a specified range as to keep the thermal shifts in the turbine within its safe boundaries and to increase the life, the operating range for online generators is controlled by their ramp rate limits (RRL) as follows. Mathematically,

$$P_n^G - P_0^{Go} \leq UR_n \quad n = 1, 2, 3, \dots, NG \quad (12)$$

$$P_n^{G_o} - P_n^G \leq DR_n \quad n = 1, 2, 3, \ldots, NG \tag{13}$$

$$\max[P_{n(max)}^G, (UR_n - P_n^G)] \leq P_n^G \leq \min[P_{n(max)}^G, (P_n^{G_o} - DR_n)] \quad n = 1, 2, 3, \ldots, NG \tag{14}$$

Prohibited Operating Zones. The thermal power generating units may lie in a certain specified range where operation of the generating unit is impossible due to some physical constraints like vibration in shaft, steam valve, other machine components, Such constrained or restricted regions are acknowledged as prohibited operating zones (POZ). Under such constraints, the operational region splits into isolated sub-regions, thus forming a non-convex problem.

$$\begin{cases} P_{n(min)} \leq P_n \leq P_{n(min),1}^{POZ} \\ P_{n(max),m-1}^{POZ} \leq P_n \leq P_{min,m}^{POZ}; \quad m = 2, 3, \ldots.N_{POZ} \\ P_{n(max),m}^{POZ} \leq n_i \leq P_{n(max)}; \quad m = N_{POZ} \end{cases} \tag{15}$$

3 Proposed Methodology

In the proposed research, a memetic slime mould optimizer combined with pattern search optimizer has been used and named as hSMA-PS. Slime Mould algorithm in its simple version simulates action and a transition in Physarum polycephalum slime mould n foraging, and its entire life cycle does not model. Simultaneously, the usage of SMA weights replicates positive and negative criticism of slime mould during foraging, shaping 3 distinct morphotypes. The venous configuration of the slime mould grows according to the contraction mode phase difference [9]. 1) Thick veins from around the radius as the contraction frequency varies from outwards to inward. 2) Anisotropy begins to turn up when the mode of contraction is unstable 3) If the slime mould reduction series is no matter how long ordered in space and time the venous system will no longer be relevant. If sources of food are of high quality, use region-limited search method for slime mould [10], thereby concentrating the check on sources of food found. If the density of the original food source is at a low level, the slime mould will finish up leaving the food source to search other optional regional food sources [11]. This innovative research method can be expressed more often when various qualities of food blocks in an area are dispersed.

3.1 Mathematical Modeling of SMA.

This section illustrates mathematical modeling of SMA and describes various methodologies for finding food. Which are namely approaching food, wrap of food, grabble food.

Approaching Food. Depending upon the smell in the air, slime mould should address food. In order to describe its reaching nature in mathematics, the following equations are suggested to mimic the process of contraction.

$$\overrightarrow{S(i+1)} = \overrightarrow{S_b(i)} + \overrightarrow{vb}.\left(\overrightarrow{W} \cdot \overrightarrow{S_A(i)} - \overrightarrow{S_B(i)}\right), r < p \tag{16}$$

$$\overrightarrow{S(i+1)} = \overrightarrow{vc} \cdot \overrightarrow{S(i)}, r \geq p \qquad (17)$$

In this case $\overrightarrow{vc}$ a parameter variable with a linear decrease from one to zero, $\overrightarrow{vb}$ a parameter variable with a range of $[-a, a]$, i reflect the current iteration, $\overrightarrow{S_b}$ individual position with the highest currently observed odor concentration, $\overrightarrow{S}$ individual location of slime mould, $\overrightarrow{S_A}$ individual and $\overrightarrow{S_B}$ individual are two of individuals randomly picked from swarm and slime mould individual weight as $\overrightarrow{W}$.

$$p = \tanh|X(t) - bF| \qquad (18)$$

Here, $t \in 1, 2, \ldots, n$, $X(t)$ reflects the fitness of $\overrightarrow{S}$, bF reflects the best fitness in all iterations. The equation $\overrightarrow{vb}$ states the following:

$$\overrightarrow{vb} = [-a, a] \qquad (19)$$

$$a = \text{arctanh}\left(-\left(\frac{i}{\text{max\_}i}\right) + 1\right) \qquad (20)$$

$$\overrightarrow{W(SmellIndex(i))} = \begin{cases} 1 + r \cdot \log\left(\frac{DF - X(t)}{DF - wF} + 1\right), condition \\ 1 - r \cdot \log\left(\frac{DF - X(t)}{DF - wF} + 1\right), others \end{cases} \qquad (21)$$

$$SmellIndex = sort(X) \qquad (22)$$

'r' indicates its random number at the duration $[0, 1]$, DF represents the optimum fitness achieved in the recent iterative process, WF indicates a worst fitness cost currently attained in the iterative course, *smell index* replicates the order of sorted attributes of fitness (goes up in the order of minimal value). The Eq. 17 and 18 results are visualized in Fig. 1. The position of individual $\overrightarrow{S}$ quest can be changed to the finest location $\overrightarrow{S_B}$ currently obtained, and the proper tuning of $\overrightarrow{vb}$, $\overrightarrow{vc}$ and $\overrightarrow{W}$ parameters will adjust the position of the item.

Wrapping Food. This section mathematically simulates the mode of contraction of slime mould venous tissue structure. It has been concluded that as the food concentration reached by the vein becomes higher, the bio-oscillator-generated wave becomes more stronger with faster flow of the cytoplasm and the vein becomes thicker as stated in Eq. 21, The heavier weight lies near the region when the food concentration is high; if the food concentration decreases, the weight of the area reduces, thereby having to turn to explore other areas. Figure 2 shows the fitness values assessment process for slime mould.

A mathematical model for upgrading its slime mould position shall be as follows:

$$\overrightarrow{S^*} = \begin{cases} rand \cdot (U_{\cup B} - U_{LB}) + U_{LB}, rand < z \\ \overrightarrow{S_b(i)} + \overrightarrow{vb} \cdot \left(W \cdot \overrightarrow{S(i)} - \overrightarrow{S_B(i)}\right), r < p \\ \overrightarrow{vc} \cdot \overrightarrow{S(i)}, r \geq p \end{cases} \qquad (23)$$

Here, U_{LB} and $U_{\cup B}$ represent the quest range's lower and upper limits, *rand* and r represent the random value in the range 0 and 1.

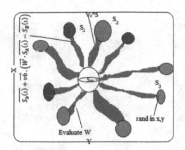

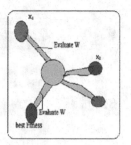

Fig. 1. 2D View of possible position   **Fig. 2.** Assessment of fitness

Food Grabble. Slime Mould evidently depends upon its wave of propagation that is generated by the biological generator/oscillator to alter the cytoplasmic flowing throughout the veins, and they appear in improved affordable food absorption role. In order to simulate the variations in the venous width of slime mould; $\overrightarrow{W}$, $\overrightarrow{vb}$ and $\overrightarrow{vc}$ are applied to realize the varieties. $\overrightarrow{W}$ replicates arithmetically the oscillatory frequency of slime moulds next to one at various locations of food concentrations, but slime moulds can enter in the food quite easily whenever they achieve food of high quality, thus approaching food very slowly when the food level is lower in the image point, thereby increase the effectiveness of slime moulds in selecting the optimum food source. $\overrightarrow{vb}$ fluctuates at random between ($-a$ and a) and turns to zero as iterations inclined up while $\overrightarrow{vc}$ swings between (-1 and 1) and finally tends to be zero.

3.2 Pattern Search Algorithm

Pattern search algorithm (PS) is considered as a derivative-free method with local exploration search capability and is ideal for solution space at which optimization problem derivative is uncomfortable or uncertain [12, 13]. The study involves two movements when conducting its own operation: the first movement is for an exploratory search and the other movement is the movement of pattern which is a greater quest for path improvement; The movement of the pattern involves two points: one is the existing location while another is some arbitrary point with improved objective function that controls the search process; and a new improved point is obtained from Eq. (24) stated as

$$x^{(iter+1)} = x^{(\text{int})} + \upsilon[x^{(iter)} - x^{(\text{int})}] \tag{24}$$

Here, υ is a positive acceleration factor, used during multiplying the path length improvement's vector.

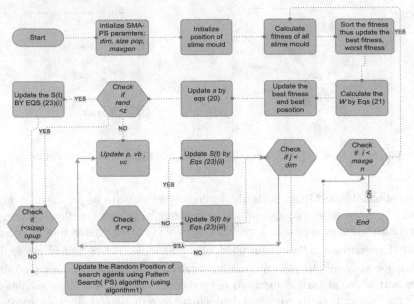

Fig. 3. Flow chart of hSMA-PS algorithm

The position vector 'X' that was randomly generated is further improved employing the PS method in the proposed hybrid Slime Mould-Pattern Search (hSMA-PS) algorithm, and the new position vector, $\vec{S}$ was applied to Slime Mould to determine the location of the food source. The heuristics technique has been introduced for hybridizing the SMA and PS. The phase of exploration in hSMA-PS is similar to that of classical SMA and the phase of exploitation is taken from PS in the proposed algorithm. The pseudo code for SMA-PS is as follows in Algorithm 2 and Flowchart is illustrated in Fig. 3.

4 Results and Discussions

In this research paper, the proposed algorithm is implemented on three IEEE test systems. Case 1: IEEE-14 Bus System (5 generating units); Case 2: IEEE-30 Bus System (6 generating units) and Case3: IEEE-57 Bus System (7 generating units). The proposed memetic optimizer has been tested on Intel® Core ™ i7–5600 CPU @2.60 GHz 2.60 GHz for 500 Iterations and 30-trial runs. The test data for all the test systems has been given in Table 1, 2 and 3. The results for these cases using the proposed memetic optimizer has been shown in Table 4 through Table 6. Comparison of results undoubtedly shows that the proposed optimizer has better efficiency as compared to many other optimizers. The total fuel cost in all the three cases has been significantly reduced using hSMA-PS method in comparison to other algorithms considered in literature.

Algorithm 1 Pseudo-code of PS (Pattern Search)

Initialize the input parameters for pattern search algorithm i.e. acceleration factor (υ), perturbation vector (P^0) and perturbation tolerance vector (τ).

Initialize the current perturbation vector $P \leftarrow P^0$ and select the value for the starting point x^{int}.

Update x^{int} to x^{iter} using exploratory search around x^{int} to find an improved point x^{iter} that has a better value of objective function.

    if $x^{iter} > x^{int}$

        $DO\ P \leftarrow P/2$.

        if $P_i < \tau$

            $DO\ \ x^{final} = x^{int}$

        else

    Go to step-3 and update the solution vector using exploratory move.

    else

        $DO\ x^{final} = x^{iter}$, $P \leftarrow P^0$ and go to step-4.

        end

    end

Apply Pattern Move using following steps:

    Obtain tentative x^{iter+1} by a pattern move from x^{int} through x^{iter}.

    Obtain final x^{iter+1} by an exploratory search around tentative x^{iter+1}.

        if $f(x^{iter+1}) > f(x^{iter})$

            $DO\ \ x^{int} \leftarrow x^{iter}$ and go to step 3.

        else

            $DO\ x^{int} \leftarrow x^{iter}$, $x^{iter} \leftarrow x^{iter+1}$ and go to step-4

end

Algorithm 2 Pseudo-code of SMA-PS

Initialize the parameters *pop size, Max_iteraition*;

Initialize the positions of slime mould $S_t (t = 1, 2, \ldots, n)$;

While $(i \le Max\_iteraition)$

Calculate the fitness of all slime mould;

    Update bestFitness, S_b

Calculate the W by Eq. (21).

For *each search portion*

    Update p, vb, vc;

    Update positions by Eq. (23);

End For

Check $\vec{S}$ *location using the pattern search method (refer algorithm 1 pseudo code)*

$i = i + 1$;

End While

Return *bestFitness, S_b*;

Table 1. Test data for IEEE-14 bus system with power demand $= 259$ MW

Unit	a	b	c	P_{min}	P_{max}
1	150.000	2.00000	0.00160	50	200
2	25.00000	2.50000	0.01000	20	80
3	0.00000	1.00000	0.06250	15	50
4	0.00000	3.25000	0.00834	10	35
5	0.00000	3.00000	0.02500	10	30

Table 2. Test data for IEEE-30 bus system with power demand = 283.4 MW

Bus no.	a	b	c	P_{min}	P_{max}
1	0.00000	2.00000	0.00375	50	200
2	0.00000	1.75000	0.01750	20	80
5	0.00000	1.00000	0.06250	15	50
8	0.00000	3.25000	0.00834	10	35
11	0.00000	3.00000	0.02500	10	30
13	0.00000	3.00000	0.02500	12	40

Table 3. Test data for IEEE-57 bus system with power demand = 1273 MW

Generator no.	a	b	c	P_{min}	P_{max}
G_1	400	7	0.007	100	575
G_2	200	10	0.0095	50	100
G_3	220	8.5	0.009	50	140
G_4	200	11	0.009	50	100
G_5	240	10.5	0.008	100	550
G_6	200	12	0.0075	50	100
G_7	180	10	0.0068	100	410

Table 4. Test results for case 1-IEEE-14 bus system.

Unit	GA [18]	FPSOGSA [14]	PSO [18]	GA-APO [14]	MSG-HP [14]	NSOA [14]	hSMA-PS*	hSMA-PS#
G1	172.765	199.5997	197.4696	172.765	199.6923	181.129	199.9999	199.9999
G2	26.6212	20	20	26.6212	20	46.7567	31.8236	31.8849
G3	24.8322	20.9133	21.3421	24.8322	20.8157	19.1526	17.1765	17.2136
G4	23.4152	15.4893	11.6762	23.4152	15.5504	10.1879	10	10.0001
G5	19.1885	12.5527	17.7744	19.1885	12.5069	10.7719	10	10
Total Power output (MW)	266.8217	268.555	268.2623	266.8217	268.5653	267.9977	269	269
Total fuel cost ($/h)	926.553	834.1308	836.4568	926.553	834.363	905.5437	830.1362	830.4457
P_{loss} (MW)	7.825	9.555	9.2623	7.825	9.5654	8.9977	0	0.0985
Time (s)	0.391	1.544	0.3484	0.391	0.4617	0.015	2.229157	2.617031

*Without Loss   # With Loss

Table 5. Test results for IEEE-30 bus system.

Unit	GA [18]	MSG-HP [16]	NSOA [14]	FPSOGSA [14]	GA-APO [14]	PSO [18]	hSMA-PS*	hSMA-PS#
G1	150.724	199.6331	182.478	199.5997	133.9816	197.8648	132.5045	133.3174
G2	60.8707	20	48.3525	20	37.2158	50.3374	80	80
G3	30.8965	23.7624	19.8553	23.9896	37.7677	15	50	50
G4	14.2138	18.3934	17.137	18.8493	28.3492	10	10	10
G5	19.4888	17.1018	13.6677	18.2153	18.7929	10	10	10
G6	15.9154	15.6922	12.3487	13.8506	38.0525	12	12	12
Total power output (MW)	292.1096	294.5829	293.8395	294.5045	294.16	295.2022	294.5045	294.5045
Total fuel cost ($/h)	996.0369	925.6406	984.9365	925.4137	1101.491	925.7581	553.6511	555.2768
P_{loss}(MW)	8.706	11.183	10.4395	11.1044	10.7563	11.8022	0	0.8129
Time (s)	0.578	0.6215	0.015	1.4108	0.156	0.3529	2.261178	2.97279

*Without Loss   # With Loss

Table 6. Test results for IEEE-57 bus system.

Unit	hSMA-PS	DEIANT [17]	PSO [17]	ACO [17]
G_1 (MW)	444.4432	139.57	142.36	140.82
G_2 (MW)	100	92.84	94.69	93.67
G_3 (MW)	140	56.66	57.79	57.17
G_4 (MW)	100	73.94	75.42	74.61
G_5 (MW)	170.1131	461.27	470.5	465.43
G_6 (MW)	81.4812	97.33	99.28	98.21
G_7 (MW)	236.9625	353.58	360.66	356.77
Total Cost ($/hour)	15581.9276	42017.46	42857.81	42395.62

5 Conclusion

In this paper the mathematical formulation of ELD problem has been framed considering all the important constraints, which is considered as the most challenging problems in power system optimization in to planning, operation, and control. The proposed memetic optimizer hSMA-PS has been tested to find the best possible solution for IEEE-14, 30 and 57 bus system and it has been proved from the results that the proposed optimizer performs better than other meta-heuristics optimizer algorithms.

This method can be implemented to dynamic, multiarea and multiobjective ELD problems. The work can also be extended to thermal solar integrated ELD systems and ELD with due consideration to electric vehicles.

References

1. Wood, A.J., Wollenberg, B.F.: Power Generation, Operation, and Control, 3rd edn.
2. Kothari, D.P., Dhillion, J.S.: Power system optimization. PHI Learning (2010)

3. Andervazh, M.R., Javadi, S.: Emission-economic dispatch of thermal power generation units in the presence of hybrid electric vehicles and correlated wind power plants. IET Gener. Transm. Distrib. **11**(9), 2232–2243 (2017)

4. Singh, P.K., Kar, A.K., Singh, Y., Kolekar, M.H., Tanwar, S. (eds.): Proceedings of ICRIC 2019: Recent Innovations in Computing, vol. 597. Springer, Cham (2020). ISBN: 978-3-030-29406-9. https://doi.org/10.1007/978-3-030-29407-6

5. Singh, P.K., Panigrahi, B.K., Suryadevara, N.K., Sharma, S.K., Singh, A.K. (eds.): Proceedings of ICETIT 2019: Emerging Trends in Information Technology. Lecture Notes in Electrical Engineering (LNEE), Springer, Cham (2020). https://doi.org/10.1007/978-3-030-30577-2

6. Kamboj, V.K., Bath, S.K., Dhillon, J.S.: Solution of non-convex economic load dispatch problem using Grey Wolf Optimizer. Neural Comput. Appl. **27**(5), 1301–1316 (2015). https://doi.org/10.1007/s00521-015-1934-8

7. Bhadoria, A., Kamboj, V.K.: Optimal generation scheduling and dispatch of thermal generating units considering impact of wind penetration using hGWO-RES algorithm. Appl. Intell. **49**(4), 1517–1547 (2018). https://doi.org/10.1007/s10489-018-1325-9

8. Jayakumar, N., Subramanian, S., Ganesan, S., Elanchezhian, E.B.: Grey wolf optimization for combined heat and power dispatch with cogeneration systems. Int. J. Electr. Power Energy Syst. **74**, 252–264 (2016)

9. Nakagaki, T., Yamada, H., Ueda, T.: Interaction between cell shape and contraction pattern in the Physarum plasmodium. Biophys. Chem. **84**(3), 195–204 (2000)

10. Kareiva, P., Odell, G.: Swarms of predators exhibit 'preytaxis' if individual predators use area-restricted search. Am. Nat. **130**(2), 233–270 (1987)

11. Latty, T., Beekman, M.: Food quality affects search strategy in the acellular slime mould, Physarum polycephalum. Behav. Ecol. **20**(6), 1160–1167 (2009)

12. Torczon, V.: On the convergence of pattern search algorithms. SIAM J. Optim. **7**(1), 1–25 (1997)

13. McCarthy, J.F.: Block-conjugate-gradient method. Phys. Rev. D **40**(6), 2149–2152 (1989)

14. Malik, T.N., ul Asar, A., Wyne, M.F., Akhtar, S.: A new hybrid approach for the solution of nonconvex economic dispatch problem with valve-point effects. Electr. Power Syst. Res. **80**(9), 1128–1136 (2010)

15. Abdullah, M.N., Tawai, R., Yousof, F.: Comparison of constraints handling methods for economic load dispatch problem using particle swarm optimization algorithm. Int. J. Ad. Sci. Eng. Inf. Technol. **7**(4), 1322 (2017)

16. Kumari, Ch.L., Kamboj, V.K.: An effective solution to single-area dynamic dispatch using improved chimp optimizer. In: E3S Web Conference, vol. 184 (2020). Article number: 01069

17. Rahmat, N.A., Aziz, N.F.A., Mansor, M.H., Musirin, I.: Optimizing economic load dispatch with renewable energy sources via differential evolution immunized ant colony optimization technique (2017). https://doi.org/10.18517/ijaseit.7.6.2328

18. Whitley, D.: An overview of evolutionary algorithms: practical issues and common pitfalls. Inf. Softw. Technol. **43**(14), 817–831 (2001)

Air Navigation: An Integrated Test Method for Airborne Objects' Identification Systems

Ivan I. Linnik[1] (iD), Elena P. Linnik[1] (iD), Igor Yu. Grishin[2](✉) (iD),
Rena R. Timirgaleeva[2] (iD), and Aleksander A. Tamargazin[3] (iD)

[1] V.I. Vernadsky Crimean Federal University, Yalta, Russia
[2] Lomonosov Moscow State University, Moscow, Russia
[3] National Aviation University, Kyiv, Ukraine

Abstract. The article analyses the methods of increasing the efficiency of the processes of airborne objects' classification along with the possible solutions to the problems of airspace operating procedure. The methods of formalizing and assessing the information quality are developed to classify airborne objects. Formulated is the verification method of the fuzzy logical system's software used to classify airborne objects. Particular attention is paid to the analysis of the completeness and reliability of the input information, the properties of the mechanism of logical conclusions having deterministic decision-making branches on airborne objects and decision-making branches based on fuzzy logical inference with the formation of the «confidence» vector towards decision options.

The article is just the first part of a group of methods proposed to the scientific community for the purpose of simplifying the processes of identifying airborne objects illegally located in controlled areas and, in particular, verifying the software used for this purpose. It also continues a series of articles dealing with the problems of air navigation.

Keywords: Airborne vehicles · Air traffic control system · Classification of airborne vehicles

1 Introduction

Searching for various objects is one of the most important types of human activity found in various fields of science and technology. The main purpose of spatial search is to detect various objects in survey areas and determine their nature and location [1, 2].

The use of such systems is primarily aimed at identifying aircraft which are located in the controlled airspace without permission. First of all, the data obtained from radar systems are used as input data, but at the same time, acoustic and visual data can (and should) be used, as well as the data obtained as a result of monitoring the electromagnetic activity of the aircraft. The latter is especially important for identifying unmanned airborne vehicles.

The vast majority of the currently existing software systems for the integrated data processing on the air situation devised in the developed countries of the world are aimed

P. K. Singh et al. (Eds.): FTNCT 2020, CCIS 1396, pp. 57–67, 2021.
https://doi.org/10.1007/978-981-16-1483-5_6

at military use and bear insular nature. On the other hand, the authors of the series of articles set a goal of developing a methodology for creating such software systems for civilian purposes, which could be easier to use and cheaper. One of the promising areas of such systems' application is monitoring the air situation in a "smart city".

One of the challenges in developing this software is testing it.

Currently, the process of testing airborne objects' identification systems is fairly standardized and based on the use of different versions of the Testing and Test Control Notation language.

Since airborne objects' identification systems are object-oriented distributed knowledge data bases in the form of Mealy finite-state machines, the Abstract Syntax Notation One language is most often used to describe the abstract data syntax in the field of various objects' classification.

An analysis of the approaches used in testing airborne objects' identification systems indicates that the existing family of languages used to present test scripts is aimed only at object-oriented distributed knowledge bases, and the standardized Unified Model Language is used to formally represent the initial requirements for airborne objects' classification.

For the laboratory modeling and accumulation of information about the research object, the Fuzzy Logic Toolbox was used (one of the Matlab/Simulink applications).

The main methods designing test suites and test cases are as follows [3]:

- breaking up into equivalence classes;
- analysis of extreme values;
- method of all pairs;
- method based on the use of decision tables;
- method based on testing state diagrams;
- method based on the user's script composed according to the tester's experience;
- method based on the Petri nets' use.

Test cases consist of a certain set of prerequisites, stimulating actions and expected responses including a certain sequence of scripts:

- normal case;
- expansion;
- exceptional situations.

Each script provides the conditions and actions performed by the subject. It demands a response on the part of the system that meets part of the actions of the test case. To design a test suite, each script is specified by setting exact values for all the attributes and objects used in the identification program [4].

The quality of airborne objects' identification systems depends, first of all, on the rules for making logical decisions. Therefore, decision tables can be effective for designing test suites and test cases. Moreover, decision tables' structure is equivalent to the structure of test suites, being simple and clear. The advantages of decision tables as a means of test suites' formalized description in the process of their creation include the availability of images of automatic verification of the description's completeness and consistency and the receipt of decision tables' control flow. But the fuzziness, blurring and qualitative nature of some values of airborne objects' classification criteria [5] do not allow taking the decision tables as the basic method for designing test suites for airborne objects' identification systems.

The adequacy of test suites and test cases can be measured using the test coverage concept and the test suites' reliability concept [6, 7].

Test coverage is one of the metric evidences of testing quality assessment indicating how densely test suites cover the requirements or executable code. The higher the required test coverage level, the more test suites will be selected for verification. At the same time, the complexity of airborne objects' identification systems makes it impossible to provide 100% test coverage.

Currently, the following approaches are used to evaluate and measure the test coverage:

- requirements coverage;
- code coverage;
- test coverage based on the control flow analysis.

In our research, the requirements coverage approach is used as the main approach while the test coverage based on the control flow analysis is used as an additional approach.

The requirements coverage consists in the assessment of coverage of functional and non-functional requirements for a software product by tests by constructing trace matrices:

$$M_c = \frac{N_c}{N_{\Sigma c}} 100\% \tag{1}$$

in which M_c is the completeness of the test requirements coverage; N_c is the number of requirements verified by test cases; $N_{\Sigma c}$ is the total number of requirements represented by use cases.

Test coverage based on the control flow analysis assesses how tests cover the test routes for executing the code of a program module or graph of control flows.

The calculation of the completeness of the test coverage based on the control flow analysis is carried out according to the following formula:

$$M_w = \frac{N_w}{N_{\Sigma w}} 100\% \tag{2}$$

in which M_w is the completeness of the test coverage based on the control flow analysis; N_w is the number of control flow graph elements checked by test cases; $N_{\Sigma w}$ is the total number of control flow graph elements represented by use cases.

The reliability of the developed test suites characterizes the measure of confidence in the design method of test suites. According to [1], the value of the reliability indicator is equal to:

$$D = 1 - \sum_{j=1}^{4} \beta_j \sum_{i \in q_j} \alpha_i \tag{3}$$

in which α_i indicates how important it is to take into account the developed method in test suites of the i-th factor in relative units; q_j is the set of factors taken into account in test suites in the j-th generalization manner; β_j is the relative average error value, which is introduced into the calculation decisions due to the inaccurate consideration of factors.

At present, a great number of scientific works are known on the problem of testing systems for various purposes.

So, in [8], algorithms were developed for conducting the dynamic testing of the correspondence between the predefined automaton stochastic multi-agent mathematical model and the model constructed during the system's operation.

[9] studies the models, methods and algorithms for testing object-oriented programs on graph-models of finite-state machines' transitions with the aim of finding an error in the initial program code.

Research [10] deals with the development of an automated software testing system based on stratified and diagnostic models allowing for the real-time control of the workability and reliability of the developed software product. But the formalized presentation of test suites and the control of their correctness are not considered in the above-mentioned research.

[11, 12] studies the criteria and temporal indicators of testing software tools for data processing aimed at reducing the risk of failures during operation without considering the problems of designing test suites.

In addition, numerous research papers address the problems of improving the reliability of software products' testing by identifying hidden errors by means of retesting, as well as stochastic testing, breakdown testing, script-based testing and state-based testing.

Analyzing these research papers, we can conclude that the software model using fuzzy rules in knowledge bases based on fuzzy logic and Petri nets can be represented by a tuple:

$$S(f) = <P, T, F, I, O, M> \qquad (4)$$

in which $P = \{p_j : \mu_{pj}\}$ is the finite set of fuzzy positions p_j, $\mu_{pj}(k)$, which correspond to the membership function $\mu_{pj}(k)$, k is a variable determining the value of the function $\mu_{pj}(k)$, $j = 1...m$, $P \neq \varnothing$, $|P| = m$; $T = \{t_i : \mu_{ti}\}$ is the finite set of fuzzy transitions t_i, $\mu_{ti}(h)$, which correspond to the membership function $\mu_{ti}(h)$, h is the variable determining the value of the function $\mu_{ti}(h)$, $i = 1...n$, $T \neq \varnothing$, $|T| = n$;

$$F : (P \times T) \cup (T \times P) \rightarrow \{x_{ij}(v), y_{ij}(v)\} \qquad (5)$$

the fuzzy incidence function P и T, $x_{ij}(v)$, $y_{ij}(v)$ are the membership functions of the input $I:(P \times T)$ and the original $O:(T \times P)$ incidents of some fuzzy positions $p_j \in P$ and fuzzy transitions $t_i \in T$, v is the variable determining the value of the corresponding function; $M:(P) \rightarrow N$ is the function defining positions' marking.

Such a structure is distinguished by the possibility of representing fuzzy processes and the dynamics of their interaction. But it does not take into account many parameters, indicators and characteristics that really describe the physical processes of a particular system. The quality of the above-mentioned system's functioning is also limited by the possibility of forming indicators of fuzzy labeling and components of the incidence function.

To improve the testing process of systems used for identifying airborne objects, it is essential to solve the problems of formalizing the processes of determining the classes of objects in the air during its control and verify the software of a fuzzy logical system used for classifying airborne objects based on the requirements for the subject area.

Thus, the present-day situation in science and practice is characterized, on the one hand, by the need for effective testing of software used for classifying airborne objects at the system level, taking into account the advanced requirements regarding the correctness and adequacy of test suites used for this purpose, and on the other hand, by the absence of appropriate methods for formalizing the processes of airborne objects' classification and the verification method of the fuzzy logical classification system's software.

2 Main Part

The process of identifying an airborne object is a multi-step procedure:

- selecting and analyzing information on the air situation;
- determining the reliability of information obtained from heterogeneous sources;
- transforming the semantic information on airborne objects' behavior properties into a binary set of membership functions of detailed properties;
- building a knowledge base;
- calculating the quality of information;
- determining the degree of preference;
- forming an inference apparatus;
- automatic determination of the membership index by the totality of properties allowing for an unambiguous decision;
- clarification of input data on an airborne object, which is difficult to identify, using other sources or recognition procedures;
- automated identification of a set of properties with the corresponding membership index;
- the ownership index's possible assessment and offering of possible solutions;
- making the final decision on an airborne object's index of affiliation.

The decision making process implies the use of weight coefficients:

$$W_i = 1 - D_i(B_k, A_k), \tag{6}$$

in which D_i is the normalized Kemeny distance; $B_k = \|b(i,\ j)\|$ is the matrix of an airborne object's current properties; $A_k = \|a(i,\ j)\|$ is the matrix of reference properties for the i-th class of an airborne object.

The proposed classification method includes:

- the method of formalization of airborne objects' properties to form a knowledge base;
- the method of selecting and analyzing information about airborne objects;
- the method of assessing the quality of information about airborne objects;

- the system of airborne objects' classification;
- inference method;
- the method of assessing the quality of classification;
- clarification of the input data about airborne objects;
- procedures for the automatic determination of identifiers of a set of properties with appropriate index accessories;

To improve the classification procedures for airborne objects, it is necessary to accumulate data in the course of monitoring the use of airspace and have appropriate tools for assessing quality.

It is possible to use the indicator of the control systems' efficiency indicator as the identification efficiency criterion. So, recognition algorithms can be estimated by the formula:

$$E = \frac{N^P - N}{N} \tag{7}$$

in which N^p, N is the number of targets detected with and without the recognition system.

Such a criterion is inconvenient in decision-making or recognition systems. It is advisable to analyze dynamic situations in the air space using multi-stage decision-making procedures based on statistical laws. Most often, such procedures use Bayesian algorithms based on the use of likelihood functions. Calculation of the conditional probabilities of distortion of the air situation allows determining the average probability of erroneous decisions. The disadvantage of this method of recognizing the air situation is the difficulty of formalizing the multidimensional distribution density of random values of the multidimensional vector's components describing the signs of a crisis situation.

When assessing the quality of the air situation's recognition, the following probabilistic indicators are used:

- recognition probability

$$P = \sum_{k=1}^{M} (1 - P_y), \tag{8}$$

in which P_y is the conditional probability of correct recognition;
- the average risk of recognition errors

$$r = \sum_{i,k=1}^{M} r_{ij} P\left(\frac{A'_i}{A_k}\right) \tag{9}$$

in which $\|r_{ik}\|$ is the cost matrix, $r_{ik} = r_{kk} = 0$.

The average risk is a generalized indicator of the recognition quality in the process of decision-making. But the problem consists in determining the cost ratios;

To assess the quality of airborne objects' classification, we apply the comprehensive performance criterion and average values of particular indicators. It is a known fact that the rule of super-additive nonlinear summation is applied to evaluate a complex system's behavior. According to the rule, the efficiency function does not equal the sum of the efficiency functions of its constituent parts:

$$F(x, y) \neq F(x) + F(y).$$ (10)

Average estimates are used if only one type of relationship between the objects' properties is taken into account and do not reflect the real relations between properties. Therefore, in order to develop the method of integrated assessment, it is necessary to take into account causal relations between the system's elements.

We represent the functional of the integral quality indicator as a normalized dimensionless value:

$$E = \log_2 \left[1 + (-1)^m \prod_{i=1}^{m} \left(1 - 2^{-K_i^{r_i}} \right) \right]$$ (11)

or

$$E = \log_2 \left[1 + \prod_{i=1}^{m} \left(2^{-K_i^{r_i}} - 1 \right) \right]$$ (12)

in which K_i is the indicator's value; r_i is the i-th indicator's degree of importance $\left(\sum_{i=1}^{m} r_i = 1 \right)$.

A larger value of E performance indicator corresponds to a better classification process. The maximum value of E can reach unity. Such a criterion is invariant to external parameters, has a clear meaning and can characterize air objects' identification efficiency.

The weighted coefficients in this expression can be determined by the Delphi method. The coefficients' value can be subject to different indices of airborne objects' affiliation and the air situation's complexity.

The requirements for partial indicators and the procedure for their calculation are defined in [11–13]. For the task in question, it is necessary to use the following partial indicators K_i of the classification quality of all identified and tracking airborne objects:

- reliability of classification - P_{kl};
- efficiency coefficient of decision-making on every airborne object - T_{kl};
- completeness of airborne objects' classification during the time allowed for its implementation - H_{kl}.

The reliability of airborne objects' classification will be evaluated according to the approach proposed for assessing the quality of the fuzzy logical output of objects with discrete outputs [14–16].

Suppose Q is the total number of situations for describing a fuzzy model:

$$Q = Q_1 + Q_2 + \ldots + Q_m,$$ (13)

in which Q_j is the number of situations requiring the d_j solution:

$$Q_j = Q_{j1} + Q_{j2} + \ldots + Q_{jm}, j = 1 \ldots m, \tag{14}$$

in which Q_{ij} is the number of situations where the d_j solution was necessary, but the d_i solution was taken.

It is necessary to distribute situations Q according to the tree, which can be built on the basis of the inference algorithm.

The validity of the classification is evaluated as:

$$P_j = \frac{Q_{jj}}{Q_j}, \; P_{ij} = \frac{Q_{ji}}{Q_j}, \; P = \frac{1}{Q} \sum_{j=1}^{m} Q_{jj}, \tag{15}$$

in which P_j is the reliability of the correct d_j decision-making; P_{ij} is the reliability of d_i decision making subject to the objective necessity of choosing the d_j decision; P is the average reliability of making the right decision.

The efficiency K_t of decision-making for each airborne object is evaluated as:

$$K_t = \frac{1}{1 + \left(\frac{T_R}{T_D}\right)^2}, \tag{16}$$

in which T_D is the allowed classification time of an air object; T_R is the real classification time of an air object.

The nonlinear form of expression for this indicator makes it sensitive to the T_R parameter. When $T_R = T_D$, $K_t = 0{,}5$ and rapidly decreases with a further increase in the classification time.

The completeness of airborne objects' classification H_{kl} is estimated according to the following formula:

$$H_{kl} = \frac{M_{kl}}{M} \tag{17}$$

in which M is the total number of detected objects in the air; M_{kl} is the number of classified objects. Undefined airborne objects are not classified objects.

The quality of classification of each individual airborne object is evaluated according to the depth of classification. This indicator takes into account the importance of the target:

$$H_{gl\,kl} = \sum_{i=1}^{m} r_{kli} a_{kli} \tag{18}$$

in which $r_{kl\,i}$ is the weight of the i-th class in the general set for all levels; $a_{kl\,i}$ (1 - the i-th class was defined, 0 - the i-th class was not defined).

The maximum depth $H_{gl} = 1$. The m value is different for different airborne objects, as is the distribution of weight among all $r_{kl\,i}$.

The classification depth clearly shows the a priori classification quality of airborne objects. It is achieved by using different sources of information on airborne objects and depends on the quality of information support for airspace control.

Below, it is shown how it is possible to assess the effectiveness of airborne objects' classification in case the obtained information is incomplete and uncertain by comparing the estimates obtained by experts in the field of airborne objects' management and the results obtained using the developed classification method.

In the experiment, we chose $N = 18$ airborne objects with a full set of features a priori belonging to different classes. The random data generator randomly eliminated several features from $K = 15$ of them. The rest of the features were obtained from various sources of information. A set of these features was issued in the form of a questionnaire to $n = 9$ experts and a data package for the airborne objects' identification program.

The probability of N targets' correct classification conducted by experts was about 0.59 and practically did not change during the tests. At the beginning of the tests, the classification depth was 0.29 on average. Upon expert training, the classification depth increased to 0.68, which is due to the experts' attention mainly to the classification at the targets' higher danger levels. The depth of automatic classification in the presence of a set of relevant features was 1. In the case of a limited set of available features, the depth of automatic classification was equal to the coefficient of feature completeness (the ratio of the number of available features to the number of features needed at each classification level) - 0.81… 0.92.

When some features' values changed, new values appeared and some features maintained their values, the experts, as a rule, did not react or reacted with delay. The decision-making system reacted to any changes.

The experts' classification lasted from 90 to 260 s. The decision-making system's classification period was no longer than 11 s.

The results of target classes' expert evaluation according to the proposed scheme show an increase of the classification efficiency by 82% on average and an increase of classification reliability by 17% in case data processing automation is used. The high depth level of automatic classification and the instant reaction to features' changes are due to the exclusion of the human factor.

The analysis and comparison of the results will be considered in our further research. To make such a comparison, we will need to write two or three scientific articles, since the volume of the comparative results is currently about 120 published pages.

3 Conclusion

The improved hierarchical method of airborne objects' classification differs from the already existing ones. Its peculiarities are the formalization of airborne objects' features based on binary relations and divisible procedures and the structural features of the singleton knowledge base. We put to use this method to propose an improved method of assessing information quality when classifying airborne objects. Unlike the already known ones, this method considers the minimum distance of the available information from the reference information to be the criterion of completeness.

The proposed method is based on the fuzzy logic apparatus and allows for the evaluation of the reliability of information about airborne objects coming from heterogeneous sources. In particular, it was determined that the reliability depends on the source types, the methods of issuing and obtaining information and the delay time.

All this should allow developing a formalized representation of the sets of rules for identifying airborne objects based on the fuzzy production model and the Mamdani fuzzy logical conclusions. The most suitable software environment for solving this problem is the Fuzzy Logic Toolbox.

Acknowledgment. The reported study was funded by RFBR, project number 19-29-06081.

References

1. Hellman, O.: Introduction to the Optimal Search Theory, p. 248. Nauka Publishing, Moscow (1985)
2. Tamargazin, A.A., Linnik, I.I.: Process control of single information space usage in securing technological processes at airports. Naukoemni tekhnologiï: Nauk. zhurnal **4**(44), 494–499 (2019). Kiïv: NAU. https://doi.org/10.18372/2310-5461.44.14326
3. Tamre, L.: Introduction to Software Testing: Per. s angl, p. 386. «Vil'yams» Publ., Moscow (2003)
4. Makgregor, D., Sajks, D.: Object-Oriented Software Testing. Prakticheskoe posobie: Per. s angl, p. 432. OOO «TID DS», Kiev (2002)
5. Linnik, I.I., Tamargazin, A.A., Linnik, E.P.: Efficiency of controlling the production system at airports using the single information space for ensuring technological processes. In: CEUR Workshop Proceedings, pp. 88–99 (2019)
6. Rudnickij, D.: Basic principles of biometric systems' designing for preventing unauthorized aircraft use. Trudy SPIIRAN (4), 405–415. https://doi.org/10.15622/sp.4.30
7. Kotlyarov, V.P., Kolikova, T.V.: Fundamentals of Software Testing, p. 246. Internet-Universitet Informacionnyh tekhnologij, Moscow (2006)
8. Staroletov, S., Dubko, A.A.: Method to verify parallel and distributed software in C# by doing Roslyn AST transformation to a Promela model. Syst. Inform. (15), 13–43 (2019). https://doi.org/10.31144/si.2307-6410.2019.n15
9. Malinin, S.N.: Object-oriented software testing based on finite state machine modeling. Synopsis of a thesis: Cand. of Science in Engineering. Avtoreferat dissertacii na soiskanie uchyonoj stepeni kandidata tekhnicheskih nauk, p. 20. Nizhegorodskij gosudarstvennyj tekhnicheskij universitet, Nizhnij Novgorod (2010)
10. Volkov, G.V.: Models and algorithms for software testing based on their stratified description. Synopsis of a thesis: Cand. of Science in Engineering. Avtoreferat dissertacii na soiskanie uchyonoj stepeni kandidata tekhnicheskih nauk, p. 18. Nizhegorodskij gosudarstvennyj tekhnicheskij universitet, Nizhnij Novgorod (2010)
11. Korotun, T.M.: Models and methods of engineering software systems' testing under the conditions of limited resources. Synopsis of a Thesis. Avtoreferat disertaciï na zdobuttya vchenogo stupenyu kandidata fiziko-matematichnih nauk, p. 21. Institut programnih sistem NAN Ukraïni, Kiïv (2005)
12. Chumakov, N.M., Serebryanyj, E.I.: Technical Devices' Effectiveness Evaluation, p. 192. Sov.radio Publ, Moscow (1980)
13. Pljonkin, A.P.: Vulnerability of the synchronization process in the quantum key distribution system. Int. J. Cloud Appl. Comput. **9**(1), 50–58 (2019). https://doi.org/10.4018/IJCAC.2019010104
14. Pljonkin, A., Singh, P.K.: The review of the commercial quantum key distribution system In: 2018 Fifth International Conference on Parallel, Distributed and Grid Computing. IEEE (2018). https://doi.org/10.1109/PDGC.2018.8745822

15. Pljonkin, A., Rumyantsev, K.: Single-photon synchronization mode of quantum key distribution system. In: International Conference on Computational Techniques in Information and Communication Technologies, pp. 531–534. https://doi.org/10.1109/ICCTICT.2016.751 4637
16. Rotshtejn, A.P.: Intelligent Identification Technologies: Fuzzy Sets, Genetic Algorithms, Neural Networks, p. 320. UNIVERSUM Publ., Vinnica (1999)

The Study of Synchronization in Quantum Key Distribution System

Anton Pljonkin[1][(✉)], Pradeep Kumar Singh[2], Sandeep Joshi[3], and Lilia Sabantina[4]

[1] Southern Federal University, Taganrog, Russian Federation
pljonkin@mail.ru
[2] Jaypee University of Information Technology, Waknaghat, India
[3] Manipal University Jaipur, Jaipur, Rajasthan, India
sandeep.joshi@jaipur.manipal.edu
[4] Bielefeld University of Applied Sciences, Bielefeld, Germany
lilia.sabantina@fh-bielefeld.de

Abstract. The paper considers the main methods of synchronization in quantum cryptography systems. A generalized structure of a quantum key distribution system with phase coding of photon states is described. The results of experimental studies of the synchronization process in a two-pass quantum communication system are presented and the features of optical pulse detection are shown. Analytical expressions are given for calculating the error of detecting the length of a quantum channel during synchronization. The estimation of the security of the synchronization process using a multiphoton pulse is given. An optical signal detection algorithm that reduces the probability of an attack on the quantum key distribution system during synchronization is proposed.

Keywords: Quantum key distribution · Synchronization · Photon impulse · The algorithm · Unauthorized access

1 Introduction

The technological developments in today's world are increasing rapidly and the essential possibility of secure communication is becoming more essential. At this point, security plays an important role and the confidentiality and integrity of data in wireless and wired networks is crucial. Quantum cryptography offers promising solutions to the problem of information security and represents a branch of quantum informatics [1, 2]. The relevance of the idea of quantum cryptography is that a method for creating an absolutely random secret key between users of a quantum communication line is proposed. The secrecy of key formation and the impossibility of unauthorized access to the communication line are based on the laws of quantum physics [3, 4]. Classical cryptography, as opposed to quantum cryptography, is based on mathematical regularities and is theoretically decipherable [5]. The complete secrecy of messages transmission can be achieved only by solving the key distribution problem.

Quantum key distribution techniques (QKD) allow two parties to distribute a secret key in such a way that eavesdropping is detected. Any information obtained about the

P. K. Singh et al. (Eds.): FTNCT 2020, CCIS 1396, pp. 68–80, 2021.
https://doi.org/10.1007/978-981-16-1483-5_7

exchanged key by an unauthorized third party leads to an increase in the quantum bit error rate (QBER) of the transmitted files [6, 7].

The first quantum key distribution protocol is based on the ideas of Stephen Wiesner from 1983 [8] and was introduced in 1984 by Charles Bennett and Gilles Brassard as the BB84 protocol [9], which is based on the laws of quantum mechanics and is used to realize key distribution polarization coding. This protocol is based on Heisenberg's uncertainty principle, which states that the properties of a photon such as spin, polarization, etc. cannot be measured without introducing deviations or errors in normal photon transfer [10, 11]. This means that if an eavesdropper would try to interfere with the information and measure the photon, the state of the photon would be disturbed in a relatively noticeable way. Quantum key distribution technology allows two parties to encrypt and decrypt the message using a random secret shared key [12, 13].

One of the physical solutions to the key distribution problem is quantum cryptography, which is based on the fundamental properties of quantum physics. Quantum cryptography methods are implemented in quantum key distribution systems (QKDS), the principle of operation of which is based on encoding the quantum state of a single particle. Physically, the QKDS consists of two stations that are connected by fiber-optic communication channel. Stationsexchangelow-poweropticalsignals. Quantum key distribution functions under the control of quantum cryptography protocols. For a detailed description of how the protocols work, see [14].

In general, the work of the QKD system can be divided into two functional parts: statistical and technical.The technical part includes the operation of components, modules, and software. The statistical part includes the operation of the quantum protocol and the synchronization process. The most important aspect of quantum cryptography is the security of quantum key distribution systems, and various approaches are proposed to enhance the security of quantum cryptography [15].The study of Hasani and Naimee 2019 shows that by mixing quantum key and chaotic signal, the security of quantum cryptography can be enhanced. Here, the use of one-time pad technology and a chaotic signal is shown and the chaotic signal is generated by a semiconductor laser with optical feedback, resulting in ultimate security [12].

The papers [16, 17] describe the main methods of attacks on QKD systems.In most cases an imperfection of technical part is used to carry out attacks. Thus, avalanche photodetectors, phase modulators, quantum generators and optical emission sources are attacked. Another type of attack uses vulnerabilities in the software of the QKD system, but this type of attack is based on flaws in the software and is not directly related to quantum key distribution systems. A little-studied method of attacks is to analyze the statistical properties of the photoelectron flux. This attack exploits vulnerabilities in the preparatory processes and post processing processes of accumulated key material.

We conducted experimental studies of the preparatory processes of the quantum communication system and proposed a new synchronization technique. The technique provides higher protection of the synchronization process from unauthorized access compared to the classical scheme for detecting an optical synchronizing signal.The technique is applicable in two pass-through quantum key distribution systems, where synchronization is performed over the same optical communication channel as the quantum keys distribution. Live experiments were conducted on the basis of the quantum key distribution system with phase photons coding Clavis 3110 (IDQuantique).This system operates on the principle of automatic compensation of polarizing distortions.

2   Research Objective

2.1   Synchronization in Optical Channels

When transmitting digital information, the decoding device of the receiver must work synchronously with the received signal. Time synchronization of the receiver is provided by the synchronization subsystem, which is an integral part of the receiver. In [18] it is shown that imperfection of synchronization can cause a significant deterioration in the efficiency of the information transmission system in general.The problem of time synchronization in classical communication systems is described by a model with additive Gaussian noise. Optical quantum communication systems are completely different from traditional ones. The difference is primarily in the models of the output signal of the photodetector (compared to conventional noise models). This is explained by the quantum nature of the photodetector's output signal, which is shot noise. The consequence of this is that the classical procedures for analyzing basic equations lead to noticeable differences from the well-known procedures for Gaussian channels. Therefore, for optical channels of quantum communication systems, it is necessary to transform a number of states underlying the design of synchronization subsystems.

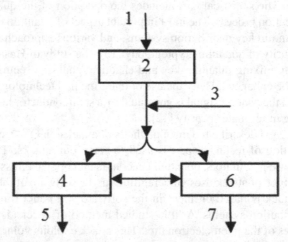

Fig. 1. Synchronization subsystem of information signal receiving. *1—input optical signal; 2— photodetector; 3—noise of electrical circuits; 4—information allocation system; 5—decoded information; 6—synchronization system; 7—time stamps.*

In most cases, the synchronization receiver is an integral part of the synchronization subsystem and is installed after the photodetector. If the system's capabilities allow, the receiver works in parallel with the information channel (Fig. 1). The sync signals allocated by the receiver are used for synchronization of the information decoding device and (or) for generating marker signals. Some receivers may use decoded information signals for synchronization. Synchronization information is generally received by the receiver in the form of a synchronizing signal or in the form of timestamps sent by the transmitter. In the receiver, synchronizing signals are used to generate marker pulses that initiate the start of a pulse or long sequences of pulses (frames).

Another method involves the imposition of synchronizing signals on the information. In this combined form the signals are transmitted in the communication channel. To detect these signals in the receiver, the well-known principles of time or frequency separation are used. In time division, synchronizing signals are sent during one-time interval, and information signals are sent in other time intervals. In frequency division, information and synchronization signals are placed in non-overlapping regions of the frequency spectrum. In both cases, the task of the synchronization subsystem is to allocate synchronizing signal. The task of allocation of synchronizing signal is solved either by time gating, or by frequency filtering. Ideally the allocated synchronizing signal does not depend on the information and such synchronization is called "pure".

A less effective technique is the synchronization procedure, where the synchronization subsystem generates marker pulses. Such pulses are allocated directly from information signals. In this case, there are no longer the benefits that are due to the use of "pure" synchronizing signals in the system, but power and frequency band are saved. Systems that separate the synchronizing signal directly from the information signal must make minimal distortion in the modulation. Since in this case, the process of detecting information signals and synchronization are directly related, even minimal distortion can have a negative impact on the decision-making procedure of the decoding device.

In the general theory of synchronization for optical communication systems the most suitable form of synchronizing signal is a periodic sequence of optical pulses. The time markers in this case are the pulses themselves, and synchronization is achieved by measurement of the time points of arrival of optical pulses. In this case, the problem of analytical study of the synchronization procedure of a periodic sequence of optical pulses is formulated as a problem of estimating the time of arrival of the synchronizing signal.

Two ways of synchronization are considered in relation to optical quantum communication systems. The first is based on a two-pass scheme, and the second is based on a one-way communication channel. Synchronization methods in quantum key distribution systems rely on quantum protocols and depend on how they are implemented.

2.2 The Synchronization in Quantum Channel Between QKD Stations

Recent developments in quantum cryptography focus on creating quantum key distribution systems for open space. Optical signal transmission systems through the atmosphere have a number of features. In such systems, one-way quantum protocols are used, and the calculation of probabilistic characteristics of signal detection is fundamentally different from the calculations in fiber-optic transmission systems. From the signal detection perspective, the concept of certainty is applied in fiber-optic systems, i.e. the reflected signal will arrive at the photodetector with a probability of 0.99(9). The task of detection is reduced to determining the time interval. In contrast, an optical signal in open communication systems does not have such a high probability of detection. The latter is due, firstly, to one-way transmission, and secondly, to the presence of external interference

(including noise).In this case, it is necessary to take into account a number of probabilistic characteristics that are entered into the calculations. Synchronization in one-way
protocols is implemented by means of paired pulses at a priori known distance between
the receiver and the transmitter. Two pulses that are rigidly connected in time are sent
over a communication channel with a specified period of time and frequency (Fig. 2).
The first pulse has a much greater intensity (power) relative to the second. The first pulse
has a much greater intensity (power) relative to the second. A powerful pulse is detected
on the receiving side and serves as a time stamp. When the first pulse is detected, the
synchronization subsystem accurately determines the timestamp of the second pulse.
Note that the second impulse maybe informational.

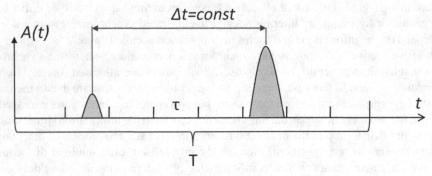

Fig. 2. Coupled momentum method. Time diagram.

Consider the time synchronization of an autocompensation quantum key distribution
system. It will be recalled that in autocompensation systems the signal propagates along a
single fiber in two directions, i.e. the pulses go the same way [19–21]. Photodetectors are
installed in the sender station (Bob). The pulses propagate along the quantum channel
to the recipient station (Alice), are detected, reflected, and follow back to the sender
station. Pulse registration is performed by avalanche photodiodes.

Fiber-optic autocompensation quantum key distribution systems use a periodic
sequence of pulses as timestamps. Synchronization consists in detecting the moment of
registration of the reflected pulse by the Bob station's photodetectors. The pulse detection
operation requires searching for all possible positions of the pulse on the time axis. Synchronization in this case is a preparatory stage of the system, i.e. the sequence of pulses
is transmitted before the start of the key generation session. This way, synchronization
will be set before the information is transmitted.

The synchronization process itself is divided into three stages. The first two of them
are probabilistic, and the third is a test.

The period of optical pulses is determined based on the maximum range of the
quantum channel. The problem of detecting an optical signal is solved by analyzing the
time axis. As mentioned earlier, in two pass-through systems, the probability of detecting
a signal is reduced to determining the probability of detecting a time interval, i.e., the
moment when the reflected pulse enters the avalanche photodiodes.

The probability of no signal in this case is almost completely absent, and its presence can only mean physical damage to the fiber-optic communication line.

The entire period of movement is divided into time intervals. Each of these intervals is analyzed sequentially. The position of the time intervals at which the synchronizing pulse can be located is determined by counting the photoelectrons in each interval. Physically this search is performed by switching the counter step by step. You can use a threshold test at each position of a pair of intervals on the time axis. Threshold tests continue until the threshold level is exceeded. The search procedure consists of accumulating samples in each position over a fixed search interval. The operation of the photodetector in this search is segmented, i.e. the voltage is applied with a variable delay. Experimental studies show that photodetectors operate in linear mode during synchronization. The latter means that all photoelectrons received by the photodetector will be recorded. In this case, the electrical signal at the output of the photodetector will be either "0" or "1", i.e. the presence or absence of a signal. Repetitive checking of each analyzed interval is used to exclude false positives of photodetectors. Let us introduce the concept of time delay detection. This is the time when the photodetector is not active. Thus, each time you switch to the next time interval, the time delay of detection increases by the duration of the interval. Accordingly, the time of active operation of the photodetector will be equal to the duration of the scanning interval. Only one-time interval is analyzed per period of movement. The latter allows you to ignore such a parameter of the photodetector as the recovery time of the operating mode.

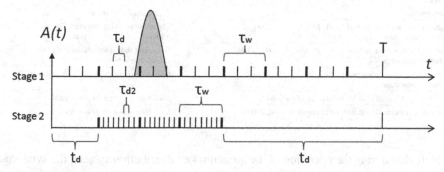

Fig. 3. Synchronization pulse detection process. τd—*search interval;* τw—*big search interval (1ns); T—period; td—photodetector delay;* $\tau d2 = \tau w/17$—*small search interval.*

Considering the features of pulse blurring, it is necessary to record the detection error. The first stage is considered completed when all the time intervals of the period of movement are surveyed and the interval with the maximum number of avalanche photodiode triggers is found. Note that the noise in this case can be the own noise of avalanche photodiodes, which form false positives. Since each interval is analyzed many times, the difference between the signal and noise is unambiguous. The signal is several tens, hundreds, or even thousands of times higher than the noise. After detecting the interval with the maximum number of registered photoelectrons, the system proceeds to the second synchronization stage. Here, by the analogy with the first stage, the analysis of time intervals takes place. The difference is that at the second stage, the search area is narrowed, i.e. the duration of scanning intervals is reduced (Fig. 3). The detection error is expressed in the analysis of two adjacent time intervals bordering the signal interval (in which the maximum number of triggers is recorded).

The synchronizing pulse detection procedure is identical to the first stage. All time intervals are polled sequentially and the interval with the maximum number of triggers is allocated. The time difference between the first two stages is obvious. The first stage analyzes the entire period of movement, and the second stage analyzes only three time intervals. At the third stage of synchronization the detected time interval is checked repeatedly with the maximum number of triggers. Table 1 summarizes the parameters of the synchronizing signal detection process.

Table 1. The parameters of the synchronizing signal

Parameter	Value	Comment
Optical pulse		
Duration, ns	~1	Pulse duration is the same for all stages of synchronization
Frequency	800 Hz; 800 Hz; 5 MHz	Measurements for the first, second and third stages, respectively
Average power, dBm	−48.3; −55.8; −24.2	Measurements for the first, second and third stages, respectively. Connection point - after leaving the sender station
Amplitude, mV	48/21;13/6; 13/6	Measurements for the first, second and third stages, respectively. Connection point - after leaving the sender station
Algorithm		
Period, ms	1.2	Permanent for all stages
Duration of the analysis interval for the first synchronization stage	~300 ps/1 ns	The entire period is analyzed. 300 ps – subinterval, 1 ns – interval
Duration of the analysis interval for the second synchronization stage	~60 ps/1 ns	Only three time intervals are analyzed (51 subintervals)
Duration of the analysis interval for the third synchronization stage	~10 ps	Only five, six time intervals are analyzed
Number of iterations of each interval (1, 2 stages)	800	Each time sub-interval is analyzed
Number of iterations of each interval (3 stage)	~20 000	Each time sub-interval is analyzed

Note that during the operation of the quantum key distribution system, the synchronization process must be initiated with a certain periodicity. Commonly, this function is provided by industrial designs. Elaboration is required due to the instability of the physical length of the optical fiber. Especially the effect of changing the length of the optical communication channel is noticeable at large quantum channel lengths. At the same time, external changes in the environment can affect the physical parameters of the optical fiber.

Note another feature of the QKD system operation. Experimental studies were conducted in the laboratory at room temperature (~23°) and the system functioned stably. However, when the air temperature increased to 30°, the system stopped running, i.e. the control board did not allow to start the software and enter the operating mode. When the temperature dropped to 26°, the system started up again and functioned stably. Thus, we can say that the quantum key distribution system functions stably at the upper limit of the ambient temperature of 26.5 °C.

The synchronization process is considered complete when the time interval with the maximum number of triggers was found. The duration of this interval is 10 ps.

2.3   The Issue of Determining the Length of a Quantum Channel

During the experimental studies, a discrepancy between the theoretical length of the quantum channel and its actual length was found. Let's explain that the quantum channel is a single-mode optical fiber.Since the installation of the quantum key distribution system is organized on existing fiber-optic communication lines, it's length can be determined by the reflectometric method.

The synchronization process of the QKD system provides a detection mode in which the approximate length of the quantum channel is set with an error. The error in this case should be understood as the interval of length on both sides of the estimated length of the optical path. The length of the quantum channel is specified in kilometers, and the error value in meters.

Experimental studies have shown that the length of the quantum channel measured by the system differs from the actual length. The measurement error varies from a few meters to a kilometer.

To determine the error, experiments were conducted, the essence of which is to scan several variants of communication lines with a pre-known length and compare the scanning results with the actual length of each communication line. The next step was to calculate the scanning error and determine its dependence on the length of the studied communication line.

As a quantum channel the connection cords with lengths of 2, 3 and 20 m, and the fiber optic coils with lengths of 0.5, 1, 2, 4, 7, 25, 50 km were used. To determine the length of the fiber coils used, reflectometric measurements were made using a reflectometer YokogawaAQ7275. To improve accuracy measurements were made in both directions with subsequent averaging of the results. When performing measurements, the effective refraction index of the fiber is set to 1.4682 (the certified value for single-mode Corning SMF-28e fiber used in fiber coils).

Figure 4 shows reflectograms of two quantum channel lengths 7072 m and 50494 m. A 50 km long quantum channel consists of two 25 km long bobbins, and 7 km long includes coils 1, 2 and 4 km.The total losses in the fiber and on the connecting adapters do not exceed the acceptable values (0.12 dB/km).

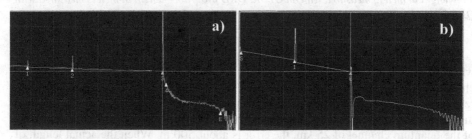

Fig. 4. Quantum channels - 7072 m (a) and 50494 m (b)

After measuring all the lengths of the quantum channel using the reflectometric method, we measured the same lengths using the software of the quantum key distribution system. Each measurement was performed 3 times to get more accurate data and avoid possible errors. The measurement results are shown in Table 2.

Table 2. The measurement results of quantum channel

Method/Iteration	1	2	3	4	5	6	7	8	9
Reflecto-meter, m	4.2	22	504	1004	2003	4001	7028	25253	50494
QKD program, m	991	1010	1481	1966	2947	4904	7875	25732	50461

According to the obtained data, the dependences of the actual lengths on the measured lengths are plotted (Fig. 5).

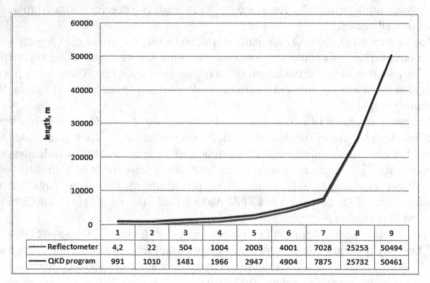

Fig. 5. Quantum channel length measurement graphs. *Values from 1 to 9—iterations; Reflectometer—length in meters measured with an OTDR; QKD program—length in meters measured with QKDS.*

The graphs in Fig. 5 show the general dependence of the length measurement error when using nine different fiber optics coils. It is shown that as the length of the quantum channel increases, the error decreases. The general trend of error change shows its reduction with increasing length of the quantum channel. So, with the actual length of the quantum channel of several meters, the error is about 1 km, and with the actual length of the quantum channel of 25 km, the error is about 500 m. When the actual length of the quantum channel is 50 km, there is almost no error.

3 Analytical Expressions and Algorithm

3.1 Experimental Studies

As a result of experimental studies of the synchronization process of the fiber-optical system of quantum key distribution, the dependence of the error of measuring the length of the quantum channel is established. From the obtained data the values of the error change can be calculated.

Approximation of the obtained experimental dependence using the least square method allows us to obtain the following expression:

$$\Delta L_{[m]} = -2.0133 * 10^{-2} * L_{[m]} + 985 \tag{1}$$

where ΔL – the estimated value of error in determining the communication line length; L – the actual value of line length (with an effective refraction index of the fiber $n_x = 1.4682$).

The non-constant error value indicates the influence of two factors: incorrect accounting of the length of the internal delay line in the encoding station and mismatch of the fiber refraction index (the value of the refraction index used by the QKD system differs from the value of the coefficient used in a standard single-mode fiber).

From the expression (1) for a known link length L, determined by the reflectometric method, and a known refractive index n_x, used for reflectometric measurements, a formula can be obtained for calculating the value of the link length L_{rs}, which must be specified when scanning the link in the QKD system:

$$L_{rs[m]} = L_{[m]} * \left(\frac{n_x}{1.49837}\right) + 985 \tag{2}$$

To check the validity of the obtained formulas, we will conduct experimental tests on the current system of the QKD. The testing algorithm includes measuring the actual length of the quantum channel using the reflectometric method, calculating the error and corrected length of the quantum channel using formulas, entering the calculated length into the software of the quantum communication system, and recording the results.

Measurements were made at the same length values as before. The graphs in Fig. 6 show the difference between the length of the quantum channel obtained by (2) and the length measured by the QKD software.

The Fig. 6 show that the difference between the estimated length and the measured length is no more than 5 m on the entire measurement axis (from 900 m to 50 km). There are two dependencies in the Fig. 6, but visually they are practically indistinguishable.

3.2 Security Improving Method

In this section we will briefly describe the proposed method for improving the security of the quantum communication channel from unauthorized data retrieval. Unauthorized information retrieval in the quantum communication system should be understood as the removal of part of the optical emission from the fiber optic during synchronization or operation of the quantum protocol.

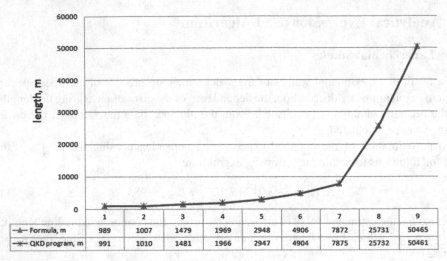

Fig. 6. Dependencies of measurement error

As shown in the study [22], at the preparatory stage of the QKD system the determination of fiber optic length is performed. At the same time, no power control algorithms function, and the photodetectors operate in linear mode. Experimental studies have shown that a powerful optical pulse is used in the synchronization process. The pulse power does not depend on the length of the quantum channel and is constant.

Known attacks on the quantum communication channel allow to implement optical power couplers in the fiber optic, while remaining unnoticed by legal users. A powerful optical pulse in the process of detecting the length of the communication line allows you to set synchronization with embedded couplers. A detailed description of the method of attack on the quantum channel and the method of counteraction are described in [23].

Having data about the features of the QKD system in synchronization mode, it is recommended to modify the QKDS software. One of the options for detecting couplers in the communication channel can be an additional check for power control of the synchronizing pulse. In conjunction with the preliminary analysis of the link length by the reflectometric method, it is possible to set the necessary power of the synchronizing pulse in advance. The latter allows to control the level of the synchronization signal and, when it drops to the threshold value, issue an alarm [24].

At the time of writing, experimental studies of the modes of operation of the QKDS are continuing. The results of the research will be presented in the near future.

4   Conclusion

The paper considers the main methods of synchronization in quantum cryptography systems. The results of experimental studies of the synchronization process in a two-pass quantum communication system are presented and the features of optical pulse detection are shown. Analytical expressions are given for calculating the error of detecting the length of a quantum channel during synchronization. The empirical formulas obtained in this work allow us to calculate the error ΔL based on the results of reflectometric measurements of the length of the existing communication line, take this error into account as an amendment to the original data, and determine the corrected value of the quantum channel length. The results of experimental tests showed that the difference between the calculated length and the measured length is no more than 5 m. The received data can be used in the current QKD system when setting it up or during synchronization. Knowing the length of the quantum channel with an error of up to 10 m, you can significantly reduce the time spent on installation and configuration of the QKD system. The technique that reduces the probability of an attack on the quantum key distribution system during synchronization is proposed.

Acknowledgements. The study was supported by Institute of Computer Technology and Information Safety, Southern Federal University and International Pljonkins Corporation.

References

1. Huang, D., Huang, P., Lin, D., Zeng, G.: Long-distance continuous-variable quantum key distribution by controlling excess noise. Sci. Rep. **6**, 19201 (2015)
2. Wang, C., Huang, D., Huang, P., Lin, D., Peng, J., Zeng, G.: 25 mHz clock continuous-variable quantum key distribution system over 50 km fiber channel. Sci. Rep. **5**(4), 102–108 (2015)
3. Gisin, N., Ribordy, G., Tittel, W., Zbinden, H.: Quantum cryptography. Rev. Mod. Phys. **74**, 145–195 (2002)
4. Bennett, C.H., Bessette, F., Brassard, G., Salvail, L., Smolin, J.: Experimental quantum cryptography. J. Cryptol. **5**(1), 3–28 (1992). https://doi.org/10.1007/BF00191318
5. Renuka, D., Chenna Reddy, P.: Integrated classical and quantum cryptography scheme using three party authenticated key distribution protocols. Mater. Today Proc. **5**(1), Part 1, 1017–1023 (2018)
6. Tchoffo, M., Tene, A.G.: Privacy amplification of entanglement parametric-down conversion based quantum key distribution via quantum logistic map for photon bases choice. Chaos, Solitons Fractals **140**, 110110 (2020)
7. Liu, R., et al.: Analysis of polarization fluctuation in long-distance aerial fiber for QKD system design. Optic. Fiber Technol. **48**, 28–33 (2019)
8. Wiesner, S.: Conjugate coding. Sigact News **15**(1), 78–88 (1983). The original paper, written around 1970, had been refused for publication and remained unpublished until 1983
9. Bennett, C.H., Brassard, G.: Quantum cryptography: public key distribution and coin tossing. In: Proceedings of International Conference on Computers, Systems, and Signal Processing, Bangalore, India, pp. 175–179 (1984)
10. Aggarwal, R., Sharma, H., Gupta, D.: Analysis of various attacks over BB84 quantum key distribution protocol. IJCA Int. J. Comput. Appl. **20**(8), 28–31 (2011)
11. Lomonaco, S.J.: A quick glance at quantum cryptography. Cryptologia **23**(1), 1–41 (1999)
12. Al Hasani, M.H., Al Naimee, K.A.: Impact security enhancement in chaotic quantum cryptography. Opt. Laser Technol. **119**, 1055755 (2019)
13. Lopes, M., Sarwade, N.: Modeling optimized decoy state protocol for enhanced quantum key distribution. J. Inf. Secur. Appl. **38**, 1–7 (2018)
14. Stucki, D., Gisin, N., Guinnard, O., Ribordy, G., Zbinden, H.: Quantum key distribution over 67 km with a plug & play system. New J. Phys. **4**, 41 (2002)
15. Kammüller, F.: Attack trees in Isabelle extended with probabilities for quantum cryptography. Comput. Secur. **87**, 101572 (2019)

16. Makarov, V.: Quantum cryptography and quantum cryptanalysis. Ph.D. thesis, Norwegian University of Science, Trondheim, Norwegian (2007)
17. Qin, H., Kumar, R., Makarov, V., Alléaume, R.: Homodyne-detector-blinding attack in continuous-variable quantum key distribution, Phys. Rev. **A98**, 012312 (2018)
18. Gagliardi, R.M., Karp, S.: Optical Communications. Wiley, New York (1976). Translated to Russian, 1978; translated to Japanese, 1979. (Second Edition, 1995)
19. Pljonkin, A., Rumyantsev, K., Singh, P.K.: Synchronization in quantum key distribution systems. Cryptography **1**, 18 (2017). https://doi.org/10.3390/cryptography1030018
20. Rumyantsev, K.E., Pljonkin, A.P.: Preliminary stage synchronization algorithm of auto-compensation quantum key distribution system with an unauthorized access security. In: International Conference on Electronics, Information, and Communications, pp. 1–4. https://doi.org/10.1109/ELINFOCOM.2016.7562955
21. Pljonkin, A.P.: Features of the photon pulse detection algorithm in the quantum key distribution system. In: Proceedings of the 2017 International Conference on Cryptography, Security and Privacy, pp. 81–84. https://doi.org/10.1145/3058060.3058078
22. Lydersen, L., Wiechers, C., Wittmann, C., Elser, D., Skaar, J., Makarov, V.: Hacking commercial quantum cryptography systems by tailored bright illumination. Nat. Photonics **4**, 686 (2010)
23. Pljonkin, A.P.: Vulnerability of the synchronization process in the quantum key distribution system. Int. J. Cloud Appl. Comput. **9**(1), 9 (2019). https://doi.org/10.4018/IJCAC.2019010104.
24. Scarani, V., Bechmann-Pasquinucci, H., Cerf, N.J., Dušek, M., Lütkenhaus, N., Peev, M.: The security of practical quantum key distribution. Rev. Mod. Phys. **81**, 1301–1350 (2009)

Modeling the Acoustoelectric Effect in a Telephone Using COMSOL Multiphysics

Lukmanova Oksana$^{(\boxtimes)}$ (iD) and Anatoly Horev

National Research University of Electronic Technology (MIET), Zelenograd, Moscow, Russia
oksanlukman@yandex.ru, horev@miee.ru

Abstract. Telephones are one of the most common telecommunication devices
in the protected premises. The telephone includes various acoustic transducers
(speaker, microphone), as a result of which these devices have a microphone
effect and can cause leakage of speech information into the telephone network.
This paper describes the model of the piezoelectric speaker of the Gigaset DA210
telephone connected to the buzzer circuit using simulations in COMSOL Multiphysics. The piezoelectric (Lead Zirconate Titanate 8) actuator is investigated,
a comparison based on the obtained results of acoustic transducers is made with
the parameters specified by the piezoelectric speaker designers. The paper studies
the characteristics of this piezoelectric speaker as a sensor under the influence of
an acoustic field, as a result of which a technical channel of speech information
leakage channel. Based on the data obtained, the speech intelligibility assessment
in the telephone network is made using the developed model. The results can be
used in the development of secure telephones and the educational process in the
training of specialists in the area of information security.

Keywords: Telephone · Acoustoelectric effect · Piezoelectric speaker · Speech
information leakage channel · Speech intelligibility

1 Introduction

Telephones connected to a telephone line are among the telecommunications device
often installed in protected premises. It is possible to create acoustoelectric leakage
channels of speech information.

The reason for the emergence of such a channel of information leakage is some of
the elements included in the device, capable of converting acoustic vibrations into electrical energy. Such elements are often called acoustic transducers (speaker, microphone,
buzzer) [1].

The electromotive force arises in piezoelectric transducers under the action of an
acoustic field created by a source of acoustic vibrations and changes according to the
law of the acting field. There are three main types of such transducers in the telephone:
electrodynamic, electromagnetic, and piezoelectric.

In this paper, a piezoelectric transducer is considered in detail, its principle of operation is based on the use of the piezoelectric effect, according to which an electromotive

© Springer Nature Singapore Pte Ltd. 2021
P. K. Singh et al. (Eds.): FTNCT 2020, CCIS 1396, pp. 81–90, 2021.
https://doi.org/10.1007/978-981-16-1483-5_8

force arises on the surface of crystals having two types of atoms during compression and deformation. An example of such devices is piezoelectric actuators, which have a microphone effect.

To intercept speech information in a passive acoustoelectric channel, special low-frequency amplifiers are used, connected to the telephone network (Fig. 1) [2].

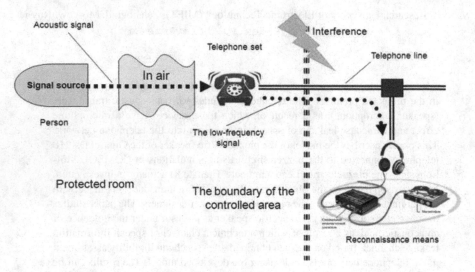

Fig. 1. The scheme of a passive acoustoelectric channel of speech information leakage

To study the acoustoelectric channel of information leakage, expensive measuring equipment is required. One of the possible ways to reduce the cost of laboratory equipment in the study of acoustoelectric channels of information leakage in the process of teaching students is the use of modeling methods in laboratory work. For these purposes, the authors chose the COMSOL Multiphysics environment, which contains the acoustics, mechanics, and AC/DC module [3].

The research is aimed at developing a virtual laboratory stand for studying of the acoustoelectric information leakage channels, using virtualization methods. Based on Gigaset DA210 telephone, in the buzzer circuit of which the piezoelectric transducer TFM-27DA [4] is installed, a model of the piezoelectric element has been designed using COMSOL Multiphysics. The model is used to study the piezoelectric transducer of the buzzer circuit of a telephone in normal operation and when using it as a sensor of acoustic signals.

2 Design of the Model of a Piezoelectric Transducer

2.1 Designing Model Geometry

The construction of the model is carried out in a 3D symmetric system concerning the axis r = 0. The investigated model of a telephone buzzer is based on a cylindrical piezoelectric with a diameter of 30 mm and a height of 9 mm (Fig. 2). The piezoelectric transducer is made of PZT-8 piezoceramic [5]. The polarization of the material is directed in the negative direction of the Z-axis.

In this model, the hemisphere adjacent to the piezoelectric element simulates the boundless air space around the sound vibration exciter (Fig. 3).

Figures 2 and 3 shows the grid diagram from which the finite element calculation is performed. To refine the mesh, the following characteristics are taken as the basis for calculations: the speed of sound in air is 343 m/s, the maximum investigated frequency is 20 kHz [6].

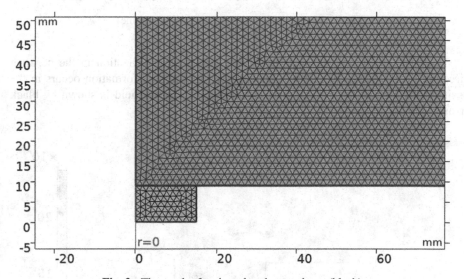

Fig. 2. The mesh of a piezoelectric transducer (black)

2.2 Simulation of the Converse Piezoelectric Effect of the Telephone Buzzer

The piezo converse simulation takes into account the voltage applied to the telephone circuit to generate the required sound pressure level (SPL). A voltage of 9 V is applied to the top bounding of the piezoelectric transducer, and the ground is connected to the bottom bounding.

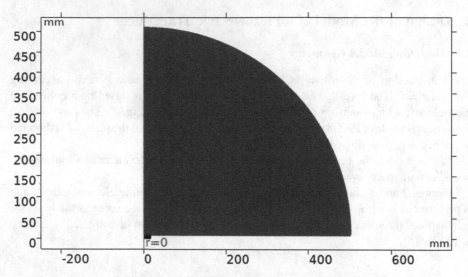

Fig. 3. The mesh of air (blue) (Color figure online)

The basic settings of the material in this model are polarization in the negative direction of the Z-axis, therefore, when exposed to stress, deformation occurs in the positive direction of the Z-axis, the direction of the electric field is shown by black arrows (Fig. 4).

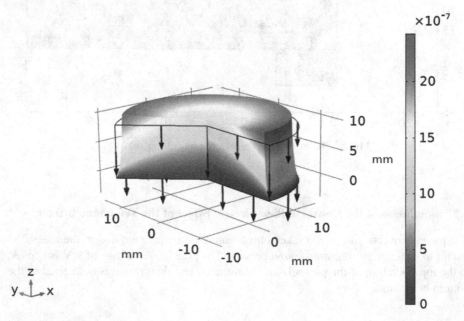

Fig. 4. The total displacement of the piezoelectric transducer (mm)

Consider the diagram obtained in the study of sound pressure levels and acoustic pressure field in the air at a frequency of 4 kHz when voltage is applied to the 9 V piezoelectric transducer. With the given initial parameters, the sound pressure level without re-reflections in the air at a distance of 0.5 m is approximately 20 dB (Fig. 5). A similar figure is repeated when considering the acoustic pressure field graph (Fig. 6).

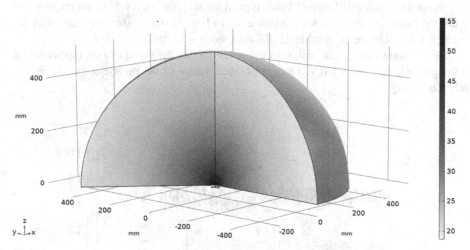

Fig. 5. The sound pressure level in the air (dB)

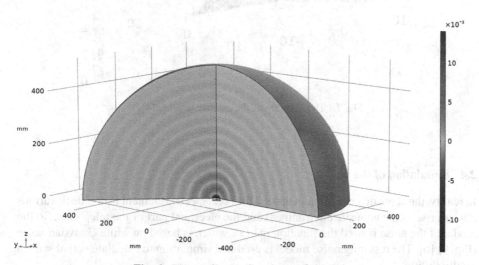

Fig. 6. The total acoustic pressure field (Pa)

2.3 Simulation of the Direct Piezoelectric Effect of the Telephone Buzzer

The study of the direct piezoelectric effect in a stationary study is conducted (without time parameter). The parameters of the piezoelectric transducer are changed in order functions in the sensor mode: the bottom bounding is fixed; a probe is placed on the top bounding to measure the level of induced voltages.

For simulation at a distance of 1 m, a typical sound pressure level is applied, directed to the top bounding of the sensor (black cone in Fig. 7). The sound pressure level for research is equal to the integral level of loud speech – 75 dB.

In Fig. 7 shows a diagram of the electric potential (V), the voltage in the top bounding of the piezoelectric is 16.7 μV. The deformation vector of the piezoelectric element is indicated in Fig. 8.

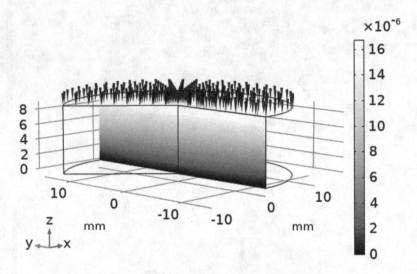

Fig. 7. The diagram of the electric potential (V)

2.4 Simulation of the Noise

In reality, the acoustic environment around the piezoelectric element is not ideal; various noises arise in the acoustic environment and the electrical part of the telephone. To the model of the noise is used the function rn1 (x), which is based on white Gaussian noise (Fig. 9) [6]. The resulting noise model is used in a simulation to calculate verbal speech intelligibility.

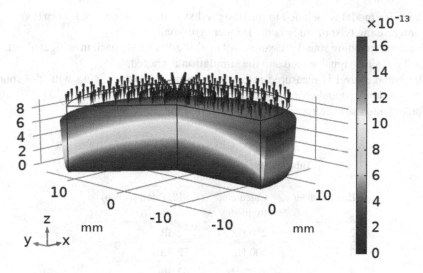

Fig. 8. The total displacement of the piezoelectric transducer (mm)

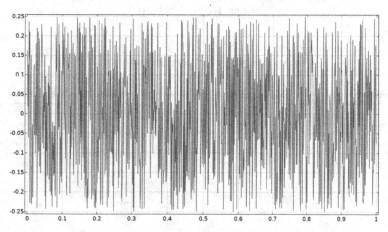

Fig. 9. The noise model

3 Methods for Controlling the Susceptibility of the Buzzer Piezoelectric Transducer

3.1 The Procedure for Making Measurements a Study Model

Consider the procedure for making measurements of the piezoelectric transducer model when controlling the susceptibility of the telephone buzzer:

1. Build the initial model of the piezoelectric element with the original characteristics.
2. The developed model of the piezoelectric element is adjusted to the sensor, a signal source is installed at a distance of 1 m, a probe is installed on the top bounding of the piezoelectric element.

3. The noise model is included in the designed system using the function rn1(x).
4. Configure the type of study is the frequency domain.
5. The corresponding sound pressure level in Table 1 is set for each investigated octave band from the signal source and the simulation is started.
6. The voltage level is measured at the probe for each octave band with the sound pressure level on and off from the signal source.
7. The obtained simulation values are shown in Table 2.

Table 1. Typical SPL in octave bands

Band number	Calculated frequency	SPL (loud speech)
2	250 Hz	72 dB
3	500 Hz	72 dB
4	1000 Hz	67 dB
5	2000 Hz	62 dB
6	4000 Hz	59 dB

Table 2. Signal voltage level measurements

Calculated frequency	Measured signal level U_i	Measured noise level U_n
250 Hz	16.7 μV	2.2 μV
500 Hz	16.7 μV	2.1 μV
1000 Hz	48.7 μV	47.2 μV
2000 Hz	51.2 μV	50.9 μV
4000 Hz	54.2 μV	48.9 μV

3.2 Procedure for Calculating Speech Intelligibility

Calculation of voltage acoustic signal Us and SNR (dB) for each octave band is performed [2]:

$$U_s = \sqrt{U_i^2 - U_n^2} \tag{1}$$

$$SNR = 20 \cdot \log\left(\frac{U_s \cdot \sqrt{\Delta F_u}}{U_n \cdot \sqrt{\Delta F_i}}\right) \tag{2}$$

where ΔF_i is the width i-octave band, ΔF_u is the width measuring receiver bandwidth.

The characteristics of the octave bands of the speech frequency range and the experimentally determined values of the formant parameter of the spectrum of the speech signal Ai, and the weight coefficients k_i for the octave bands are presented in Table 3 [2].

Table 3. Characteristics of the octave bands of the frequency range of speech

Band number	Calculated frequency	The weighting factor of the band ki	The formant parameter Ai
2	250 Hz	0.03	18 dB
3	500 Hz	0.12	14 dB
4	1000 Hz	0.20	9 dB
5	2000 Hz	0.30	6 dB
6	4000 Hz	0.26	5 dB

The speech intelligibility W_s is calculated according to the following formulas, the input parameter is the SNR [2]:

$$Q_i = SNR_i - A_i \tag{3}$$

$$p_i = \begin{cases} \dfrac{0{,}78+5{,}46 \cdot \exp(-4{,}3 \cdot 10^{-3} \cdot (27{,}3-|Q_i|)^2)}{1+10^{0{,}1 \cdot |Q_i|}}, & \text{если } Q_i \leq 0; \\ 1 - \dfrac{0{,}78+5{,}46 \cdot \exp(-4{,}3 \cdot 10^{-3} \cdot (27{,}3-|Q_i|)^2)}{1+10^{0{,}1 \cdot |Q_i|}}, & \text{если } Q_i > 0; \end{cases} \tag{4}$$

$$R_i = p_i \cdot k_i \tag{5}$$

$$R = \sum_{i=1}^{N} R_i \tag{6}$$

$$W_s = \begin{cases} 1{,}54 \cdot R^{0{,}25}(1 - \exp(-11 \cdot R)), & \text{если } R < 0{,}15; \\ 1 - \exp\left(-\dfrac{11 \cdot R}{1+0{,}7 \cdot R}\right), & \text{если } R \geq 0{,}15; \end{cases} \tag{7}$$

When comparing layered speech intelligibility to a threshold value $W_s \leq W_p$, the device is considered to be subject to acoustoelectric transformations.

Based on Eq. (1)–(7), the intelligibility of speech was calculated for the studied model $W_s = 0.44$, the obtained value indicates the susceptibility of the telephone to acoustoelectric transformations.

4 Conclusion

Based on the developed model, a method was designed to control the susceptibility of a piezoelectric element of a telephone buzzer to acoustoelectric transformations to electric energy was designed and all the main measurements were carried out. According to the results of calculations, speech intelligibility is Ws = 0.44. The obtained value of speech intelligibility indicates not only the possibility of establishing the fact of the conversation but also the possibility of revealing the content of the conversation if this telephone set is installed in the protected premises.

Investigations were carried out for the first time not only to consider the usual characteristics of piezoelectric elements but also with the use of calculations regarding indicators of information security.

The introduction of the developed models into the educational process and the creation of virtual laboratory stands on the topic, which makes it possible to study of the acoustoelectric speech information leakage channels, will increase the quality of education due to the clarity of the studied models and will allow the use of distance technologies in education, which corresponds to the main direction of the digital economy development. The research results can be used in the educational process when studying acoustoelectric information leakage channels.

Acknowledgments. The reported study was funded by Russian Ministry of Science (information security) № 4/2020.

References

1. Tichý, J., Erhart, J., Kittinger, E., Privratska, J.: Fundamentals of Piezoelectric Sensorics: Mechanical, Dielectric, and Thermodynamical Properties of Piezoelectric Materials. Springer, Heidelberg (2010). https://doi.org/10.1007/978-3-540-68427-5
2. Lukmanova, O.R., Horev, A.A: Modelling the acoustoelectric leakage channel of speech information in a telephone set. In: 2017 IEEE Conference of Russian Young Researchers in Electrical and Electronic Engineering (EIConRus), St. Petersburg, pp. 493–495. IEEE (2017). https://doi.org/10.1109/EIConRus.2017.7910599
3. COMSOL Multiphysics Documentation. https://www.comsol.com/. Accessed 12 Aug 2020
4. East Electronics. https://www.east-elec.com/sounder/tfm-27da. Accessed 12 Aug 2020
5. Sahul, R., Nesvijski, E., Hackenberger, W.: Optimization of piezoelectric transducer design by modeling and simulation. In: 2014 Joint IEEE International Symposium on the Applications of Ferroelectric, International Workshop on Acoustic Transduction Materials and Devices & Workshop on Piezoresponse Force Microscopy, State College, PA, USA, pp. 1–3. IEEE (2014). https://doi.org/10.1109/ISAF.2014.6923003
6. Kumar, S., Jain, Y.K.: Simulation of circular-shaped PZT-5H sensor for train measurement using COMSOL multiphysics. IEEE Sens. J. **15**(8), 4380–387 (2015). https://doi.org/10.1109/JSEN.2015.2419281

Automatic Parallelization of Affine Programs for Distributed Memory Systems

Artem S. Lebedev[✉] and Shamil G. Magomedov

MIREA - Russian Technological University, 78 Vernadsky Avenue, 119454 Moscow, Russia
{lebedev_a,magomedov_sh}@mirea.ru

Abstract. The paper addresses problems of spatial distribution of data and computations, organizing data exchange within pool of parallel processes to perform parallelizing optimization with data locality improvement when compiling affine programs for distributed memory systems with MPI support. The presented method of spatial distribution of data and computations rely on polyhedral framework implementing the idea of reducing construction of affine transformations of the program to multi-objective optimization problem. Data and computation placements are constructed accordingly spatial locality principle and satisfies forward communication only property. There is no single master node orchestrating the computational process and storing all the data to be processed – all the parallel processes are equal. Finally, an MPI-program with MPI_send and MPI_recv invocations is generated. A concept of communication polyhedron is introduced for modeling of information exchange within MPI communicator. Three algorithms of linear algebra are taken for benchmarks: LU decomposition, syr2k, atax. Results of parallelization are compared with Pluto compiler output in the aspect of performance.

Keywords: Polyhedral model · Distributed memory systems · Parallel processes · MPI

1 Introduction

Effective programming of parallel computing systems has always been a challenging task, and it becomes especially difficult with the increasing demands on the performance of modern software with a large code base created in the course of many years of development. In addition, researchers and engineers who develop software code for their own research prefer to focus on solving an applied problem, rather than on the technical aspects of parallel programming of a specific computing system, which may result in inefficient use of hardware resources. One of the approaches to solving the indicated problems is automatic code parallelization, which frees the programmer from the effort related to data flow analysis, parallelism identification, and synthesis of the parallel computational code.

Most computationally intensive scientific and engineering applications spend a significant part of CPU time during execution on nesting loops, which often meet the

© Springer Nature Singapore Pte Ltd. 2021
P. K. Singh et al. (Eds.): FTNCT 2020, CCIS 1396, pp. 91–101, 2021.
https://doi.org/10.1007/978-981-16-1483-5_9

program affinity criteria. The polyhedral model provides a powerful mathematical background that simplifies the analysis and transformation of such programs in order to improve performance by increasing the degree of parallelism and optimizing data locality in computations. Various methods based on polyhedral model find their use in static compilation, primarily in C and FORTRAN compilers which optimize code for specific microarchitecture (multicore processors and accelerators like GPUs).

Parallelization of an affine program in the polyhedron model is carried out in five stages:

1. Analysis of information dependencies. The method developed by Feautrier [1] and further extended by Collard and Griebl [2] gives an exact solution to the problem of data flow analysis (thanks to the use of parametric integer programming for solving the problem of lexicographic optimization) and is used in practice. Collard's and Griebl's extensions were implemented in the LooPo project (development stopped). The original Feautrier's method is implemented in the candl [3] project, the development of which continues, and software components are used in third-party projects, such as the Pluto translator.
2. Construction of a multidimensional computation schedule. Feautrier [4, 5] proposed a method for constructing one-dimensional schedules that optimize the temporal locality of data (bounded delay schedule), and then a greedy algorithm that minimizes the dimension of a multidimensional schedule. Bondhugula [6] developed Feautrier's ideas for optimizing the temporal locality of data, and implemented them without minimizing the dimension of the schedule in the Pluto parallelizing translator using lexicographic optimization when choosing alternatives.
3. Constructing the placement of calculations and data. For systems with shared memory, only the problem of constructing the computations placement is solved. Bondhugula [7] in the Pluto project continues to construct linearly independent transformations that optimize the locality of the program, preserving the dimension of the instruction domains with respect to the original program. Griebl [8] proposes a full enumeration of alternatives and the choice of the most preferable one from the point of view of the researcher, without giving any cost model. For distributed memory systems like clusters, the placements of computations and data are constructed together. Feautrier [9, 10] proposed a greedy algorithm to completely eliminate communications for as many data dependencies as possible. Griebl [8] proposes a complete enumeration of alternatives, as for systems with shared memory.
4. Tiling the time and space domain. Iteration cycles of logical time and virtual processors can be aggregated into blocks to further improve the temporal and spatial locality of the data. Modern methods are actively developed by Bondhugula [11] and have an experimental implementation in the Pluto project.
5. Synthesis of a parallel program and code generation. For systems with shared memory, the problem of generating a parallel program is exhaustively solved by Bastoul's method, which has a software implementation in the cloog [12] project supported by developers and used in other projects like Pluto. For systems with distributed memory, the problem of generating a parallel program is complicated by the need to organize information exchange between parallel processes. Dathatri and others [13] proposed and implemented in the Pluto project (distmem branch) the FOP

(flow-out partitioning) method, which determines the data flow between iterations of distributed loops along the vectors of information dependencies, and eliminates duplication of information when sending information packets. The input data is placed on all computing devices, and the calculation of the data placement is not performed.

The paper addresses problems of finding spatial distribution of computations and data to optimize data reuse distance in distributed memory systems and proposes a method to generate parallel code using message passing interface. The method of construction of data and computation placement proposed in the paper does not require full enumeration of alternatives according to Griebl scheme – it allows to effectively optimize the spatial locality of data according to Feautrier's idea, but with weakened restrictions: the key idea is to reduce communication distances, but not to completely eliminate inter-process information exchange. The method to generate parallel programs for distributed memory systems proposed in the paper takes into account the optimal placement of computations and data found at the third stage, introduces the concept of communication polyhedrons, and converts a parallel OpenMP-program generated by the Bastoul method into a parallel MPI-program with two-way communication of processes.

2   Basic Concepts of the Polyhedral Model

Any program (parallel or sequential) with static control flow can be modeled by polyhedra. Points of a polyhedron can model computations, which may be dependent on other computations modelled by other polyhedra. Dependences are constrained to be regular and local, and may be determined using analysis of data flow [1]. A program may have global parameters of integer type (called «structure parameters»), whose values become known only in runtime. In the assumption that there are q_z such parameters, we represent them as integer vector $\vec{z} \in \mathbb{Z}^{q_z}$.

Each instruction X is associated with its domain D_X – a polyhedron whose points with integer-valued coordinates model iterations of loops surrounding X. A symbolic notation for these points is an index vector $\vec{i} \in D_X$, which identifies an operation (dynamic instance of the corresponding instruction X) denoted as $\langle \vec{i}, \vec{z}; X \rangle \in \Omega$, where Ω is the set of all operations.

Any data dependent operations u and v must satisfy the causality condition to preserve correctness of the computation process: $u \rightarrow v \Rightarrow \theta(v) > \theta(u)$, where θ is the function modelling logical time, called schedule. Any two non-dependent operations may be executed at the same time (in parallel). The set of operations with the same logical time t is called parallel front at t: $F(t) = \{u \in \Omega | \theta(u) = t\}$. The value $L = \max_{u \in \Omega}(\theta(u))$ is called the schedule latency.

Sequential execution of parallel fronts with increasing logical time index is the common scheme used to construct programs with synchronous parallelism:

for $(t = 0; t \leq L; \mathrm{inc}(t))$ {

    information exchange;

    parallel execution of $F(t)$;

    barrier synchronization;

}

Polyhedron model introduces the infinite set of virtual processors to associate operations execution with. Since the number of operations is finite, only finite subset of virtual processors is sufficient to model computations. In the assumption that virtual processors space is one-dimensional, a function $\pi : \Omega \rightarrow \mathbb{N}_0$, called computation placement, maps operations to virtual processors identified with non-negative integer indexes. The practical way to define such placement in polyhedral model is to associate an affine function with every instruction X, which maps related operations to virtual processors:
$\pi_X(\vec{i}, \vec{z}) = \vec{\zeta}_X \cdot \vec{i} + \vec{\zeta}'_X \cdot \vec{z} + \zeta^0_X, \quad \zeta^0_X \in \mathbb{Z}, \vec{\zeta}_X \in \mathbb{Z}^{p_X}, \vec{\zeta}'_X \in \mathbb{Z}^{q_z}, \quad \vec{i} \in D_X.$

By analogy, the concept of placement for data arrays is introduced. We denote by $\langle g_a, \vec{z}; A_a \rangle$ an access to array A_a with affine index function $g_a(\vec{i})$ in some position a in instruction X. Then $\eta \langle g_a, \vec{z}; A_a \rangle$ is the virtual processor number the datum $A_a[g_a(\vec{i})]$ is placed to. The dimensionality of the array A is denoted with p_A, the set of its legal indices is denoted by D_A. One-dimensional affine placement for array A is a function of the form $\eta_A(\vec{g}, \vec{z}) = \vec{\zeta}_A \cdot \vec{g} + \vec{\zeta}'_A \cdot \vec{z} + \zeta^0_A, \quad \zeta^0_A \in \mathbb{Z}, \vec{\zeta}_A \in \mathbb{Z}^{p_A}, \vec{\zeta}'_A \in \mathbb{Z}^{q_z}, \quad \vec{g} \in D_A.$

3 Construction of Affine Transformations

Consider a function $v_a(\vec{i}, \vec{z}) = \left| \pi_X(\vec{i}, \vec{z}) - \eta_{A_a}(g_a(\vec{i}), \vec{z}) \right|$ for access $\langle g_a, \vec{z}; A_a \rangle$ in some position a in instruction X. It gives the measure of data reuse distance. Minimization of this distance forces data-dependent operations to be placed on possibly nearest virtual processors, which leads to reducing of the communication overhead. The measure given by $v_a(\vec{i}, \vec{z})$ may be bounded by a constant value, which is considered optimal. However, this is not always possible.

Theorem 1. Given a bounded domain D_X, two affine mappings: $\pi_X(\vec{i}, \vec{z})$ and $\eta_{A_a}(g_a(\vec{i}), \vec{z})$ for some position a in instruction X, then there exists at least one affine form in structure parameters $L_a(\vec{z})$, such that $L_a(\vec{z}) - v_a(\vec{i}, \vec{z}) \geq 0, \quad \vec{i} \in D_X$.

Definition 1. Let $\left\{ \varphi : \varphi = \langle \{\pi_{S_i} : i = 1, \ldots, m\}; \{\eta_{A_k} : k = 1, \ldots, l\} \rangle \right\}$ be the set of all collections φ of one-dimensional affine mappings π_{S_i} and η_{A_k} for all instructions and arrays respectively. Collection φ is called optimal for the program, if it minimizes functionals $f_{a_j}(\varphi) = L_{a_j}(\vec{w}) = \vec{l}_{a_j} \cdot \vec{w} + l^0_{a_j}$ for all positions $a_j, j = 1, \ldots, n$ in instructions of the program, performing memory accesses, such that $\neg \exists \varphi' \in \{\varphi\} (\forall j \in \{1 \ldots n\} (f_{a_j}(\varphi') \leq f_{a_j}(\varphi)) \wedge \exists j \in \{1 \ldots n\} (f_{a_j}(\varphi') < f_{a_j}(\varphi)))$, where $\vec{w}$ stands for vector of weighting coefficients for variables in $\vec{l}_{a_j}$ associated with structure parameters.

The problem of finding spatial distribution reduces to a multiple-criteria decision-making problem with the following scalar form: $\sum_{j=1}^{n} \alpha_{a_j} f_{a_j} = \sum_{j=1}^{n} \alpha_{a_j} \left(\vec{l}_{a_j} \cdot \vec{w} + l_{a_j}^0 \right) \rightarrow$ min, where α_{a_j} are non-negative weighting coefficients, which encode the priorities of different data dependencies. This formulation more accurately reflects the preferences of the decision maker than Feautrier's scheme, since it allows to order the accesses by priority in accordance with the frequency of their execution. It is recommended to set α_{a_j} to the number of points with integer coordinates of the domain of the instruction which performs access a_j. In contrast to the well-known Griebl's scheme, the proposed approach does not require a complete enumeration of alternatives since the minimization of the scalar form may be done with integer linear programming machinery.

Considering only one-dimensional affine placements does not mean a significant narrowing of the practical applicability of the method, since processing elements of a cluster can be modeled with one-dimensional virtual processors space by assigning sequential numbers to the cores at the level of individual processor, as well as at the level of an individual node and a whole cluster.

4 Organizing Information Exchange

Let the computing system has Q physical processors with indices $r = 0, \ldots, Q - 1$. Let v be the non-negative index of the virtual processor, $r(v)$ be the index of the physical processor to which the virtual processor with index v is assigned. In the works of Feautrier [9], Bondhugula [14], Griebl [8], two practical methods of distributing virtual processors between physical ones were mentioned: block, if $r(v) = \lfloor v/Q \rfloor$, and cyclic, if $r(v) = v \bmod Q$. The proposed method for organizing information exchange between parallel processes is based on a block distribution scheme.

Each physical processor r processes a segment of the space of virtual processors $l(r), \ldots, u(r)$ such that $l(r + 1) = u(r) + 1$, where $l(r) = L + r\lfloor (U - L + Q)/Q \rfloor$, $L = \min\left(\min_{X}(\pi_X), \min_{A}(\eta_A) \right)$, $U = \max\left(\max_{X}(\pi_X), \max_{X}(\eta_A) \right)$. In this case, not all Q physical processors can be loaded, but all loaded ones will have the same number of virtual processors. Information exchange between physical processors is caused by remote read and remote write operations, when the processor with index R accesses data elements located on the processor with index r: $R > r$ for remote read operations, $R < r$ for remote write operations, since the calculated placement satisfy the FCO-property [8].

A refined scheme to construct program with synchronous parallelism for distributed memory systems:

```
for ( t = 0 ; t ≤ ScheduleLatency ; inc( t )) {
    information exchange for remote reads;
    parallel execution of F(t) ;
    barrier synchronization;
    information exchange for remote writes;
}
```

Before the front is executed, the data is sent for remote read operations, after the front is executed, the data induced by the remote write operations is sent. The implementation of parallelism is assumed within the MPI standard with two-way communication of processes (MPI_Send, MPI_Recv). Define a set of data that will participate in the acts of information exchange. Let D'_S be the domain of the instruction S in a parallelized program, p'_S denotes its dimensionality, $\vec{i}'_S \in D'_S$ is an integer vector of the iteration index, $\vec{i}_S^{\prime(p)}$ is the index of the loop iterating in the space of virtual processors. Let D'_S be the polyhedron described with constraints $\vec{b}_{S,k} \cdot \vec{i}'_S + \vec{c}_{S,k} \cdot \vec{z} + d_{S,k} \geq 0, k = 1, \ldots, p_{D'_S}$.

Definition 2. The instantaneous domain of an instruction S for a physical processor R is a parametrically defined polytope $D''_{S,R}$:

$$
\vec{i}''_S = \begin{bmatrix} \vec{i}_S^{\prime(p)} \\ \cdots \\ \vec{i}_S^{\prime(p'_S)} \end{bmatrix} \in D''_{S,R} \Leftrightarrow \begin{cases} l(R) \leq \vec{i}_S^{\prime(p)} \leq u(R) \\ \vec{b}_{S,k} \cdot \vec{i}'_S + \vec{c}_{S,k} \cdot \vec{z} + d_{S,k} \geq 0, k \in K_S^{D''} \end{cases}, \tag{1}
$$

where $K_S^{D''}$ is the set of indices of constraints including at least one of the components of $\vec{i}_S^{\prime(l)}$, $l = p+1, \ldots, p'_S$. Let $\tilde{g}_a(\theta', D''_{S,R})$ be the set of indices of all elements of array A_a, which are accessed by the instruction S in the position a by the physical processor R at the moment $\theta' = \begin{bmatrix} \vec{i}_S^{\prime(1)} & \cdots & \vec{i}_S^{\prime(p-1)} \end{bmatrix}$.

Definition 3. Sets $Q_*^{r/w-r/s}$ (2–5) are communication polyhedrons. In the first part of the top index r and w denotes remote read and remote write respectively. In the second part of the top index r and s denotes receiving and sending data respectively.

$$
Q_a^{r-r}(\vec{g}_{A_a}, R, r) : \begin{cases} r < R \\ \vec{g}_{A_a} \in g_a(\theta', D''_{S,R}) \\ l(r) \leq \eta(\langle \vec{g}_{A_a}, \vec{z}; A_a \rangle) \leq u(r) \end{cases} \tag{2}
$$

$$
Q_a^{r-s}(\vec{g}_{A_a}, R, r) : \begin{cases} r > R \\ \vec{g}_{A_a} \in g_a(\theta', D''_{S,r}) \\ l(R) \leq \eta(\langle \vec{g}_{A_a}, \vec{z}; A_a \rangle) \leq u(R) \end{cases} \tag{3}
$$

$$
Q_a^{w-s}(\vec{g}_{A_a}, R, r) : \begin{cases} r > R \\ \vec{g}_{A_a} \in g_a(\theta', D''_{S,R}) \\ l(r) \leq \eta(\langle \vec{g}_{A_a}, \vec{z}; A_a \rangle) \leq u(r) \end{cases} \tag{4}
$$

$$
Q_a^{w-r}(\vec{g}_{A_a}, R, r) : \begin{cases} r < R \\ \vec{g}_{A_a} \in g_a(\theta', D''_{S,r}) \\ l(R) \leq \eta(\langle \vec{g}_{A_a}, \vec{z}; A_a \rangle) \leq u(R) \end{cases} \tag{5}
$$

These polyhedra can be scanned by loops nest, which the CLooG tool is suitable for generating. The code of these nests can be used in the formation of packets to implement information exchange between processes in the MPI communicator. Let's clarify steps of information exchange in the parallel program:

```
// information exchange for remote reads
for (int j = 1; j <= n; j++) {
  if ( a_j is read) {
    for (int r = 0; r < R; r++)
      MPI_Recv(data for Q_{a_j}^{r-r}(g_{A_{a_j}}, R, r) );
    for (int r = R+1; r < Q; r++)
      MPI_Send(data for Q_{a_j}^{r-s}(g_{A_{a_j}}, R, r));
  }
}
// information exchange for remote writes
for (int j = 1; j <= n; j++) {
  if ( a_j is write) {
    for (int r = 0; r < R; r++)
      MPI_Recv(data for Q_{a_j}^{w-r}(g_{A_{a_j}}, R, r) );
    for (int r = R+1; r < Q; r++)
      MPI_Send(data for Q_{a_j}^{w-s}(g_{A_{a_j}}, R, r) );
  }
}
```

The R variable stores the value of the physical processor's own index (the rank of the MPI process). The r variable is used to index other physical processors (ranks of other MPI processes).

5 Benchmarks

The developed methods for automatic parallelization of affine programs were applied to three implementations of linear algebra algorithms: LU-decomposition of a square matrix, matrix products atax and syr2k. A method developed earlier was used to compute schedules [15]. Each program has been parallelized for distributed memory systems using MPI. Calculations were performed with double precision (double type of C language). The experiments were done on two machines of the cluster of the Institute of Integrated Safety, Security and Special Instrumentation (MIREA) (Table 1). MPI programs were launched on two machines. The performance of a parallel program obtained using the implementation of the proposed methods and the modern compiler Pluto 0.11.4 was compared. Acceleration was estimated relative to running a sequential version of the program on machine 1.

Table 1. Computing environment configuration.

Parameter	Value
Machine 1 configuration (node0)	Intel Xeon E5-2690 v2, 8 GB RAM, InfiniBand: Mellanox ConnectX VPI
Machine 2 configuration (node1)	Intel Xeon E5-2640 v3, 4 GB RAM, InfiniBand: Mellanox ConnectX-3
Interconnect network	InfiniBand 40 Gb/sec
OS	Linux CentOS 7.3 x64
Compiler	gcc 4.8.5
MPI library	openmpi-1.10.5a1
Compilation (ILP)	mpicc -O2 -std = c99 -fopenmp
Compilation (pluto)	lu: mpicc -O2 -fopenmp -D__MPI -DTIME \ -D__DONT_USE_INV_BLOCK_DIST_FUNCTION atax and syr2k: mpicc -O2 -fopenmp -D__MPI -DTIME
Pluto keys	polycc --distmem --mpiomp --commopt_fop --isldep \ --lastwriter --cloogsh --timereport
MPI processes layout	2 processes: mpirun -np 2 -host node0, node1 4 processes: mpirun -np 4 -host node0, node0, node1, node1 6 processes: mpirun -np 6 -host node0, node0, node0,\ node1, node1, node1 8 processes: mpirun -np 8 -host node0, node0, node0, node0,\ node1, node1, node1, node1

Table 2 shows the results of parallelization of three linear programs. The variants of parallel programs obtained using the developed system are marked as ILP, and the variants obtained using the Pluto compiler are marked as Pluto.

Parallel code was run for execution in 2, 4, 6, 8 threads. In the MPI experiments, single threads were running inside multiple MPI processes running on both machines (the number of processes was divided equally between the machines). The Pluto compiler, considered as an analogue of the developed system, is at the stage of an experimental prototype at the time of this writing, and therefore its operation is unstable. The resulting parallel code of the lu program was successfully compiled only with the additional definition (Table 1). The presence of this definition for other considered examples atax and syr2k led to a noticeable decrease in the performance, and therefore was not used when comparing the performance of parallel versions of programs.

Despite the presence of undesirable build parameters, the lu parallel program (Pluto-MPI) turned out to be 14% faster than the lu (ILP-MPI) version, showing a 2.94 times speedup versus 2.56 times when executing in 8 threads. The gain was achieved due to a more even loading of processes with dynamically distributed workload, as opposed to the static approach used in the developed system, which allows processes to be idle.

Table 2. Results of parallelizing of affine programs.

Sequential programs	Results of parallel runs

// LU-decomposition
for (**int** k = 0; k < N; k++) {
  for (**int** l = k + 1; l < N; l++)
   A[l][k] /= A[k][k];
  for (**int** i = k + 1; i < N; i++)
   for (**int** j = k + 1; j < N; j++)
    A[i][j] −= A[i][k] * A[k][j];
}	

$\vec{y} = A^T (Ax)$
// atax
for (**int** i = 0; i < N; i++)
  y[i] = 0;
for (**int** i = 0; i < M; i++) {
  t[i] = 0;
  for (**int** j = 0; j < N; j++)
   t[i] = t[i] + A[i][j] * x[j];
  for (**int** j = 0; j < N; j++)
   y[j] = y[j] + A[i][j] * t [i];
}	

$C_{out} = \alpha AB^T + \alpha BA^T + \beta C$
// syr2k
for (**int** i = 0; i < N; i++) {
  for (**int** j = 0; j <= i; j++)
   C[i][j] *= beta;
  for (**int** k = 0; k < M; k++)
   for (**int** j = 0; j <= i; j++)
    C[i][j] += alpha * (A[j][k] *
B[i][k] + B[j][k] * A[i][k]);
}	

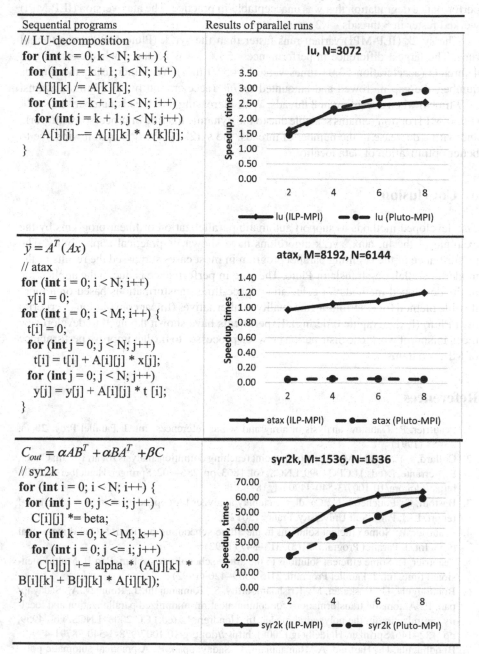

For the atax program, all the results obtained using the pluto compiler showed a performance degradation that was unacceptable in practice. The atax version (ILP-MPI) worked faster in 8 threads - 1.2 times faster.

The syr2k (ILP-MPI) variant runs faster than the syr2k (Pluto-MPI) variant in all runs. The largest difference in performance - 53% - was achieved when executing in 4 threads (acceleration 53.03 times versus 34.51 times). With increasing the threads number, the gap narrowed and amounted to 7% (acceleration by 63.97 times against 59.7 times) when executing in 8 threads. With increasing the threads number, the syr2k (Pluto-MPI) option remains scalable due to the dynamic loading of processes with work, and with a decrease in the number of threads, the syr2k (ILP-MPI) option wins due to better optimization of data locality.

6 Conclusion

The developed methods to support automatic parallelization of linear programs by the example of the lu, atax, syr2k algorithms have shown its practical applicability. The performance of the resulting parallel program in most cases surpassed the results of the modern parallelizing translator Pluto. The gain in performance is due to the application of the developed methods for calculating space-time transformations based on a more flexible method for determining the quality of alternatives (linear convolution of criteria) than Pluto (lexicographic ordering). Experiments have shown the need to develop new mechanisms of workload distribution between processes to further improve performance of MPI programs.

References

1. Feautrier, P.: Dataflow analysis of array and scalar references. Int. J. Parallel Prog. **20**(1), 23–53 (1991)
2. Collard, J.-F., Griebl, M.: A precise fixpoint reaching definition analysis for arrays. In: Carter, L., Ferrante, J. (eds.) LCPC 1999. LNCS, vol. 1863, pp. 286–302. Springer, Heidelberg (2000). https://doi.org/10.1007/3-540-44905-1_18
3. Bastoul, C., Pouchet, L.N.: Candl: the chunky analyzer for dependences in loops. Technical report. LRI, Paris-Sud University, France (2012)
4. Feautrier, P.: Some efficient solutions to the affine scheduling problem. I. One-dimensional time. Int. J. Parallel Program. **21**(5), 313–347 (1992)
5. Feautrier, P.: Some efficient solutions to the affine scheduling problem. Part II. Multidimensional time. Int. J. Parallel Program. **21**(6), 389–420 (1992)
6. Bondhugula, U., Baskaran, M., Krishnamoorthy, S., Ramanujam, J., Rountev, A., Sadayappan, P.: Automatic transformations for communication-minimized parallelization and locality optimization in the polyhedral model. In: Hendren, L. (ed.) CC 2008. LNCS, vol. 4959, pp. 132–146. Springer, Heidelberg (2008). https://doi.org/10.1007/978-3-540-78791-4_9
7. Bondhugula, U., Hartono, A., Ramanujam, J., Sadayappan, P.: A practical automatic polyhedral parallelizer and locality optimizer. In: Proceedings of the 29th ACM SIGPLAN Conference on Programming Language Design and Implementation, pp. 101–113, June 2008
8. Griebl, M.: Automatic parallelization of loop programs for distributed memory architectures. University of Passau (2004)

9. Feautrier, P.: Toward automatic distribution. Parallel Process. Lett. **4**(03), 233–244 (1994)
10. Feautrier, P.: Automatic distribution of data and computations. In In Technical Report 2000/3 (2000)
11. Bondhugula, U., Bandishti, V., Pananilath, I.: Diamond tiling: tiling techniques to maximize parallelism for stencil computations. IEEE Trans. Parallel Distrib. Syst. **28**(5), 1285–1298 (2016)
12. Bastoul, C.: Code generation in the polyhedral model is easier than you think. In: Proceedings. 13th International Conference on Parallel Architecture and Compilation Techniques, PACT 2004, pp. 7–16. IEEE, October 2004
13. Dathathri, R., Reddy, C., Ramashekar, T., Bondhugula, U.: Generating efficient data movement code for heterogeneous architectures with distributed-memory. In: Proceedings of the 22nd International Conference on Parallel Architectures and Compilation Techniques, pp. 375–386. IEEE, September 2013
14. Reddy, C., Bondhugula, U.: Effective automatic computation placement and data allocation for parallelization of regular programs. In: Proceedings of the 28th ACM International Conference on Supercomputing, pp. 13–22, June 2014
15. Lebedev, A.S.: Construction of optimal space-time mappings for automatic parallelization of loop nests with static control flow. In: 2017 IEEE 11th International Conference on Application of Information and Communication Technologies (AICT), pp. 1–7. IEEE, September 2017

Influence of Signal Preprocessing When Highlighting Steady-State Visual Evoked Potentials Based on a Multivariate Synchronization Index

Sergei Kharchenko[1]([✉]), Roman Meshcheryakov[2], and Yaroslav Turovsky[2,3]

[1] Tomsk State University of Control Systems and Radioelectronics, Tomsk, Russia
[2] Institute of Control Sciences Academician VA Trapeznikov, Moscow, Russia
[3] Voronezh State University, Voronezh, Russia

Abstract. This article covers the issue of the data preprocessing when highlighting steady-state visual evoked potentials using preliminary band-pass filtering of the EEG signal. In the introduction part the authors illustrate relevance of the system integration such as human-machine interaction and brain-computer interface. The integration of the above-mentioned systems as well as the ways of the signal preprocessing for highlighting of steady-state visual evoked potentials in electroencephalograms were examined. The article contains researches of the electroencephalogram signals with steady-state visual evoked potentials for photostimulation frequencies of 8 and 14 Hz with sampling frequency of 5 kHz based on the multivariate synchronization index method. Influence of preliminary band-pass filtering on recognition accuracy of the signal frequency under study is considered. Ratio of the correctly recognized states is considered in the function of accuracy metric. Butterworth filters, Chebyshev filters of I and II types, elliptic filters as well as Bessel filters of different orders are considered as bend-pass filters. The result of the authors' investigation is a number of recommendations on parameters used while signal preprocessing for highlighting of steady-state visual evoked potentials in the multivariate synchronization index method. The results obtained are of considerable practical importance as they can be used for brain-computer interface producing on the basis of steady-state visual evoked potentials and later can be taken for building of control theory of robot systems of different application and for implementation of decisions on human-machine interaction within narrow practical tasks.

Keywords: Steady-state visual evoked potentials · Multivariate synchronization index · Human-machine interaction · SSVEP · Electroencephalography · EEG · Signal preprocessing · Butterworth filter · Chebyshev filter · Elliptic filter · Bessel filter

1 Introduction

Over the last years development of brain-machine interfaces (BCI) of different types has become not only like an experimental trend but also more and more of practical

© Springer Nature Singapore Pte Ltd. 2021
P. K. Singh et al. (Eds.): FTNCT 2020, CCIS 1396, pp. 102–111, 2021.
https://doi.org/10.1007/978-981-16-1483-5_10

use. The first reference to the brain-machine interface creation is primarily connected to the capability development of the electroencephalography and attempts to interpret isolated impulses of brain signals [1]. The basis of all brain-computer interfaces is a biofeedback training method providing information acquisition about current state of this or that physiological function for human training of a conscious brain control and control of this function [2]. Biofeedback utilization involves the use or either positive or negative reinforcement [3].

Electroencephalogram data as well as electromyography or analysis of a human's ocular motility can be used for the brain-machine interface implementation. Both real and false responses, used for BCI development while patient's rehabilitation after nervous system damage can be used as brain responses [4].

One of the ways of realization of such systems is the usage of steady-state visual evoked potentials (SSVEP). Registration of the evoked brain potentials (EP) is a non-invasive method of testing functions of the central nervous system [5]. Evoked potentials are brain electrical responses to visual, auditory or sensory stimuli. The important thing is that the signals of the evoked potentials on any irritant are similar to signals generated in case when a person acts as an irritant. SSVEP are evoked potentials of the brain on visual stimuli, where in most cases the following can be used as an irritant: screen image, image in AR goggles or LED glow of different flicker frequencies. Flicker frequency range of an irritant establishes a command set, which can be used for development of brain-computer interfaces or human-machine interactions.

Electroencephalogram (EEG) is a graphical presentation of an oscillatory electrical process registered when electrodes being placed on a brain or a scalp surface. Usually signals are recorded from electrodes to be placed on a scalp surface of a patient. EEG registration required usage of different sets of electrodes from 8 to 75 and different placement on a scalp [6].

The maim problems of using steady-state visual evoked potentials are spontaneous EEG due to external irritants and low signal-to-noise ratio. While the first problem can be solved only by organizational measures – a patient has to be concentrated on an object during the procedure, increase of signal-to-noise ratio often requires coherent integration and/or averaging on a software or hardware level. In addition, it is relevant to reduce an analysis window while highlighting EEG state as it contributes to development of brain-computer interfaces and human-machine interaction systems on the biofeedback basis, which work in real-time mode.

Analysis of research articles and references at scientific conferences in the area of development [7–9], implementation [10–12] and practical application [13–16] of human-machine interaction interfaces and development of brain-computer interfaces shows that relevance of recording of steady-state visual evoked potentials only increases with accuracy increase of their highlighting in the EEG signal.

2 Methods and Results

This article looks at the method which shows the highest results from the perspective of various researchers - multivariate synchronization index method [17–20]. Synchronization principle of multichannel EEG and reference signals, meant to be in line with visual stimulus frequency (photostimulation frequency) is a core of the multivariate synchronization index method. Selection of reference signals are based on Eq. 1.

$$Y(t) = \begin{bmatrix} sin(2\pi ft) \\ cos(2\pi ft) \\ ... \\ sin(2\pi Nft) \\ cos(2\pi Nft) \end{bmatrix}, t = \frac{1}{F_s}, \frac{2}{F_s}, ... \frac{K}{F_s} \tag{1}$$

where N – the harmonic sequence number, K – the number of samples, Fs – the sampling frequency, $Y(t)$ – the reference signal, $X(t)$ – the original EEG signal. Initially, the correlation matrix between two signals is calculated using Eqs. 2–3.

$$D_{11} = \left(\frac{1}{M}\right) XX^T \tag{2}$$

$$D_{22} = \left(\frac{1}{M}\right) YY^T \tag{3}$$

$$D_{21} = D_{12} = \left(\frac{1}{M}\right) XY^T \tag{4}$$

A linear transformation is calculated to eliminate the effect of autocorrelation on the measure of synchronization (Eq. 5).

$$T = \begin{bmatrix} \frac{1}{\sqrt{D_{11}}} & 0 \\ 0 & \frac{1}{\sqrt{D_{22}}} \end{bmatrix} \tag{5}$$

After that the correlation matrix is calculated by the Eq. 6.

$$S = \begin{bmatrix} I_{1\times 1} & \frac{1}{\sqrt{D_{11}}} D_{12} \frac{1}{\sqrt{D_{22}}} \\ \frac{1}{\sqrt{D_{22}}} D_{21} \frac{1}{\sqrt{D_{11}}} & I_{2N_h\times 2N_h} \end{bmatrix} \tag{6}$$

Then multivariate synchronization index is determined by the Eq. 7.

$$R_i = 1 + \frac{\sum \lambda_i' \log(\lambda_i')}{\log(P)} \tag{7}$$

where λ_i' - normalized eigenvalues S, P = N + Nh и Nh note the number of lines in the reference signal B(t). The frequency of photostimulation is defined as the frequency corresponding to the maximum value of R.

The use of multivariate synchronization index for highlighting of steady-state visual evoked potentials within brain-computer interfaces makes it possible to use signals from several EEG channels at a time that could in perspective contribute to development of human-machine interaction systems of higher quality (Fig. 1).

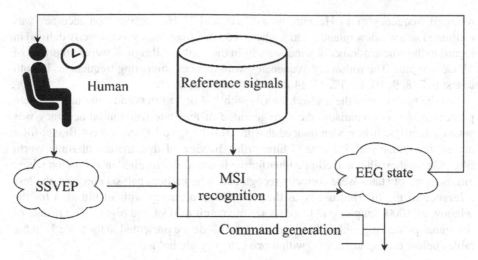

Fig. 1. Scheme of the use of multivariate synchronization index within brain-computer interfaces.

Butterworth filter is a filter that is different in that its amplitude-frequency character-istic (AFC) is max smooth on band pass frequencies [21]. Chebyshev filter is a filter that is different in that its AFC possesses steeper roll-off and more significant pulsations on band-pass frequencies (Chebyshev filter of type I) and stopband frequencies (Chebyshev filter of type II) than those of filters of other types. They can be used, where with the help of the filter of a small order it is required to provide suppression of frequencies from the stopband and at the same time smoothness of AFC on band-pass and stopband frequencies is not of a big importance [22]. Elliptic filter is a filter that is different in that its AFC possesses very steep roll-off, that it why with the help of this filter it becomes possible to achieve more efficient frequency separation in comparison with other filters [23]. Bessel filter is a filter, which specific feature is a maximally smooth group delay such that waveform of a filtrated signal in output of this filter within the band pass remains almost the same [24].

EEG signals with steady-state visual evoked potentials were explored basing on the multivariate synchronization index with the use of the MATLAB [25] application pro-gram package. 60 signals of 30 adult patients, men and women of various age groups without contraindications to EEG and photostimulation reading were studied. LED glow was used as a source of photostimulation. All signals were preliminarily subjected to coherent integration in order to increase the signal-to-noise ratio because a big number of noises triggered by the brain spontaneous activity is typical for clear EEG signals. Photostimulation frequency for the signals from the first group amounted to 8 Hz and 14 Hz for the second group. Discretization frequency for all signals amounted to 5 kHz. Each signal was divided into windows of 500, 1000 and 1500 samples, which is equiva-lent of the analysis epoch of 100, 200 and 300 ms respectively. Band-pass filtering with the usage of the Butterworth filter, Chebyshev filter of type I, Chebyshev filter of type II, elliptic filter and Bessel filter was preliminarily used for each analysis window. Filter order used lay in the range from 1 to 4. Band edges of the filter for signals with required frequency of 8 Hz were set as 4 Hz and 12 Hz. Band edges of the filter for signals with required frequency of 14 Hz were set as 7 Hz and 21 Hz. Recognition accuracy was estimated as a window quantity ratio, where required frequency was correctly defined in regard to the whole number of windows within the signal. All signals were comprised of 15000 samples. The following frequencies were used as competing frequencies in both cases: 6, 7, 8, 9, 10, 11, 12, 13, 14, 15, 16, 17, 18, 19, 20 Hz.

At the first stage of the research signals with 1–4 order filters and without them were processed. As a comparison, the average value of the state recognition accuracy was set as a metrics. It has been noticed that the results for all filters except Bessel filter are getting worse with increase of filter order. In view of this, the use of Butterworth filter, Chebyshev filter and elliptic filter for the fourth order resulted in a situation where almost none of states were correctly recognized. The higher analysis epoch is, the less relevance of the filtering use is, as the recognition accuracy without filtration for the window of 1000 samples and more shows the result of 0.94 and higher. The results of the signal processing within the single-channel mode are presented in the table 1. In the tables below the highest results within one category are bolded.

Table 1. Single-channel mode results.

Freq.	Window	Order	Filter type					
			But.	ChebI	ChebII	Ellip	Bes.	Basic
8 Hz	500	1	**0,81**	**0,80**	**0,80**	**0,80**	0,62	0,62
		2	**0,79**	**0,70**	0,35	0,57	0,62	0,62
		3	0,47	0,01	0,62	0,51	0,62	0,62
		4	0,00	0,00	0,00	0,00	**0,62**	**0,62**
	1000	1	0,93	**1,00**	**1,00**	**1,00**	**1,00**	**1,00**
		2	0,93	0,93	**1,00**	**1,00**	**1,00**	**1,00**
		3	0,93	0,50	**1,00**	0,93	**1,00**	**1,00**
		4	0,04	0,05	0,01	0,00	**1,00**	**1,00**
	1500	1	**1,00**	**1,00**	**1,00**	**1,00**	**1,00**	**1,00**
		2	0,89	0,89	**1,00**	**1,00**	**1,00**	**1,00**
		3	0,89	0,89	**1,00**	**1,00**	**1,00**	**1,00**
		4	0,00	0,00	0,00	0,00	**1,00**	**1,00**
14 Hz	500	1	**0,86**	**0,87**	**0,87**	**0,87**	0,81	0,81
		2	0,41	0,33	0,73	0,70	**0,80**	**0,81**
		3	0,01	0,00	0,78	0,79	**0,80**	**0,81**
		4	0,00	0,00	0,00	0,00	**0,80**	**0,81**

(continued)

Table 1. (*continued*)

Freq.	Window	Order	Filter type					
			But.	ChebI	ChebII	Ellip	Bes.	Basic
	1000	1	0,90	0,90	0,90	0,90	**0,94**	**0,94**
		2	0,54	0,51	0,89	0,85	**0,94**	**0,94**
		3	0,03	0,00	0,88	0,88	**0,94**	**0,94**
		4	0,00	0,00	0,00	0,00	**0,94**	**0,94**
	1500	1	0,86	0,87	0,87	0,87	**0,99**	**0,99**
		2	0,61	0,58	0,87	0,96	**0,99**	**0,99**
		3	0,03	0,01	0,96	0,86	**0,99**	**0,99**
		4	0,00	0,00	0,00	0,00	**0,99**	**0,99**

The results obtained within the dual-channel mode of the multivariate synchronization index correspond to the results for the single-channel mode. With increase of the analysis epoch the highest results were obtained without filtration and recognition accuracy for analysis window of 1000 samples showed the result of at least 0.9. The results of the signal processing within the dual-channel mode are presented in the Table 2.

Table 2. Dual-channel mode results.

Freq.	Window	Order	Filter type					
			But.	ChebI	ChebII	Ellip	Bes.	Basic
8 Hz	500	1	**0,57**	**0,56**	**0,56**	**0,56**	0,38	0,37
		2	**0,55**	0,50	0,29	0,36	0,39	0,37
		3	0,00	0,00	0,03	0,00	**0,40**	0,37
		4	0,00	0,00	0,00	0,00	**0,40**	0,37
	1000	1	0,96	**1,00**	**1,00**	1,00	1,00	1,00
		2	0,93	0,93	**1,00**	1,00	1,00	1,00
		3	0,80	0,44	**0,95**	0,91	1,00	1,00
		4	0,00	0,02	0,00	0,02	1,00	1,00
	1500	1	**1,00**	**1,00**	**1,00**	**1,00**	1,00	1,00
		2	0,91	0,90	**1,00**	1,00	1,00	1,00
		3	0,89	0,85	**1,00**	0,99	1,00	1,00
		4	0,00	0,00	0,00	0,00	1,00	1,00

(*continued*)

Table 2. (*continued*)

Freq.	Window	Order	Filter type					
			But.	ChebI	ChebII	Ellip	Bes.	Basic
14 Hz	500	1	**0,78**	**0,83**	**0,83**	**0,83**	0,34	0,33
		2	0,16	0,12	0,36	0,30	0,34	0,33
		3	0,00	0,00	**0,76**	0,09	0,34	0,33
		4	0,00	0,00	0,00	0,00	**0,34**	0,33
	1000	1	0,89	**0,94**	**0,94**	**0,94**	**0,90**	**0,90**
		2	0,26	0,24	0,89	0,86	**0,89**	**0,90**
		3	0,00	0,00	0,96	0,35	0,89	0,90
		4	0,00	0,00	0,00	0,00	**0,90**	**0,90**
	1500	1	0,86	0,93	0,93	0,93	**1,00**	**1,00**
		2	0,30	0,27	0,91	1,00	**1,00**	**1,00**
		3	0,00	0,00	0,98	0,77	**1,00**	**1,00**
		4	0,00	0,00	0,00	0,00	**1,00**	**1,00**

The results obtained within the four-channel mode of the multivariate synchroniza-tion index were mixed. With the photostimulation frequency equal to 8 Hz the results correspond to the single-channel and dual-channel modes of filtration. And for the pho-tostimulation frequency equal to 14 Hz with the window of 1000 samples the highest results are obtained with the use of Chebyshev filter and elliptic filter. In the authors' opinion, it can be ascribed to non-optimal choice of channels for the analysis. For the rest the results correspond to the preceding frequency highlighting modes with the help of the multivariate synchronization index. The results of the signal processing within the four-channel mode are presented in the Table 3.

Table 3. Four-channel mode results.

Freq.	Window	Order	Filter type					
			But.	ChebI	ChebII	Ellip	Bes.	Basic
8 Hz	500	1	**0,39**	**0,39**	**0,39**	**0,39**	0,25	0,24
		2	0,13	0,10	**0,24**	0,23	0,25	0,24
		3	0,00	0,00	0,01	0,00	0,25	0,24
		4	0,00	0,00	0,00	0,00	**0,26**	0,24
	1000	1	**1,00**	**1,00**	**1,00**	**1,00**	**1,00**	**1,00**
		2	0,93	0,92	**1,00**	**1,00**	**1,00**	**1,00**

(*continued*)

Table 3. (*continued*)

| Freq. | Window | Order | Filter type | | | | | |
			But.	ChebI	ChebII	Ellip	Bes.	Basic
		3	0,74	0,60	**0,98**	0,87	**1,00**	**1,00**
		4	0,00	0,00	0,00	0,00	**1,00**	**1,00**
	1500	1	**1,00**	**1,00**	**1,00**	**1,00**	**1,00**	**1,00**
		2	**1,00**	0,99	**1,00**	**1,00**	**1,00**	**1,00**
		3	0,88	0,83	**1,00**	**1,00**	**1,00**	**1,00**
		4	0,00	0,00	0,00	0,00	**1,00**	**1,00**
14 Hz	500	1	**0,49**	**0,55**	**0,55**	**0,55**	0,07	0,07
		2	0,01	0,01	**0,07**	**0,06**	**0,07**	**0,07**
		3	0,00	0,00	**0,45**	0,02	**0,07**	**0,07**
		4	0,00	0,00	0,00	0,00	**0,07**	**0,07**
	1000	1	0,81	**0,95**	**0,95**	**0,95**	0,50	0,50
		2	0,08	0,07	**0,54**	0,48	0,50	0,50
		3	0,00	0,00	**0,98**	0,35	0,50	0,50
		4	0,00	0,00	0,00	0,00	**0,50**	**0,50**
	1500	1	0,84	0,95	0,95	0,95	**0,99**	**0,99**
		2	0,12	0,11	0,92	**0,98**	**0,99**	**0,99**
		3	0,00	0,00	**0,99**	0,80	**0,99**	**0,99**
		4	0,00	0,00	0,00	0,00	**0,99**	**0,99**

3   Conclusion

This research was made to discover influence of prefiltration of signals when using the multivariate synchronization index to highlight SSVEP in EEG within different MSI modes. Single-channel, dual-channel as well as four-channel modes of the multivariate synchronization index were studied. It is shown that for the current research the use of the prefiltration is required with the analysis window of 500 samples, which is equal to 100 ms. When the analysis epoch increases up to 1000 samples (equal to 200 ms) and higher the use of prefiltration becomes no longer of relevance, except Bessel filter, the use of which shows the results similar to recognition without filtration. Besides, it is relevant to use filters of the first order, because the higher order is, the worse results become. On the basis of the results obtained the authors consider the use of Chebyshev filter of type II as the most efficient as it shows the best results with the analysis window of 500 samples in comparison with elliptic filter and Chebyshev filter of type I, but it also shows higher results when increasing analysis window. In the future it makes sense to examine EEG state recognition with sufficient accuracy on a smaller analysis window, as decrease of analysis window makes it possible to count on integration of human-machine interaction systems running in real-time mode on the basis of the biofeedback. In this case sufficient accuracy is considered as 0.5 and higher because in this case the required frequency will be selected among the competing frequencies.

Acknowledgment. The reported study was partially funded by RFBR according to the research projects № 19-08-00331 and № 19-29-01156.

References

1. Nam, C.S., Nijholt, A., Lotte, F.: Brain–Computer Interfaces Handbook: Technological and Theoretical Advances. CRC Press, Boca Raton, 788 p. (2018)
2. Pfurtscheller, G., et al.: Current trends in Graz Brain-Computer Interface (BCI) research. IEEE Trans. Rehabil. Eng. **8**(2), 216–219 (2000)
3. Kharchenko, S.S.: Investigation of the influence of the positive reinforcement method using biofeedback. Int. J. Biosen Bioelectron. **2**(2), 73–75 (2017)
4. Gnezditsky, V.V.: Evoked Brain Potentials in Clinical Practice, p. 252. Publishing House of TSURE, Taganrog (1997). (in Russian)
5. Tyagi, A., Semwal, S., Shah, G.: Article: a review of Eeg sensors used for data acquisition. IJCA Proc. Nat. Conf. Future Aspects Artif. Intell. Ind. Autom. 2012 **NCFAAIIA**(1), 13–18 (2012). https://www.ijcaonline.org/proceedings/ncfaaiia/number1/6725-1004
6. Malmivuo, J., Plonsey, R.: Bioelectromagnetism - Principles and Applications of Bioelectric and Biomagnetic Fields. Oxford University Press, Oxford, 641 p. (1995)
7. Ma, W., Tran, D., Le, T., Lin, H., Zhou, S.: Using EEG artifacts for BCI applications. In: 2014 International Joint Conference on Neural Networks (IJCNN), Beijing, pp. 3628–3635 (2014)
8. Han, J., Ji, S., Shi, C., Yu, S., Shin, J.: Recent progress of non-invasive optical modality to brain computer interface: a review study. In: The 3rd International Winter Conference on Brain-Computer Interface, Sabuk, pp. 1–2 (2015)
9. Chueshev, A., Melekhova, O., Meshcheryakov, R.: Cloud robotic platform on basis of fog computing approach. In: Ronzhin, A., Rigoll, G., Meshcheryakov, R. (eds.) ICR 2018. LNCS (LNAI), vol. 11097, pp. 34–43. Springer, Cham (2018). https://doi.org/10.1007/978-3-319-99582-3_4
10. Wan, X., et al.: A review on electroencephalogram based brain computer interface for elderly disabled. IEEE Access **7**, 36380–36387 (2019)
11. Turovsky, Y.A., Kurgalin, S.D., Vahtin, A.A., Borzunov, S.V., Belobrodsky, V.A.: Event-related brain potential investigation using the adaptive wavelet recovery method. Biophysics (Russ. Fed.) **60**(3), 443–448 (2015). article № A018
12. Lee, M., Fazli, S., Mehnert, J., Lee, S.: Hybrid brain-computer interface based on EEG and NIRS modalities. In: 2014 International Winter Workshop on Brain-Computer Interface (BCI), Jeongsun-kun, pp. 1–2 (2014)
13. Reda, R., Tantawi, M., shedeed, H., Tolba, M.F.: Analyzing electrooculography (EOG) for eye movement detection. In: Hassanien, A.E., Azar, A.T., Gaber, T., Bhatnagar, R., F. Tolba, M. (eds.) AMLTA 2019. AISC, vol. 921, pp. 179–189. Springer, Cham (2020). https://doi.org/10.1007/978-3-030-14118-9_18
14. Jo, S., Choi, J.W.: Effective motor imagery training with visual feedback for non-invasive brain computer interface. In: 2018 6th International Conference on Brain-Computer Interface (BCI), GangWon, pp. 1–4 (2018)
15. Clerc, M., Bougrain, L., Lotte, F.: Brain-Computer Interfaces 2: Technology and Applications. Wiley, Hoboken, 364 p. (2016)

16. Shepelenko, M., Meshcheryakov, R.: Algorithm for automated calculation of a segmented electromechatronic module of robotic system motion. MATEC Web Conf. **113**, article № 02005 (2017)

17. Zhang, Y., Xu, P., Cheng, K., Yao, D.: Multivariate synchronization index for frequency recognition of SSVEP-based brain-computer interface. J. Neurosci. Methods **221**, 32–40 (2014)

18. Purushothaman, G., Prakash, P.R., Kothari, S.: Investigation of multiple frequency recognition from single-channel steady-state visual evoked potential for efficient brain–computer interfaces application. IET Signal Process. **12**(3), 255–259 (2018)

19. Zhang, Y., Guo, D., Xu, P., Zhang, Y., Yao, D.: Robust frequency recognition for SSVEP-based BCI with temporally local multivariate synchronization index. Cogn. Neurodyn. **10**(6), 505–511 (2016). https://doi.org/10.1007/s11571-016-9398-9

20. Kharchenko, S., Turovsky, Y., Meshcheryakov, R., Iskhakova, A.: Restrictions of the measurement system and a patient when using visually evoked potentials. In: 2019 12th International Conference on Developments in eSystems Engineering (DeSE), Kazan, Russia, pp. 15–19 (2019)

21. Oppenheim, A.V., Schafer, R.W., Yuen, C.K.: Digital signal processing. IEEE Trans. Syst. Man Cybern. **8**(2), 146 (1978)

22. Smith, S.: Digital signal processing. Newnes, Boston (2003)

23. Daniels, R.: Approximastion Methods for Electronic Filter Design. McGraw-Hill, New York (1974)

24. Paarmann, L.: Design and Analysis of Analog Filters. Springer, Boston (2003). https://doi.org/10.1007/b100752

25. Turovsky, Y.A., Kharchenko, S.S., Meshcheryakov, R.V., Iskhakova, A.o., Iskhakov, A.Y.: Algorithmic support of the interface of management of robot-human with the steady state visual evoked potentials based on the multivariate synchronization index. Izvestiya SFedU. Eng. Sci. **1**, 66–78 (2020). (in Russian)

Unmanned Vehicles: Safety Management Systems and Safety Functions

Elena Jharko⬡, Ekaterina Abdulova⬡, and Andrey Iskhakov$^{(\boxtimes)}$ ⬡

V.A. Trapeznikov Institute of Control Sciences of the Russian Academy of Sciences,
65 Profsoyuznaya, Moscow 117997, Russia
{zharko,consoft,iay}@ipu.ru

Abstract. The paper describes the stages of a smart city's concept from the point of view of transport. Simultaneously, the concept of smart cities is intimately interconnected with the use of unmanned vehicles. The hardware components resolve the unmanned vehicle to see, communicate, and move. The unmanned vehicle software provides the perception of sensor data, planning, and motion control based on the processed data. But the use of the unmanned vehicle is associated with risks and security issues associated with vulnerabilities in both software and hardware. In this regard, the necessity of developing safety management systems for unmanned vehicles is shown, based on identifying risk factors and assessing their degree of danger, as well as examples of sources of the main vulnerabilities of intelligent unmanned vehicles. The necessity of using safety functions is shown to determine how the control system of an unmanned vehicle meets the requirements for this system at all stages of the life cycle.

Keywords: Unmanned vehicles · Safety management systems · Safety functions

1 Introduction

In [1, 2], it was noted that Industry 4.0 is defined by advanced digitization and integration of industrial production and logistics, and the apply of the Internet and smart objects and the merging of the virtual and physical worlds via the introduction of information and communication technologies (ITT). Various aspects of the Internet of things (IoT) and the prospects for their applications in industries and development prospects are some works [3, 4].

Today's cities are undergoing a global transformation caused by the digital economy. The development of a modern city is impossible without creating a digital ecosystem formed based on intelligent networks. Besides, modern information and communication technologies should not only become the basis for building new cities, which are already called smart cities but also integrate seamlessly into existing technologies and systems.

The concept of smart cities has been actively discussed for the past 10 years. The term Smart City can be explained wide and in different ways. However, in any interpretation, the key role is given to ITTs that help decide social problems in the framework of a multilateral partnership between government, businesses, and citizens [5, 6]. A smart

P. K. Singh et al. (Eds.): FTNCT 2020, CCIS 1396, pp. 112–121, 2021.
https://doi.org/10.1007/978-981-16-1483-5_11

city strategically approaches the development of transport. Table 1 shows the correspondence between the stages of development of a smart city and the state of the transport environment.

Transport infrastructure is becoming intelligent. A trend towards the use of dynamic and multimodal information is noticeable in urban logistics management. Big data is collected from car sensors, security cameras, RFID tags, sensors on roads, and railroad tracks. Data on the state of urban road systems, transit systems, bicycle roads, and pedestrian zones are used to optimize traffic flows depending on passenger traffic, business needs, environmental conditions, as well as to monitor the condition of roads. Such systems require an integrated management and maintenance approach, which means removing institutional barriers. A special place in the transport infrastructure is occupied by unmanned vehicles, which require the development of technology, artificial intelligence, telecommunication systems, cyberphysical interfaces, information, and cybersecurity [7–10].

Table 1. Table captions should be placed above the tables.

	Smart city 1.0	Smart city 2.0	Smart city 3.0
Stage characteristic	Improving the management of the city. City managers have access to integrated real-time data on the status of services, energy, and infrastructure	City development and management based on digital infrastructure models	Smart City as a City Development Strategy with a Common Vision
Results	The architecture develops for the deployment of intelligent systems and services, and technologies introduced in pilot projects		Pilot platform forms for access to open data developed
Transport	Centralized monitoring and transport management systems	Intelligent transport (hybrid systems for transport) - automated traffic management systems	Associated transport (renewable energy for transport) - unmanned control, autonomous servicing (connected transport, autonomous vehicle)

The approach to conception a smart city focused on security should respond not only to existing but also to emerging vulnerabilities and take into account the hazards arising from the development of new technologies.

2   Unmanned Vehicles: Decision-Making Architecture

The decision-making architecture of the unmanned vehicle is shown in Fig. 1 and consists of the following levels: perception, decision making, network, and computational multilevel analytics.

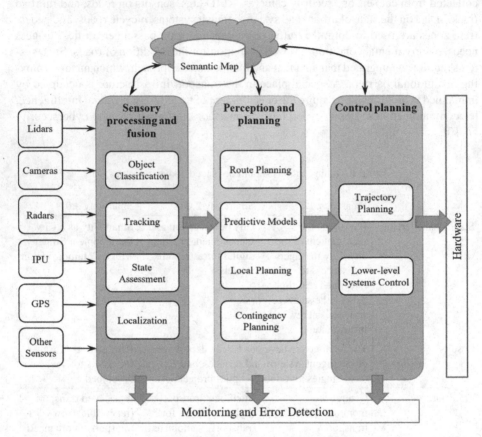

Fig. 1. Decision-making architecture

At the perceptual level, the system helps create high-resolution maps of laser reflectivity and transforms into real-time unmanned vehicle positioning mode in urban environments. Localization significantly improves navigation accuracy. Achieving this accuracy in city environments is impossible with GPS-based inertial guider. The system uses wheel odometry, IMU, GPS and lidar data with the unmanned vehicle to generate high-resolution environmental maps. Localization of the moving unmanned vehicle relative to the maps is carried out using the particle filtration method [11]. This approach relieves to increase the relative accuracy of position determination by more than an order of magnitude compared to traditional odometry methods of GPS-IMU [12]. The system can also use other methods of dynamic mapping of the urban environment, which ensure accuracy at the centimeter level by determining the vehicle's location in real-time [13, 14].

Automatical calibration of multibeam sensors can be executed applying algorithms that allow the vehicle to move exactly along a given trajectory [15]. Also, at this level, methods can be used to display and detect light signals, and their state in real-time [16].

At the decision-making level for the operation of the unmanned vehicle, algorithms are required to prediction situations in complicated dynamic conditions to ensure the safe mobility of the unmanned vehicle. To plan and make decisions on the movement of the unmanned vehicle, it is necessary to:

- determine the destination,
- use sensor readings,
- ensure data exchange with other vehicles,
- to train the system to use historical data in the field of vehicle driving,
- ensure the safety and reliability of the decision-making process,
- manage mobility based on coordination with other vehicles [17].

The network layer uses the Internet of Things (IoT) technologies to permit devices to execute tasks without human intervention [18].

Data from sensors installed on the unmanned vehicle (cameras, lidars) are analyzed at the level of computational multilevel analytics. To collect data from the unmanned vehicle, a cloud is created where driving data is stored and creates an opportunity to improve the quality of unmanned vehicle control based on artificial intelligence methods.

3 "Safety Management Systems" Properties in Transport

One of the main priorities for the development of unmanned vehicles is increasing the security level, including information and cybersecurity. But due to the increase in various threats related to the improvement of information technology, the application of traditional approaches to reducing risk to an acceptable level is not enough. The systemic causes of many incidents related to unauthorized access to management systems have executed an essential increase to interest in identification and risk management procedures, and the design and growth of safety management systems (SMS) [19–26] characterized by systemicity, proactivity, and clarity.

The functioning of the SMS of unmanned vehicles should represent a closed cycle of sequentially executable operations: risk factor identifying, estimating the degree of danger of identified risk factors, developing choices for localizing risk factors, informing management bodies and decision support, and effectiveness analysis the taken measures. Figure 2 and 3 show a safety estimation scheme founded factor analysis, which apply the PDCA (the Deming's Shewhart cycle) approach to continuously improvement safety.

The corporate approach to security directs for permanent perfecting of the security system and haves as the ensuing central purposes:

- promptly and constantly decrease the residual system risk (see Fig. 4);
- the estimation of the actual adaptability and real effectiveness of the security policy, with the purpose of its permanent improvement.

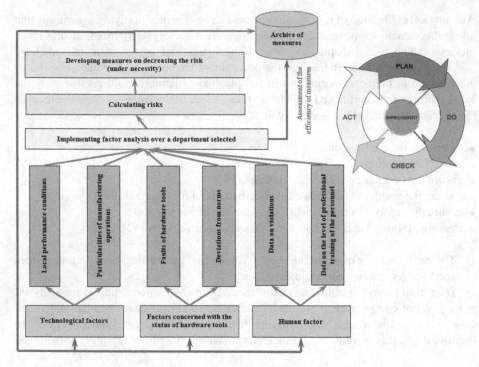

Fig. 2. Safety analysis based on factor analysis

	Input information (*critical safety parametersu*)	Current safety level (*requirements*)	Actions (*action for each requirement*)
P	Determining possible status of each CSP	Determining possible efficiency of requirement on the status basis of each CSP	Determining the safety for each proposed action
D	Report on factors led to changing CSP		
C		Analysis of obtained levels of possible efficiency of CSP	Checking the safety level for each recommended action
A			Implementing actions providing higher safety level

Fig. 3. Monitoring concept

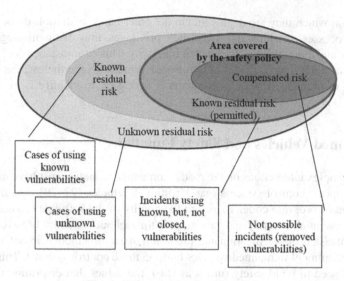

Fig. 4. Relationship of residual risks

In turn, when analyzing the security of unmanned vehicles, as with any cyberphysical or robotic system, it is important to highlight and assess the criticality of its elements. Almost all elements of unmanned vehicles are connected by different data transmission channels and multiple semantic relationships, and the assets used in them can be significantly distributed. Under assets in this case we understand all information technology objects of unmanned vehicles (including sensors, controls, databases, applications, users, services, etc.). At the same time, in modern unmanned vehicles infrastructure can change over time - new unregistered elements, new communication channels and semantic relationships can appear, which is associated with the appearance of vulnerabilities and configuration errors. Under such conditions, defining assets and their criticality with the involvement of experts requires significant time and human resources. Automating the identification of elements and a hierarchy of relationships between them, as well as assessing their criticality will allow for a more accurate and detailed risk model for security analysis. Criticism in this case means the importance of the object for the functioning of unmanned vehicles. Determining the criticality of all information technology objects is also important for the task of choosing protection measures, since their implementation in distributed unmanned transport systems with complex interconnections can lead to unexpected collateral damage to critical assets through the disconnection or removal of auxiliary assets. In this regard, the task of evaluating the security of an unmanned vehicle includes not only evaluating the security of information transmitted, processed, stored in it and the systems interacting with it, but also evaluating the security of correctness and continuity of technological processes.

At the heart of the interaction of modern unmanned vehicles components is often reflected in the interaction of devices based on network protocols, which allow to convert transmitted data into messages of a certain format. On the one hand, the use of network scanners makes it possible to identify various network objects such as services, ports and devices on which they are deployed. On the other hand, such tools do not allow to single out processes, sessions, users and their privileges, thus distinguishing different types of static and dynamic objects and their hierarchy. This circumstance does not allow to obtain an actual dynamic model of unmanned vehicles. Nevertheless, the definition and analysis of unmanned vehicles elements is necessary to identify its most critical elements.

4 Unmanned Vehicles and Safety Functions

Due to the complex interactions on the roads, unmanned vehicles must have much more coherent computer control systems than traditional vehicles [27–29], and therefore a larger amount of program code. To ensure the quality of the software of an unmanned vehicle, it is essential to verify and validate it is throughout the entire life cycle.

An urgent task is the verification and validation of existing models in order to ensure the safe functioning of unmanned vehicles built on these control systems. This problem to solve is a need to build safety functions (SF), the values that determine the degree of compliance of the unmanned vehicle with the requirements for cybersecurity for monitoring. This approach can be applied to significant objects of critical information infrastructure, which are objects of transport information infrastructure. The safety function [30] is a formalized condition in relation to the verified system, the implementation of which allows us to draw a conclusion about the safety of operation.

Control systems for unmanned vehicles are of high complexity, both in the view of algorithms and in the programs that implement them, which complicates the formalization. Therefore, it is necessary to define a SF in these shortcomings are absent. As a safety function, there can be either function that meets the conditions in Fig. 5.

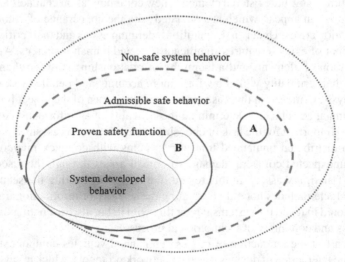

Fig. 5. Choosing a proven SF: Domain A – to some causes, the system not realizes the condition of the proven SF, but this did not conduct a hazardous fault; Domain B – the system behavior corresponds to the SF condition.

For the same unmanned vehicle, the SF can define in various ways, and the choice of the proven conditions can make at differing stages of the system's life cycle. For example, the SF can determine based on the system functionality, determination of the safety function around the security strategy for the entire system, safety requirements for the unmanned vehicle system under consideration, and interactive interfaces.

5 Examples of Basic Vulnerabilities

The main difference between such attacks against conventional IoT devices and attacks in a is increasing connected or autonomous vehicle is the likelihood of increasing the risk of life and property in the vehicle context. The following are examples of the sources of the principal vulnerabilities of intelligent unmanned vehicles:

- Software errors. Connected vehicles today contain hundreds of millions of code lines. More code means more errors and hacking opportunities;
- Lack of a single source of knowledge and control over source code. Different developers write software for different components of connected vehicles, and no source has knowledge or controls overall safety;
- As the use of connected functions increases, there is an increased need for continuous updates to correct failures and protect vehicles. There is a risk that these updates may be missed or that intruders may infect regular updates.

The following can be identified as basic vulnerable locks of unmanned vehicle:

- Application for remote operator connection;
- Electric control units (ECU). They control systems such as engine and transmission, steering and brakes, infotainment system, lighting, etc.;
- Onboard diagnostic ports (e.g., OBD II, etc.);
- Dedicated communication receivers;
- TPMS-type diagnostic systems, etc.;
- Passive Keyless Entry/Remote Key.

6 Conclusions

The paper (see Table 1) shows the trend in the development of transport in a smart city towards an increase in intelligence and the transition to unmanned vehicles. Unmanned vehicle control systems require an integrated management approach with compensation for new threats caused by the development of information technologies and telecommunication systems. To increase security, it is proposed to introduce safety management systems for the smart city's transport system. In order to guarantee the safe functioning of vehicles, it is proposed to monitor the safety functions.

Nowadays, M2M/IoT technologies imply almost limitless possibilities for solving tasks within the framework of "smart city." In this regard, the use of unmanned vehicles equipped with the latest software and hardware is an ideal tool for solving any practical and scientific problems within the framework of "smart city." The main problem of stagnation in the development of engineering solutions for process automation today is the lack of technical regulations for cybersecurity in the development, as well as regulations governing the use of unmanned vehicles in the airspace in urban environments.

Acknowledgment. The reported study was partially funded by RFBR, project number 19-29-06044 (sections 4, 5), and project number 19-01-00767 (section 3).

References

1. Fonseca, L.M.: Industry 4.0 and the digital society: concepts, dimensions and envisioned benefits. In: Proceedings of the International Conference on Business Excellence, vol. **12**, no. 1, pp. 386–397 (2018)
2. Saucedo-Martínez, J.A., Pérez-Lara, M., Marmolejo-Saucedo, J.A., Salais-Fierro, T.E., Vasant, P.: Industry 4.0 framework for management and operations: a review. J. Ambient Intell. Human. Comput. **9**(3), 789–801 (2018)
3. Molano, J.I.R., Lovelle, M.C., Montenegro, C.E., Granados, J.J.R., Crespo, R.G.: Ruben Metamodel for integration of Internet of Things, Social Networks, the Cloud and Industry 4.0. J. Ambient Intell. Human. Comput. **9**(3), 709–723 (2018)
4. Mozzaquatro, B.A., Agostinho, C., Goncalves, D., Martins, J., Jardim-Goncalves, R.: An ontology-based cybersecurity framework for the Internet of Things. Sensors **18**(9), 3053 (2018)
5. Chamoso, P., González-Briones, A., De La Prieta, F., Venyagamoorthy, G.K., Corchado, J.M.: Smart city as a distributed platform: toward a system for citizen-oriented management. Comput. Commun. **152**, 323–332 (2020)
6. Kummitha, R.K.R.: Smart cities and entrepreneurship: an agenda for future research. Technol. Forecast. Soc. Change **149**, article 119763 (2019)
7. Abdulov, A.V., Abramenkov, A.N., Shevlyakov, A.A.: Visual odometry approaches to autonomous navigation for multicopter model in virtual indoor environment. Adv. Syst. Sci. Appl. **18**(3), 17–28 (2018)
8. Abdulov, A.V., Abramenkov, A.N.: Is face 3D or 2D on stereo images? In: Proceedings of the 2019 International Russian Automation Conference (RusAutoCon), Sochi, Russia, pp. 1–5. IEEE (2019)
9. Iskhakova, A., Iskhakov, A., Meshcheryakov, R., Jharko, E.: Method of verification of robotic group agents in the conditions of communication facility suppression. IFAC-PapersOnLine **52**(13), 1397–1402 (2019)
10. Promyslov, V.G., Sakrutina, E., Meshcheryakov, R.: Coherence criterion for security architecture of digital control system. In: Proceedings of the 2019 International Russian Automation Conference (RusAutoCon), Sochi, Russia, pp. 1–5. IEEE (2019)
11. Carvalho, G.P.S., Costa, R.R.: Localization of an autonomous rail-guided robot using particle filter. IFAC-PapersOnLine **50**(1), 5642–5647 (2017)
12. Cai, G., Lin, H., Kao, S.: Mobile robot localization using GPS, IMU and visual odometry. In: Proceedings of the 2019 International Automatic Control Conference (CACS), Keelung, Taiwan, pp. 1–6. IEEE (2019)
13. Forster, C., Zhang, Z., Gassner, M., Werlberger, M., Scaramuzza, D.: SVO: semi direct visual odometry for monocular and multicamera systems. IEEE Trans. Rob. **33**(2), 249–265 (2017)
14. Engel, J., Stckler, J., Cremers, D.: Large-scale direct SLAM with stereo cameras. In: Proceedings of the 2015 IEEE/RSJ International Conference on Intelligent Robots and Systems (IROS), Hamburg, Germany, pp. 1935–1942. IEEE (2015)

15. Bar Hillel, A., Lerner, R., Levi, D., Raz, G.: Recent progress in road and lane detection: a survey. Mach. Vis. Appl. **25**(3), 727–745 (2012). https://doi.org/10.1007/s00138-011-0404-2

16. Russakovsky, O., et al.: ImageNet large scale visual recognition challenge. Int. J. Comput. Vis. **115**, 211-252 (2015)

17. Russell, H.E.B., Harbott, L.K., Nisky, I., Pan, S., Okamura, A.M., Gerdes, J.C.: Motor learning affects car-to-driver handover in automated vehicles. Sci. Robot. **1**(1), eaah5682 (2016)

18. Philip, B.V., Alpcan, T., Jin, J., Palaniswami, M.: Distributed real-time IoT for autonomous vehicles. IEEE Trans. Industr. Inf. **15**(2), 1131–1140 (2019)

19. Liou, J.H., Yen, L., Tzeng, G.H.: Building an effective safety management system for airlines. J. Air Transp. Manage. **14**(1), 20–26 (2008)

20. Li, C.-Y., Wang, J.-H., Zhi, Y.-R., Wang, Z.-R., Gong, J.-H.: Simulation of the chlorination process safety management system based on system dynamics approach. Procedia Eng. **211**, 332–342 (2018)

21. Hsu, Y.-L.: From reactive to proactive: using safety survey to assess effectiveness of airline SMS. J. Aeronaut. Astronaut. Aviat. Ser. A **40**(1), 41–48 (2008)

22. Jharko, E., Sakrutina, E.: Towards the problem of creating a safety management system in the transportation area. IFAC-PapersOnLine **50**(1), 15610–15615 (2017)

23. Jharko, E., Promyslov, V.G., Iskhakov, A.: Extending functionality of early fault diagnostic system for online security assessment of nuclear power plant. In: Proceedings of the 2019 International Russian Automation Conference (RusAutoCon), Sochi, Russia, pp. 1–6. IEEE (2019)

24. Shumskaya, O.O., Iskhakova, A.O.: Application of digital watermarks in the problem of operating signal hidden transfer in multi-agent robotic system. In: Proceedings of the 2019 International Siberian Conference on Control and Communications (SIBCON), Tomsk, Russia, pp. 1–5. IEEE (2019)

25. Kalashnikov, A., Sakrutina, E.: Safety management system and Significant Plants of Critical Information Infrastructure. IFAC-PapersOnLine **52**(13), 1391–1396 (2019)

26. Iskhakov A., Meshcheryakov, R.: Intelligent system of environment monitoring on the basis of a set of IoT-sensors. In: Proceedings of the 2019 International Siberian Conference on Control and Communications (SIBCON), Tomsk, Russia, pp. 1–5. IEEE (2019)

27. Victoria Transport Policy Institute. https://www.vtpi.org/avip.pdf. Accessed 17 Aug 2020

28. Pieroni, A., Scarpato, N., Brilli, M.: Industry 4.0 revolution in autonomous and connected vehicle. A non-conventional approach to manage big data. J. Theoret. Appl. Inf. Technol. **96**(1), 10–18 (2018)

29. SAS. https://www.sas.com/content/dam/SAS/en_us/doc/whitepaper1/connected-vehicle-107832.pdf. Accessed 17 Aug 2020

30. Jharko, E.: Formalizing the safety functions to assure the software quality of NPP safety important systems. In: Proceedings of the 16th International Conference on Informatics in Control, Automation and Robotics. ICINCO 2019, Prague, Czech Republic, vol. 2, pp. 637–644. SCITEPRESS, Setúbal (2019)

Probabilistic Characteristics of a Two-Channel Detector with Two Inertial Single-Photon Photoemission Devices and an Electronic Adder

A. E. Ampliev[⊠]

Southern Federal University, Taganrog, Russia
aeampliev@sfedu.ru

Abstract. Analytical expressions are Obtained for calculating the probabilities of correct detection and false alarm of a two-channel inertial detector of pulsed optical radiation in the photon counting mode, containing a receiving optical complex of two-lens antennas, two single-photon photoemission devices and an electronic adder.

Keywords: Optical radiation · Two-channel detector · Photon count · Probability of correct detection · Probability of false alarm

1 Introduction

The need to reduce the weight of the equipment is very relevant when placing laser communication systems on mobile (aircraft, space) vehicles. For example, the cost of just putting a kilogram of payload into space is estimated in thousands of dollars [1–9]. Table 1 shows the cost of launching a payload into outer space.

It can be seen that the cost of withdrawing 1 kg of cargo varies depending on the type of ship and its loading, but in any case it is in the order of thousands and tens of thousands of USD, not counting the cost of the launch itself. So, the cheapest – 1136 USD – was the launch of 1 kg of cargo into geostationary orbit in 2004 by a single-use proton launch vehicle when it was fully loaded. One of the most expensive – up to 50,000 USD – was from 1981 to 2011, the withdrawal of 1 kg of cargo to earth orbit by a reusable space Shuttle ship when it was not fully loaded.

It is known [10] that the receiving antenna of the laser communication system is frequently used lens telescope, contribute most to the mass of the entire system and the actual aperture of the receiving antenna provides the area of the input lens, as a rule, are thin. Note that the mass of a thin lens according to [11] is proportional to the fourth power of its diameter. Based on this, it is shown in [12] that the transition from a complex with a single-lens optical antenna to a complex consisting of two-lens optical antennas allows to reduce its mass twice at a fixed reception area.

In long-range laser systems, the energy of the received optical radiation is so small that the photodetector channel operates in the photon counting mode, separately registering each act of converting a photon into a primary electron (photoelectron, PE). This

P. K. Singh et al. (Eds.): FTNCT 2020, CCIS 1396, pp. 122–131, 2021.
https://doi.org/10.1007/978-981-16-1483-5_12

Table 1. Cost of launching cargo into outer space.

Carrier	Cost, USD per kg	Launch cost, million USD	Load capacity, tons	Note
Zenit-2/3SL	2 567–3 667	35–50	13,7	
The space Shuttle (a reusable spacecraft)	13 000–17 000	500	25	When the ship is fully loaded 29,5 tons; increases to 40–50 thousand USD/kg when partially loaded 10 tons. The maximum mass of delivery to orbit is about 120–130 tons (together with the ship), the maximum payload mass is 24,4 tons, and the maximum return mass to earth is 14,5 tons
«Soyuz» (single-use launch vehicle)	4 242–11 265	35–78,858	8,25	Up to 25 thousand USD/kg per geostationary orbit. The maximum cargo that can be taken to the «Soyuz TMA» ship launched by the «Soyuz» launch vehicle is about 300 kg. The maximum mass of delivery to orbit is 7–7,5 tons. If used for satellite output, the launch cost is: - since 2002, 35–40 million USD; - from the Kourou cosmodrome – from 40 to 60 million EUR per launch (from the Equatorial cosmodrome, the payload mass can be increased to 3 tons in geostationary orbit and up to 10 tons in low orbit)
«Vostok»	1 586	7,5	4,73	In the early 90's, it was 7–8 million USD to attract foreign clients. Since 1991, it has been decommissioned

(*continued*)

Table 1. (*continued*)

Carrier	Cost, USD per kg	Launch cost, million USD	Load capacity, tons	Note
«Proton» (single-use launch vehicle)	1 136–4 546	25–100	22	The launch price changes over the years; recently, it has been constantly increasing. Data on the cost of launches on GSO: - in 1999, the launch of one proton-K with the DM block was 70–90 million USD; - in 2004, due to increased global competition, the launch cost "was reduced almost to cost" – 25 million USD - in 2005, the cost was 800 million rubles for proton-K and 900 million rubles for proton-M (36 – 40 million USD); - at the end of 2008 -100 million USD for GPO using proton-M with the Briz-M block o since the beginning of the global economic crisis in 2008, the exchange rate of the ruble to the dollar has decreased by 33%, which has reduced the launch cost to approximately 80 million USD; - since 2010, the launch cost is about 70 – 100 million USD, depending on the configuration
«Atlas-5» (single-use launch vehicle)		187	9,75–29,42 т (НОО); 4,95–13 т на ГПО	(only unmanned satellites), the maximum mass of delivery to low orbit is 30 tons, 13 tons in geostationary orbit. The launch cost is about 187 million USD
«Dnepr» (single-use launch vehicle)	2 703	10	3,7	(only unmanned satellites), the maximum mass of delivery to orbit is 3.7 tons. The launch cost is about 10 million USD

mode will also be typical for the subsystem of communicating with mobile devices 3 when performing spatial (or spatial-temporal) search and detecting correspondent signals.

The issues of detecting weak optical radiation in noise are discussed in a number of monographs [13–16] and articles [16–18]. However, the analysis of registration processes was performed under the assumption that the photodetector channel is able to distinguish each incoming photon. At the same time, the inertia of a single-photon photoemission device (SPPD) and a discrete counter (DC) leads to overlapping responses to the appearance of PE (single-photon pulses, SPP), which affects the probability characteristics of the detector.

2 Purpose of Research

The purpose of the study is to compare the effectiveness of systems with one and two optical lens antennas and inertial SPPD and processing path, to obtain analytical expressions for calculating the probability of correct detection and false alarm.

Patent studies [20] devoted to recorders of weak light signals give a retrospective view of inventions since 1968. The analysis of patenting dynamics on the problem of registration of weak light signals and its application in various fields of science and technology, conducted in 2019, indicates a steady interest of scientists and research centers in Russia and around the world in this topic.

The analysis shows that the registration of optical fluxes by counting individual photons is continuously developing, mainly in two directions: the scope of the method is expanding and the registration efficiency is increasing as a result of the development of new single-photon photodetectors and the use of methods that increase the sensitivity of photodetectors and expand the dynamic range of recorded light signals.

Such prominent Russian scientists as Vetokhin S.S., Shubnikov E.N., Sheremetyev A.G., Oganesyan A.V., Bychkov S.I., Kazaryan S.A., Shchelkunov K.N., Gulakov N.R., Pertsev A.N., Rumyantsev K.E. and many others devoted many of their works to solving the problems of single-photon registration of optical radiation.

To implement the limiting characteristics of optical telecommunications systems and to ensure high accuracy of optical radiation registration in laser communication systems (as well as in communication entry systems), the photodetector channel must operate in single-photon mode, separately registering each act of photon-to-photoelectron conversion. The latter involves the use of highly sensitive single-photon counters as photodetector equipment [21–23].

The structure of a two-channel system with two optical antennas (OA), two SPPD and an electronic adder (EA) is shown in the Fig. 1. Here, each optical channel of the system includes a series of connected OA and a guide optical medium (GOM). As a GOM, a mirror-lens or fiber-optic medium can be used to supply energy from the optical antenna to the SPPD photocathodes. The output of the first SPPD is connected to the first port of the electronic adder, and the output of the second is connected to its second port. The third output port of the electronic adder is connected via a pulse amplifier (PA) and an amplitude discriminator (AD) to the counting input of the DC, the output signal of which corresponds to the number of registered PE during the measurement.

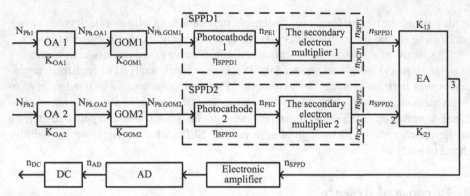

Fig. 1. Structure of a two-channel system with two optical antennas, two SPPD and an electronic adder.

Let OA receive N_{Ph1} and N_{Ph2} photons, respectively, during the measurement τ, the number of which is subject to Poisson's law with mathematical expectations $\overline{N_{Ph1}}$ and $\overline{N_{Ph2}}$. At the transmission coefficients OA K_{OA1} and K_{OA2}, we find the number of photons $N_{Ph.OA1}$ and $N_{Ph.OA2}$ that passed through the optical antennas OA1 and OA2:

$$N_{Ph.OA1} = K_{OA1} \cdot N_{Ph1}; \tag{1}$$

$$N_{Ph.OA2} = K_{OA2} \cdot N_{Ph2}. \tag{2}$$

The number of photons $N_{Ph.GOM1}$ and $N_{Ph.GOM2}$ that passed through the guide optical media GOM1 and GOM2 with transmission coefficients K_{GOM1} and K_{GOM2} is equal to

$$N_{Ph.GOM1} = K_{GOM1} \cdot N_{Ph.OA1}; \tag{3}$$

$$N_{Ph.GOM2} = K_{GOM2} \cdot N_{Ph.OA2} \tag{4}$$

respectively.

The average number of photons that passed through the OA and GOM during the measurement is determined by the formulas

$$\overline{N_{Ph.GOM1}} = K_{OA1}K_{GOM1} \cdot \overline{N_{Ph1}}; \tag{5}$$

$$\overline{N_{Ph.GOM2}} = K_{OA2}K_{GOM2} \cdot \overline{N_{Ph2}}. \tag{6}$$

As a result of interaction with SPPD photo cathodes photon flux is converted into a stream of photoelectrons. In this transformation, the number of PE n_{PE1} and n_{PE2} during the measurement τ:

$$n_{PE1} = \eta_{SPPD1} \cdot N_{Ph.GOM1}; \tag{7}$$

$$n_{PE2} = \eta_{SPPD2} \cdot N_{Ph.GOM2}, \tag{8}$$

where η_{SPPD1} and η_{SPPD2} are the quantum efficiencies of the first and second SPPD photocathodes, respectively.

The number of generated SPP n_{SPP1} and n_{SPP2} by secondary electronic multipliers in each of the SPPD during measurement is equal to the corresponding number of PE n_{PE}, and the mathematical expectations of their distributions coincide, which in General for both channels has the form

$$\overline{n_{SPP}} = \overline{n_{PE}} = \eta_{SPPD} \cdot \overline{N_{Ph.GOM}}. \tag{9}$$

Dark current pulses (DCP) n_{DCP1} and n_{DCP2} with the corresponding mathematical expectations $\overline{n_{DCP1}}$ and $\overline{n_{DCP2}}$ will be generated at the output of each of the SPPD during the measurement. Therefore, the average number of pulses generated by the SPPD during the observation period will be

$$\overline{n_{SPPD1,2}} = \overline{n_{SPP1,2}} + \overline{n_{DCP1,2}}. \tag{10}$$

In the structure of the two-channel system shown in the figure, SPP flows from the outputs of the SPPD are summed in an electronic adder. For the transmission coefficients K_{13} and K_{23} between ports 1–3 and 2–3 EA, we find the number of pulses on port 3

$$n_{SPPD} = K_{13} \cdot n_{SPPD1} + K_{23} \cdot n_{SPPD2}, \tag{11}$$

which is also distributed by Poisson's law with mathematical expectation

$$\overline{n_{SPPD}} = K_{13} \cdot \overline{n_{SPPD1}} + K_{23} \cdot \overline{n_{SPPD2}}. \tag{12}$$

Let's analyze the situation when the area of optical radiation reception is the same in single-channel and two-channel systems. The latter is equivalent to assuming that the condition for a single-channel system is fulfilled with respect to the average number of photons during measurement

$$\overline{N_{Ph}} = \overline{N_{Ph1}} + \overline{N_{Ph2}} \tag{13}$$

and assuming that the average number of SPP at the output of EA

$$n_{SPPD} = K_{13} \cdot \left(\eta_{SPPD1} \cdot K_{GOM1} \cdot K_{OA1} \cdot \overline{N_{Ph1}} + \overline{n_{DCP1}} \right) \\ + K_{23} \cdot \left(\eta_{SPPD2} \cdot K_{GOM2} \cdot K_{OA2} \cdot \overline{N_{Ph2}} + \overline{n_{DCP2}} \right). \tag{14}$$

A comparison of the process of processing the photon flux in systems with one and two optical antennas shows that the functional chain "PA−AD−DC" is common to them. As a result, for a single-channel system, the average number of pulses generated by SPPD during measurement will be

$$n_{SPPD} = \eta_{SPPD} \cdot K_{GOM} \cdot K_{OA} \cdot \overline{N_{Ph}} + \overline{n_{DCP}}. \tag{15}$$

Let the conditions

$$K_{OA} = K_{OA1} = K_{OA2} \tag{16}$$

for the transmission coefficients of optical antennas,

$$K_{GOM} = K_{GOM1} = K_{GOM2} \tag{17}$$

for the transmission coefficients of GOM,

$$\eta_{SPPD} = \eta_{SPPD1} = \eta_{SPPD2} \tag{18}$$

for the quantum efficiency of photocathodes, and

$$\overline{n_{DCP1}} = \overline{n_{DCP2}} = \overline{n_{DCP}} \tag{19}$$

for the number of dark current pulses are met for a single-channel system (assuming that the same SPPD is used in a single- and two-channel system). Then, for

$$K_{13} = K_{23} = 1, \tag{20}$$

the average number of pulses generated by the SPPD can also be calculated using the formula (15).

It should be noted that in the presence of two SPPD, dark current pulses will be generated by each of the optoelectronic devices and the total rate of DCP receipt will be twice higher than when using a single SPPD. However, the average frequency of dark current pulses is units – tens of Hertz, and the average frequency of signal photons is in the range of tens – hundreds of megahertz. It can be assumed that doubling the frequency of DCP receipt will have almost no effect on the probability characteristics of the detector, at least on the probability of correct detection.

This shows that up to the transmission coefficients K_{13} and K_{23} between ports 1–2 and 2–3 of the electronic adder, switching from a single-channel to a two-channel system does not improve the probabilistic characteristics of the detector while maintaining the same receiving area.

Due to the inertia of the SPPD, a partial overlap of the generated pulses is possible [19]. In addition, due to the imperfection of the discrete counter, closely spaced pulses may be indistinguishable [12]. As a result, the number of calculated DC pulses at the output of the amplitude discriminator n_{AD} may not coincide with the number of pulses generated by the SPPD, and

$$n_{SPPD} \geq n_{AD}. \tag{21}$$

In [19], an analytical expression was obtained for calculating the conditional probability of $Pr\{n_{DC}|n_{SPPD}\}$ registration of n_{DC} pulses by a discrete counter under the condition that n_{SPPD} pulses are generated by an SPPD:

$$Pr\{n_{DC}|n_{SPPD}\}$$
$$= \frac{(n_{SPPD}-1)!}{(n_{SPPD}-n_{DC})!\cdot(n_{DC}-1)!} \frac{n_{SPPD}!}{n_{DC}!} \cdot \alpha^{n_{SPPD}-n_{DC}}[1-(n_{SPPD}-1)\alpha]^{n_{DC}}. \tag{22}$$

Here

$$\alpha = \frac{\Delta t_{SPPD.Cr}}{\tau} + \frac{\Delta t_{DC.Cr}}{\tau} \tag{23}$$

is a generalized parameter, where $\Delta t_{SPPD.Cr}$ is the critical value of the time difference between the moments of appearance of two PE, at which the SPPD responses are distinguishable by an amplitude discriminator, and $\Delta t_{DC.Cr}$ is the critical gap between the pulses for their separate registration in the DC.

The decision to detect the signal is made based on comparing the number of electric pulses counted in a discrete counter n_{DC} during the measurement time τ with the threshold level n_T in accordance with the decision rule

$$\Psi(n_{DC}) = \begin{cases} n_{DC} \geq n_T - the\ presence\ of\ a\ signal; \\ n_{DC} < n_T - no\ signal. \end{cases} \tag{24}$$

Let the average number of photons of signal and background radiation for the duration of measurement in the i-th channel (i = 1, 2) be equal to $\overline{N_{Ph.Si}}$ and $\overline{N_{Ph.Bi}}$, with

$$\overline{N_{Ph.S1}} = \overline{N_{Ph.S2}} = \overline{N_{Ph.S}}/2 \tag{25}$$

and

$$\overline{N_{Ph.B1}} = \overline{N_{Ph.B2}} = \overline{N_{Ph.B}}/2. \tag{26}$$

Then for a two-channel system when testing the hypothesis of the presence of a signal is accepted

$$\overline{n_{SPPD.S}}$$
$$= \eta_{SPPD}(K_{1-3}K_{GOM1}K_{OA1} + K_{2-3}K_{GOM2}K_{OA2})(\overline{N_{Ph.S}} + \overline{N_{Ph.B}})/2 + 2\overline{n_{DCP}}. \tag{27}$$

On the contrary, when checking the alternative about the absence of a signal

$$\overline{n_{SPPD.B}} = \eta_{SPPD}(K_{1-3}K_{GOM1}K_{OA1} + K_{2-3}K_{GOM2}K_{OA2})\overline{N_{Ph.B}}/2 + +2\overline{n_{DCP}}. \tag{28}$$

The probability of correct detection and false alarm can be calculated using the following formulas

$$Pr_{CD} = exp(-\overline{n_{SPPD.S}} - \overline{n_{SPPD.B}})$$
$$\times \sum_{n_{SPPD}=n_T}^{\infty} \left(\frac{(\overline{n_{SPPD.S}}+\overline{n_{SPPD.B}})^{n_{SPPD}}}{n_{SPPD}!} \sum_{n_{DC}=n_T}^{n_{SPPD}} Pr\{n_{DC}|n_{SPPD}\} \right); \tag{29}$$

$$Pr_{FA} = exp(-\overline{n_{SPPD.B}}) \times \sum_{n_{SPPD}=n_T}^{\infty} \left(\frac{(\overline{n_{SPPD.B}})^{n_{SPPD}}}{n_{SPPD}!} \sum_{n_{DC}=n_T}^{n_{SPPD}} Pr\{n_{DC}|n_{SPPD}\} \right), \tag{30}$$

where n_{SPPD} is the number of pulses generated by the SPPD.

Function

$$Y_T = \sum_{n_{DC}=n_T}^{n_{SPPD}} Pr\{n_{DC}|n_{SPPD}\} \tag{31}$$

takes into account the possibility of making a decision to exceed the threshold level $n_{DC} \geq n_T$ even under condition $n_{DC} < n_{SPPD}$. For example, for $n_T = 3$ and $n_{SPPD} = 5$ we have

$$Y_T = \sum_{n_{DC}=3}^{5} Pr_{CD}\{n_{DC}|5\} = Pr_{CD}\{3|5\} + Pr_{CD}\{4|5\} + Pr_{CD}\{5|5\}. \tag{32}$$

The terms $Pr_{CD}\{3|5\}$, $Pr_{CD}\{4|5\}$, and $Pr_{CD}\{5|5\}$ determine the probabilities of registering 3, 4 and 5 pulses by a discrete counter when generating 5 pulses SPPD. The decision to detect the signal will be made, even if one or two of the 5 pulses are lost due to the inertia of the SPPD and the imperfection of the DC.

3 Conclusion

The process of detecting pulsed optical radiation by a two-channel single-photon detector with an inertial photoemission device in the photon counting mode is analyzed. Analytical expressions are obtained for calculating the probabilities of correct detection and false alarm by a detector with two optical lens antennas. It is proved that the transition from a complex with one optical antenna to a complex with two optical antennas does not worsen the probabilistic characteristics of a detector with a single-photon photoemission device while maintaining the same receiving area, guaranteeing a reduction in the mass of the receiving optical lens complex.

References

1. The Russian-French project of Starsem to launch the "Soyuz" rocket from the Kourou cosmodrome in French Guiana. Center for Arms Control, Energy and Environmental Studies [Electronic resource]: Center for the study of problems of arms control, energy and ecology [website]. Access mode: https://www.armscontrol.ru/atmtc/space/baikonur_eads_france_paper_publ.htm
2. On launches of Russian Soyuz launch vehicles from the Kourou cosmodrome [Electronic resource]: Analysis. Forecast. Comments. IAC "space-inform" [website]. Access mode: https://www.space.com.ua/inform/number44/analiz_prognoz.html
3. Amos-2 [Electronic resource]: Telesputnik [website]. Access mode: https://www.telesputnik.ru/archive/100/article/59.html
4. "Proton" launch vehicles [Electronic resource]: project "Silent space" [website]. Access mode: https://tihiy.fromru.com/Rn/RN_Proton.htm
5. Europe "will launch a rocket" to Russia and the USA [Electronic resource]: GN [website]. Access mode: https://emigration.russie.ru/news/6/5680_1.html
6. Viasat drops Ariane-5 for Lower-Cost Proton Launch [Electronic resource]: Space News [website]. Access mode: https://www.spacenews.com/resource-center/sn_pdfs/SPN_20090316_Mar_2012.pdf
7. Europe calls Russia to Mars [Electronic resource]: business newspaper "Izvestia" [website]. Access mode: https://www.izvestia.ru/news/504020
8. United Launch Alliance. Technical data RN Atlas V [Electronic resource]: Wikipedia – Free encyclopedia [site]. Access mode: https://en.wikipedia.org/wiki/United_Launch_Alliance
9. Space News. U.S. Air Force To Request $1.8 Billion for EELV Program as Costs Skyrocket [Electronic resource]: Space News [website]. Access mode: https://www.spacenews.com/military/110114-eelv-program-costs-skyrocket.html
10. Pratt, W.K.: Laser Communication System. Wiley, Hoboken (1969)
11. Galperin, D.Y.: Reducing the weight of the optical system. Optical-Mechanical Industry, vol. 3 (1976). (in Russian)
12. Rumyantsev, K.E., Ampliev, A.E.: The accuracy of single photon registration in a dual-channel optical system. News South. Federal Univ. Tech. Sci. 4(129), 74–79 (2012). (in Russian)

13. Gagliardi, R.M.: Optical Communication. Wiley, New York (1976)
14. Bychkov, S.I., Rumyantsev, K.E.: Search and Detection of Optical Signals. Monograph. Radio and Communication, Moscow (2000). (in Russian)
15. Sheremetev, A.G.: Statistical Theory Laser Communication. Svyaz, Moscow (1971). (in Russian)
16. Bogdanovich, V.A., Vostretsov, A.G.: The Theory of Robust Detection, Discrimination and Estimation of Signals. Phyzmatlit, Moscow (2003). (in Russian)
17. Rumyantsev, K.E.: Methods of registering the flow of single-photon pulses. Radiotechnics **3**, 75–81 (1991). (in Russian)
18. Rumyantsev, K.E., Sukovatyi, A.N.: Breeding techniques of single-electron noise pulses: a review. Radiotechnics **6**, 56–61 (2004). (in Russian)
19. Rumyantsev, K.E.: Single-Photon Registrars Light Signals. TREI, Taganrog (1991). (in Russian)
20. Development of radio-technical processors on acousto-optical, fiber-optical and optoelectronic structures: report on patent research on the state of the art on the topic "Strobable recorders". Part 4. Between. R & d report 11351/TRTU; Head Rumyantsev K.E. no. GR 01.9.60.004349. inv. no. 02.9.70.001265. Taganrog (1999). (in Russian)
21. Bychkov, S.I., Rumyantsev, K.E.: Search and detection of optical signals. Monograph. Rumyantsev, K.E. (eds.) Radio and Communications, Moscow, TRTU, Taganrog (2000). (in Russian)
22. Vetokhin, S.S., Gulakov, N.R., Pertsev, A.N., Reznikov, I.V.: Single-Photon Photodetectors. Atomizdat, Moscow (1979). (in Russian)
23. Artemyev, V.V.: Photoelectronic Photon Counters: An Overview. Opt. Mech. Ind. **1**, 62–68 (1974). (in Russian)

Energy and Spectrum-Aware Cluster-Based Routing in Cognitive Radio Sensor Networks

Veeranna Gatate$^{(\boxtimes)}$ and Jayashree Agarkhed

Computer Science and Engineering Department, Poojya Doddappa Appa College of Engineering, Kalaburagi, Karnataka, India

Abstract. Spectrum awareness with energy preservation is a primary requirement in Cognitive Radio Sensor Networks as the sensor nodes are energy constrained and operate in physically unattended areas. Cluster based routing coupled with channel allocation achieves energy efficient path selection as a countermeasure to conserve energy. The proposed protocol in this work implements reliable routing with cluster based channel allocation which contributes in enhancement of network performance. Shortest path is computed for source to destination using Dijkstra's algorithm and simulation results show that proposed protocol achieves higher packet delivery with minimum delay, optimizing energy consumption than the existing approach.

Keywords: Energy-aware · Spectrum-aware · Cluster-based routing · Dijkstra

1 Introduction

Wireless Sensor Network (WSN) is defined as a distributed collection of sensor nodes deployed in an unattended environment. WSN applications today are regulated by governmental agencies using a fixed radio frequency (RF) spectrum assignment policy. The RF spectrum is categorized as a licensed band designated to licensed users called Primary Users (PUs) and unlicensed band being employed by non-licensed users called Secondary Users (SUs) [1]. As per the reports of Federal Communications Commission (FCC), portions of the RF spectrum is sparsely utilized and major portions are unutilized. These unoccupied portions of spectrum is referred to as white spaces. The licensed band is utilized for limited time period and average spectrum utilization ranges from 15% to 85% [2]. These white spaces can be identified and exploited for SU communication. Therefore there is a considerable requirement of research attention to design methodologies to acquire white spaces for efficient spectrum utilization. Recent research works carried out reveals that Cognitive Radio (CR) technology has emerged as a promising technology which can play an important role in enhancing the effectiveness of spectrum utilization without intervening the basic operations of PUs [2, 3].

If CR technology is integrated in WSN, challenges of conventional WSNs can be mitigated. The new system model thus formed is termed as Cognitive Radio Sensor Networks (CRSNs) [4]. PUs have higher priority and can access the licensed spectrum anytime, whereas SUs gain opportunity over the vacant spectrum only when a PU has

P. K. Singh et al. (Eds.): FTNCT 2020, CCIS 1396, pp. 132–143, 2021.
https://doi.org/10.1007/978-981-16-1483-5_13

moved out of licensed spectrum band [5]. Hence a SU has to monitor the time duration for which the PU is allocated with the spectrum to grab the opportunity of spectrum access. This constraint enables SUs to avoid crowded licensed band and hence the RF spectrum can be utilized in a more efficient manner [4, 5].

CRSN nodes expedite significant energy in sensing the spectrum for PU activites, to switch over an alternate vacant channel on PU detection, data transmission on spectrum availability. Therefore designing energy preservation mechanisms is essential for prolonged network lifetime. Clustering approach can be used in achieving energy-efficiency for SU communication in CRSN. The primary objectives of clustering are to optimize the total power expenditure, aggregated over the nodes in the routing path determined, with balancing the energy consumption and network load on sensor nodes to enhance the lifetime of network. Each cluster has an elected leader called Cluster-Head (CH) [6]. CH is mainly responsible for controlling and coordinating the data transmission activities of Cluster Members (CMs). CMs communicate to the CH and CHs in turn communicate with their nearest CH till the data reaches Base Station (BS). Therefore communication takes place only between the CHs which can minimize the routing protocol overheads. Selecting a CH within a cluster for improving energy efficiency largely depends on node's initial energy, average energy of network, residual energy or rate of energy consumption [7].

Some of the other relevant objectives of clustering with this presented work are outlined below as cited from [7, 8].

1. The clustering approach can preserve the channel bandwidth as it restricts the communication to among CHs and therefore preventing redundant exchange of messages among sensor nodes.
2. Cluster formation reduces the topology maintenance overhead. Clustering topology can localize the route set up within the cluster and thus reduce the size of the routing table stored at the individual sensor nodes.
3. Data aggregation by CH is the process of aggregating the data from multiple nodes to prevent redundant transmission and provides fused data to the BS, which saves member node's energy.

In this work a novel cluster based routing mechanism for efficient channel utilization and energy efficient shortest path routing protocol is designed. The proposed Energy and Spectrum-aware Cluster-based Routing (ESCR) implements clustered approach for reducing energy for intra-cluster communication (IA-C) and the implementation of Dijkstra's algorithm in CH communication to determine reliable shortest path for routing mainly contribute in enhancing the overall network performance. The contributions of this paper include: a) Design of cluster based channel allocation scheme b) Implementation of shortest path routing for inter-cluster communication. The rest of the paper is structured as follows: Sect. 2 provides the literature works for spectrum aware and energy efficient routing protocols. Section 3 provides the implementation details of the proposed ESCR protocol. Section 4 presents the performance analysis of ESCR along with real time applications and challenges of proposed mechanism and finally Sect. 5 concludes the paper.

2 Related Work

Since energy conservation is an important aspect in CRSN energy efficient clustering is been a critical area of research in sensor networks. An Energy-aware cluster based Routing Algorithm referred to as ERA is proposed in [6]. In this protocol, CH is selected based on the node residual energy as CHs have to perform many tasks and hence energy can deplete easily. And the distance between CHs varies increasing IA-C distance. This contributes to additional energy depletion at CH. A directed graph of CHs is constructed as a virtual network backbone to aid in data routing. In this way, ERA balances the energy consumption among its CHs. In [9] an Equalized Cluster Head Election Routing Protocol in WSN (ECHERP) is proposed. Energy efficiency is accomplished by implementing a balanced clustering approach for sensor nodes. Using Gaussian Elimination algorithm ECHERP determines the total power consumption and selects the nodes that optimize the total power consumption as CHs such that the overall network lifetime is enhanced. Time Division Multiple Access (TDMA) slots are created by CHs and CMs transfer the data packets in scheduled timeslots between sensor nodes. In [10] an algorithm called Event-driven Clustering with Spectrum Awareness (ESAC) is proposed which forms event-based clusters. By exchanging control messages such as EFC_REQ, C_REQ, EFC_REP, and C_REP the cluster formation takes place. In dynamic networks like CRSN control message exchange results in delay hence the protocol suffers from delay in cluster formation. In [11] an Energy-Aware Routing Protocol (EAP) is proposed which aims at conserving the node's energy using clustering approach. As CH consumes more energy when compared to other member nodes in receiving sensed information, data aggregation, and forwarding the data to BS, the CH rotation policy is implemented. The nodes with least distance to CH become its cluster members thus EAP minimizes the energy by forming clusters with cluster members joining the nearest CH. A Spectrum Aware Cluster-based Energy-Efficient Multimedia (SCEEM) routing protocol is proposed in [12] for CRSN. In this protocol optimal number of clusters is determined to reduce the latency and packet retransmissions thus saving energy. SCEEM combines Carrier Sense Multiple Access (CSMA) mechanism for inter-cluster (IE-C) communication and TDMA for IA-C communication. Expected Availability Ratio (EAR) is estimated for each sensor node at a particular time t. Based on the EAR computed value, a CH gets allocated with a vacant channel. In [13] authors propose CogLEACH protocol an extension of LEACH for cognitive environment. Using the number of nodes needed for area coverage and probability of channel availability at a node, the expected cluster count is computed. CH is chosen based on the channel availability probability value. Once clusters are formed, CH nodes frame static TDMA schedules and CMs begin data transmission in their allotted timeslots. Our previous work Improved Cluster-Based Channel Allocation proposed in [15] focuses on routing by minimizing SU interference with fairness based channel selection. A channel availability probablity (CAP) value is computed for each node and the node with highest CAP becomes the CH. CH builds static TDMA schedules and broadcasts to all non-CH members similar to CogLEACH and data transmission takes place within the allocated timeslots for IA-C. But for IE-C Communication the underlying AODV routing selects routes by using RREQ and RREP messages which increases delay in route selection resulting in degraded routing performance. An On-demand cooperative routing protocol is proposed in [14] which constructs routes from source to destination nodes using RREQ and RREP messages to achieve optimized throughput and minimum delay. Minimum end to end cost path is determined by computing the cumulated cost between the two communicating nodes. The channel utilization is not properly addressed and is assumed to be obtained from MAC layer but practically it requires cross coupling mechanisms between MAC layer and network layer to fulfill the routing objectives satisfying the channel requirements. Some of the recent works are studied from [16–20].

2.1 Identifying the Research Gaps

The existing spectrum aware routing protocols have focused on either spectrum awareness or energy preservation, there are very few works incorporating both these aspects efficiently. Clustering approach for communication in CRSN is less explored which can offer several advantages as described in Sect. 1. The clustering metrics in existing works do not consider channel allocation to CHs. Routing protocols performance can be significantly enhanced if channels are allocated to only CHs thus contributing in efficient spectrum utilization. To fulfill these research gaps the proposed work presents cluster based channel allocation for efficient spectrum aware routing.

3 ESCR Protocol – Implementation Details

The detailed working of the ESCR protocol is presented in this section. Subsects. 3.1 and 3.2 provide the network and channel allocation model. Subsect. 3.3 provides the details of clustering and routing algorithms. Table 1 provides the list of abbreviations used in this paper.

Table 1. List of abbreviations.

Abbreviation	Meaning
PU	Primary User
SU	Secondary User
BS	Base Station
N_S	Network Size
CM_P	Cluster Member Probability
C_u	Channel Usage
CV	Channel Value
K_{opt}	Optimal Cluster Count
CIC	Channel Incentive Cost
CH_{value}	Channel Allocation Value
V_{ch}	Vacant Channel
Cho	Channel Overlap count
CH_A	Available Channels

3.1 Network Model

The network considered is a CRSN with distributed collection of sensor nodes $S = \{s_1, s_2, ...s_n\}$ where n denotes the total number of nodes in CRSN. All the nodes are randomly positioned and the network is built with the PUs and SUs having the channel sensing ability and BS. The channel sensing ability is imbibed in sensor nodes which make them aware of selecting a spectrum aware routing path.

3.2 Channel Allocation Model

Each channel is assigned with a Channel Incentive Cost (CIC) to make channel allocation task much easier and is computed based on the probability of channel availability to the PUs. The sensor nodes collect and update information about the neighbors to determine the optimal quantity of clusters (K_{Opt}) needed to cover the entire network area. The optimal number of clusters is derived from the Eq. (1) as

$$K_{Opt} = \frac{S}{(D_m \times \sqrt{3D})} + 0.5 \tag{1}$$

Suppose m indicates total channels and initially the SUs are occupied with some channels, which is denoted as O_{Ch} therefore the total vacant channels V_{Ch} is computed as in Eq. (2)

$$V_{Ch} = m - O_{Ch} \tag{2}$$

Cluster states (C) for the available vacant channels V_{Ch} are computed and a channel value (CV) is computed as in Eq. (3)

$$CV = \frac{m}{C} \tag{3}$$

Since CRSN is dynamic network and the PU activities are uncertain, the channel states always needs to be updated to ensure dynamicity in spectrum availability. Based on the computed values of V_{Ch}, K_{Opt} and CV Channels are updated by computing the Channel usage (C_U) factor which helps in computing the Channel Allocation probability CA_P between any two neighboring clusters. To know the channel allocation status between two neighboring clusters we compute CA_P and based on CA_P Channel Selection (Ch_S) factor is estimated. Let Ch_A denote the channels available and let Ch_O indicate the count of overlapped channels. A channel allocation value (CH_{Value}) is computed using the Eq. (4)

$$CH_{Value} = Ch_A \times Ch_S \tag{4}$$

Finally the CIC for the channel is computed as shown in the Eq. (5)

$$CIC = \frac{CH_{Value}}{Ch_A + Ch_O} \tag{5}$$

3.3 Working of Proposed Protocol

The proposed protocol has two stages:

1. Cluster formation and IA-C Communication: In this stage clusters of nodes are formed and a CH is selected based on the channel availability probability. CH constructs the TDMA schedules for IA-C communication.
2. IE-C Communication: Once all the CMs forward their sensed data their respective CHs then a particular CH node communicates to the BS via neighboring CH nodes by executing Dijkstra's shortest path routing algorithm.

Cluster formation and IA-C Communication: Initially BS broadcasts its location information in the network. The clustering algorithm begins by the SU nodes expediting their location information and available vacant channels to BS after performing the local sensing. Nodes discover the distance to their neighbor using Euclidean distance formula. By identifying the vacant channels available for SU node the Cluster member probability (CM_P) is computed. Let x be the total number of channels and y be the total vacant channels and let p_i denote vacant channels at node i then CM_P is computed as shown in Eq. (6).

$$CM_P = \frac{x \times p_i}{y} \tag{6}$$

Let N_S define the Network Size. Suppose there are S SUs and each node has maximum transmission distance D_m. Then the size of each cluster denoted as (k) is computed as shown in Eq. (7).

$$k = \frac{S}{D \times 2 \times D_m} \text{ where } D = \frac{S}{N_s} \tag{7}$$

Among the CMs the node bearing highest CM_P will be elected as tentative CH. Now the tentative CH broadcasts its location information in CH-announcement message. All non CH nodes within the tentative-CH transmission range D_m join as cluster members. Thus clusters are formed with maximum k size. The cluster formation is explained in Algorithm 1. If a new node that has greater CM_P joins the formed cluster then it becomes the tentative-CH and broadcasts CH-announcement message. If no node with greater CM_P joins the cluster then the current tentative-CH becomes the stable-CH. Once stable CH is elected then TDMA schedules are constructed by CH and forwarded to all CMs for data transmission. All the CMs perform routing the data to their respective CHs in allotted time-slots.

IE-C communication: In this stage the data aggregated from CMs at the CH nodes is forwarded to the BS via the neighboring CH nodes. The location information of BS is known to all the nodes including CHs therefore the source CH node executes the Dijkstra's shortest path algorithm to determine the shortest routing path to the BS [18]. Dijkstra's algorithm computes all pair possible source destination routing paths and selects the shortest path from a source CH node to the BS. Algorithm 2 explains the data transmission mechanism.

Cluster-Head Selection and Data Transmission

In the proposed work the nodes having highest CM_P is elected as CH. During IA-C communication CHs constructs the static TDMA schedules and all the non-CH nodes forward their sensed data to nearest elected CH in allotted time schedules. Once the CHs receive the sensed data from all CMs, CHs execute the Dijkstra's Algorithm to determine the shortest path to reach BS. CH now communicates by sending RREQ messages to nearest CH identified on the selected shortest path by including the CIC information as discussed in Subsect. 3.2. This message traverses the selected path to reach BS and in reply RREP message is constructed by BS and forwards this message on the selected route back to the source CH. Thus routes are constructed and data packets are forwarded by executing Dijkstra's algorithm to reduce the routing overhead and to enhance the performance of routing protocol. Figure 1 shows the overall flow of ESCR protocol.

Algorithm-1 for cluster formation

1. BS → broadcasts its location all nodes in the network
2. for each non-CH nodes
3.   SU nodes → send location and vacant channels information
4.   Compute CM_P for each CM
5.   Compare CM_P of each CM
6.   If node i has highest CM_P among all other CMs then
7.   node i is eligible to become a CH
8.   else repeat step 4 to step 7 for other nodes in CRSN
9.   for each non-CH node
10.   If CM_P for a SU node $j > CM_P$ of remaining nodes
11.   Node j becomes the tentative-CH and broadcasts CH-announcement
12.   All SU nodes that listen CH-announcement become CMs
13.   When new node k joins the formed cluster
14.   if CM_P of $k > CM_P$ of j
15.   Node k becomes CH and broadcasts CH-announcement
16.   else
17.   Node j is elected as CH and constructs TDMA schedules
18.   end-for
19. end-for

Algorithm-2 for Data transmission

1. *for* each CM i within the cluster
2.   Perform data transmission to elected CH within TDMA time-slots
3.   *for* each CH j
4.   Compute all-pair shortest paths to BS using Dijkstra's algorithm
5.   Among the possible paths identified
6.   Select the shortest path with minimum distance to BS
7.   Forward the data packets over shortest path
8.   *End-for*
9. *End-for*

4 Performance Analysis

The proposed ESCR protocol is implemented in Network Simulator (NS-2) and its performance is compared with IACFC routing approach [15]. The performance of the proposed protocol is compared on the basis of routing metrics like node energy consumption, packet delivery ratio (PDR), delay experienced by packets. The energy consumption metric is defined as the average energy consumption of nodes in the network. The PDR is considered as a ratio of the total received packets at the destination to the total sent packets by the source. The end-to-end packet delay is defined as the difference between the packet send time from source CH and the packet received time by the BS.

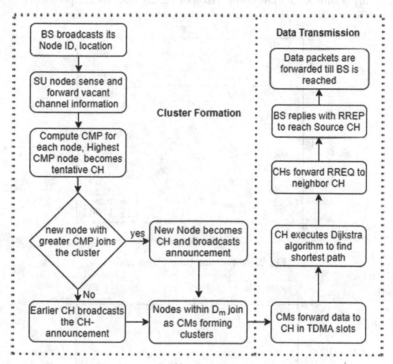

Fig. 1. Flow Diagram of ESCR protocol

4.1 Energy Consumption

As discussed in the literature the clustering approach saves significant energy as only CHs involve in communication. In IACFC, IE-C data transmission takes place using RREQ and RREP packets randomly as in [14] which consumes significant node energy whereas in ESCR only CHs are involved in communication and the channels are assigned to SU-CH after forming the clusters thus saving energy. Routes are determined by finding the shortest path from source CH to BS which reduces unnecessary node energy depletion and contributes in energy savings. As shown in the Fig. 2 both protocols initiate with the same values but as there is increase in simulation time approximately (9–10)% of node energy is preserved in ESCR.

4.2 Packet Delivery Ratio (PDR)

The protocols having higher PDR values are considered to be more efficient. As shown in the Fig. 3 with the increase in communication range of the sensor nodes the IACFC protocol suffers from packet loss due to the lack of route stability for data transmission whereas in ESCR algorithm channels are allocated to clusters for CH-CH communication and converges finding reliable with shortest routing path and hence shows higher values of PDR. Figure 3 shows the PDR comparison of ESCR and IACFC protocols.

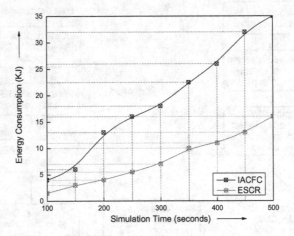

Fig. 2. Simulation time v/s energy

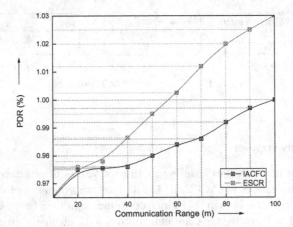

Fig. 3. Communication range v/s PDR

4.3 Packet Delay

Delay in recieving packets at the destination causes applications to experience uneven waiting periods. Lesser the packet delay experienced by packets and higher the PDR, more efficent is the routing protocol. The packet delay is mainly due to the hop-to-hop distance to reach destination from source, route instability which results in packet retransmissions. In ESCR only CH involves in data communication and channel allocation to CH communication results in more spectrum awareness thus minimizing packet delay. The proposed protocol achieves lesser delay in comparison with IACFC protocol as shown in Fig. 4.

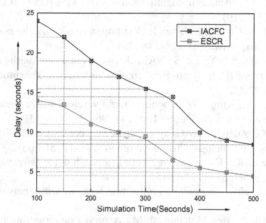

Fig. 4. Simulation time v/s delay

5   Real Time Applications and Challenges of the Proposed Solution

The proposed work is designed focusing on real time surveillance applications like military applications, disaster management and environment monitoring. These applications demand higher rate of data delivery causing minimum delay. CRSNs with thier self learning abilities are more suitable for surveillance applications, capable of adapting to varying environmental conditions. ESCR can perform much better causing minimum packet delay with higher percentage of data delivery consuming minimum energy. The real time challenges would be varying data packet rate in emergency situations and CIC estimation of channels as SUs have to switch over the channels dynamically.

6   Conclusion and Future Work

In this work a novel spectrum and energy efficient cluster based routing protocol is proposed to mitigate the promising issues of CRSN like optimizing energy consumption, achieving higher PDR with minimum delay. Routing is performed using cluster based channel allocation and channels are selected by estimating CIC which contributes in effective spectrum utilization. As compared to IACFC, simulation results show that ESCR executes with minimum delay and higher PDR values due to the Dijkstra's shortest path routing to find reliable routing paths. As data transmitted by users in CRSN can easily be manipulated by malevolent nodes, routing algorithms need secure mechanisms. In future ESCR can be further improved by incorporating data security mechanisms to ensure secure data transmission in CRSN.

References

1. Wang, B., Liu, K.J.R.: Advances in cognitive radio networks: a survey. IEEE J. Sel. Top. Sign. Process. **5**(1), 5–23 (2010)
2. Liu, X., Cesana, P.M., Cuomo, F., Ekici, E.: Routing in cognitive radio networks: Challenges and solutions. Ad Hoc Netw. **9**(3), 228–248 (2011)
3. Pefkianakis, I., Wong, S.H.Y., Lu, S.: SAMER: spectrum aware mesh routing in cognitive radio networks. In: 3rd IEEE Symposium on New Frontiers in Dynamic Spectrum Access Networks, pp. 1–5 (2008)
4. Joshi, G.P., Nam, S.Y., Kim, S.W.: Cognitive radio wireless sensor networks: applications, challenges and research trends. Sensors **13**(9), 11196–11228 (2013)
5. Kim, H., Shin, K.G.: Adaptive MAC-layer sensing of spectrum availability in cognitive radio networks. University of Michigan, Technical report CSE-TR-518-06 (2006)
6. Amgoth, T., Jana, P.K.: Energy-aware routing algorithm for wireless sensor networks. Comput. Electr. Eng. **41**, 357–367 (2015)
7. Liu, X.: A survey on clustering routing protocols in wireless sensor networks. Sensors **12**(8), 11113–11153 (2012)
8. Gherbi, C., Aliouat, Z., Ben Mohammed, M.: A survey on clustering routing protocols in wireless sensor networks. Sens. Rev. **37**, 12–25 (2017)
9. Nikolidakis, S., et al.: Energy efficient routing in wireless sensor networks through balanced clustering. Algorithms **6**(1), 29–42 (2013)
10. Ozger, M., Akan, O.: Event-driven spectrum-aware clustering in cognitive radio sensor networks. In: 2013 Proceedings IEEE INFOCOM, pp. 1483–1491 (2013)
11. Liu, M., Cao, J., Chen, G., Wang, X.: An energy-aware routing protocol in wireless sensor networks. Sensors (Basel) **9**(1), 445–462 (2009). https://doi.org/10.3390/s90100445
12. Shah, G.A., et al.: A spectrum-aware clustering for efficient multimedia routing in cognitive radio sensor networks. IEEE Trans. Veh. Technol. **63**(7), 3369–3380 (2014)
13. Eletreby, R.M., Elsayed, H.M., Khairy, M.M.: CogLEACH: a spectrum aware clustering protocol for cognitive radio sensor networks. In: 9th International Conference on Cognitive Radio Oriented Wireless Networks and Communications (CROWNCOM), pp. 179–184. IEEE (2014)
14. Sheu, J., Lao, I.: Cooperative routing protocol in cognitive radio ad-hoc networks. In: IEEE Wireless Communications and Networking Conference (WCNC), Paris, France, pp. 2916–2921 (2012). https://doi.org/10.1109/WCNC.2012.6214302
15. Agarkhed, J., Gatate, V.: Interference aware cluster formation in cognitive radio sensor networks. In: Bindhu, V., Chen, J., Tavares, J.M.R.S. (eds.) International Conference on Communication, Computing and Electronics Systems. LNEE, vol. 637, pp. 635–644. Springer, Singapore (2020). https://doi.org/10.1007/978-981-15-2612-1_61
16. Basak, S., Acharya, T.: Spectrum-aware outage minimizing cooperative routing in cognitive radio sensor networks. Wireless Netw. **26**(2), 1069–1084 (2018). https://doi.org/10.1007/s11276-018-1844-7

17. Stephan, T., Al-Turjman, F., K, S.J., Balusamy, B.: Energy and spectrum aware unequal clustering with deep learning based primary user classification in cognitive radio sensor networks. Int. J. Mach. Learn. Cybern. **1**, 34 (2020). https://doi.org/10.1007/s13042-020-011 54-y
18. Razzaq, M., Shin, S.: Fuzzy-logic Dijkstra-based energy-efficient algorithm for data transmission in WSNs. Sensors (Basel) **19**(5), 1040 (2019).https://doi.org/10.3390/s19051040
19. Raj, R.N., Nayak, A., Kumar, M.S.: A survey and performance evaluation of reinforcement learning based spectrum aware routing in cognitive radio ad hoc networks. Int. J. Wireless Inf. Networks **27**(1), 144–163 (2020). https://doi.org/10.1007/s10776-019-00463-6
20. Dhingra, H., Dhand, G.D., Chawla, R., Gupta, S.: An integrated service model to support user specific QoS routing in cognitive radio ad hoc network. Peer-to-Peer Netw. Appl. **14**(1), 18–29 (2020). https://doi.org/10.1007/s12083-020-00965-8

The Hybrid Approach for the Partitioning of VLSI Circuits

Vladimir Kureichik, Dmitry Zaporozhets$^{(\boxtimes)}$, and Vladimir Kureichik Jr.

Southern Federal University, Rostov-on-Don, Russia
{vkur,duzaporozhets}@sfedu.ru

Abstract. Partitioning is one of the most important problems at the design stage during the Very Large Scale Integrated (VLSI) manufacture. The article provides a description of this problem and its formal statement as partitioning of a hypergraph into parts. Partitioning belongs to the NP-hard class of optimization problems. A combination of swarm intelligence and genetic search methods made it possible to develop a hybrid approach to partitioning of VLSI circuits. A distinctive feature of this approach is to divide search process in two stages. At the first stage, search space is reduced by allocation of areas with high objective function values on the basis of a bee colony optimization method. As a result, an effective initial population of alternative solutions is generated. At the second stage, optimization of obtained solutions can be implemented with the use of the genetic search method. The suggested approach is supported by a hybrid algorithm which can obtain quazi-optimal solutions in polynomial time and avoid falling into local optima. A new software application has been developed to confirm the effectiveness of the suggested approach and hybrid algorithm. Experiments have been carried out on the basis of IBM benchmarks. The results of experiments show that the quality of solutions obtained by the suggested algorithm exceeds on average of 5% the well-known partitioning algorithm hMetis. Time complexity of the developed algorithm can be represented as $O\left(n^2\right)$ in the best case and $O\left(n^3\right)$ in the worst case.

Keywords: VLSI · Partitioning problem · Hypergraph · Bee colony optimization · Genetic algorithm

1 Introduction

Currently, the development of Very Large Scale Integrated (VLSI) circuits implies a generally accepted sequence of design stages: system specification, functional design, algorithmic design, structural design, technological design (manufacture of crystals (chips)), assembly, testing and control [1].

The development of structural, functional, and schematic diagrams of the device is carried out at the functional design stage. Then, algorithms for the functioning of computing systems and computers are developed at the algorithmic design stage. Structural design includes the implementation of the results obtained at the functional design

© Springer Nature Singapore Pte Ltd. 2021
P. K. Singh et al. (Eds.): FTNCT 2020, CCIS 1396, pp. 144–153, 2021.
https://doi.org/10.1007/978-981-16-1483-5_14

stage. Technological design is associated with the implementation of the of the design stage results, namely the development of technological processes for the manufacture of devices. At this stage, the schematic representation of each component is converted to a geometric representation, i.e. a set of geometric images that perform the logical functions of the corresponding components. The connections between the various components of the circuit are used as geometric images. At the same time, it is imperative to take into account various types of verification in circuit topology design. The result of the work at the design stage is a set of photomasks (masks), which are necessary for the VLSI manufacture [1–4].

Also, the optimal construction needs to take into account both technological capabilities and requirements of the technical specification. The main challenges at this stage are partitioning and placement of elements and routing of electrical connections.

These issues belong to the class of NP-hard optimization problems. Therefore, it is not possible to create a general mathematical model which can integrate design and technological features. In addition, an universal algorithm to search for the optimal constructive solution cannot be developed in terms of unified cycle of VLSI design. In this regard, it is necessary to create new effective methods and approaches to solve the VLSI design problems.

Note, partitioning of VLSI components is one of the most complex issues at the design stage as it is not possible to develop the whole topology of the circuit, because it contains hundreds of millions of elements. Therefore, the circuit should be divided into blocks. To put it simply, a set of blocks and a set of connections between them are formed by grouping components in blocks.

To date, new design standards and increasing of VLSI integration cause the modernization and development of new effective approaches and methods for circuit design. One such approach is the multilevel optimization and combined approaches based on evolutionary modelling and bioinspired search methods.

2 Problem Formulation

Partitioning of a VLSI circuit is to find such mutual position of elements that all requirements have met. Formalization of solutions to this problem is impossible without an adequate mathematical model. The primary requirement to the mathematical model is choosing an appropriate way for the electrical circuit representation. Therefore, as we know from the [1, 2], the adequate model for the circuit representation is a hypergraph, which can accurately assess number of electrical connections between parts of the circuit.

Let us formulate the problem of circuit partitioning of the hypergraph into parts (blocks, modules, etc.) with the limitation on the number of elements assigned to nodes [1]. Given a hypergraph $H = (X, E)$, where $X = \{x_i | i = 1, 2, \ldots, n\}$ is a set of vertices, $E = \{e_j | j = 1, 2, \ldots, m\}$ is a set of hyperedges. Let weight of vertices will be assigned as $\Phi = \{\varphi_i | i = 1, 2, \ldots, n\}$ and weight of edges - $\Psi = \{\psi_j | j = 1, 2, \ldots, m\}$. It is necessary to find K nodes. In other words, the set X needs to divide in K non-empty and non-intersecting sets X_v such as $X = \cup X_v$, $(\forall i, j), X_i \cap X_j = \emptyset, X_v = \emptyset$. Then, a total cost of hyperedges is calculated according with the formula:

$$F = \sum_{j=J} \psi_j, J = \{j | e_j \in C\} \tag{1}$$

where $C = \{e_j|(\forall v)[e_j \cap X_v \neq e_j]\}$ is a set of hyperedges.

The expression (1) is a partitioning criterion for the hypergraph and it should be minimized.

Obviously, this criterion is significant since a number of external connections between circuit modules is a major factor the implementation of which increase an interference, simplify the construction of device, and, therefore, increase the VLSI reliability. As a result of optimization of this criterion, the VLSI design is simplified and its reliability is also increased.

3   The Hybrid Approach

Recent studies show that NP-complex design problems are effectively solved by bio-inspired methods, as well as their combination and hybridization [3–8]. These methods, in contrast to the classical ones, work with a variety of solutions, are able to operate with preliminary knowledge about the problem, obtain sets of quasi-optimal solutions in polynomial time, and can avoid local optima.

Bioinspired algorithms involve the parallel processing of several alternative solutions to the optimization problem. All bioinspired algorithms belong to the class of heuristic algorithms, that is, algorithms for which convergence to the global optimum has not been theoretically proven, but it has been empirically established that the probability of obtaining an optimal or quasi-optimal solution is high.

The general scheme of bioinspired algorithms includes the following steps [8–12]:

1. Initialization of the initial population. A given number of initial agents that are to varying degrees close to the optimal solution are created in each search area
2. Generation of new agents. New agents are generated or existing ones are changed in such a way that each agent iteratively approaches the optimum one. For this, a set of operators is used that are specific to each of the bioinspired algorithms.
3. Completion of the search process. The stopping criterion is checked, and if it is fulfilled, the best of the found solutions is taken as an approximate solution to the problem. Otherwise, the process is repeated iteratively upon reaching the stopping criterion (the number of iterations, the specified value of the objective function, the running time).

Deterministic or random algorithms can be applied to obtain an initial population. Agents cover the search area to generate the initial population (breadth-first search). If the neighborhood of the global extremum is known, agents fill the neighborhood and search near the global extremum of the optimized function (depth search). This approach can significantly reduce the time required to solve the problem. But in most cases there is no information about the global extremum, so the agents of the initial population are distributed over the search area.

As is known from [3, 4, 6], one of the most important stages in the implementation of bio-inspired algorithms, the results of which have a significant impact on its further work, is the formation of the initial population of solutions. So, in the case of a successful choice of the initial values, the set of alternative solutions can fall into the global optimum, and, conversely, in the case of an unsuccessful choice of the initial population, with a low degree of determinism, the algorithm can fall into the local optimum. In this regard, a hybrid approach based on the combination of swarm intelligence and genetic search methods is proposed to effectively solve the problem of partitioning VLSI circuits [13, 14].

At the first level, it is proposed to use the bee colony optimization method as a swarm intelligence. This can reduce the search area and form an effective initial population of alternative solutions. At the second level, optimization is performed based on genetic search methods.

Encoding and decoding of alternative solutions are the main problems in dealing with applied problems of science and technology with the use of bioinspired algorithms. The authors suggest using a unified approach to data presentation for all stages of the hybrid algorithm. It can speed up the encoding and decoding of alternative solutions, as well as the calculation of the objective function. The authors propose to encode the solution of VLSI fragments partitioning in the form of a sequence of fragments processing. An alternative solution (chromosome) is a sequence of numbers of VLSI fragments, divided into partition groups. For example, partitioning of a circuit which contain 10 blocks into 2 equal partition groups shown in Fig. 1.

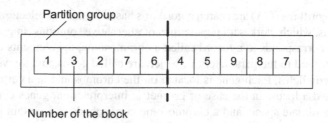

Fig. 1. An example of an alternative solution

Let us consider a more complex example. Suppose it is need to encode a partition of a 20 block circuit into 4 different sized partition groups. The Group 1 contains 5 elements, the Group 2–2 elements, the Group 3–10 elements, the Group 4–3 elements. In this case, an alternative solution takes the form shown in Fig. 2.

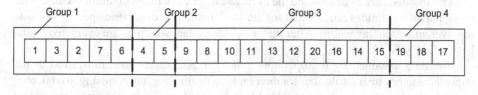

Fig. 2. Complex example of an alternative solution

In this example, the Group 1 contains blocks # 1, 3, 2, 7, the Group 2 – blocks # 4, 5, the Group 3 – blocks # 9, 8, 10, 11, 13, 12, 20, 16, 14, 15, and the Group 4 – blocks #

19, 18, 17. The quantity and size of each partition group are set by the decision-maker in accordance with the terms of reference.

4 The Hybrid Algorithm

Based on the proposed and described approach, the authors suggest a scheme of the hybrid algorithm for partitioning VLSI circuits shown in Fig. 3 [10–15].

Let us consider the given scheme of the hybrid algorithm and describe the purpose of each of its blocks in more detail.

According to this scheme, the search process is implemented at two levels. At the preliminary stage, there are entered the initial data in the form of a hypergraph model, the number of parts and the parameters of the bee and genetic algorithms. At the first level, there are applied the basic operations of the bee optimization method, which can quickly divide the search space into areas with a high value of the objective function (OF) [16]. The initial bee population is generated based on known principles [17–19]. Further, search areas are formed and the elite areas with a high OF value are distinguished among them [20]. The result of the bee optimization method is the creation of an effective population of alternative solutions for the genetic algorithm which is implemented at the second search level.

Genetic algorithms (GA) are search algorithms based on natural selection and genetics mechanisms, which work with populations of alternative solutions. In genetic methods, the set X corresponds to a record called a chromosome, the elements of the chromosome correspond to the parameters x_i, which are called genes, and the values of the genes are called alleles. Each gene is located on the chromosome in a certain position which are called a locus. In the case of geometric interpretation, genes correspond to axes of the coordinate space, and a chromosome corresponds to a certain point in the search space [21].

Obviously, the number of possible alternatives is so great in most practically significant problems that an explicit representation of the set of alternatives is impossible. Therefore, the genetic algorithm operates with a set of alternatives N representing some N structural parameters at each moment of the search. This set is called the population, and N is called the population size.

At the second level, the population is realized on the basis of the Lamarck's evolutionary model [21, 22].

The solutions are evaluated and the average OF value of the population is calculated. Next, parental solutions are selected for the implementation of genetic operators (crossing over, mutation, inversion). After that, new descendant solutions are evaluated on the basis of the OF.

The data, obtained by the operators and their assessment, are transferred to the analysis of unpromising solutions for their ranking (promising, unpromising, trivial, etc.) and subsequent selection. Note that this block makes it possible to take into account all available solutions in genetic search and increases the efficiency of the hybrid algorithm as a whole.

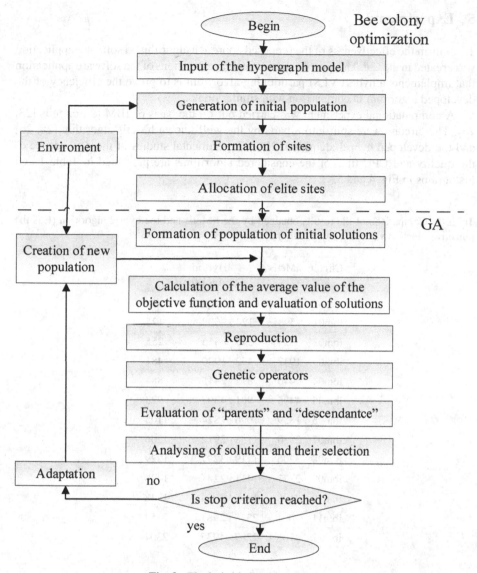

Fig. 3. The hybrid algorithm scheme

Next, the condition of the stopping criterion is checked, and if it is not reached, then the results are transferred to the block of evolutionary adaptation. This block has a direct impact on the process of restructuring the current population and creating a new population of alternative solutions. The environment block manages all variable parameters of the hybrid search. Note, that the search continues iteratively until a set of quasi-optimal solutions is obtained.

5 Experiments

To confirm the effectiveness of the proposed approach algorithm, a software application was created in the C #. The aim of experimental investigations of the software application that implements a hybrid VLSI partitioning algorithm is to prove the efficiency of the developed algorithm in comparison with similar ones.

A computational experiment was carried out on the basis of IBM test circuits [23, 24]. The circuits were split into 8 parts by the well-known hMetis algorithm [25, 26] and the developed hybrid algorithm (HA). Experimental studies of the dependence of the quality and CPU time of the considered algorithms are presented in Table 1 and histograms in Fig. 4 and 5.

Table 1. Comparison of the results obtained by the hMetis and the hybrid algorithm (F is the objective function value, t is a CPU time)

Circuit	hMetis		Hybrid algorithm	
	F, (pc.)	t, (s)	F, (pc.)	t, (s)
ibm01	598	124	608	125
ibm02	823	249	815	255
ibm03	1947	472	1920	481
ibm04	2446	872	2415	884
ibm05	4405	981	4397	993
ibm06	1859	1096	1824	1105
ibm07	2930	1198	2912	1206
ibm08	3306	1219	3297	1229
ibm09	2277	1411	2247	1428
ibm10	3108	1810	3084	1848
ibm11	3001	2315	2981	2354
ibm12	4966	2287	4937	2304

The analysis of the table and histograms shows that the developed hybrid algorithm loses insignificantly in time to the known hMetis algorithm but surpasses it in quality by an average of 5%, which indicates the effectiveness of the proposed approach.

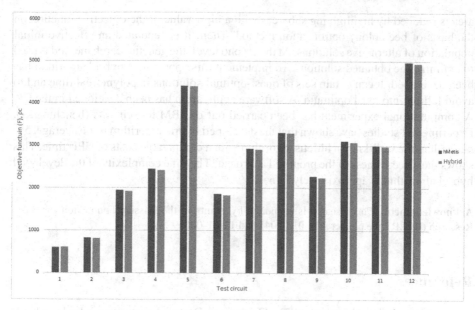

Fig. 4. Histogram of the dependence of the objective function value

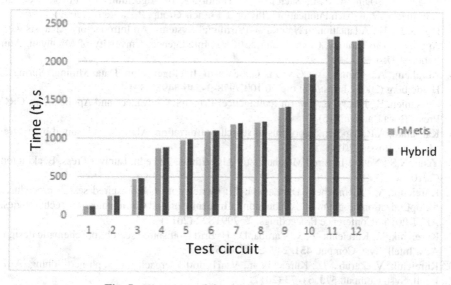

Fig. 5. Histogram of the dependence of CPU time

6 Conclusion

The paper considers one of the main tasks of VLSI design - the problem of circuit partitioning. For its effective solution, a hybrid approach based on the combination of swarm intelligence and genetic search methods is proposed. At the first level, the search area is reduced by highlighting subareas with a high value of the objective function on the basis of bee colony optimization method. Then, it is generated an effective initial population of alternative solutions. At the second level, the genetic search method is used to optimize the obtained solutions. To implement this approach, a hybrid algorithm has been developed. It can obtain sets of quasi-optimal solutions in polynomial time and to avoid falling into local optimum. A software application has been developed in the C#. A computational experiment has been carried out on IBM test circuits (benchmarks). Experimental studies have shown that the developed hybrid algorithm is, on average, 5% better than the well-known hMetis algorithm with a comparable costs of CPU time. This shows the effectiveness of the proposed approach. The time complexity of the developed hybrid algorithm is approximately $O(n^2)$.

Acknowledgment. This research is supported by grants of the Russian Foundation for Basic Research (RFBR), the project # 18-01-00041 and 19-01-00059.

References

1. Sherwani, N.A.: Algorithms for VLSI Physical Design Automation, 3rd edn. Kluwer Academic Publisher, Dordrecht (2013)
2. Alpert, C.J., Dinesh, P.M., Sachin, S.S.: Handbook of Algorithms for Physical design Automation. Auerbach Publications Taylor & Francis Group, Boca Raton (2009)
3. Holland, J.H.: Adaptation in Natural and Artificial Systems: An Introductory Analysis with Application to Biology, Control, and Artificial Intelligence. University of Michigan, Ann Arbor (1975)
4. Abraham, A., Ramos, V., Grosan, G.: Swarm Intelligence in Data Mining. Springer, Heidelberg (2007). https://doi.org/10.1007/978-3-540-34956-3_1
5. Hassanien, E., Emary, E.: Swarm Intelligence: Principles Advances and Applications. CRC Press, Boca Raton (2015)
6. Karpenko, A.P.: Modern algorithms of search optimization. Algorithms inspired by nature. Moskow, Russia (2014)
7. Yang, X.S.: Nature-Inspired Metaheuristic Algorithms, 2nd edn. Luniver Press, Beckington (2010)
8. Kureichik, V., Zaporozhets, D., Zaruba, D.: Generation of bioinspired search procedures for optimization problem. In: Application of Information and Communication Technologies, AICT 2016 - Conference Proceedings, № 7991822 (2017)
9. Kureichik, V., Kureichik Jr., V., Zaruba, D.: Hybrid bioinspired search for schematic design. Adv. Intell. Syst. Comput. **451**, 249–255 (2016)
10. Kureichik, V., Zaruba, D., Kureichik Jr., V.: Hybrid approach for graph partitioning. Adv. Intell. Syst. Comput. **573**, 64–73 (2017)
11. Hendrickson, B., Leland, R.: A multilevel algorithm for partitioning graphs. In: Proceedings of the 1995 ACM/IEEE Conference on Super Computing, pp. 626–657 (1995)
12. Schloegel, K., Karypis, G., Kumar, V.: Multilevel diffusion schemes for repartitioning of adaptive meshes, pp. 109–124. Department of Computer Science, University of Minnesota (1997)
13. Kureichik, V., Zaporozhets, D., Zaruba, D.: Generation of bioinspired search procedures for optimization problems. In: Application of Information and Communication Technologies, AICT 2016 - Conference Proceedings, № 7991822 (2016)

14. Kureichik Jr., V., Bova, V., Kureichik, V.: Hybrid approach for computer-aided design problems. In: International Seminar on Electron Devices Design and Production (SED). Proceedings, Prague, pp. 151–156 (2019)

15. De Jong, K.: Evolutionary computation: recent development and open issues. In: Proceedings 1st International Conference on Evolutionary Computation and Its Application, Moscow, pp. 7–18 (1996)

16. Karaboga, D.: An idea based on honeybee swarm for numerical optimization, p. 110. Erciyes University, Engineering Faculty, Computer Engineering Department (2005)

17. Zaruba, D., Zaporozhets, D., Kureichik, V.: Artificial bee colony algorithm—a novel tool for VLSI placement. J. Adv. Intell. Syst. Comput. **450**, 433–442 (2016)

18. Akay, B., Karaboga, D.: A modified artificial bee colony algorithm for real-parameter optimization. J. Inf. Sci. **192**, 120–142 (2012). https://doi.org/10.1016/j.ins.2010.07.015

19. Ning, J., Zhang, B., Liu, T., Zhang, C.: An archive-based artificial bee colony optimization algorithm for multi-objective continuous optimization problem. Neural Comput. Appl. **30**(9), 2661–2671 (2016). https://doi.org/10.1007/s00521-016-2821-7

20. Harfouchi, F., Habbi, H., Ozturk, C., Karaboga, D. Modified multiple search cooperative foraging strategy for improved artificial bee colony optimization with robustness analysis. Soft Comput. **22**(19), 6371–6394 (2018). https://doi.org/10.1007/s00500-017-2689-1

21. Kureichik, V.V., Kureichik, V.M., Sorokoletov, P.V.: Analysis and a survey of evolutionary models. J. Comput. Syst. Sci. Int. **46**(5), 779–791 (2007). https://doi.org/10.1134/S10642307 07050103

22. Karypis, G., Kumar, V.: Analysis of multilevel graph partitioning. Department of Computer Science, University of Minnesota (1995)

23. Kacprzyk, J., Kureichik, V.M., Malioukov, S.P., Kureichik, V.V., Malioukov, A.S.: Experimental investigation of algorithms developed. Stud. Comput. Intell. **212**, 211–223+227–236 (2009)

24. IBM-PLACE 2.0 benchmark suits. https://er.cs.ucla.edu/benchmarks/ibm-place2/bookshelf/ibm-place2-all-bookshelf-nopad.tar.gz. Accessed 25 May 2020

25. Alpert, C.J.: The ISPD-98 circuit beanchmark suit. In: Proceedings of the ACM/IEEE International Symposium on Physical Design, pp. 80–85 (1998)

26. Karypis, G., Kumar, V.: METIS: a software package for partitioning unstructured graphs, partitioning meshes, and computing fill–reducing orderings of sparse matrices version 5.1.0: Department of Computer Science and Engineering, University of Minnesota Minneapolis, MN (2013)

Maximization of IoT Network Lifetime Using Efficient Clustering Technique

N. N. Srinidhi[1]([✉]), Dharamendra Chouhan[2], A. N. Savitha[2], J. Shreyas[2], and S. M. Dilip Kumar[2]

[1] Department of Computer Science and Engineering, Sri Krishna Institute of Technology, Bangalore, India
[2] Department of Computer Science and Engineering, University Visvesvaraya College of Engineering, Bangalore, India

Abstract. Internet of Things (IoT) consists of heterogeneous nodes that consumes more network resources due to this network lifetime is foreshorten. To enhance network lifetime, dynamic cluster head selection algorithm (DCHSA) is propounded in this work. This algorithm combines both tree and cluster based data aggregation that classifies cluster head (CH) into primary cluster head (PCH) and secondary cluster head (SCH) to improve energy efficiency and network lifetime. The proposed work provides fault tolerance whenever primary cluster head fails and secondary cluster head takes over the task of primary cluster head. The data sent from individual node in the cluster is collected and aggregated by the cluster head. Further tree based data aggregation scheme is proposed to send the data from PCH to base station. The results obtained through simulation outperforms with respect to energy efficiency, lifetime of the network and energy dissipation in comparison with existing works.

Keywords: Cluster head · Data aggregation · Energy conservation · Internet of Things · Network lifetime

1 Introduction

The Internet of Things (IoT) is a new paradigm of heterogeneous networks which are distributed over the globe and exchanges information between them [11]. This provides the more flexibility in various applications which are used daily that includes smart home, smart farming, smart healthcare, military etc. In IoT, Wireless Sensor Networks (WSN) is responsible for collecting surrounding information [8]. WSN consists of wirelessly communicating nodes which are randomly deployed and are intended to sense data. It suffers failure due to large amount of data in sensor network hence, similar data collected by nodes leads to redundancy. Therefore, data aggregation method is an efficient method in sensor networks [12]. Due to less power of nodes redundant data become necessary to reduce energy dissipation at every sensor node to enhance the overall time

© Springer Nature Singapore Pte Ltd. 2021
P. K. Singh et al. (Eds.): FTNCT 2020, CCIS 1396, pp. 154–166, 2021.
https://doi.org/10.1007/978-981-16-1483-5_15

period of wireless device network. Since nodes waste their power in processing redundant information thus, removing data redundancy has putforth solution for improving WSN lifetime [4]. Data aggregation is a technique that gathers the data and aggregates the data to reduce redundancy and increases network lifetime. Data aggregation focus on the issues like redundancy, delay, accuracy and traffic load. To overcome these issues some of the data aggregation strategies such as centralized approach aggregation, in network aggregation, tree based aggregation, cluster based aggregation as been used. Different sensors such as temperature sensor, pressure sensor, humidity sensor etc., in which data packets are correlated to each other. In these kind of issues, aggregation is done together and removal of redundant data to make the data aggregation more efficient [1]. Hence, data aggregation technique to enhance energy efficiency and lifetime of the network is propounded in this work.

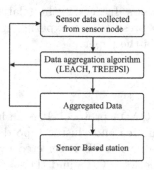

Fig. 1. Aggregation of data in WSN

The data is received from different nodes and aggregates these data using different algorithms such as LEACH, TREEPSI, TAG etc. The sensor readings from various nodes are considered as input and aggregated data is produced as output. To transmit collected data towards sink node an efficient shortest path is chosen by the sink node and an efficient routing methid is required to select optimal route which is suitable for sending data from sensor node to base station as shown in Fig. 1 [2]. In cluster based scheme, sensor nodes are grouped into clusters. Every cluster has a leader, known as CH. Every non sensor nodes transmits data towards receptive CH for the process of aggregation. CH aggregates and forwards data towards sink node for further processing. Cluster based WSN has following benefits. (1) Making cluster head to combine data to reduce redundancy, unrelated data and also minimizes energy dissipation of nodes. (2) Cluster head will maintain the local route setup of other cluster head so that, the routing will be carried out more efficiently. (3) Communication with nodes is done only with the CHs, it conserves bandwidth [13]. Tree based scheme is another type used in data aggregation, which finds a efficient path and shortens the distance between sensor node and sink node by constructing a tree based aggregation. In WSN, there is an issue of limited power supply due to which the CH's will die quickly. So, this failure will affect the overall lifetime of the network. Hence, to overcome from this limitations DCHSA is proposed which combines cluster and data aggregation based on tree which consist of dynamic cluster head such as PCH and SCH [5].

1.1 Contributions of This Work

Various contributions of this work are as follows:

1) To optimize the energy consumption.
2) To optimize network parameters of DCHSA when compared with QADA, LEACH, TREEPSI in terms of network lifetime.
3) Failure of PCH effects the overall network lifetime, so to overcome SCH will acts PCH for that round.

Paper is furnished as follows. In Sect. 2, the related work. Section 3 explains problem statement, Sect. 4 presents the experimental evaluation and finally, Sect. 5 provides conclusion of the paper.

2 Related Works

Rahman et al. [9] proposed QADA protocol. It is an homogeneous network protocol, which combines both tree and cluster type data aggregation. On basis of distance and energy information CH is selected by the base station and the logical tree is constructed between CH's and thereafter CH combines data and transmits it to upper parent node. In case of failure of cluster head and due to homogeneous network leads to decrease of the network lifetime. The work has been carried out in proposed LEACH protocol [3]. In this approach election of CH and CF is done based on the RSS and threshold value. Aggregation of the received data from the non sensor node is done by cluster head. Each and every node gets a chance to act as CH for a particular time, to balance the network lifetime. In this approach it addresses some issues like low energy consumption and low network lifetime. Here, CH is selected on basis of random number ranges from 0 and 1, if value is smaller than threshold then that node acts as CH for that round. Node having lesser energy is possibly selected as CH, leads in shortening lifetime of the network. In [14], proposed CIDT protocol. In this, DCN and CH is selected on basis of residual energy of sensor nodes, RSS and connection time. This protocol shows better performance than LEACH protocol. However, it has issue in data rate. Liu et al. [6], designed EAP protocol which is an method for data collection. Nodes are grouped into intra-cluster communication and tree construction is done between the clusters to establish communication. This protocol is not well suited for mobile type WSN, because it will not establish link when the nodes are mobile. Gaurav and Mohamed [2], propounded the fault-tolerant clustering approach. In this approach detection and recovery are carried in two phases. It makes the network in which sensors recover from the failed gateways by not re-clustering the system however, it as an issue while maintaining the data rate, delay and coverage distance. In [7], proposed TTDCA protocol, which minimizes transmission of data towards sink and this is based on additive as well as divisible aggregation function. But here CH directly send combined data towards base station which leads to more energy consumption and this decreases overall network lifetime.

3   Problem Statement and Objectives

To select dynamic cluster head to maximize lifetime of heterogeneous IoT network with the following objectives: 1) To optimize energy consumption. 2) To increase network lifetime. 3) To decrease overhead of network. 4) To reduce transmission of duplicate data.

4   Proposed Algorithm

4.1   Notations

Various notations used in this algorithm is shown in Table 1.

Table 1. Basic notations used in this paper

Terms	Description
S	Sensor nodes
K	Expected number of clusters
Avg_Eng	Average energy of the nodes
d	Distance of the Nodes
N	Number of nodes
E	Energy of the nodes
$X_i\,Y_i$	Coordinates for node i
PCH	Primary cluster head
SCH	Secondary cluster head
T_round	Total rounds the system runs
CSMA	Carrier sense multiple access

4.2   Algorithm Phases

The proposed DCHSA technique consists of two phases as: 1) Cluster setup phase 2) Cluster steady phase.

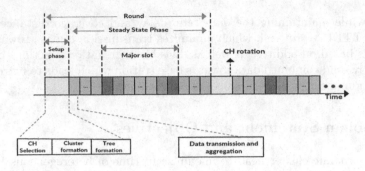

Fig. 2. Phase diagram

4.3   Cluster Setup Phase

Cluster set-up phase corresponds to the cluster head selection, cluster formation and tree formation. As shown in the Fig. 2

1. Start round r = 0
2. Every sensor nodes S send their energy and distance information towards base station.
3. Based on that information PCH will be selected by sink node.
4. PCH send ADV message to all sensor nodes.
5. Initially, the NonCH nodes are supposed to keep their receiver on to receive broadcast messages.
6. NonCH nodes send JOIN-Req message to choose PCH node inside cluster.
7. Formation of cluster is done based on step 6.
8. SCH is selected by the PCH.
9. Tree Construction is done by sink node on basis of energy and distance of cluster head.

4.3.1   Cluster Head Selection

In set-up phase, selection of CH is the main phase in heterogeneous network. The CH is divided into PCH and SCH. Initially, every node will send their distance information and current energy information towards base station. Based on that information, sink selects PCH. After that sink node broadcast a Adv_message by utilizing $CSMA$ (Carrier sense multiple access) and MAC protocol to distribute the PCH information. The sensor nodes receive the Adv_message and matches their ID with the received ID, If both ID matches then that sensor node will acts as a PCH node for that round as shown in below Fig. 3.

4.3.2   Cluster Formation

After the PCH selection, each PCH node sends a PCH_Adv (Advertisement message) to non-cluster nodes. Adv_message contains an(PCH_ID). Nodes receive this message which contain an (PCH_ID) and matches their id with

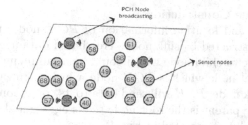

Fig. 3. Cluster head selection

PCH_ID, if both the id's are matched then that NonCH will belong for that primary cluster head node for that round. Now, NonCH will send (JOIN_Req) message to selected *PCH* using carrier sense multiple access(CSMA) and received signal strength(RSS). The requesting message contains node id, PCH_ID, using *CSMA* as a MAC protocol. NonCH nodes choose the nearest *PCH* to minimize the energy consumption. Now each *PCH* announces NonCH to facilitate the data using *TDMA* schedule as shown in below Algorithm 1. Each NonCH node will wakes up during TDMA timeslot to transmit its data to *PCH* and then goes to sleep mode. After the cluster is formed all the nodes are grouped into clusters. Nodes in particular cluster will broadcast energy details to *PCH*. The *PCH* will select *SCH* on highest energy basis among the nodes and send the Adv_message(Node_ID) to the non sensor nodes. The nodes whose ID matches with the PCH_ID becomes a *SCH* for the particular cluster.

Algorithm 1. Formation of Cluster and SCH selection

1: **Input:** Energy and distance information
2: **Output:** Selection of SCH
3: PCH node broadcasts an PCH_Adv message to nonCH nodes
4: Message Broadcast PCH_Adv(PCH_ID)
5: NonCH node sends JOIN_Req message to selected PCH nodes
6: JOIN_Req contains (NodeID, PCH_ID)
7: Schedule of TDMA is created by PCH within the cluster
8: SCH Selection (E, N)
9: Nodes send (Energy, ID) to the PCH of respective clusters
10: PCH selects the highest energy among the them
11: PCH sends a Adv_Msg to all nonCH node
12: **if** PCH_ID == NodeID
13:    | **then**
14:    | Node becomes an SCH for that round
15: **else**
16:    | N = NonCH node
17:    | Repeat for all rounds
18: **end if**

4.3.3   Tree Construction

On energy and location information of PCH nodes tree construction is done. Tree is constructed by sink node. Tree-based data aggregation is done from the parent node to child node which could be a minimum spanning tree. Each node has a parent node which is PCH node, which aggregates the data and forwards data to sink node. PCH will send data to its corresponding parent nodes. Parent node whose parent is the root node sends aggregated data towards base station or (sink node) as depicted in Fig. 4.

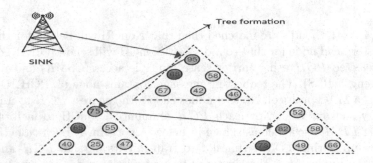

Fig. 4. Tree construction

Algorithm 2. Tree construction

1: **T_msg:** Message used while constructing the tree
2: **P_node:** For each CH node their will be an parent node
3: **P_node:** For each CH node their will be an parent node
4: **C_node:** Child node j, in For each CH node their will be an child node
5: **if** (Initiator _node=TRUE)
6: $\quad$ **then**
7: $\quad$ P_node$_i \leftarrow (Id_i)$
8: $\quad$ br_1$< T\_msg, Id_i,$ P_node$_i >$
9: **end if**
10: Any CH_j receives T_msg from any CH_i
11: **if** $(Id_j == P_node_i)$ **then**
12: $\quad$ $C\_node(j) \leftarrow C\_node(j) \cup Id_i$
13: **else**
14: $\quad$ **if** (Parent_selected$_j$=FALSE)
15: $\quad\quad$ **then**
16: $\quad\quad$ Br_1$< T\_msg, Id_j, Parent\_node >$
17: $\quad\quad$ **else**
18: $\quad\quad$ Packet drop
19: $\quad\quad$ **end if**
20: **end if**

4.4   Cluster Steady Phase

Cluster steady phase corresponds to the data transmission and aggregation.

1. In this phase all NonCH nodes send its data towards corresponding primary CH.
2. PCH nodes schedules the communication of NonCH nodes with itself based on TDMA.
3. If the energy consumption NonCH nodes are less then the transmitter will be switched off.
4. All the Primary CH aggregates the data which are received from the NonCH nodes.
5. CHs finally transmits the data to their CH based on the tree formation.
6. Now CH parent will send their data to the Base station.

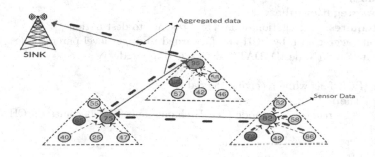

Fig. 5. Aggregation and transmission of data

4.4.1   Data Aggregation and Transmission

After tree construction, each NonCH nodes send the data to its designated PCH node and then PCH combines data which is received and send them towards upper level parent node until it reaches to the sink node. Figure 5 shows how data is forwarded towards sink node.

5   Simulation Settings

The proposed work, has been evaluated in $NS-2$ simulator. The simulation has been carried out in an terrain size of 100 * 100 m, with 120 number of nodes has been considered with DSDV as routing protocol and different parameters accounted during simulation are shown in the Table 2.

5.1   Results and Discussion

Proposed DCHSA consists of cluster based and tree based data aggregations and compared with QADA [9], TREEPSI [10] protocols.

Algorithm 3. Aggregation and Transmission of Data

1: **procedure**
2:    | **Collection phase**
3:    | **Requires:** PCH node collects data from Non sensor node
4:    | NonCH node send data (Node_ID,DATA,datasize) in TDMA frame
5:    |
6:    | **if** (No data to send)
7:    | **then**
8:    | Goes to sleep mode
9:    |
10:   | **end if**
11:   | **if** (Node_ID = current PCH)
12:   | **then**
13:   | PCH go to sleep mode
14:   |
15:   | **end if**
        Aggregation phase
16:   | **Requires:** Aggregation of data and reaches to destination
17:   | Data aggregation by PCH and forwarded to upper level parent node
18:   | Data Send (Node_ID, DATA, data size, Parent_ID)
19:   |
20:   | **if** (PCH fails while receiving the data)
21:   | **then**
22:   | PCH request Sink node for CH change and SCH becomes an CH for that round
23:   | |
24:   | **end if**
25:   | **if** (PCH_ID = Parent_ID) **then**
26:   |
27:   | PCH enters sleep mode
28:   |
29:   | **end if**
30:   |
31:   | PCH sends data towards upper level parent node until data reaches to the sink node
32:   |
33: **end procedure**

5.1.1 Energy Dissipation over Time

The DCHSA, QADA and TREEPSI protocols were examined and compared on energy consumption basis of sink as shown in Fig. 6 and Fig. 7. In DCHSA scheme the distance communication between CH and sink decreases so that energy dissipation decreases. In QADA and TREEPSI protocols energy dissipation increases with increasing time. QADA dissipates more energy due to homogeneous network. TREEPSI consumes more energy than QADA by reducing the distance between CH and the base station.

Table 2. Simulation parameters

Metrics	Value
Nodes used	120
Area	100 * 100 m
Protocol in routing	DSDV
MAC type	802.11
Transmission range (m)	250
Time duration	20 s
Delay while data processing	25
Size of the packet	500 Bytes
Antenna type	Omni Antenna
Model for mobility	Random wave point
Nodes initial energy	100 J

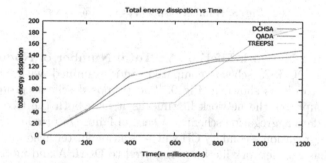

Fig. 6. Total energy dissipation vs time

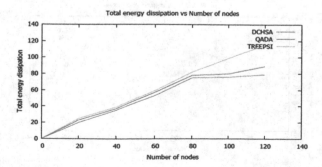

Fig. 7. Total energy dissipation vs number of nodes

5.1.2   Number of Packets Reached at Sink Node

The proposed scheme DCHSA, QADA and TREEPSI protocols were examined and compared with the total packets received at the sink node which is shown in Fig. 8. As per the results, the number of packets reached in the DCHSA is less than that of QADA and TREEPSI models as it reduces operation of CH and energy is exhausted. In the proposed protocol data aggregation which removes the duplicate data and send to the base station conserves energy.

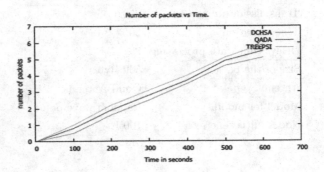

Fig. 8. Number of packets vs time

5.1.3   Varying Network Lifetime Vs Total Number of Nodes

The proposed DCHSA scheme compared and examined with QADA and TREEPSI protocols as shown in Fig. 9. The proposed scheme protocol which significantly improves the network lifetime as it uses both the tree based and cluster based data aggregation scheme. In case of failure of primary cluster head during data aggregation secondary CH will acts as an cluster head for that round. The QADA has less network lifetime compared to DCHSA and more than that of TREEPSI protocol due to lack of fault tolerance mechanism and TREEPSI has less network lifetime compared with DCHSA and QADA.

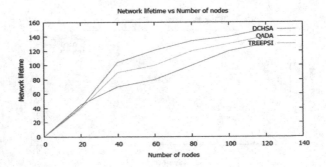

Fig. 9. Lifetime of network vs nodes number

6 Conclusion

DCHSA scheme is proposed in this work in context to improve IoT network lifetime by classifying cluster into PCH and SCH. The cluster-based scheme maximizes the network lifetime by selecting the highest energy nodes as a primary CH node and also by selecting secondary cluster head in the failure of primary CH. Reduction in power consumption results due to tree based scheme, which reduces distance between CH and Base station. Results obtained by simulations concludes that DCHSA provides improved performances than the QADA & TREEPSI protocol on network lifetime, power consumption and packet delivery. Future work in terms of enhancing proposed work is by providing security and fault tolerance in routing.

Acknowledgment. This research work has been funded by the Science and Engineering Research Board (SERB-DST) Project File No: EEQ/2017/000681.

References

1. Adya, A., Sharma, K.P., et al.: Energy aware clustering based mobility model for FANETs. In: Singh, P., Panigrahi, B., Suryadevara, N., Sharma, S., Singh, A. (eds.) Proceedings of ICETIT 2019, pp. 36–47. Springer, Cham (2020). https://doi.org/10.1007/978-3-030-30577-2_3
2. Gupta, G., Younis, M.: Fault-tolerant clustering of wireless sensor networks. In: 2003 IEEE Wireless Communications and Networking, 2003. WCNC 2003, vol. 3, pp. 1579–1584. IEEE (2003)
3. Heinzelman, W.R., Chandrakasan, A., Balakrishnan, H.: Energy-efficient communication protocol for wireless microsensor networks. In: Proceedings of the 33rd Annual Hawaii International Conference on System Sciences, pp. 10–16. IEEE (2000)
4. Kaur, S., Mahajan, R.: Hybrid meta-heuristic optimization based energy efficient protocol for wireless sensor networks. Egypt. Inform. J. **19**(3), 145–150 (2018)
5. Liu, G., Huang, L., Xu, H., Xu, X., Wang, Y.: Energy-efficient tree-based cooperative data aggregation for wireless sensor networks. Int. J. Sens. Netw. **13**(2), 65–75 (2013)
6. Liu, M., Cao, J., Chen, G., Wang, X.: An energy-aware routing protocol in wireless sensor networks. Sensors **9**(1), 445–462 (2009)
7. Mantri, D., Prasad, N.R., Prasad, R., Ohmori, S.: Two tier cluster based data aggregation (TTCDA) in wireless sensor network. In: 2012 IEEE International Conference on Advanced Networks and Telecommunciations Systems (ANTS), pp. 117–122. IEEE (2012)
8. Negi, A.S., Garg, N., Singh, A.P.: Role of clustering in achieving energy efficient coverage in wireless sensor network: a short review. Int. Res. J. Eng. Technol. (IRJET) **2**(02) (2015)
9. Rahman, H., Ahmed, N., Hussain, M.I.: A QoS-aware hybrid data aggregation scheme for Internet of Things. Ann. Telecommun. **73**(7–8), 475–486 (2018). https://doi.org/10.1007/s12243-018-0646-3
10. Satapathy, S.S., Sarma, N.: TREEPSI: tree based energy efficient protocol for sensor information. In: 2006 IFIP International Conference on Wireless and Optical Communications Networks, p. 4. IEEE (2006)

11. Srinidhi, N., Nagarjun, E., Kumar, S.D.: HMCRA: hybrid multi-copy routing algorithm for opportunistic IoT network. In: 2019 International Conference on Smart Systems and Inventive Technology (ICSSIT), pp. 370–375. IEEE (2019)
12. Srinidhi, N.N., Sagar, C.S., Deepak Chethan, S., Shreyas, J., Dilip Kumar, S.M.: Machine learning based efficient multi-copy routing for OppIoT networks. In: Saha, A., Kar, N., Deb, S. (eds.) ICCISIoT 2019. CCIS, vol. 1192, pp. 288–302. Springer, Singapore (2020). https://doi.org/10.1007/978-981-15-3666-3_24
13. Srinidhi, N., Sunitha, G., Nagarjun, E., Shreyas, J., Kumar, S.D.: Lifetime maximization of IoT network by optimizing routing energy. In: 2019 IEEE International WIE Conference on Electrical and Computer Engineering (WIECON-ECE), pp. 1–4 (2019)
14. Velmani, R., Kaarthick, B.: An energy efficient data gathering in dense mobile wireless sensor networks. ISRN Sens. Netw. **2014** (2014)

Wireless Networks and Internet of Things (IoT)

A Hybrid Metaheuristic to Solve Capacitated Vehicle Routing Problem

Prahlad Bhadani[1]([✉]), Kamakshi Puri[1], Ankur Choudhary[2], Arun Prakash Agrawal[2], and Neha Agarwal[1]

[1] Amity University, Noida, Uttar Pradesh, India
[2] Sharda University, Greater Noida, India
{ankur.choudhary,arun.agrawal}@sharda.ac.in

Abstract. Many real life problems that play a major role in human lives are mostly optimization problems and need to be solved in order to judiciously utilize vital resources. The vast solution space consists of a large number of feasible solutions. Solving these problems requires finding the most optimal solution while satisfying the constraints imposed (if any). Vehicle Routing is a real life problem originated primarily in the logistics industry where the consignments are to be delivered to the clients in such a way, that there is minimal usage of resources like fuel, and time. In addition, the consignments are to be successfully delivered to the clients through the shortest route and utilizing the maximum capacity of each vehicle. Automation is the key to solve such large problems while reducing effort and complexity of the solution. Literature reveals that nature inspired algorithms have proved their ability for solving such large complex optimization problems. These algorithms are inspired from various natural phenomena and are supported by their successful survival. This paper proposes a hybrid framework to solve Vehicle Routing Problem (VRP) utilizing Differential Evolution and Marine Predators algorithm. We have considered the variant called Capacitated Vehicle Routing Problem (CVRP) to conduct experiments and compared the results to evaluate the performance of proposed hybrid approach DEMPA with Differential Evolution (DE). Results indicate the superiority of the proposed approach over Differential Evolution.

Keywords: Optimization · Solution Space · Vehicle Routing Problem · Nature Inspired Algorithms · Differential Evolution · Marine Predator Algorithm · Brute-force · Capacitated VRP

1 Introduction

Vehicle Routing Problem (VRP) is a generalized version of most studied Travelling Salesman Problem and was introduced first in 1959 by Dantzig et al. [1] where they attempted to solve petrol delivery problem. It requires finding the optimal path for the set of deliveries to be made. Being an N-P hard problem, here the objective is to minimize the cost in terms of distance travelled by the vehicle. This can be achieved by finding an optimal route from source to multiple destinations and then back to the source station.

© Springer Nature Singapore Pte Ltd. 2021
P. K. Singh et al. (Eds.): FTNCT 2020, CCIS 1396, pp. 169–180, 2021.
https://doi.org/10.1007/978-981-16-1483-5_16

This problem can also be formulated in other words as finding a Hamiltonian cycle which is a closed loop graph and describes the path actually traversed by the vehicle to optimize the cost (distance travelled). Each depot is represented as a node in the graph. Each node in the graph needs to be visited only once except the starting node which is traversed first and last.

There are other variants of the problems also where there can be a single-depot for the vehicles from where pickup and delivery is performed or there can be multiple depots for one or many vehicles.

Here in this paper, we will discuss single – depot VRP in detail. Fig. 1 shows the basic route map for a state of the VRP. The black dots represent the various nodes, or cities (application specific). The hollow square in the center shows the depot from which the vehicles originate and return after their circuit is completed. The line segments connecting these nodes represents the path chosen by the vehicles to reach a specific node. It basically is a set of more than one Hamiltonian paths.

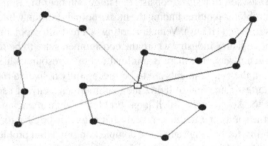

Fig. 1. Illustration of the vehicle routing problem

2   Related Work

- Yeun et al. (2008) [2] conducted a study that sought to define the theoretical and mathematical formulation of VRP and its variants i.e. Classical VRP, CVRP, VRP with Time Windows and also with Pick-up and Delivery. It also discussed the algorithms being used to optimize the same.
- Kromer et al. (2013) [3] carried out an experimental study which works upon using an evolutionary algorithm i.e. Differential Evolution (DE) to optimize a variant of the VRP which is the Stochastic VRP with Real Simultaneous Pickup and Delivery and a set of CVRP. The evolution of the model designed is evaluated using a fitness function and the required crossover, mutation and selection was performed to obtain the desired results.
- Gomez and Salhi (2014) [4] solved the CVRP by artificial bee colony algorithm. They approach of a bee colony to efficiently handle the coordinated tasks and focus on group work. It simulates the behavior of a colony of bees where it is led by the queen bee.

- Stodola et al. (2014) [5] used the Ant Colony Optimization Algorithm to solve the CVRP. The ant colony is also a nature inspired metaheuristic that simulates the behavior of how the ants gather their food. They used the benchmark instances of Christofides, Mingozzi and Toth. Instances here mean datasets.
- Nazif and Lee (2012) [6] optimized the crossover Genetic Algorithm to solve the CVRP. The genetic algorithm is based on how living beings acquire their traits and characteristics. This algorithm has been tested on benchmark instances and the results have been compared.
- Faramarzi et al. (2020) [7] introduced the Marine Predators Algorithm (MPA) which is inspired by the movement in the predators of the ocean. MPA's performance is evaluated on 29 test functions, the test suite of CEC-BC-2017, 3 benchmark problems of engineering and 2 real-world engineering design problems. The performance of MPA was then compared with pre-existing meta-heuristic algorithms.

3 Metaheuristics

According to Sörensen and Glover, "A metaheuristic is a high-level problem-independent algorithmic framework that provides a set of guidelines or strategies to develop heuristic optimization algorithms [8]".

A metaheuristic may find a good solution to an optimization problem under conditions of limited processing power or resources as it samples sets of data that is too large to be sampled in a single pass. The fact that metaheuristics make some assumptions before solving the optimization problem makes it problem independent and hence a very popular method for solving optimization problems. Although metaheuristics do not guarantee a globally optimal solution for the problem under study, it usually finds reasonably good solutions. Researchers may combine the metaheuristic with other metaheuristics to tune parameters and get improve convergence.

Metaheuristics are majorly classified into the following categories based upon the various properties they exhibit [9]:

- Local vs. Global Search Methods:

  The search strategy of a metaheuristic can be Local or Global. Local search strategy focuses on finding the local minima/maxima (collectively referred to as optima) of the optimization problem and hence does not guarantee the global optima.

- Single Solution vs. Population Based:

  Some metaheuristics are single solution based i.e. they keep on improving a single solution iteratively to get to the optimum whereas population based techniques work on improving a collection of solutions.

- Hybrid vs. Memetic Approach:

  Hybrid Approach involves the combination of both metaheuristic and mathematical algorithms to guide the search, whereas memetic approach involves the combination of local search methods with some population based approach to guide the search process.

- Nature inspired metaheuristics:

  Algorithms like Genetic Algorithm take inspiration from living beings and how their DNA are programmed to produce a particular human being. Particle Swarm Optimization is inspired from how a swarm of birds approaches a food particle and Simulated Annealing is inspired from the process of strengthening the metal by heating and cooling it.

4 Capacitated VRP

The case discussed here is **Capacitated Vehicle Routing Problem (CVRP).** Let $G = \{V. E\}$ is a graph (undirected) where V is the set of vertices $(n + 1)$ between $(0, n)$ and E is the set of edges. The initial vertex O represents the depot and as we are discussing single – depot problems so all the vehicles will start their journey from this point i.e. O. An initial cost, say d_{ij} is associated with each edge. Each vehicle holds a particular capacity, say m which is uniform throughout the journey [10, 11].

Feasibility: The feasibility of solution lies in the condition that the uniform capacity of each vehicle should not be exceeded at any point during the vehicle's journey and subsequent delivery.

Aim: The main objective of this type of optimization problem is to obtain the best cost (i.e. minimum time to complete the deliveries) without violating the conditions for the hard constraint of uniform capacity not being exceeded.

The CVRP can be mathematically formulated as (Fukasawa et al. 2004) [12, 13]:

$$Minimise \sum\nolimits_{e=(u,v)\in A} d(e)x_e \tag{1}$$

Subject to:

$$\sum\nolimits_{e\in\delta(\{v\})} x_e = 2, \forall u \in N\setminus\{0\}, \tag{2}$$

$$\sum\nolimits_{e\in\delta(\{v\})} x_e \geq 2k^*, \tag{3}$$

$$\sum\nolimits_{e\in\delta(\{S\})} x_e \geq 2k(S), \forall S \in N\setminus\{0\}, \tag{4}$$

$$x_e \leq 1, \forall e \in A\setminus\delta(\{0\}), \tag{5}$$

$$\sum_{l=1}^{p} q_l^e \lambda_l - x_e = 0, \forall e \in A, \tag{6}$$

$$x_e \in \{0, 1, 2\}, \forall e \in A, \tag{7}$$

$$\lambda_l \geq 0 \forall l \in \{1, \ldots, p\}. \tag{8}$$

Where:

x_e is the frequency of travel on edge 'e' by the vehicle.

λ_l variables are allied to a group of all routes fulfilling the vehicle capacity constraint. A route is a walk that is initiated from the depot, travels to a series of clients with maximum collective demand Q, and finally returns to the depot.

5 Algorithms Used

5.1 Differential Evolution

The Differential Evolution algorithm, popularly known, as DE is an evolutionary meta-heuristic algorithm. As mentioned above, DE tries to improve upon a candidate solution iteratively as long as it converges to the optima. It does not guarantee to find an optimal solution as metaheuristics are problem independent, which may be considered as both an advantage and a disadvantage [14, 15].

It is a population based algorithm that is used to solve optimization problems that fall in the nonlinear category. Storn and Price introduced it in 1996 [16]. Figure 2 illustrates the flow of evolutionary algorithms.

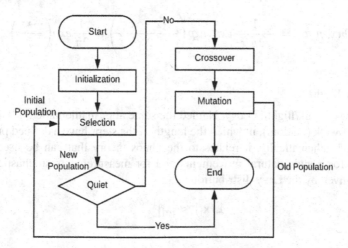

Fig. 2. Flow of differential evolution algorithm [14]

Steps for DE algorithm:

1. Initialize Population: The initial population for most of the Evolutionary Algorithms is generated randomly and is between an upper and a lower bound.
2. Mutation: For each parameter vector, we choose three other vectors randomly and add the third vector to the weighted difference of the other two vectors.
3. Recombination: Using the donor vector and the target vector, we develop a trial vector.
4. Selection: The target and the trial vector are compared and the one, which has the lowest function value, is selected.

5.2 Differential Evolution

As Darwin's theory suggests 'Survival of the fittest', so in order to live in the wildlife, the predators need to hunt their prey and gather food. Like land, water bodies also have a wide range of species of autotrophs and heterotrophs. Here in this algorithm basically the walk of the predators are analyzed which suggest search strategies based on the current location and how to go to the next position in order to reach the prey i.e. final destination [7].

5.2.1 Brownian Movement

Derived from the Brownian motion, which is a non-uniform, irregular motion of particles when left suspended in a fluid, this movement defines the random walk of predators in search of food. Here the step length, say of the predator in this case, is the probability function of a normal distribution where the mean is 0 and the variance is 1. The probability density function is defined by (Einstein 1956):

$$fb(x; \mu, \sigma) = \frac{1}{\sqrt{2\pi\sigma^2}} exp\ exp\left(-\frac{(x-\mu)^2}{2\sigma^2}\right) = \frac{1}{2\pi} exp\left(\frac{-x^2}{2}\right) \qquad (9)$$

5.2.2 Levy Flight

Another type of walk/flight is Levy. Named the same after mathematician 'Paul Lévy', it is a type of walk (random), in which the length of the steps have a defined probability distribution. Mathematically, it relates to the chaos theory that can be used to form simulations for pseudo-natural movements and for measurements stochastically. The step size is given by the Levy distribution:

$$L(x_j) \approx |x_j|^{1-\alpha} \qquad (10)$$

6 Methodology

We have tried to develop a hybrid metaheuristic by optimizing the DE with MPA. In simple terms, there are two optimization problems being solved in this framework:

1. The problem of finding optimal parameters for DE algorithm.
2. The Vehicle Routing Problem

MPA solves the first problem and Differential Evolution Algorithm solves the second one. Figure 3 shows the flowchart used for the framework.

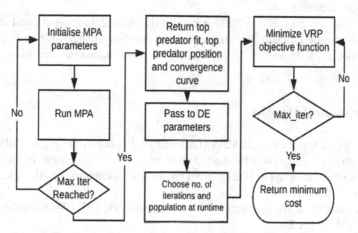

Fig. 3. Flowchart for Hybrid Metaheuristic

6.1 Functionality of MPA

Each metaheuristic has some initialization parameters that decide the performance of the algorithm. One of the most important problem is to find an optimal combination of initialization parameters that lead to a good result. The MPA here is assigned the job of finding the good combination of initialization parameters.

We have converted the MPA algorithm into a function that takes as argument, the number of search agents, maximum number of iterations, the lower and upper bound of decision variables, dimension of objective function, the objective function itself and the model structure. It returns the top predator fit, the top predator position and the convergence curve [17].

Using these returned values, we optimize the DE parameters. The working of MPA has been discussed above. The parameters of the DE are acting as the decision variables here. The decision variables of any optimization problem are the number of unknown values that have to be optimally found out.

6.2 Functionality of DE

DE has been converted to a function that returns the best cost of the VRP. The number of search agents, lower and upper bound of scaling factor, crossover probability and the model structure are supplied as arguments to the function and that returns the best cost for the corresponding VRP model [11].

6.3 Main Function

We first set some parameters like the maximum iterations and population for DE. Then, get the lower and upper bound, dimensions and the name of the objective function. Afterwards, it calls the MPA with appropriate call structure passing arguments and gets the required values. These values are then passed to DE and the program runs 15 times. The results are recorded.

The DE runs for 500, 800 or 1000 iterations depending upon what combination of parameters is returned. In addition, the population size also changes during runtime and switches between 25, 35 and 45. Multiple combination of parameters are tried to get the best results.

7   Experimental Results

As the developed framework DEMPA (Differential Evolution guided by MPA) gives better results i.e. smaller values for the best cost or least best cost, it can be said that the performance of the simple DE (Differential Evolution) is enhanced as the optimization is done more efficiently [18].

The least as well as the greatest cost for our framework, DEMPA is smaller in value than that of the simple DE.

The results further prove that optimizing the same problem with pre-existing meta-heuristic DE costs more on average as well as on a single run than the developed hybrid meta-heuristic DEMPA. Figure 4 shows the difference in the best and worst case values for DE and DEMPA (Tables 1, 2 and 3).

MODEL 50×7		
RUNS	**DE**	**DEMPA**
1	619.0505975	590.1338667
2	671.6037683	629.867512
3	621.9684539	644.2949014
4	669.958604	633.6395283
5	683.0938364	632.5450503
6	651.5325112	633.7650221
7	656.1058995	658.1686235
8	681.8432085	627.3253069
9	666.6405333	636.0089229
10	668.018899	629.4836619
11	667.8144811	645.0977703
12	664.0656509	658.0759657
13	638.3706644	632.1578391
14	622.7825623	646.7257164
15	671.3820173	610.0380826
Average =	**656.9487792**	**633.8218513**

Fig. 4. Comparison of values between the frameworks

Table 1. Comparison of DE and DEMPA on models 10 × 3, 14 × 4, 18 × 4

RUNS	MODEL 10 × 3		MODEL 14 × 4		MODEL 18 × 4	
	DE	DEMPA	DE	DEMPA	DE	DEMPA
1	284.979	284.979	276.352	275.402	260.673	259.808
2	284.979	284.979	275.525	275.529	261.854	257.627
3	284.979	284.979	275.402	276.526	265.256	257.202
4	284.979	284.979	275.652	275.529	258.234	260.583
5	284.979	285.26	277.055	275.947	261.983	261.677
6	284.979	284.979	276.201	276.201	264.21	257.512
7	284.979	284.979	278.059	275.402	259.946	257.512
8	284.979	284.979	276.327	275.529	261.456	259.31
9	284.979	284.979	276.327	275.402	264.79	260.583
10	284.979	284.979	277.055	276.566	263.037	258.362
11	284.979	284.979	276.201	275.402	264.243	257.644
12	284.979	284.979	277.055	275.402	266.157	261.048
13	284.979	284.979	275.663	275.529	270.576	257.512
14	284.979	285.26	276.201	276.07	266.343	266.037
15	284.979	284.979	276.327	275.402	261.948	257.512
AVG	**284.979**	**285.017**	**276.36**	**275.723**	**263.38**	**259.328**

Table 2. Comparison of DE and DEMPA on models 20 × 4, 25 × 5, 27 × 5

RUNS	MODEL 20 × 4		MODEL 25 × 5		MODEL 27 × 5	
	DE	DEMPA	DE	DEMPA	DE	DEMPA
1	358.106	351.425	364.549	338.946	358.557	352.248
2	355.693	357.892	353.637	343.333	360.572	353.369
3	359.291	345.662	354.312	341.842	370.645	371.895
4	366.261	354.865	357.366	344.216	360.791	365.085
5	367.84	349.969	347.058	348.777	363.486	356.169
6	362.891	337.034	346.733	356.603	370.965	355.438
7	352.997	349.2	396.418	346.327	344.217	364.279
8	364.493	356.842	384.556	351.226	353.922	355.4
9	347.984	357.003	384.604	351.604	367.498	352.506
10	353.676	342.897	379.48	347.596	368.041	352.37
11	362.861	356.542	354.002	342.824	372.414	350.969
12	359.457	357.476	354.134	361.577	359.181	349.326
13	351.942	351.513	372.366	368.425	359.607	361.322
14	365.203	348.843	371.295	353.027	371.611	350.198
15	362.294	343.456	377.385	336.776	357.835	354.144
AVG	**359.399**	**350.708**	**366.526**	**348.873**	**362.623**	**356.314**

Table 3. Comparison of DE and DEMPA on models 30 × 5, 40 × 6, 50 × 7

RUNS	MODEL 30 × 5		MODEL 40 × 6		MODEL 50 × 7	
	DE	DEMPA	DE	DEMPA	DE	DEMPA
1	435.526	448.167	571.028	546.117	619.051	590.134
2	430.157	443.36	567.704	554.522	671.604	629.868
3	467.713	414.672	566.012	547.664	621.968	644.295
4	483.673	441.737	552.647	545.136	669.959	633.64
5	447.665	434.132	589.458	534.294	683.094	632.545
6	473.207	410.569	512.082	526.279	651.533	633.765
7	449.431	384.346	568.307	544.884	656.106	658.169
8	458.069	421.817	572.5	560.943	681.843	627.325
9	440.284	412.284	528.499	523.455	666.641	636.009
10	448.277	426.094	592.86	518.983	668.019	629.484
11	438.949	447.324	567.256	505.026	667.814	645.098
12	445.122	433.087	588.285	513.676	664.066	658.076
13	426.551	432.272	547.484	533.204	638.371	632.158
14	463.174	434.562	553.455	551.219	622.783	646.726
15	470.022	445.514	577.397	546.951	671.382	610.038
AVG	**451.855**	**428.663**	**563.665**	**536.823**	**656.949**	**633.822**

8 Conclusion

From the above study, it can be inferred that a hybrid technique consisting of two or more algorithms can yield better results as compared to a single meta-heuristic technique [19]. As in case of a hybrid meta-heuristic, the shortcomings of one algorithm are fulfilled by another.

DE is itself a very efficient algorithm to optimize the VRP, but the initial parameters are set to certain values at the beginning of execution and they remain constant throughout the process. Had the parameters been tuned after each iteration, the results i.e. best cost and position would be more optimized for the given vehicles and their journeys.

By creating a hybrid of DE and MPA named DEMPA, the parameters of DE are tuned by MPA at each iteration and hence, instead of a set of pre-defined parameter values, a combination of refined parameter values are used to optimize the CVRP. This is the reason why the best cost and position values are more optimized in case of DEMPA.

9 Future Work

We can develop a multi-level architecture with a number of metaheuristic algorithms on the lower level that optimize the initialization parameters of the upper level meta-heuristic during the runtime [20]. This helps in refining the parameters which in turn produce more optimal results. Even though the process is more intensive, the outcome is far more efficient in case of larger models as compared to a simple meta-heuristic algorithm [21].

The framework in this project has only been applied to one variant of the VRP. It can be applied to other variants with Time Windows, simultaneous Pickup and delivery or one-way (Open) VRP.

Similarly, hybrid can be created with other meta-heuristic algorithms and can be checked for efficiency by optimizing benchmark and other optimization problems [22].

References

1. Dantzig, G., Ramser, J.: The truck dispatching problem. Manage. Sci. **6**, 80–91 (1959)
2. Zirour, M., Oughalime, A., Liong, C.-Y., Ismail, W.R., Omar, K.: A model for routing problem in quay management problem (2014)
3. Kromer, P., Abraham, A., Snasel, V., Berhan, E., Kitaw, D.: On the differential evolution for vehicle routing problem. In: 2013 International Conference on Soft Computing and Pattern Recognition (SoCPaR) (2013)
4. Gomez, A., Salhi, S.: Solving capacitated vehicle routing problem by artificial bee colony algorithm. In: 2014 IEEE Symposium on Computational Intelligence in Production and Logistics Systems (CIPLS) (2014)
5. Stodola, P., Mazal, J., Podhorec, M., Litvaj, O.: Using the ant colony optimization algorithm for the capacitated vehicle routing problem. In: Proceedings of the 16th International Conference on Mechatronics - Mechatronika (2014)
6. Nazif, H., Lee, L.S.: Optimised crossover genetic algorithm for capacitated vehicle routing problem. Appl. Math. Model. **36**, 2110–2117 (2012)
7. Faramarzı, A., Heidarinejad, M., Mirjalili, S., Gandomi, A.H.: Marine predators algorithm: A nature-inspired metaheuristic. Expert Syst. Appl. **152**, 113377 (2020)
8. Talbi, E.-G.: Metaheuristics: From Design to Implementation. Wiley, Hoboken (2009)
9. Blum, C., Roli, A.: Metaheuristics in combinatorial optimization. ACM Comput. Surv. **35**, 268–308 (2003)
10. Lei, J.-J., Li, J.: Solving capacitated vehicle routing problems by modified differential evolution. In: 2010 2nd International Asia Conference on Informatics in Control, Automation and Robotics (CAR 2010) (2010)
11. Jian, L.: Solving capacitated vehicle routing problems via genetic particle swarm optimization. In: 2009 Third International Symposium on Intelligent Information Technology Application (2009)
12. Fukasawa, R., Lysgaard, J., Poggi de Aragão, M., Reis, M., Uchoa, E., Werneck, R.F.: Robust branch-and-cut-and-price for the capacitated vehicle routing problem. In: Bienstock, D., Nemhauser, G. (eds.) IPCO 2004. LNCS, vol. 3064, pp. 1–15. Springer, Heidelberg (2004). https://doi.org/10.1007/978-3-540-25960-2_1
13. Liong, C.Y., Ismail, W.R., Omar, K., Zirour, M.: Vehicle routing problem: models and solutions. J. Qual. Meas. Anal. **4**, 205–218 (2011)
14. Teoh, B.E., Ponnambalam, S., Kanagaraj, G.: Differential evolution algorithm with local search for capacitated vehicle routing problem. Int. J. Bio-Inspired Comput. **7**, 321 (2015)
15. Silva, A.L., Ramírez, J.A., Campelo, F.: A statistical study of discrete differential evolution approaches for the capacitated vehicle routing problem. In: Proceeding of the Fifteenth Annual Conference Companion on Genetic and Evolutionary Computation Conference Companion - GECCO 2013 Companion (2013)

16. Storn, R., Price, K.: Differential evolution – a simple and efficient heuristic for global optimization over continuous spaces. J. Global Optim. **11**, 341–359 (1997). https://doi.org/10.1023/A:1008202821328

17. Capacitated Vehicle Routing Problem (VRP) using SA - Yarpiz, https://yarpiz.com/372/ypap108-vehicle-routing-problem

18. Pu, E., Wang, F., Yang, Z., Wang, J., Li, Z., Huang, X.: Hybrid differential evolution optimization for the vehicle routing problem with time windows and driver-specific times. Wireless Pers. Commun. **95**(3), 2345–2357 (2017). https://doi.org/10.1007/s11277-017-4107-5

19. Blum, C., Puchinger, J., Raidl, G.R., Roli, A.: Hybrid metaheuristics in combinatorial optimization: a survey. Appl. Soft Comput. **11**, 4135–4151 (2011)

20. Garrido, P., Castro, C.: Stable solving of CVRPs using hyperheuristics. In: Proceedings of the 11th Annual conference on Genetic and evolutionary computation - GECCO 2009 (2009)

21. Kumar, Y., Singh, P.K.: A chaotic teaching learning based optimization algorithm for clustering problems. Appl. Intell. **49**(3), 1036–1062 (2018). https://doi.org/10.1007/s10489-018-1301-4

22. Abdel-Basset, M., Mohamed, R., Elhoseny, M., Chakrabortty, R.K., Ryan, M.: A hybrid COVID-19 detection model using an improved marine predators algorithm and a ranking-based diversity reduction strategy. IEEE Access. **8**, 79521–79540 (2020)

Energy Conservation in IOT: A Survey

Kartik Aggarwal[✉] and Nihar Ranjan Roy[✉]

GD Goenka School of Engineering, Gurugram, India

Abstract. Internet of things (IoT) basically refers to anything that is connected with the internet. IoT is one of the emerging technologies which acts as a bridge between the physical and cyber world. There are many places where the data collection is important but continuous supply of energy is not possible. Energy consumption is one of the most important issues faced in the IoT devices which are battery operated. This paper addresses such issues and techniques for energy conservation. In this paper we have discussed various sources of energy dissipation, causes for energy dissipation and their solutions. We have also surveyed some of the mile stone papers in the area of energy conservation along with the latest protocols. We have critically analyzed and tabulated our findings.

Keywords: Energy efficiency · Energy harvesting · Energy conservation · IoT

1 Introduction

Any device connected to internet is IoT device. This new era of IoT devices (smart watches, smart phones, voice assistants, etc.) have the capability to serve human needs in an efficient manner. IoT is the network of physical devices and other items embedded with sensors, electronics, actuators, software, and network connectivity which enables these objects to collect, exchange data and help in analysis. It is a global infrastructure for information society which enables advanced services by connecting objects to the internet. The vision of IoT is making almost every object connect to internet which can collect the data and provide the data for analyzing, optimizing and controlling.

IOT plays an important role in energy sector. Trains and aeroplanes have been using IoT since a long time, IoT based intelligent transportation system are designed to support the vision of smart city. Environmental monitoring, modelling and management helps us to get a close understanding of natural environmental processes. Many industries such as construction industry being the least digitalized sector in the world, the current trend is bending towards smart construction (Patel et al. 2019) where machinery, components and devices are linked with technologies in order to get insights about the structure, strength and architecture. Application of IoT in medical and health sector includes (Ahmmad et al. 2020a) patient surveillance, chronic disease management, UV radiation, sleep control, dental health, medical fridges, etc. Home Automation (Ahmmad et al. 2020b) provides more comfort, as most of the things get automated.

Energy efficiency in IoT are very important. Energy consumption is one of the most important issues faced as the IoT devices are battery constrained and not fully

© Springer Nature Singapore Pte Ltd. 2021
P. K. Singh et al. (Eds.): FTNCT 2020, CCIS 1396, pp. 181–193, 2021.
https://doi.org/10.1007/978-981-16-1483-5_17

self- dependent. Also, there is no such battery which can support a device for lifetime, therefore, there is an emerging demand to overcome this problem. Also, seeing the applications of Iot, this problem cannot be ignored. The energy is dissipated in various forms and there are a lot of issues in energy conservation.

The paper goes with Sect. 2 consisting the IoT architecture wherein all the three layers of architecture will be discussed. The two techniques used to extend the lifespan of an IoT device is energy conservation and energy harvesting which is discussed in Sect. 3 i.e. green Iot. Ways of harvesting (Shaikh and Sherali 2016) energy from external sources is also discussed in this section. It is important to address the sources of energy dissipation as discussed in Sect. 4 to counter the energy conservation problems. The main core of this paper is to understand the need to and use that energy in a very conservative manner without compromising the efficiency of the IoT devices. Various techniques are introduced which come with their advantages and disadvantages as discussed in Sect. 5. Various clustering methods (Cacciagrano et al. 2019) and wireless sensor network protocols are discussed which can be used in wireless sensor networks to conserve energy followed by the conclusion in Sect. 6 and references in Sect. 7. Also, it may provide help in the direction for the future clustering techniques or protocols to expand the IoT devices life span.

In this survey, important wireless sensor networks are evaluated which are very much important and is the base of most of the protocols. IoT devices are discussed in depth and with the basic diagram (Fig. 3) that can explain how each protocol works. The routing protocols act on the node management and every protocol tries to work faster and use less energy. This paper provides an overview of the current scenario in the field of routing protocols. The variety of protocols discussed in this paper tells the emergence and time to time improvements done

2 IOT Architecture

In this section we have discussed the most popular architecture of IoT. There are three layers in IoT architecture:

- Device layer (client side)
- Gateway layer (operators on server side)
- Platform layer (pathway for connecting clients and operators)

IoT architecture (Rafiullah et al. 2012) include functionality, availability, scalability and maintainability. The IoT ecosystem has five horizontal layers that are essential elements which is common to all IoT use-cases.

1. Sensors and Actuators
2. Gateway device to integrate and transmit data via network
3. Communication network to exchange data
4. Software for data analysis and translation
5. End application service

Now elaborating each and every part of ecosystem (Gaurav and Jain 2016) would include.

Stage 1. Network Physical Devices and Actuators

The lowest layer of IoT Eco-system includes sensors. There are basically two types of sensors, active sensors and passive sensors. The first i.e. active, requires an additional external power source for monitoring event environment while passive ones do not require a power source to operate. An important IoT concept, Edge Intelligence, which is to allow low latency reaction to field events and to allow higher levels of autonomy and distributed processing, needs to be implemented at this layer.

The lowest layer of IoT Eco-system includes sensors. There are basically two types of sensors, active sensors and passive sensors. The first i.e. active, requires an additional external power source for monitoring event environment while passive ones do not require a power source to operate. An important IoT concept, Edge Intelligence, which is to allow low latency reaction to field events and to allow higher levels of autonomy and distributed processing, needs to be implemented at this layer.

Connectivity: We can use many alternatives for communications. This layer includes the mapping of field data to the logical and physical technologies used as well as the backhaul to the on premise or cloud and the next layer, Edge Computing.

Stage 2. Data Aggregation Systems and Data Conversion

Data Accumulation- now the internet gateway and data acquisition come into play. Here it is required to provide incoming data storage for integration, processing, normalization. Basically, the raw data is collected from the sensors and actuators i.e. the previous stage data is squeezed to its optimal size for further analysis. Therefore, here the data is digitalized and aggregated.

Stage 3. Edge IT Systems

Here the data is preprocessed and advanced level analysis is done using edge IT systems. This stage is very close to previous stage. Here the data is prepared or finally processed before entering the data centre.

Stage 4. Storage, Management and Analysis of Data

Coming to the final stage of IoT architecture, the main processes are done in the data Centre or cloud. Now the visualizations are correlations are found in order to use it for predictions making decisions. The data is stored, finally managed and relations are found.

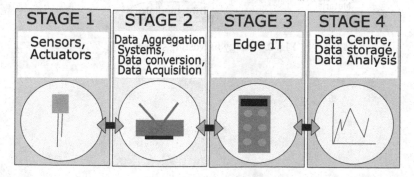

Fig. 1. IoT architecture

3 GREEN IOT: Energy Conservation and Harvesting

There are certain situations where continuous supply of power is not possible and the IoT devices are totally dependent on their battery. Considering those situations, it is very important to conserve the energy and also to harvest energy from external natural resources in order to extend the life of these devices. Green Iot (Albreem et al. 2017) is the that key to unlimited energy.

- Energy Conservation - A technique to save energy in IoT devices and extend their life without compromising their efficiency is called energy conservation. There could be several applications where IoT devices needs to be placed in an unattended environment such as border surveillance in such scenarios it is either difficult or impossible to even change the battery of these devices. Thus, it leaves with one of the possible solutions to use the battery wisely.
- Energy Harvesting - In the current scenario, most of the IoT devices work on battery and no battery has unlimited lifetime, therefore, there is a strong need of self-powered devices or an alternative source of energy that can continuously power the IoT devices. Energy harvesting is the process of capturing energy from renewable source of energy such as solar energy, wind energy etc. and using that form of energy for IoT devices that is usable electrical energy as shown in Fig. 2. Energy harvesters extract the energy from external sources. Then that energy is transferred to transducer which converts that energy into electricity and transfer it to power management system which is initially powered by primary battery. Also, an intermediate battery storage is connected with power management system where the energy is stored and used when required by power management system. Finally, the power management system then transfers the energy to sensors, actuators and micro controllers in order to perform tasks.

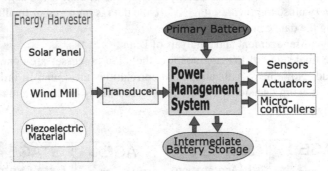

Fig. 2. Energy harvesting system

There are different ways of energy harvesting. Some of them are listed below

a) Solar energy - The most efficient source of environmental energy is the solar energy. Photo-voltaic cells are used to harvest solar energy which are made up of semiconductor material i.e. silicon. To make the solar energy harvester, more efficient, maximum power point tracking (MPPT) controller is used which tracks the voltage and current from solar panel and adjusts the duty cycle accordingly.

b) Wind energy - There are two ways to convert wind energy into electrical energy. In the first method, the wind rotates the turbine piezoelectric material is used to convert that rotational movement into usable electrical energy. Stoppers are placed in order to produce electricity as piezoelectric material require to undergo stress to do so.

c) Thermal energy - It is produced when the rise in temperature causes the atoms and molecules to move at a faster rate and collide against each other. Now this process takes place in thermoelectric generators which contain p type and n type semiconductors where the heat is converted with the Seebeck effect phenomenon. Basically, the temperature difference s attained across a conductor which helps in generating voltage. Thermal diffusion provokes the motion of the charge carrier against temperature difference in conductors.

d) Piezo-electricity - It is the electric charge that is accumulated on certain solid material such as quertz, soft and hard lead ziconate titone piezoceramics, barium titanate etc. in response to applied mechanical stress. This mechanical stress or strain can come from different sources such as how frequency seismic vibrations, acoustic noise etc. the electric charge of dipoles become aligned and leads to net polarization when a crystal is under mechanical stress. This forms an electric potential across the crystal providing electrical oscillation output that can lead to a power source.

e) RFD - It plays an important role in the IoT. Wireless identification and sensing platform can lead to more efficient and less power consumption. There are passive RFD's (Tahiliani and Digalwar 2018) present that extract energy from radio frequency signals which are present around them. Then this energy is stored in the capacitors that can be used for performing task that require more power. The first transmission equation (Nintanavongsa 2014) related power with distance as

$$P_r = P_t G_t G_r \left(\frac{\lambda}{4\pi R}\right)^2$$

Where, P_r = power received
P_t = power transmitted
G_t and G_R are antenna gain
R = distance
λ = wavelength of transmitted signal

A comparative analysis of the about mentioned energy harvesting techniques is presented in Table 1. The major disadvantage of energy harvesting technique is that it increases the cost of the device and size.

Table 1. Comparison of various energy harvesting techniques (Garg and Garg 2017; Adu-Manu et al. 2018)

Energy source	Harvester	Characteristics	Advantages	Disadvantages	Power density
Solar energy	PV panel	Predictable, ambient, uncontrollable	Limitless availability, high output, consistent, eco-friendly, requires little maintenance	Unavailable at night, can be used outdoor only for high output, expensive, takes a lot of space, weather dependent	15 mW/cm^2
Wind energy	Anemometer	Predictable, ambient, uncontrollable	Cost effective, clean, eco-friendly, renewable source	Fluctuations of wind, threat to wildlife	16.2 μW/cm^3
Piezoelectric energy	Piezo electric solid	Predictable, ambient, uncontrollable	Available when needed, indoor as well as outdoor availability, takes less space	Small lifespan, brittle material	330 μW/cm^3
Thermal energy	Thermocouple	Partly Predictable, non-ambient, controllable	Large life span, requires less maintenance	Less power density	40 μW/cm^2
RFD	Rectennas	Non-ambient, partly controllable, partly predictable	Freely available, allow mobility	Low power density, less availability in suburbs	0.01 μW/cm^2

4   Sources of Energy Dissipation

Several issues (Bhargav et al. 2020) are there which influence the energy efficiency and performance of the network. Below are some of the broad issues (Bhargava et al. 2020) that need to be addressed as they are the major factors responsible for the performance and lifetime of the network.

a) Idle listening - It is a major issue (Khan et al. 2012) faced in low power network. When a node is in the active state i.e. ready to receive but currently is not receiving any data is referred as idle listening. In applications such as event detection, the sensor node is waiting for the incoming packets most of the time. The time taken by nodes to switch between different states is called duty cycle which takes a significant amount of energy. Therefore, idle listening is always a big challenge in low power radio scenarios.

b) Collisions - Collision is a one of the major problems in wireless network. Basically, the collision occurs when a node receives multiple data packets at the same time. The data becomes useless due to this. The transmission process has to be repeated again and again till the data is transferred while the energy gets dissipated. The collision also increases latency.

c) Over hearing - Interference is when an unwanted signal destroys the original signal. High density sensor nodes lead to the interference with the neighboring nodes during data conveyance. This process is called over hearing. Since the chance of interference is increased when multiple radios share the bandwidth on a single channel therefore, assigning default value to each radio set may lead to severe interference. This results in burn up the energy resources owing to receiving and processing useless information.

d) Network overload - The nodes which are close to the base station carry a huge amount of data traffic when compared to other nodes which results in uneven energy consumption and quick node drain out, this is referred to as energy hole problem. Nodes carry their own data and forwarded data of other nodes which are near to the base station which results in huge overload and sometimes quick node death. Network overload may also lead to congestion.

e) Phantom energy - while the sensors are in sleep mode, they still consume energy as they use energy to process the wake-up signal in order to get fully activated. The power consumption is low but still it adds up to energy usage.

f) Heat energy - while the sensors are in active state and performing some tasks, the energy is also released in the form of heat and gets wasted. A more detailed analysis of sources of energy dissipation and their mathematical model for estimation of dissipation rate is done in (Roy and Chandra 2019).

5 Ways of Energy Conservation

In the past decade a plethora of energy conservation techniques have been proposed by the researchers. Some of the techniques in general are discussed here. Broadly these techniques can be categorized in to two categories: Node activity management and Clustering.

a) Node activity management - Node activity is divided into two partitions that are sleep scheduling and on-demand node activity. Here, sleep scheduling is basically scheduling the sleep time of a node. For example, if we require the data in the day time only by the sensor, then the sensor sleep schedule is set accordingly where the node takes bare-minimum energy in its sleep mode. On demand node activity does not include the schedule link process like in case of sleep scheduling, but the node is always in its active state. Here if the wake-up signal is transmitted, the neighbor node switches to active node with which data transmission starts. Since start-up nodes do not require decoding, all the nearby nodes are switched on.

b) Clustering - Data transmission and data processing are the processor that also require energy in IoT devices. To save energy, a new method is proposed known as clustering (Sreenivasamurthy and Obraczka 2018) where clusters help in reducing the amount of data coming from different sources is combined into a single data pocket. It helps in reducing redundancy and minimizing the number of transmissions i.e. same data is clustered and transmitted without causing any traffic load.

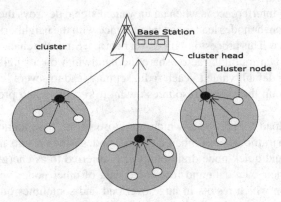

Fig. 3. Basic Clustering protocol

One of the most popular and oldest clustering protocol is LEACH. Its popularity is such high that even today it is being used to either compare new protocols or to create a new variant of its old form. Leach where cluster-based routing is used in order to reduce the energy consumption. LEACH stands for low energy adaptive clustering hierarchy protocol. It helps in improving the life span of wireless sensor networks by using minimum amount of energy for creating and maintaining cluster heads. It is divided into two phases (Kansal et al. 2010); setup phase and steady phase.

Setup Phase - In set up phase, initially the cluster head sends advertisement pockets so as to inform cluster nodes that they became cluster head by formula

$$T(n) = \begin{cases} \dfrac{P}{1-p\left(r+mod\left(\frac{1}{p}\right)\right)}, & \text{if } n \in G \\ 0, & otherwise \end{cases}$$

Where,

N = Given node
P = Probability
R = Current Round
G = Set of nodes that were not cluster heads in the previous rounds
T(n) = Threshold

Once a cluster node becomes cluster head cannot become cluster head again until all the cluster nodes become cluster head once, it helps in balancing energy consumption. After that the non-cluster head nodes join the cluster head and finally the cluster head creates the transmission schedule for the member nodes. Here non cluster head nodes are the primary source of energy saving by using energy while interacting with cluster head only. A lot many variations of LEACH protocols have been proposed, the latest being (Roy and Chandra 2018) where new formula for estimation of number of clusters is proposed (Roy and Chandra 2019).

There is a huge scope of saving energy in the whole network where the dense sensors nodes deployed in the sensing field have data that is highly correlated in the sensor nodes. It is very much important to turn off the unnecessary nodes which produce same readings so as to extend WSN lifetime. Sensor activity scheduling (SAS) protocol (Idrees and Huseein 2017) measures the degree of similarity among the sensed data that is collected initially. With the help of which it makes a decision about which sensor should stay active during the sensing phase and put the rest of the sensor nodes to sleep node in order to keep up with the accuracy level of data received, conserve the power and enhance the lifetime of node.

It is observed that clustering protocols are leading the trend for energy conservation. Due to this we have survey cluster based protocols for energy conservation. Table 2 contains a comparative analysis of cluster based protocols form the last two decades.

Table 2. Some energy efficient protocols (Parul and Ajay 2010; Deepak and Malay 2012; More and Vijay 2017)

Protocols	Year	Advantages	Disadvantages
PEGASIS (power efficient gathering in the sensor information system)	2002 (Lindsey and Raghavendra 2002)	Almost doubles the lifetime, avoids extra clusters.	Dynamical topology adjustment is required.
PEAS (Probing Environment and Adaptive Sleeping)	2003 (Ye et al. 2003)	Neighbouring node information is not available.	Varying energy consumption, high node density required.
PECAS (Probing Environment and Collaborating Adaptive Sleeping)	2004 (Gui and Prasant 2004)	No local state information, energy is balanced in network.	Less energy saving.
DCCA (Distributed Coverage Calculation Algorithm)	2007 (Tezcan and Wenye 2007)	No sensing void in the beginning.	High energy consumption, coverage redundancy.
PCPP (Probabilistic Coverage Preserving Protocol)	2007 (Sheu and Lin 2007)	Works for $C_d >= 1$	Centralized algorithm.
CACP (Coverage-aware Clustering Protocol)	2012 (Wang et al. 2012)	No sensing void in the beginning; reduced coverage redundancy.	Multi-hop communication; higher messaging overheads; partial coverage.
BECG (Balanced Energy and Coverage Guaranteed) Protocol)	2013 (Le et al. 2013)	Probing based on residual energy, no sensing void.	Incomplete coverage, high messaging overhead.

(*continued*)

Table 2. (*continued*)

Protocols	Year	Advantages	Disadvantages
ECDC (Energy and Coverage-aware Distributed Clustering Protocol)	2014 (Gu, et al.)	Probability based cluster head selection (similar to LEACH), good for point and area coverage.	Non-uniform distribution of cluster heads, energy loss.
C3 Protocol (Energy Efficient Protocol for Coverage, Connectivity and Communication)	2014 (Akhlaq et al. 2014)	Layered architecture, good connectivity.	Partial coverage; multi-hop communication overheads
R-HEED (Rotated Hybrid, Energy-Efficient and Distributed) Clustering Protocol	2014 (Wail et al. 2014)	Does not perform clustering at each round, advancement of HEED protocol	Poor cluster election, may cause higher communication overhead
RBSP (Random Back-off Sleep Protocol)	2014 (More and Vijay 2014)	Residual energy- based searching	Sleep time is random
DCBSP (Discharge Curve Back-off Sleep Protocol)	2015 (Avinash and Vijay 2015)	Effective wake-up rate	Saves less energy
Fuzzy Logic-Based Clustering Protocol	2015 (Quan et al. 2018)	converts multiple inputs to a single output, resolves 'hot spot problem'	Unbalanced cluster size, Node mobility is not considered
LCP (Load-balancing Cluster Based Protocol)	2015 (Mohamed et al. 2015)	Selects node with higher residual energy	Execution cost is high, more control packets are transferred in making clusters
CESS (Coverage and Energy Strategy for Wireless Sensor Networks)	2015 (Le and Yeong 2015)	No sensing void in the beginning	High energy consumption, higher number of active nodes.
CTC (Connected Target K-Coverage)	2016 (Yu et al. 2016)	Disjoint set of sensor nodes	High energy consumption, multi-hop connectivity
DWCA (Dynamic Weight Clustering based Algorithm)	2017 (Essa et al. 2017)	Balanced energy consumption, improved scalability	Process of Weight estimation and degree estimation is complicated and incurs cost
Energy Efficient K-means Clustering-based Routing Protocol	2018 (Razzaq et al. 2018)	Considers different power levels for data transmission from cluster head to cluster member and base station	Comparison with state of the art algorithms for energy conservation is missing
SAVEER (Secure Anti-Void Energy-Efficient Routing) Protocol	2020 (Tabassum et al. 2020)	better routing efficiency, highly secure	Encryption and decryption process incur cost
Threshold sensitive clustering in SEP	2020 (Roy and Chandra 2020)	Heterogeneous Hierarchical clustering approach is used with better cluster size estimation technique	Only three levels of heterogeneity is considered

6 Conclusion

There are different ways to conserve energy ranging from managing node activity to clustering. Among all the techniques clustering is one of the most popular technique. We have also discussed the energy harvesting techniques along with the reason why it cannot be used in some applications. Finally, we have surveyed latest clustering protocols, analyzed them and tabulated them. Most of the research focuses on estimation of number of clusters, cluster head selection criteria and level of heterogeneity among nodes. Less work has been done on data fusion and compression.

References

Adu-Manu, K.S., Nadir, A., Cristiano, T., Hoda, A., Wendi, H.: Energy-harvesting wireless sensor networks (EH-WSNs) a review. ACM Trans. Sensor Netw. **02**, 1–50 (2018)

Ahmmad, S.N.Z., Eswendy, M.A.G., Muchtar, F., Singh, P.K.: Implementation of automated retractable roof for home line-dry suspension area using IoT and WSN. In: Singh, P.K., Bhargava, B.K., Paprzycki, M., Kaushal, N.C., Hong, W.-C. (eds.) Handbook of Wireless Sensor Networks: Issues and Challenges in Current Scenario's. AISC, vol. 1132, pp. 546–565. Springer, Cham (2020a). https://doi.org/10.1007/978-3-030-40305-8_26

Ahmmad, S.N.Z., Mokhtar, M.T., Muchtar, F., Singh, P.K.: Implementation of automated aroma therapy candle process planting using IoT and WSN. In: Singh, P.K., Bhargava, B.K., Paprzycki, M., Kaushal, N.C., Hong, W.-C. (eds.) Handbook of Wireless Sensor Networks: Issues and Challenges in Current Scenario's. AISC, vol. 1132, pp. 520–545. Springer, Cham (2020b). https://doi.org/10.1007/978-3-030-40305-8_25

Akhlaq, M., Tarek, R., Elhadi, M.S.: C3: an energy-efficient protocol for coverage, connectivity and communication in WSNs. Pers. Ubiquitous Comput. **5**(18), 1117–1133 (2014)

Albreem, M.A., et al.: Green internet of things (IoT): an overview. In: IEEE 4th International Conference on Smart Instrumentation, vol. 4, pp. 1–6 (2017)

Avinash, M., Vijay, R.: Discharge curve backoff sleep protocol for energy efficient coverage in wireless sensor networks. Procedia Comput. Sci. **57**, 1131–1139 (2015)

Singh, P.K., Bhargava, B.K., Paprzycki, M., Kaushal, N.C., Hong, W.-C. (eds.): Handbook of Wireless Sensor Networks: Issues and Challenges in Current Scenario's. AISC, vol. 1132. Springer, Cham (2020). https://doi.org/10.1007/978-3-030-40305-8

Cacciagrano, D., Culmone, R., Micheletti, M., Mostarda, L.: Energy-efficient clustering for wireless sensor devices in internet of things. In: Al-Turjman, F. (ed.) Performability in Internet of Things. EICC, pp. 59–80. Springer, Cham (2019). https://doi.org/10.1007/978-3-319-935 57-7_5

Deepak, G., Malay, R.T.: Routing protocols in wireless sensor networks: a survey. In: Second International Conference on Advanced Computing & Communication Technologies, pp. 474–480 (2012)

Essa, A., Al-Dubai, A.Y., Romdhani, I., Eshaftri, M.A.: A new dynamic weight-based energy efficient algorithm for sensor networks. In: Hu, J., Leung, V.C.M., Yang, K., Zhang, Y., Gao, J., Yang, S. (eds.) Smart Grid Inspired Future Technologies. LNICST, vol. 175, pp. 195–203. Springer, Cham (2017). https://doi.org/10.1007/978-3-319-47729-9_20

Garg, N., Garg, R.: Energy harvesting in IoT devices: a survey. In: International Conference on Intelligent Sustainable Systems, pp. 127–131 (2017)

Gaurav, C., Jain, A.K.: Internet of Things: a survey on architecture, technologies, protocols and challenges. In: International Conference on Recent Advances and Innovations in Engineering (ICRAIE), pp. 1–8 (2016)

Gill, R.K., Chawla, P., Sachdeva, M.: Study of LEACH routing protocol for wireless sensor networks. In: International Conference on Communication, Computing & Systems (ICCCS) (2014)

Gu, X., Jiguo, Y., Dongxiao, Y., Guanghui, W., Yuhua, L.: ECDC: an energy and coverage-aware distributed clustering protocol for wireless sensor networks. Comput. Electric. Eng. **40**, 384–398 (2014)

Gui, C., Prasant, M.: Power conservation and quality of surveillance in target tracking sensor networks. In: Proceedings of the 10th Annual International Conference on Mobile Computing and Networking, pp. 129–143 (2004)

Idrees, A.K., Huseein, W.: Sensor activity scheduling protocol for lifetime prolongation in wireless sensor networks. Kurdistan J. Appl. Res. **02**(03), 7–13 (2017)

Jayakumar, H., Raha, A., Kim, Y., Sutar, S., Lee, W.S., Raghunathan, V.: Energy-efficient system design for IoT devices, pp. 298–301. In: 2016 21st Asia and South Pacific Design Automation Conference (2016)

Kansal, P., Kansal, D., Balodi, A.: Compression of various routing protocol in wireless sensor networks. Int. J. Comput. Appl. **05**(11), 0975–8887 (2010)

Khan, R., Khan, S.U., Zaheer, R., Khan, S.: Future internet: the internet of things architecture, possible applications and key challenges. In: 10th International Conference on Frontiers of Information Technology, Islamabad, pp. 257–260 (2012)

Le, N.T., Nirzhar, S., Ratan, K.M., Sunghun, C., Yeong, M.: Balanced energy and coverage guaranteed protocol for wireless sensor networks. In: International Conference on Electrical Information and Communication Technology (EICT), pp. 1–6 (2013)

Le, N.-T., Yeong, M.J.: Energy-efficient coverage guarantees scheduling and routing strategy for wireless sensor networks. Int. J. Distrib. Sens. Netw. **8**, (2015)

Lindsey, S., Raghavendra, C.S.: PEGASIS: power Efficient gathering in sensor information systems. In: The Proceedings of the IEEE Aerospace Conference, vol. 3, p. 3 (2002)

Mohamed, E., Ahmed, Y.-D., Imed, R., Muneer, B.Y.: A new energy efficient cluster based protocol for wireless sensor networks. In: Federated Conference on Computer Science and Information Systems (FedCSIS), pp. 1209–1214 (2015)

More, A., Raisinghani, V.: Random backoff sleep protocol for energy efficient coverage in wireless sensor networks. In: Kumar Kundu, M., Mohapatra, D.P., Konar, A., Chakraborty, A. (eds.) Advanced Computing, Networking and Informatics-Volume 2. SIST, vol. 28, pp. 123–131. Springer, Cham (2014). https://doi.org/10.1007/978-3-319-07350-7_14

More, A., Vijay, R.: A survey on energy efficient coverage protocols in wireless sensor networks. J. King Saud Univ. Comput. Inf. Sci. **29**(04), 428–448 (2017)

Nintanavongsa, P.: A survey on RF energy harvesting: circuits and protocols. Energy Procedia **56**, 414–422 (2014)

Parul, S., Ajay, K.: Energy efficient scheme for clustering protocol prolonging the lifetime of heterogeneous wireless sensor networks. Int. J. Comput. Appl. **06**(02), 30–36 (2010)

Patel, D., Narmawala, Z., Tanwar, S., Singh, P.K.: A systematic review on scheduling public transport using IoT as tool. In: Panigrahi, B.K., Trivedi, M.C., Mishra, K.K., Tiwari, S., Singh, P.K. (eds.) Smart Innovations in Communication and Computational Sciences. AISC, vol. 670, pp. 39–48. Springer, Singapore (2019). https://doi.org/10.1007/978-981-10-8971-8_4

Quan, W., Lin, D., Yang, P., Zhang, Z.: A fuzzy-logic based energy-efficient clustering algorithm for the wireless sensor networks. In: 2018 26th International Conference on Software, Telecommunications and Computer Networks (SoftCOM), pp. 1–6 (2018)

Rafiullah, K., Sarmad, U., Rifaqat, Z., Shahid, K.: Future internet: the internet of things architecture. In: International Conference on Frontiers of Information Technology, vol. 10, pp. 257–260 (2012)

Razzaq, M., Devarani, D.N., Seokjoo, S.: Energy efficient K-means clustering-based routing protocol for WSN using optimal packet size. In: International Conference on Information Networking (ICOIN), pp. 632–635 (2018)

Roy, N.R., Chandra, P.: A note on optimum cluster estimation in leach protocol. IEEE Access 6, 65690–65696 (2018)

Roy, N.R., Chandra, P.: Energy dissipation model for wireless sensor networks: a survey. Int. J. Inf. Tech. 12(4), 1343–1353 (2019). https://doi.org/10.1007/s41870-019-00374-y

Roy, N.R., Chandra, P.: Threshold sensitive clustering in SEP. Sustain. Comput. Inf. Syst. 25, (2020)

Sandhya, R., Sengottaiyan, N.: S-SEECH secured-scalable energy efficient clustering hierarchy protocol for wireless sensor network. In: International Conference on Data Mining and Advanced Computing (SAPIENCE), pp. 306–309 (2016)

Shaikh, F.K., Sherali, Z.: Energy harvesting in wireless sensor networks: a comprehensive review. Renew. Sustain. Energy Rev. 55, 1041–1054 (2016)

Sheu, J.-P., Lin, H.-F.: Probabilistic coverage preserving protocol with energy efficiency in wireless sensor networks. In: IEEE Wireless Communications and Networking Conference, pp. 2631–2636 (2007)

Sreenivasamurthy, S., Obraczka, K.: Clustering for load balancing and energy efficiency in IoT applications, vol. 26, pp. 319–332 (2018)

Tabassum, A., Sadaf, S., Sinha, D., Das, A.K.: Secure anti-void energy-efficient routing (SAVEER) protocol for WSN-based IoT network. In: Sahana, S.K., Bhattacharjee, V. (eds.) Advances in Computational Intelligence. AISC, vol. 988, pp. 129–142. Springer, Singapore (2020). https://doi.org/10.1007/978-981-13-8222-2_11

Tahiliani, V., Digalwar, M.: Green IoT systems: an energy efficient perspective, vol. 3, pp. 1–6 (2018)

Tezcan, N., Wenye, W.: Effective coverage and connectivity preserving in wireless sensor networks. In: IEEE Wireless Communications and Networking Conference, pp. 3388–3393 (2007)

Heinzelman, W.B., Chandrakasan, A.P., Balakrishnan, H.: An application specific protocol architecture for wireless microsensor networks. IEEE Trans. Wirel. Commun. 1(4), 660–670 (2002)

Wail, M., Muneer, B.Y., Yaser, K., Barraq, A.G.: Rotated hybrid, energy-efficient and distributed (R-HEED) clustering protocol in WSN. WSEAS Trans. Commun. 13, 275–290 (2014)

Wang, B., Hock, B., Di, M.: A coverage-aware clustering protocol for wireless sensor networks. Comput. Netw. 56(5), 1599–1611 (2012)

Weiping, Z., Jiannong, C., Michel, R.: IEEE Commun. Lett. Energy-efficient composite event detection in wireless sensor networks 22, 177–180 (2018)

Ye, F., Gary, Z., Jesse, C., Songwu, L., Lixia, Z.: PEAS: A robust energy conserving protocol for long-lived sensor networks, vol. 23, pp. 28–37 (2003)

Yu, J., Ying, C., Liran, M., Baogui, H., Xiuzhen, C.: On connected target k-coverage in heterogeneous wireless sensor networks. Sensors 16(01), 104 (2016)

Identification of Implicit Threats Based on Analysis of User Activity in the Internet Space

D. Yu. Zaporozhets, Yu. A. Kravchenko, E. V. Kuliev, I. O. Kursitys$^{(\boxtimes)}$, and N. A. Lyz

Southern Federal University, Rostov-on-Don, Russia
nlyz@sfedu.ru

Abstract. The article is devoted to the problem of identifying implicit information threats of user's search activity in the Internet based on the analysis of activity during the interaction process. Application of knowledge stored in the Internet space for the implementation of criminal intentions poses a threat to the whole society. Identifying malicious intents in the users' actions in the global information network is not always a trivial task. Modern technologies for analyzing the context of users' interests can fail in terms of cautious and competent actions of malicious users, who do not demonstrate their intentions explicitly. The paper analyzes the threats related to certain scenarios for implementing the search procedures, which are expressed in the search activity. Authors present an approach to classification of the mentioned threats considering the given criteria of estimating different scenarios of the user's behavior in the global information space. The article describes the developed algorithm of machine learning to identify the problem scenarios by comparing them with the key patterns of behavior. To implement the proposed approach, the authors developed software implementing the subsystem for identifying information threats. The experimental research proves the effectiveness of the developed subsystem.

Keywords: Information search · Implicit threats · Analysis of user activity · Feature vector · Machine learning · Optimization · Intelligent systems

1 Introduction

As a trend, online education requires developing the methods of managing students' activity in the Internet. Broad understanding of online education allows us to consider the diversity of the informational and educational activities: cognitive and training, search and cognitive, communicative and cognitive, information and creative, and entertaining and cognitive [1]. Search and cognitive activities are one of the most popular related to searching for information and include the technologies of information search and processing, selection, verification, and application of the relevant information [1]. The search and use of information are very important for the students in terms of formal, non-formal, and informal education. This activity can contribute to the accumulation of not only the "knowledge" experience but also experience of working with information, learning the search and analysis technologies, and cognitive and personal development by expanding the interests and increasing the motivation of cognitive activity [2].

© Springer Nature Singapore Pte Ltd. 2021
P. K. Singh et al. (Eds.): FTNCT 2020, CCIS 1396, pp. 194–206, 2021.
https://doi.org/10.1007/978-981-16-1483-5_18

However, the studies show that the students are not ready for effective search activity and do not use scientific databases and electronic scientific journals properly. More than 80% of students consider general-purpose search systems as more important and reliable sources of academic information [3]. Most students tend to repeat the strategies that were previously successful rather than find new approaches [4]. Their search behavior is biased, and they prefer using higher-ranked search results even if those do not meet their needs [3]. Searching and processing of information is a complex process that includes setting a problem, searching for the appropriate sources, extracting and organizing relevant information from the source [5–7]. This requires using the regulative, cognitive, and metacognitive abilities, which are not always developed properly. The clip-like thinking of modern youth can imply plagiarism, irrelevant information, incorrect conclusions [5, 7–9].

The additional problems can appear since the search activity have an "addictive" nature and is often implemented in the segments of the Internet, where the is no control over the flow of academic activity rather than in the special electronic educational environment. Hence, the risks of reducing the effectiveness of the activity are enhanced with the cyber, communicational, content, and other risks including Internet addiction. Students can experience dysfunctional conditions due to uncertainty and anxiety [8]. Many of them feel lost in the hyperspace through disorientation, information overload, and aimless clicking the hyperlinks [10]. Information search and common surfing are involved in high rates of problematic usage of the Internet [11]. Web surfing is considered as the most widespread and understudied activity [12]. The Internet addiction can be demonstrated and formed in terms of the search activity when it is transformed into compulsive web surfing – browsing various Internet sources and chaotic navigation.

Thus, the development of the methods for preparing students and instruments for external support of their activity (intelligent digital assistants) are relevant today.

2 Problem Analysis and Threat Assessment Criteria

The analyzed literature proposes different approaches to modeling the search activity in the Internet. The earliest psychological models introduced by B. Dervin, D. Ellis, C. Kuhlthau describe only the information searching activities; the extended model of T. Wilson includes the user, user's needs, request for information, exchange, using, and satisfaction by the search results [13]. There are several stagewise search models including the following steps: beginning and chaining, monitoring and differentiation, estimation, and extracting [14]. The models of search strategies have the following components: search planning, selecting the resources, implementation, extracting the knowledge, overcoming the difficulties, estimation, control, etc. [5–7, 15, 16].

The search activity is characterized by the strategy and particular behavior scenarios including the mechanisms of using the search systems. There are different methods of search such as comparing or investigating [6]; logical, the best relevant or combined [16]; describing the typical model of the users' behavior in terms of the thematic search [17]; building the formalized probabilistic models trained on the data on the users' activities (click logs) [18]; developing the recommendation systems supporting the directed search in education [19, 20].

To record the information, we can use the navigation flow map (NFM) method representing multilayer relations between web navigation and information search [6].

Usually, the researchers investigate increasing the search systems intelligence to meet the users' needs and reduce the information overload [17] without considering the search context, events implying the threats, and moving to the purposeless surfing.

From the point of the search safety, we can distinguish three types of threats and corresponding scenarios: 1) shifting away from the problem to the aimless surfing or attractive resources ("*distancing*"); 2) superficial search, absence of semantic immersion ("*scanning*"); 3) chaotic actions during the search process ("*spontaneity*").

Let us introduce the criteria for the identification of the features of the presence and absence of the described threats. The criteria to estimate the "distancing" scenario are the following:

1.1) y_{11} – stability of the keywords on the pages (relevant words);
1.2) y_{12} – following a lot of hyperlinks (a large number of the visited pages);
1.3) y_{13} – a gradual increase in time spent on the irrelevant pages;
1.4) y_{14} – long forward chains with no returns;
1.5) y_{15} – clicking on the advertising banners;
1.6) y_{16} – transition from the first two to the next pages of the search results;
1.7) y_{17} – holding on the "search line".

The criteria to estimate the "scanning" scenario can be described as follows:

2.1) y_{21} – a lot of visited pages with little time spent on viewing the particular pages;
2.2) y_{22} – preference of simple and brief resources;
2.3) y_{23} – using easily available resources;
2.4) y_{24} – rechecking the found information (going back to the visited pages);
2.5) y_{25} – reading the entire pages, long time spent on the pages and particular pages;
2.6) $y_{26}=y_{16}$ – transition from the first two to the next pages of the search results;

To estimate the "spontaneity" scenario, we propose the following criteria:

3.1) y_{31} – incorrect wording of the query;
3.2) y_{32} – using the search results on the first lines of the list;
3.3) y_{33} – frequent change of the query or no change of query;
3.4) y_{34} – filtering of the information at the early stage of the search cycle;
3.5) y_{35} – using the most relevant resources.

The opposite of the non-desired situations is the "effectiveness" scenario to identify the absence of threats at the first stage. To estimate it, we propose the following criteria:

1) x_1 – viewing the relevant pages;
2) x_2 – significant difference between the time spent on the pages;
3) x_3 – high-quality results of the search.

The features to describe the presence of the described effectiveness criteria include the following:

1. Query formulation (absolute number, the relative number of the relevant ones).
2. Working with the information given by the search engine (numbers of search results were clicked, transition to the second and more pages).
3. Chains: lengths, number of returns.
4. The number of the visited pages: all, relevant, irrelevant, rate of relevant pages.
5. Time spent on the page: maximal, minimal, common average, relevant average, irrelevant average, frequency distribution of the time on the particular pages.
6. At which minute of the search the irrelevant pages appear.
7. Overstated (exceeding the average and root-mean-square deviation) or understated parameters at the ratio of the average.

Let us describe a method for identifying implicit threats based on analysis of user activity in the Internet, the problem definition and constructed scenarios of presence or absence of threats.

3   The Method for Identification of Implicit Threats

This section considers the scenarios as components of a complex criterion that clearly identifies the unacceptable form of the user's behavior named "ineffective scenario". The risk is represented as accidental access to malicious content. Table 1 provides the criteria to build a feature vector for the "ineffective scenario". The presence of a feature is denoted as "1", the absence of it is denoted as "0".

Table 1. Building a feature vector for «ineffective scenario»

	y_{11}	y_{12}	y_{13}	y_{14}	y_{15}	y_{16}	y_{17}	y_{21}	y_{22}	y_{23}	y_{24}	y_{25}	y_{31}	y_{32}	y_{33}	y_{34}	y_{35}
Distancing	0	1	1	1	1	0	0	0	0	0	0	0	0	0	0	0	0
Scanning	0	0	0	0	0	0	0	1	1	1	0	0	0	0	0	0	0
Spontaneity	0	0	0	0	0	0	0	0	0	0	0	0	1	1	1	0	0
Common feature vectors																	
Max threat	0	1	1	1	1	0	0	1	1	1	0	0	1	1	1	0	0
Min threat	1	0	0	0	0	1	1	0	0	0	1	1	0	0	0	1	1

The feature vector for identification of the "ineffective scenario" is composed of the vectors of criteria sets of three described negative scenarios (Fig. 1).

Let us denote the scenarios "distancin", "scanning", and "spontaneity" as Q_1, Q_2, Q_3 respectively. Thus, the common criterion have the following form:

$$Q_{int} = \tau_1 Q_1 + \tau_2 Q_2 + \tau_3 Q_3 \rightarrow max, \tag{1}$$

where τ_i denotes the weight of each scenario based on the expert assessments.

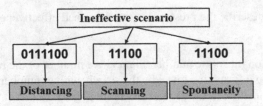

Fig. 1. Components of the feature vector «ineffective scenario»

The possible "effective scenario" is considered as a positive form of the user's activity in the Internet. It is based on the previously described "effectiveness" scenario, the main criteria of which are: x_1 – scanning the relevant pages; x_2 – significant difference between time spent on the pages; x_3 – availability of the qualitative search results.

Let us assume that in the case of the most effective scenario of users' activity represented by the enhanced feature vector (Table 2), there is a possibility of appearing of implicit threats that are important and dangerous to the whole society.

Table 2. The most effective scenario of users' activity in the Internet space

x_1	x_2	x_3	y_{11}	y_{12}	y_{13}	y_{14}	y_{15}	y_{16}	y_{17}	y_{21}	y_{22}	y_{23}	y_{24}	y_{25}	y_{31}	y_{32}	y_{33}	y_{34}	y_{35}
1	1	1	1	0	0	0	0	1	1	0	0	0	1	1	0	0	0	1	1

Application of the knowledge in the Internet for the malicious intent implies a significant threat. The task of revealing the malicious intents in terms of the users' activity cannot always be trivial. The proven technologies for analyzing the context of the users' interests can fail in terms of careful and intelligent actions of malicious users who do not demonstrate their intents explicitly.

The simple analysis of the user interest context cannot identify the threats on time due to the lack of explicit features of the malicious intents. Thus, the authors propose the additional criteria: x_4 – studying the content with double-purpose information; x_5 – studying the content of information that is not directly related to the professional or educational activities of the subject (Table 3).

Table 3. Identification of threats in terms of effective scenario

№		x_1	x_2	x_3	x_4	x_5
1	No threats	1	1	1	0	0
2		1	1	1	0	1
3		1	1	1	1	0
4	Threats	1	1	1	1	1

The first three options of this component of the feature vector have non-significant weigh in terms of identification of the possible threats. In the first option, there are no additional features x_4 and x_5 at all. In the second one, there is no data on the information of dual purpose. In the third option, the interest can be related to direct professional or education activity of the subject.

The most dangerous case is the maximal values of x_1, x_2, x_3, x_4, x_5 representing the obsession and must be the reason to consider the perspectives of application of the obtained information in detail. Further classification of the information is based on the method of semantic similarity estimation (Fig. 2) allows us to avoid the threats, e.g. in the context of the person's hobbies, or confirm the suspicions and require intervention.

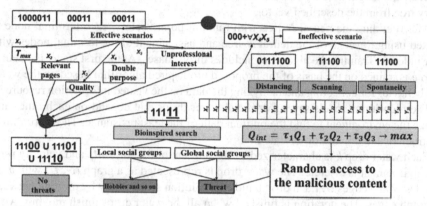

Fig. 2. The scheme of identifying implicit threats based on analysis of user activity

The authors propose to identify the threats using combined biologically plausible machine learning methods. The first stage studies local and global social groups. The search is performed effectively on the basis of the decentralized swarm methods. They allow us to make the maximal comparison of the local feature vectors with a sufficient number of global ones. At the second level, we use the swarm methods with sequential search mechanisms in the information spaces based on the described scenarios and simple context subject search to confirm or deny the presence of threats.

4   Bioinspired Algorithm for Identification of Implicit Threats

In the context of the intelligence analysis, the method for augmented intelligence (AUI) uses the idea where artificial intelligence (AI) supports the decision, training, and planning. Instead of a group of learners, we have a final user and a machine finding the solution together for a certain problem of the context communicating. The final user presents the datasets for a machine learning algorithm that builds the model. The role of the final user is active. The purpose is to adjust the model rather than modify the number of clusters or training speed affecting building the model.

Based on the information changes given by the final user, the computer builds a new model using the obtained knowledge and data. This process iteratively generates new knowledge on the context and studied phenomenon.

The AUI process leads to the cyclical discovery of the knowledge of the user and computer. Together, obtained results extend the users' previous knowledge on the context, where the datasets were collected.

To expand the AUI method, we need to develop new calculation methods for different tasks of the intelligent analysis of data in the modern intelligent education environments. In terms of the educational cluster analysis, the neural *N-Tree* algorithm represents the balanced binary tree, where each node contains a point vector. The length of the point vector equals to the length of the input vectors. The neural N-treec is built recursively by initializing each point vector with random numbers from the interval of minimal to maximal values in the dataset. At first, the algorithm considers *n* clusters and creates a vector of the length *n* × *2* − *1* with random point vectors. Then it builds the balanced binary tree from the described vector.

After building the neural N-tree with random point vectors, each terminal node is indexed using traversal of the neural N-tree and assignment of the terminal nodes with other indexes. Training the algorithm includes three phases. At the first stage, the neural *N-Tree* is trained on the basis of the proposed bioinspired algorithm based on the water drop behavior for collecting and analyzing the data on the visited information resources.

The algorithm models several artificial water drops that depend on each other and change the environment to find the optimal path of the least resistance. The algorithm is constructive and population-oriented.

Each water drop *k* is characterized by the amount of the soil $soil_k$ and velocity vel_k. The environment is discrete. The water drop is represented as a graph *(N, U)* with a set of nodes *N* and edges *U*. Each drop builds the solution sequentially by moving between the graph edges. The iteration is finished when all the water drops finish moving. After each iteration, the algorithm calculates the current best solution *F*. The set of all the best solutions is denoted as *Z*, and all the water drops gather in a flow (Fig. 3).

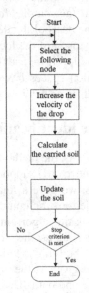

Fig. 3. Processing the solution

Each water drop belongs to the ith node and reaches the jth node from all the nodes N. The probability of reaching the jth node is calculated as follows [21]:

$$P_i^k(j) = \frac{f(soil(i,j))}{\sum_{l \notin V_{visited}^k} f(soil(i,l))},$$
(2)

where

$$f(soil(i.j)) = \frac{1}{\varepsilon + g(soil(i,j))}.$$
(3)

The numeric constant $\varepsilon \geq 0$ allows us to avoid dividing by *zero*. The function $g(soil(i,j))$ is used to denote the presence of the soil (i,j) that determines all the soil on the path between the ith and j^{th} nodes:

$$g(soil(i,j)) = \begin{cases} soil(i,j) & if min_{\forall l \notin V_{visited}^k}(soil(i,l)) \geq 0 \\ soil(i,j) - min_{\forall l \notin V_{visited}^k}(soil(i,l) & otherwise \end{cases}.$$
(4)

The new value of the velocity is calculated by the following equation:

$$vel^k(t+1) = vel^k(t) + \frac{a_v}{b_v + c_v soil(i,j)},$$
(5)

where a_v, b_v, and c_v are the minimal positive values to avoid dividing by zero, and $soil(i,j)$ defines the amount of soil from i^{th} to j^{th} node.

Let us introduce the main principles of water drop behavior [22]:

- it prefers the path with less amount of the soil;
- it prefers the easiest path from the source to the destination point;
- the difficulty of the path is determined by the amount of the soil.

The paper proposes increasing the calculation speed according to (4), where the *soil* parameter is exponential *2* [21].

1: Input: Problem statement.
2: Output: Optimal solution.
3: Formulation of the optimization problem as a connected graph.
4: Initialization of the constant parameters.
5: Repeat.
6: Initialization of the dynamic parameters.
7: Distribution of the water drop randomly among the built graph.
8: Update the list of the visited nodes ($V_{visited}^k$) including the initial node.
9: Repeat
10: For k = 1 to i do
11: i = initial node for the drop k.
12: j = next node which meets the constraints.
13: Move the drop k from the node i to the node j.
14: Update the drop velocity, amount of soil in drop k, and amount of soil at e_{ij}.

15: End for
16: Until stop criterion is met.
17: Select the best solution in the current cycle (T^{IB}).
18: Update the output soil parameter for all characteristics (T^{IB}).
19: Update the best solution among all cycles (T^{TB}).
20: If (T^{TB}quality $< T^{IB}$quality).
21: $T^{TB} = T^{IB}$.
22: Until obtaining the solution that meets all the requirements.
23: Return (T^{TB}).

At the second stage, the algorithm finds the best coincident block on the basis of comparing the randomly sampled vector with each terminal node.

At the third stage, training starts with the root node, and the following node of the input vector is a child element of the current node depending on the minimal distance to the input vector and points. The input vector passes through the N-tree from the root node to one of the terminal nodes. After each step, the algorithm calculates the level number starting from the current node (except the root node) and updates the points of the subtree level numbers. The purpose of direct training is to correct the paths for the input vectors in terms of the cluster analysis.

5 Software Implementation and Experimental Research

To approve the developed method and algorithm, we developed a subsystem for collecting and analyzing the data on the visited resources. The subsystem includes two modules. The client module is implemented as a browser extension collecting the information and metadata on each visited page and transferring this information to the server module. The server module implements the users' authentication, data collection, initial information processing and storing, and identification of the threats in terms of the effective scenario. In the current version, each scenario is considered as effective.

The server module receives information from the client module, takes the page content to terms, filters it, normalizes the terms, calculates the number of the term repetitions on the page, and saves the results in the database. The current version of the system works only with the nouns. The taboo list includes the terms that do not have any semantic meaning but are frequently met in the page content. The research shows that at least one of such terms as: "comment", "preview", "query", is included in the 10 most common terms. This can obstruct the threat identification process. The taboo filter allows us to reduce the search space, save the resources for storing, and increase the accuracy of identifying the threats.

To conduct the experiments, we used the "List of double-purpose products and technologies that can be used for building the armament and military equipment and imposed with the export control" as a benchmark. Let us denote it as a "target list". The developed subsystem highlights the terms from the target list. The terms from the target list are frequently used with the "satellite words" which can affect the threat estimation. Hence, we propose dividing the terms into the categories including the terms and their satellites in each category. The same term can be used in many categories. The initial partition was performed automatedly on the basis of the target list. The categories were then filled with the terms and satellites by the experts. Generally, the term is chosen randomly from the database, and the experts select the most appropriate category. However, this approach is ineffective due to a large number of terms. Thus, the list of terms is preassigned and can be modified by the system administrator.

The methods for AUI and neural network approach is used to estimate the threats coming from the user in the system. The values of risks for each category $R_k, R_k \in [0, 1], k \in [1, K]$, are given to the inputs of the neural network where K is the common number of the categories.

To calculate the risks for each category, we propose the following equation:

$$R_k = \frac{\sum_{x=1}^{|X^k|} (arctg(x * \alpha(t_e - t_b)) * \pi * \beta)}{|X^k|}, \tag{6}$$

where X^k denotes the set of terms belonging to the category k; α, β denote the modifying coefficients. The empirical optimal values are: $\alpha = 0.05$ and $\beta = 0.2$.

For the initial training on 10 categories, we generated 50000 training and 50000 testing samples. The results have demonstrated that the average deviation from the benchmark is 0.651%. Figure 4 shows the error distribution. The obtained deviation is acceptable as the network's answer is interpreted as a binary signal.

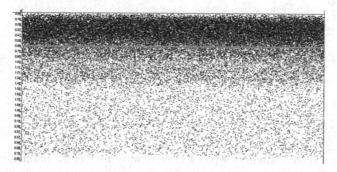

Fig. 4. Distribution of errors

To prove the necessity and sufficiency of the training samples number, we conducted the training and testing sessions (Table 4).

The results are demonstrated in Fig. 5. After performing 50000 testing samples, the network accuracy is increased insignificantly, while the execution time is quadratic.

The proposed approach allows us to analyze the activity of the users and estimate the risks of their behavior in the context of the pre-trained neural network working with categories. It does not need to be retrained if the categories are changed due to the updated distribution of the experts' opinions. The shortcoming of the approach includes the lack of possibility to expand the number of categories without retraining the network and to obtain the explanations on the presence or absence of the risk.

Table 4. Training and testing samplings

Size of the training sampling	Size of the testing sampling	Average error (%)
20000	50000	21.38
40000	50000	2.19
50000	50000	0.66
60000	50000	0.65
80000	50000	0.64
100000	50000	0.63

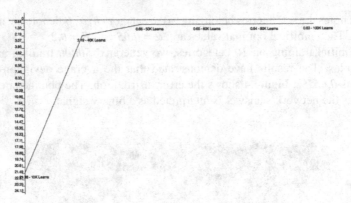

Fig. 5. The results of testing the trained neural network

6 Conclusion

The study was aimed at solving the problem of identification of the implicit information threats of the users' search activity in the Internet space. The authors built the feature vectors for classification of the users' behavior scenarios. To estimate the scenarios, we determined the corresponding criteria and developed the system of characteristics to define the criteria values. The modified bioinspired water-drop algorithm was developed for collecting and analyzing the data on the visited resources. To conduct the experiments, we developed a subsystem based on the neural network approach to collect and analyze the data on the visited information resources. The results have proven the effectiveness of the proposed approach which allows us to analyze the user's real-time activity in the Internet and estimate the risks in the context of the analyzed problem based on the previously trained neural network.

Acknowledgment. The reported study was funded by RFBR according to the research project № 18-29-22019.

References

1. Lyz', N.A., Istratova, O.N.: Informatsionno-obrazovatel'naya deyatel'nost' v internet-prostranstve: vidy, faktory, riski. Pedagogika. **4**, 16–26 (2019)
2. Raitskaya, L.K.: Vliyaniye interneta na lichnost' studenta. V sbornike: Kommunikatsiya v sovremennom polikul'turnom mire: dialog kul'tur Yezhegodnyy sbornik nauchnykh trudov. Otv. redaktor T.A. Baranovskaya. Moskva, pp. 429–441 (2014)
3. Salehi, S., Du, J.T., Ashman, H.: Use of Web search engines and personalisation in information searching for educational purposes. Inf. Res. **23**(2) (2018). http://informationr.net/ir/23-2/paper788.html
4. Cen, Y., Gan, L., Bai, C.: Reinforcement learning in information searching. Inf. Res. **18**(1) (2013). http://informationr.net/ir/18-1/paper569.html#.Xl99magzaUk
5. Goryunova, L.N., Kruglova, M.A., Provotorova, Y.A.A., Tsygan, V.N.: Strategii informatsionnogo poiska i ikh vzaimosvyaz' s lichnostnymi osobennostyami studentov. Peterburgskiy psikhologicheskiy zhurnal **2**, 1–15 (2013)
6. Lin, C.-C., Tsai, C.-C.: A navigation flow map method of representing students' searching behaviors and strategies on the web, with relation to searching outcomes. Cyberpsychol. Behav. **10**(5), 689–695 (2007). https://doi.org/10.1089/cpb.2007.9969
7. Walraven, A., Brand-Gruwel, S., Boshuizen, H.P.: Information-problem solving: a review of problems students encounter and instructional solutions. Comput. Hum. Behav. **24**(3), 623–648 (2008)
8. Porshnev, A.V.: Psikhologicheskiye aspekty effektivnogo ispol'zovaniya interneta v obrazovatel'nykh tselyakh. Kul'turno-istoricheskaya psikhologiya **3**, 43–50 (2008)
9. Lozitskiy, V.L.: Fenomen klipovogo myshleniya i informatsionno-kommunikatsionnyye tekhnologii v vysshem professional'nom obrazovanii. Nauchnyye trudy Respublikanskogo instituta vysshey shkoly **16-2**, 375–380 (2016)
10. Scholl, P., Benz, Bastian F., Böhnstedt, D., Rensing, C., Schmitz, B., Steinmetz, R.: Implementation and evaluation of a tool for setting goals in self-regulated learning with web resources. In: Cress, U., Dimitrova, V., Specht, M. (eds.) EC-TEL 2009. LNCS, vol. 5794, pp. 521–534. Springer, Heidelberg (2009). https://doi.org/10.1007/978-3-642-04636-0_48
11. Ioannidis, K., et al.: Problematic internet use as an age-related multifaceted problem: Evidence from a two-site survey. Addict. Behav. **81**, 157–166 (2018)
12. Yang, K.S.: Diagnoz – internet-zavisimost'. Mir Internet **2**, 24–29 (2000)
13. Goryunova, L.N.: Razvitiye modeley informatsionnogo povedeniya s pozitsii obobshchennoy psikhologicheskoy teorii deyatel'nosti. Vestnik Sankt-Peterburgskogo Universiteta **12**(3), 439–444 (2008)
14. Ho, L.-A., Kuo, T.-H., Lin, B.: The mediating effect of website quality on Internet searching behavior. Comput. Hum. Behav. **28**(3), 840–848 (2012). https://doi.org/10.1016/j.chb.2011.11.024
15. Ek, S.: Factors relating to problems experienced in information seeking and use: findings from a cross-sectional population study in Finland. Inf. Res. **22**(4). paper 775 (2017). http://informationr.net/ir/22-4/paper775.html
16. Ford, N., Miller, D., Moss, N.: Web search strategies and approaches to studying. J. Am. Soc. Inf. Sci. Technol. **54**(6), 473–489 (2003). https://doi.org/10.1002/asi.10233
17. Brumshteyn, Yu.M., Vas'kovskiy, Ye.Yu., Kuanshkaliyev, T.K.H.: Poisk informatsii v Internete: analiz vliyayushchikh faktorov i modeley povedeniya pol'zovateley. Izvestiya Volgogradskogo gosudarstvennogo tekhnicheskogo universiteta **1**(196), 50–55 (2017)
18. Nikolenko, S.I., Fishkov, A.A.: Obzor modeley povedeniya pol'zovateley dlya zadachi ranzhirovaniya rezul'tatov poiska. Trudy SPIIRAN **3**(22), 139–175 (2012)

19. Liu, C.-C., Chang, C.-J., Tseng, J.-M.: The effect of recommendation systems on internet-based learning for different learners: a data mining analysis. Br. J. Educ. Technol. **44**(5), 758–773 (2013). https://doi.org/10.1111/j.1467-8535.2012.01376.x
20. Bova, V.V., Kravchenko, Yu.A., Kuliev, E.V., Kureychik, V.V.: Modelirovaniye povedeniya sub"yekta v Internet-servisakh na osnove modifitsirovannogo algoritma bakterial'noy optimizatsii. Informatsionnyye tekhnologii **7**(25), 397–404 (2013). https://doi.org/10.17587/it.25.397-404
21. Pantelyuk, Ye.A., Kravchenko, Yu.A., Tsyrul'nikova, E.S.: Resheniye zadachi upravleniya znaniyami na osnove algoritma umnoy kapli vody. Informatika, vychislitel'naya tekhnika i inzhenernoye obrazovaniye **1**, 59–67 (2017)
22. Smirnova, O.S., Bogoradnikova, A.V., Yu, M.: Blinov Opisaniye royevykh algoritmov, inspirirovannykh nezhivoy prirodoy i bakteriyami, dlya ispol'zovaniya v ontologicheskoy modeli. Int. J. Open Inf. Technol. **3**(12), 28–37 (2015). ISSN: 2307-8162

EERO: Energy Efficient Route Optimization Technique for IoT Network

J. Shreyas$^{(\boxtimes)}$, Dharamendra Chouhan, Sowmya T. Rao, P. K. Udayaprasad, N. N. Srinidhi, and S. M. Dilip Kumar

Department of Computer Science and Engineering,
University Visvesvaraya College of Engineering, Bangalore, India

Abstract. In the real world, it is essential to establish efficient routes in the Internet of Things (IoT) since sensor nodes operate mainly on battery and have limited energy. In this paper, an energy efficient routing technique is proposed to select an optimal routing path from source to destination for the transmission of data. Genetic algorithm (GA) is an optimization technique which is integrated into the proposed work to select an optimal path among the available paths. Since the proposed method selects an optimal path from source cluster head to the sink, this reduces the energy consumption and improves the lifetime of network. The validity of the proposed algorithm is evaluated in MATLAB simulation tool and results generate superiority while considering parameters such as energy consumption, delay and number of rounds.

Keywords: Internet of Things · Cluster head · Genetic algorithm · Routing challenges · Optimal route

1 Introduction

IoT is considered to be one of the fast growing technologies over the past few decades across the world [1]. IoT network have a large volume of sensor nodes deployed, these nodes have the properties of being the low cost, less powerful and computational capabilities [2].

It is used for collecting information such as measuring the physical parameter like chemical composition, pressure, temperature, and others [3,4]. IoT has several advantages and one of them is that communication between the nodes and these communication takes place through Radio Frequency Identification (RFID) radio signals [5]. The main intention of the IoT is to collect the data and transmit to the particular station. Routing is one of the major essential concerns; routing protocol enables the nodes in the network, which specifies the route selection from the source to the destination node, these paths are selected using the routing algorithm [6]. A routing protocol is said to be the process that chooses an efficient and suitable path for data transmission. Routing techniques are required for transferring the data between the base stations and sensor nodes. The designing and routing have been always one of the challenging tasks

© Springer Nature Singapore Pte Ltd. 2021
P. K. Singh et al. (Eds.): FTNCT 2020, CCIS 1396, pp. 207–218, 2021.
https://doi.org/10.1007/978-981-16-1483-5_19

due to the various constraints which are shown in Fig. 1 Since, the IoT network comprised of huge sensor nodes deployed and these nodes are battery equipped and have limited energy [7]. Hence the optimal energy consumption is major challenge while transmitting the data from source to destination. Therefore, it is important to propose a technique that optimally consumes energy by balancing the QoS parameters and thereby forwards the data from source to destination. In the proposed system, the objective function is obtaining the optimal path among the available path between the source to destination node. Here, the advantage of a genetic algorithm adopted to obtain the optimal routing benefit. Therefore the proposed methodology is named energy efficient route optimization technique. The contributions of this article are as follows:

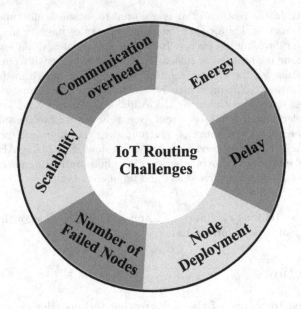

Fig. 1. Routing challenges

1. An energy efficient routing algorithm is proposed to find an efficient route from source CH to sink.
2. Fitness function $Fit\_Func(pos)$ is used to find the fitness value of the chromosomes.
3. The results of the proposed work in implemented using MATLAB simulation tool and the obtained results are compared against PMSO [10] and FPMSO [16].

The remaining part of this article is categorized as follows. Initially Sect. 2 discusses background works. Then in Sect. 3 problem statement of proposed methodology is presented. Later in Sect. 4 we present proposed methodology which consists of genetic algorithm integrated with EERO. Performance evaluation of proposed EERO is presented in Sect. 5. Finally conclusions is given in Sect. 6.

2   Related Works

In the past few decades, IoT is applicable in various places such as healthcare, agriculture, surveillance and military, several researchers have shown interest and most of them have focused on the energy consumption such as in [8,9]. It is aware that for any novel work there should be proper research behind it hence in this section various methodologies for route optimization are discussed. In [10] proposed bio-inspired particle Muli-swarm Optimization (PMSO) and Fully Particle Multi-swarm (FPMSO) for guaranteeing fault tolerance and to find optimal directions.

The authors in [11] proposed an algorithm namely EADC, here even size cluster is formed using Competition Range (CR) Characteristic as well as the area where the nodes are shared in the non- uniform in the given network. It also proposes the cluster based routing this gives the task to those available nodes. The main intention here is to force the CH to choose the node, which has more power.

The works proposed in [12] are Fuzzy Energy-Aware Unequal Clustering Algorithm (EAUCF) to get rid of the bottleneck problem. The bottleneck problem exists due to the death of nodes closure to the base station are considered idle since it has more workload. Moreover, the focus on these causes the ignorance of other nodes. Hence in [13] applied the efficient clustering mechanism, here sensing signal is increased, this helps in efficient routing. However only increasing the number of sensing signal was not enough to provide the routing.

Moreover, to overcome this [14] proposed a methodology named Geographical and Energy Aware Routing (GEAR), the authors used the Energy Aware (EA) mechanism which helps in planning the route for packet from the source to destination and two other algorithms namely Recursive Geographic Forwarding algorithm and Restricted Flooding (RGF and RF) was proposed by the same author for propagating the data in the given range. The main issue with this algorithm was that the range of this was very short.

It was mainly based on the prioritized sets, the improvised version of the same is proposed is given by the author [15], here Harmony Search Algorithm (HAS) were proposed in order to implement the CH selection for energy efficiency, this paper helped in minimizing the distance from the CH node to the sensor node. Although the performance was quite remarkable, however, Cluster head selection was very much complicated.

3   Problem Statement

The problem addressed in this article is to select an efficient cluster head and find an optimal routing path from source to the destination in the homogeneous IoT network with an objective to optimizes energy consumption and reduces the end-to-end delay to thereby increase the lifetime of the network.

The following objectives are need to be considered while addressing the defined problem:

1. To reduce end to end delay.
2. To optimize an energy consumption in the network.
3. To increase the lifetime of the network.

4   Proposed Methodology

The above discussed methodologies in the related work section are not able to find the energy efficient optimal solution. However, they lack with the efficiency and fails under various constraints. To overcome this problem an energy efficient optimized method for finding optimal path is proposed. Figure 2, presents the proposed work flow of EERO methodology, where we initialize the network, then we present a novel method to select the efficient CH, it is designed in such a way that every CH gets the same number of chances to become CH and it is assumed that all the nodes possess the same amount of energy and have data to transmit. The selected CH is given as the input to the GA. In GA selection, crossover and mutation are three major process that are performed. Through objective function the optimal path is selected and this process takes several steps which are discussed in the same section of the paper. Once the optimal path is selected, the data is sent from source to the sink.

The proposed EERO method finds an optimal path from the source CH to the sink. As shown in Algorithm 1 the chromosomes in GA are considered as the path from source CH to sink in the proposed system. The optimal path is length of the number of CHs in the routing path. In the proposed system population Initialization takes place through the random generation set and then these are evaluated using the FF (Fitness Function). The best of these are selected based on the defined fitness values and they participate for the next generation. The OF (Objective Function) is one of the methodologies in the genetic algorithm as it selects the optimal paths among given paths to process the next generation.

4.1   Selection of Cluster Head

Here the intention is to form the cluster such that there exist cluster in every round, through this intention is to distribute the energy among the nodes such that no nodes run out of energy. Each sensor node selects to be the CH by itself at first, the probability of cluster head selection is given in Eq. 1:

$$Eng = \sum_{n}^{U} Prob_n(time) * 1 \tag{1}$$

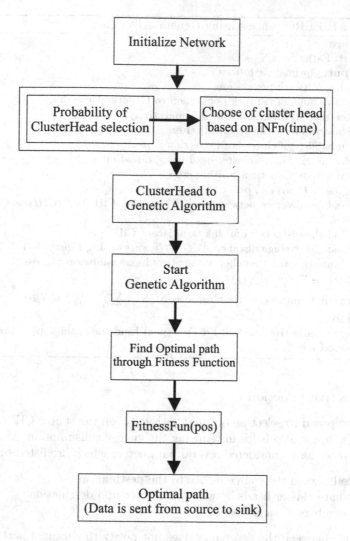

Fig. 2. EERO process using genetic algorithm

This ensures that all the nodes in the cluster get on an average energy, the equation shows the probability of cluster head selection, $INF_n(time)$ is the indicator function used which identifies whether the particular node has been cluster head or not, if the $INF_n(time) = 1$ then the node is cluster head and if $INF_n(time) = 0$ then node is not a cluster head.

Algorithm 1. EERO process using Genetic Algorithm

1: **procedure**
2: | **Input:** Paths from S → D
3: | **Output:** Optimal path from S → D
4: | Initialize Network population
5: | Input the random network population to Genetic Algorithm
6: | Choose the CH and establish Ch connectivity
7: | **if** (Sensor node != cluster head) **then**
8: | | Probability of cluter head selection is $probn(time)$
9: | | choose an efficient cluster head using Equation 1
10: | **end if**Initiate Genetic algorithm steps
11: | **for** (pos = 1, pos++, pos < p) **do**
12: | | Find the distance between one ClH to other ClH $AVG(ClHpos, ClH(pos + 1))$
13: | | Find the distance from sink to adjacent ClH
14: | | Find the average distance $AVG(ClH, sink)$ using Equation 3
15: | | Computing total number of members in transmission process
16: | | NPT = $\sum_{(pos=1)}^{(P)} NGM_i$
17: | | calculate member n the cluster as NCN = $\sum_{(pos=1)}^{(P)} NCN_pos$
18: | **end for**
19: | using the objective function Fit Func(pos) Find the optimal path from S → D
20: **end procedure**

4.2 Objective Function

EERO is proposed to select an optimal path between the source CH to destination node, hence it also helps in reducing the energy consumption. Moreover to achieve that we have considered several parameters which are listed below.

1. Distance between the source device to the destination.
2. Intermediate cluster heads between the source and destination.
3. Group members of each cluster.

The distance between the two nodes does not notify the optimal path between the source and destination node.

$$AVG(ClH, Sink) = \sum_{(pos=1)}^{(P-1)} \frac{AVG(ClH_{pos}, ClH_{(pos+1)})}{p} + \frac{AVG(ClH_P, BS)}{P}$$

$$(2)$$

$AVG(ClH_p, BS)$ is the average distance between the source station to the base station, P is the total number of cluster head in the path, $AVG(ClH_{pos}, ClH_{(pos+1)})$ is from the pos to pos+1, $AVG(ClH_P, Sink)$ is the distance from the sink to its adjacent cluster head as shown in Eq. 2.

The below objective function equation is implied for finding an optimized path.

$$Fit\_Func(pos) = AVG(ClH, Sink) + \frac{TN_{Clh}}{N} + NCN \qquad (3)$$

From Eq. 3 $Fit\_Func(pos)$ shows the value ith of chromosome, $AVG(ClH, Sink)$ is the average distance from the source to sink and TN_{Clh} is the total number of cluster heads.

5 Result and Discussion

In this section, the proposed algorithm is evaluated to prove the accuracy of the algorithm using MATLAB. The simulation is carried out by considering various parameters like energy efficiency, delay and number of rounds and henceforth compared these parameters with the existing PMSO [10] and FPMSO [16] algorithms. The sensor nodes deployed in the proposed network is 50, 100, 150, and 200.

A. *First Sensor Death Node*

Energy Consumption: Energy is defined as the quantitative attribute which needs to be transferred to the particularly given object to perform some task. Energy is considered to be one of the important parameters when the task is performed. Lesser the energy consumed by the network, more the efficient the model is. The evaluation of algorithm energy is considered as the parameters to compare with the existing algorithm. Figure 3 shows the energy consumption of network in which the energy consumption of proposed EERO is less when number of nodes are increased to 50–200 where as in FPMSO and PMSO the energy consumed by the network increases as number of nodes increase.

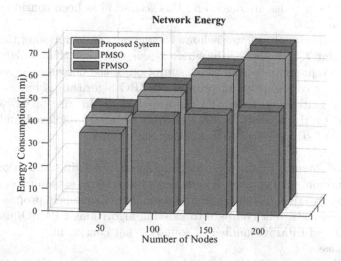

Fig. 3. Energy consumption of the network at first sensor death node

End to End Delay: Figure 4 shows the Delay time of the network at constraint first sensor node death where x-axis represent number of nodes and y-axis represent the delay time. End to End delay is defined as the time consumed for the particular packet for the transmission across the network from the source to the given destination. As seen in graph even when number of nodes are increased the delay remains constant in proposed EERO whereas in existing PMSO and FPMSO the delay is increasing.

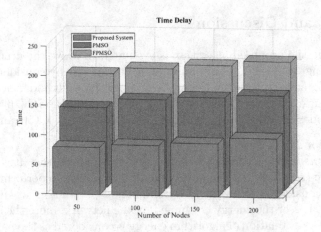

Fig. 4. Delay time at first sensor death node.

B. *75% Node Death Constraint*

Moreover, for the better evaluation of the algorithm, the constraint considered is when 75% of nodes are dead, and this scenario has been considered for 50, 100, 150 and 200.

Energy Consumption: Figure 5 shows the energy consumption of the network at constraint 75% Node Death, where x-axis represent the number of nodes and y-axis represent the energy consumption of the network. As seen in the graph energy consumption of proposed EERO algorithm is less compare to existing algorithms such as FPMSO and PMSO. In case of EERO energy consumed by the network is less when 50 nodes are deployed and again it increases but still it is less than existing algorithms.

Number of Rounds: Figure 6 shows Number of rounds in the network, where x-axis represents the number of nodes and y-axis represents number of rounds with respect to time. As shown in figure number of rounds in proposed system is more and consistent compare to existing algorithms FPMSO and PMSO. In PMSO and FPMSO number of rounds is not consistent.

C. *Netwok Loss*

Network loss represents the network where certain connections between the SNs are lost or disconnected and this is considered as one of the constraint to prove the efficiency of proposed EERO algorithm.

Energy consumption: In Fig. 7 shows the energy consumption of the network at constraint network loss, where x-axis represent the number of nodes and y-axis represent the energy consumption of the network with respect to time. As seen in the graph energy consumption of proposed EERO algorithm is less

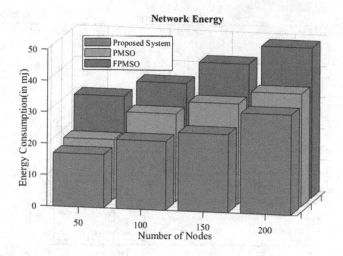

Fig. 5. Energy consumption of the network at 75% death node constraint

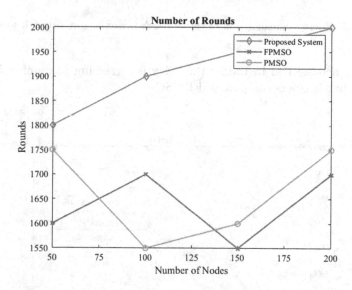

Fig. 6. Number of rounds in the network at 75% death node constraint

compare to existing algorithms but it increases as number of nodes increase which is less than existing PMSO. PMSO is Consuming more energy compare to FPMSO and EERO.

Time_Delay: In Fig. 8 shows the delay in the network at constraint network loss, where x-axis represent number of nodes and y-axis represent Delay with respect to time. As seen in graph EERO has lower Delay compare to existing algorithms FPMSO and PMSO. In FPMSO the delay is increasing as number

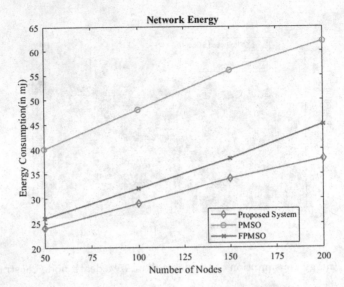

Fig. 7. Energy consumption of the network at constraint network loss

of nodes increase and in PMSO the delay is increasing as number of nodes increase but it is less compare to FPMSO.

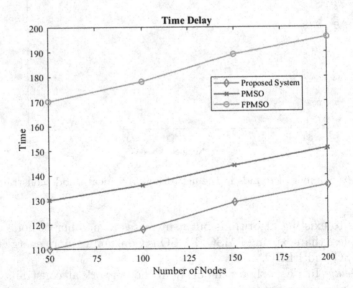

Fig. 8. Delay in the network at constraint network loss

6 Conclusion

In this paper, an energy efficient route optimization technique is proposed to find an optimal path for the transmission of data in homogeneous IoT network. The proposed algorithm finds the optimal path from source cluster head to the sink using the fitness function. The proposed work adopts genetic algorithm to obtain the optimal routing benefit. The simulation of the proposed technique is carried out using the MATLAB simulation tool. The simulation results indicates that the algorithm performs better compared to the existing routing techniques. To validate and analyze the strength of the proposed algorithm, we have considered the different scenarios such as first sensor death node, 75% node death and network loss. It has been observed that the proposed EERO performance is better in terms of energy, delay and number of rounds parameters compare to existing algorithm. As a future work, the proposed work can be improvised to further optimize the energy consumption of the network and to consider other QoS parameters for the performance analysis by increasing the network size.

References

1. Shreyas, J., Singh, H., Bhutani, J., Pandit, S., Srinidhi, N.N., Dilip Kumar, S.M.: Congestion aware algorithm using fuzzy logic to find an optimal routing path for IoT networks. In: 2019 International Conference on Computational Intelligence and Knowledge Economy (ICCIKE). IEEE (2019)
2. Malik, P.K., Wadhwa, D.S., Khinda, J.S.: A survey of device to device and cooperative communication for the future cellular networks. Int. J. Wirel. Inf. Netw. **27**(3), 411–432 (2020). https://doi.org/10.1007/s10776-020-00482-8
3. Singh, P.K., Paprzycki, M., Bhargava, B., Chhabra, J.K., Kaushal, N.C., Kumar, Y. (eds.): FTNCT 2018. CCIS, vol. 958, pp. 141–166. Springer, Singapore (2019). https://doi.org/10.1007/978-981-13-3804-5
4. Singh, P.K., Sood, S., Kumar, Y., Paprzycki, M., Pljonkin, A., Hong, W.-C. (eds.): FTNCT 2019. CCIS, vol. 1206. Springer, Singapore (2020). https://doi.org/10.1007/978-981-15-4451-4
5. Shreyas, J., Jumnal, A., Dilip Kumar, S.M., Venugopal, K.R.: Application of computational intelligence techniques for Internet of Things: an extensive survey. Int. J. Comput. Intell. Stud. **9**(3), 234–288 (2020)
6. Das, P.K., Malik, P.K., Singh, R., Gehlot, A., Gupta, K.V., Singh, A.: Industrial hazard prevention using Raspberry Pi. In: Singh Tomar, G., Chaudhari, N.S., Barbosa, J.L.V., Aghwariya, M.K. (eds.) International Conference on Intelligent Computing and Smart Communication 2019. AIS, pp. 1487–1499. Springer, Singapore (2020). https://doi.org/10.1007/978-981-15-0633-8_146
7. Shreyas, J., Chouhan, D., Akshatha, A.R., Udayaprasad, P.K., Dilip Kumar, S.M.: Selection of optimal path for the communication of multimedia data in Internet of Things. In: 2020 6th International Conference on Advanced Computing and Communication Systems (ICACCS). IEEE (2020)
8. Ramson, S.J., Moni, D.J.: Applications of wireless sensor networks–a survey. In: 2017 International Conference on Innovations in Electrical, Electronics, Instrumentation and Media Technology (ICEEIMT), pp. 325–329. IEEE (2017)

9. Roy, A., Sarma, N.: Effects of various factors on performance of MAC protocols for underwater wireless sensor networks. Mater. Today Proc. **5**(1), 2263–2274 (2018)
10. Yan, J., Zhou, M., Ding, Z.: Recent advances in energy-efficient routing protocols for wireless sensor networks: a review. IEEE Access **4**, 5673–5686 (2016)
11. Seco, F., Jim'enez, A.R., Peltola, P.: A review of multidimensional scaling techniques for RSS-based WSN localization. In: 2018 International Conference on Indoor Positioning and Indoor Navigation (IPIN), pp. 1–8. IEEE (2018)
12. Forero, P.A., Cano, A., Giannakis, G.B.: Distributed clustering using wireless sensor networks. IEEE J. Sel. Top. Sig. Process. **5**(4), 707–724 (2011)
13. Chen, C.-M., Lin, Y.-H., Chen, Y.-H., Sun, H.-M.: SASHIMI: secure aggregation via successively hierarchical inspecting of message integrity on WSN. J. Inf. Hiding Multimed. Sig. Process. **4**(1), 57–72 (2013)
14. Tuna, G., Gungor, V.C., Gulez, K., Hancke, G., Gungor, V.: Energy harvesting techniques for industrial wireless sensor networks. In: Industrial Wireless Sensor Networks: Applications, Protocols, Standards, and Products, pp. 119–136 (2013)
15. Raval, D., Raval, G., Valiveti, S.: Optimization of clustering process for WSN with hybrid harmony search and K-means algorithm. In: 2016 International Conference on Recent Trends in Information Technology (ICRTIT). IEEE (2016)
16. Hasan, M.Z., Al-Turjman, F.: SWARM-based data delivery in Social Internet of Things. Future Gener. Comput. Syst. **92**, 821–836 (2019)

Forecasting Non-Stationary Time Series Using Kernel Regression for Control Problems

S. I. Kolesnikova$^{(\boxtimes)}$, V. A. Avramyonok, and A. D. Bogdanova

St. Petersburg State University of Aerospace Instrumentation,
67, Bolshaya Morskaia Str., St. Petersburg 190000, Russia

Abstract. A combined algorithm for a time series analysis is considered based on two basic methods: the empirical mode decomposition and kernel regression. The essence of the presented algorithm is the sequential calculation of nuclear regressions and residues, which results in the decomposition of the original series into an additive mixture of the number of regressions and residual series. The illustrative examples for the application of the proposed algorithm (immunology, economics, and other fields of studies) are provided along with their statistical results of numerical simulation. The results obtained would be useful for a smart control system design and real-time decision making support as it concerns the problems of stochastic control over a wide range of poorly formalized objects from various applied areas.

1 Introduction

The problem of using mathematical methods to solve the problem of analyzing and forecasting stochastic time series $X^N = \{x_1, \ldots, x_N\} = \{x_t\}_{t=\overline{1,N}}$ is that the elements of time series are not a) statistically independent; b) equally distributed [1, 2].

In this regard, mathematical technologies for the synthesis of reliable algorithms (ref., for example, [3]) based on particular heuristic model are extremely popular. In this case, each technology shows less efficiency (when used separately).

The idea to create such combined algorithms is not new and relevant to the works of Shannon (reliable circuits using less reliable relays) or Neumann (building reliable computing circuits using unreliable elements).

The objective of this paper is to study the possibility of a combined use for two popular methods of processing time series to solve the problem of reliable forecasting, namely

- the empirical mode decomposition, hereinafter EMD, which is based on the idea of expanding time series into their component modes [4], which enables to remove a random component/noise of series to forecast and build a forecast trend with pure values; EMD-method was chosen because of its advantage. It does not rely on the analytical bases, and is determined only by the initial data. The disadvantage of this model is the end effects determined by the approximation unpredictability by the extrema of the upper and lower signal envelopes at the end portions of the local modes;

© Springer Nature Singapore Pte Ltd. 2021
P. K. Singh et al. (Eds.): FTNCT 2020, CCIS 1396, pp. 219–227, 2021.
https://doi.org/10.1007/978-981-16-1483-5_20

- the algorithm to construct kernel regression forecasting (hereinafter KR-algorithm [5]), which is based on the idea of regression modeling as a conditional mathematical expectation $M\,(Y/x)$ of a random value Y when observing x values of another random variable X. Therein, $y = M\,(Y/x)$, the estimated Y value at the observed x value, is understood as the locally weighted average;
- the weighted regression function is presented in the form of a kernel (the analog of a distribution density function) with a scalar parameter that regulates the size and shape of a core.

2   State Estimation of a Nonlinear Object. Problem Statement

Let a training sample be given in the form of a set of pairs

$$Z^L = \{z_i := (x_i, y_i)\}, i = \overline{1, L},$$

where $x^L = \{x_1, \ldots, x_L\}, y^L = \{y_1, \ldots, y_L\}, y_i = f(x_i), f$ is an unknown function, L is the depth of the historical data (a segment of observations); $y^{*L} = \{y_1^*, \ldots, y_L^*\}$ is a predicted value for a vector-object Z^L.

We set a quality criterion in the following form

$$Q(Z^L) = \frac{1}{L} \sum_{j=1}^{L} \left| y_j - y_j^* \right| \to \min_{(y^{*L})}.$$

Therefore, it is necessary to solve the following problems:

1) find the "best" forecasting segment d ("window size") of observations for the synthesized algorithm $y_j^* = a(z_j, Z^L), j = \overline{1, L}$;
2) create a forecasting algorithm $A(Z^L) = \left\{ y_j^* | y_j^* = a(z_j, Z^L), j = \overline{1, L} \right\}$ that delivers a minimum of functionality Q on the training set Z^L;

$$A(Z^L) : Z^L \to Z^{*L}; \ Z^{*L} = \{z_i^* := (x_i, y_i^*), i = \overline{1, L}\};$$

3) construct a forecast error vector and estimate the average value of the error function according to two indicators: the average value for an individual implementation and the average value for an ensemble of implementations;
4) evaluate a generalizing ability of the forecasting algorithm with an additional control sample.

3   Forecasting Problems with Solution

3.1   The Main Provisions for the Combined Forecasting Algorithm

The synthesis of the analysis and forecasting algorithm (let us call it ERD: Empirical Regression and Decomposition algorithm) based on these methods is characterized by the following provisions.

1. The initial data consists of a set of nonlinear random processes, and the average value of this set forms an axis of symmetry relative to the initial data of the time series.

2. The arbitrary time series can be divided into a finite set of functions of local $KR(i)$, $i \geq 1$ regressions (the analogue of the internal modes of EMD algorithm) and residuals.

3. ERD algorithm consists of sequentially calculating $KR(i) := \{(x_j, R_j(i)), j = \overline{1, L}\}$ regressions

$$R_j(i) = a_h(z_k; Z^L(i-1)) = \frac{\sum_{j=1}^{j=L} K(u_{kj}) y_j(i-1)}{\sum_{j=1}^{j=L} K(u_{kj})},$$

$$K(u_{kj}) = \frac{1}{\text{eg } \sqrt{2\pi}} e^{-\frac{1}{2}u_{kj}^2}, \ u_{kj} = \frac{\rho(z_k, z_j)}{h}, \ z_k, z_j \in Z^L(i-1),$$

$$Z^L(i) = \{z_j := (x_j, y_j(i)), \ y_j(i) = y_j(i-1) - R_j(i), j = \overline{1, L}\};$$

$$i = \overline{1, N_{stop}}, y_j(0) := y_j, Z^L(0) := Z^L$$

as the analogues of 'local means', when the initial series is decomposed into components as a result in the form of an additive mixture of the number of regressions KR (i) and the series of residuals $Z^L(i), i \geq 1$.

4. The process of sequential calculation of KR (i) regressions ends when the average threshold accuracy of forecasting by the sliding observation window is reached (and/or when the local threshold accuracy of forecasting is reached when compared with the real value of time series).

3.2   The Main Optimization Parameters for the Forecasting Algorithm

The optimization parameters of ERD algorithm are as follows:

- an observation "window" size d to decide on the predicted value (not to be confused with the parameter h);
- a type of a kernel function and its parameters;
- a type of a distance function $\rho (a,b), a,b \in Z^L$;
- a criterion to calculate the error of the dynamic forecast as the average difference between the forecast and the real values of the time series in the interval $d_k, k = 1,2,\ldots$;
- a criterion to stop a regression calculation process, for example,

$$N_{stop} = \arg \min\left\{i : \mathbf{D}\left(Z^L(i)\right) < \mathbf{D}\left(Z^L(i-1)\right)\right\},$$

where $\mathbf{D}(X)$ is an operation designation of the set X variance.

4   Comparative Simulation Results for Applied Problems

4.1   The Applied Problem to Forecast the Dynamics of a Currency Pair

The data used is the USD/EUR currency pair from 01/20/2020 in the interval 3.00 to 5.28 with an interval of 1 min. At each time point, the data for 20 min is displayed.

The selection of the optimal observation interval for each algorithm takes into account the same amount of the data.

Since the program runs in real time, an error is calculated at each current point in time.

The average error during the program operation for various algorithms is as follows (Table 1, Fig. 1).

Table 1. Comparative forecast quality results for three algorithms.

Names of algorithms	Average forecasting errors
ERD	4,6e−09
KR	6,4e−09
EMD	6,6e−09

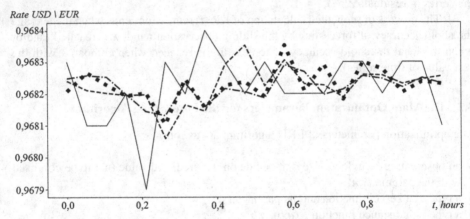

Fig. 1. Designation of predicted trajectories behaviour obtained by the algorithms: a solid line is an initial curve (the historical data); a fine-dotted and a dot line are according to ERD algorithm; a simple dotted line is according to classical EMD algorithm; a bold dotted line is according to KR-algorithm.

The attractiveness of ERD algorithm when compared with the basic EMD and KR-algorithms lies in the absence of restrictions inherent in the latter, namely, it is not required that

a) the extrema number of the series be equal to the number of the intersections with local averages up to the unity;
b) the conditions for a spline interpolation application (for example, continuous differentiability) and other restrictive requirements of these algorithms are observed.

4.2 The Applied Problem to Forecast Recovery Dynamics from COVID-19

The data used is the time series of COVID-19 incidence, recovery, and deaths from 01/02/2020 to 05/31/2020 with an interval of 1 day (Fig. 2).

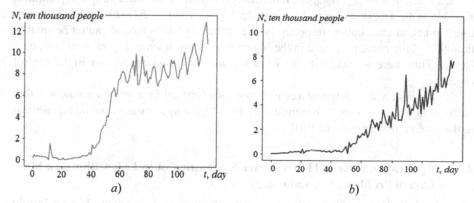

Fig. 2. The number of people who fell ill a) and b) — the number of people who recovered during the specified period, respectively.

The numerical modeling (e.g. Tables 1 and 2) of three algorithms showed that in general all algorithms show the comparable results, which essentially depend on the parameters of the algorithms and the nature of non-stationarity of the time series source. Therefore, the quality of the forecast is significantly determined by the training procedure and the criteria used to stop training.

Table 2. Comparative errors in predicting mortality using three algorithms.

Names of algorithms	Average forecasting errors	Minimum forecasting errors	Maximum forecasting errors
ERD	627,919	0,899	3116,559
KR	688,428	0,500	2986,625
EMD	703,414	0,500	3115,805

4.3 The Relevance for Correct Estimation of Time Series for a Discrete Stochastic Nonlinear Regulator

A feedback-based control over an object can be effective only given the availability of the correct data on its state.

We should note the important feature of non-linear objects, characterized by the unstable modes of operation under the conditions of uncertainty. The filtering operation is not trivial, since noise smoothing can distort useful information about the current state of such objects.

It is easy to show that in the 6-dimensional stochastic object described by a difference stochastic equations system $Y[k+1] = F[k] + u[k] + \xi[k+1] + c\xi[k]$, $k \in \{0, 1, 2, \ldots\}$, where $\{\xi[k]\}_{k \geq 0}$ are independent, equally distributed random quantities, $\mathbf{E}\{\xi[k]\} = 0$, $\mathbf{D}\{\xi[k]\} = \sigma^2$, $0 < c < 1$, $k \geq 0$; $F[k] = F(Y[k])$, $u[k]$ are a nonlinear function and control, respectively, the output signal dispersion cannot be smaller than that of the noise presented in the object's description under *any control* (see, e.g., [6–8]). Thus, here we deal with the so-called unrecoverable uncertainty in the control objects.

In this case, when designing a control, one puts forward a natural requirement to find such a state estimation tool when the dispersion of the output variable would be minimal at the given initial conditions $Y[0]$.

4.3.1   Application of Kernel Filtering in a Stochastic Control Algorithm on a Manifold in Problems of Immunology

Consider the influence of kernel filtration on the result of stochastic control on a manifold in the problem of immunology.

Let us discretize a continuous system of the simplest immunological object (according to G.I. Marchuk [9]) with a delay based on the Euler difference scheme, using phase-space extension in order to include into account the delay as follows ((see, e.g., [10]).):

$$
\begin{aligned}
&V[k+1] = V[k] + \tau_0(a_1 V[k] - a_2 F[k]V[k]), \\
&S[k+1] = S[k] + \tau_0(a_3\zeta(m[k])Y_1[k]Y_2[k] - a_5(S[k] - 1)), \\
&F[k+1] = F[k] + \tau_0(a_4(S[k] - F[k]) - a_8 F[k]V[k] + u[k]) + \xi[k+1] + c\xi[k], \quad (1) \\
&m[k+1] = m[k] + \tau_0(a_6 V[k] - a_7 m[k]), \\
&Y_1[k+1] = F[k], Y_2[k+1] = V[k], k \geq 0,
\end{aligned}
$$

where $\tau_0 > 0$ is the (Euler) discrete transformation; $Y_1[k+1] = F[k]$, $Y_2[k+1] = V[k]$ are fictitious variables for transforming a system with one step delay into a system of ordinary differential equations.

In description (1), similarly to the case in [9] the following notations are used: variables V, S, F are the concentrations of antigens in the target affected organs, plasma cells, and blood antibodies, respectively; $m(t) = 1 - M(t)/M^*$ is the fraction of the cells of the affected organ destroyed by the antigen, $M(t)$, M^* is the current number of the cells of the target affected organ at the time point t and in the normal conditions, respectively; a_i, $i = \overline{1, 8}$ are the model parameters, whose values depend on the form of the disease and its stages; function $\zeta(m)$ characterizes the disturbances of the immune system functioning due to an organ-lesion, $\zeta(m) = 1$ if $0 \leq m < m^*$, and $\zeta(m) = (m - 1)/(m^* - 1)$ if $m^* \leq m < 1$, where m^* is the maximum allowed (normal immune system functioning is still possible) fraction of the cells destroyed by the antigen.

Omitting technical details, we use the discrete method of analytical design of aggregated stochastic regulators (ADAR(S)) [7, 8] that lead to the control:

$$u^{As}[k] = -\tau_0^{-1}\psi^{(1)}[k](\omega_1 + 1 + c) - c\tau_0^{-1}\omega_1\psi^{(1)}[k-1] - a_4(S[k] - F[k]) + a_8F[k]V[k],$$
$$\psi^{(1)}[k] = F[k] - (a_2V[k]\tau_0)^{-1}(V[k] - V^*)(\omega_2 + 1) - a_1a_2^{-1}, \ k \geq 0.$$

The regulator in this form provides asymptotically stable stabilization of the control object $V[k]$ in a certain neighborhood of the target manifold $\psi[k] = V[k] - V^*$, $k \to \infty$ with the minimal dispersion for the macro variable $\psi[k]$.

4.3.2 Example 1. Object Parameters (1) that Correspond to the Fatal Disease Outcome

We assumed that the simulation parameters had the following values:

$$a_1 = 1, 54, a_2 = 0.77, a_3 = 880, a_4 = 0, 15, a_5 = 0, 5, a_6 = 12, a_7 = 0, 12, a_8 = 8,$$
$$\omega_1 = 0, 05, \omega_2 = 0, 1, V(0) = 10^{-6}, S(0) = 1, F(0) = 1, m(0) = 0, 1, t_0 = 1, V^* = 0.$$

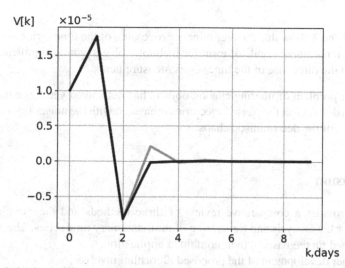

Fig. 3. The behaviour of the controlled variable $V[k]$ previously subjected to regression processing (a black line) and directly measured under a normal noise with the parameters $(0; \sigma = 0,5)$ (a red line).

4.3.3 Example 2. Object Parameters (1) that Correspond to the Chronic Disease Outcome

We assumed that the simulation parameters had the following values:

$$a_1 = 1, a_2 = 0, 8, a_3 = 1000, a_4 = 0, 17, a_5 = 0, 5, a_6 = 10, a_7 = 0, 12, a_8 = 8,$$
$$\omega_1 = 0, 05, \omega_2 = 0.1, V(0) = 10^{-6}, S(0) = 1, F(0) = 1, m(0) = 0, 1, t_0 = 1, V^* = 0.$$

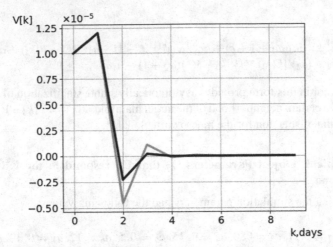

Fig. 4. The behaviour of the controlled variable $V[k]$ previously subjected to regression processing (a black line) and directly measured under a normal noise with the parameters $(0; \sigma = 0,5)$ (a red line) for the chronic disease outcome.

Figures 3 and 4 show that the preliminary processing of the time series using kernel regression in a nonlinear regulator even for a chaotic object can be significantly more effective than the direct use of the time series measurements.

Remark. The problem of filtering chaotic objects has not solved yet, since it is almost impossible to distinguish the phase trajectories measured with the noises from trajectory characteristics of the deterministic chaos.

5   Conclusion

The paper provides a comparative review of three methods and their implementing algorithms for the analysis and forecasting of non-stationary time series. The algorithm is also obtained on the basis of their combined application.

The further development of the proposed algorithm involves:

a) the optimization of the sliding window size in the forecasting process based on the maximum likelihood method (ref. its application, for example, in [11]);

b) the construction of the algebraic composition [3] based on three mentioned algorithms;

c) the construction of a single decision rule regarding the magnitude of the forecast based on a combination of several quality criteria and their additive regularization;

d) a comparative numerical testing of these algorithms on the applied problems of various applied orientation.

The obtained results when comparing the performance of all three methods for noisy non-stationary series are presented. There are reasons to believe that the synthetic use of two popular nonparametric forecasting algorithms will lead to a more efficient forecasting algorithm, at least to solve a certain class of problems.

Acknowledgments. The reported study was funded by RFBR according to the research project № 20-08-00747.

References

1. Box, G., Jenkins, G.: Time Series Analysis: Forecasting and Control. Holden-Day, San Francisco (1970)
2. Armstrong, J.S., Brodie, R.: Forecasting for Marketing. Quantitative methods in marketing. International Thompson Business Press, London (1999)
3. Vorontsov, K.V.: Time Series Forecasting. http://www.machinelearning.ru/wiki/images/c/cb/Voron-ML-forecasting-slides.pdf. Accessed 05 Feb 2020
4. Huang, H., et al.: The empirical mode decomposition and the Hilbert spectrum for nonlinear and non-stationary time series analysis. Proc. R. Soc. Lond. A **454**, 903–995 (1998)
5. Nadaraya, E.: On estimating regression. TV Appl. **9**(1), 141–142 (1964)
6. Astroem, K.J.: Introduction to Stochastic Control Theory. Academic Press, New York and London (1970)
7. Kolesnikova, S.: Stochastic discrete nonlinear control system for minimum dispersion of the output variable. Adv. Intell. Syst. Comput. **986**, 325–331 (2019)
8. Kolesnikova, S.: A multiple-control system for nonlinear discrete object under uncertainty. Optim. Methods Softw. **34**(3), 578–585 (2019)
9. Marchuk, G.I.: Mathematical modelling of immune response in infectious diseases. Math. Appl. **395**, 1–149 (1997)
10. Kolesnikova, S.I., Avramyonok, V.A.: Application of stochastic control method on manifold at immunology problem. J. Phys. Conf. Ser. **1515**(5), (2020)
11. Kolesnikova, S.: Method for recognizing and evaluating the states of a weakly formalized dynamic object based on time series marking. In: Proceedings of the Russian Academy of Sciences. Control Theory and Systems, vol. 5, pp. 41–52 (2011)

A Smart Waste Management System Based on LoRaWAN

Edwin Geovanny Flores Castro[1] and Sang Guun Yoo[2,3(✉)]

[1] Departamento de Ciencias de la Computación, Universidad de las Fuerzas Armadas ESPE,
Sangolquí, Ecuador
egflores5@espe.edu.ec
[2] Departamento de Informática y Ciencias de la Computación, Escuela Politécnica Nacional,
Quito, Ecuador
sang.yoo@epn.edu.ec
[3] Smart Lab, Escuela Politécnica Nacional, Quito, Ecuador

Abstract. Smart waste management is one of the most important services in smart cities. An efficient waste collection system based on IoT technologies allows having the streets clean and reducing resource consumption by optimizing garbage collecting trucks' routes. In this situation, the present work proposes a smart management system based on LoRaWAN. This solution seeks to mitigate the presence of containers that are at their maximum storage capacity. This solution will contribute to mitigate the spread of diseases due to it avoids having waste in the open air. Different tests of the proposed solution (i.e. communication distance, speed, and energy consumption) were performed to determinate the possibility of real implementations.

Keywords: Waste management · LoRaWAN · LPWAN · Smart cities · IoT

1 Introduction

Waste management is a task that can be result complex if traditional waste collection methods are used. It is common to see waste containers that exceed their storage capacity, making people to leave waste bags on the ground. This situation rises the possibility for dogs to break bags searching for food, making waste to scatter on the ground, drawing the attention of rodents and other animals. The efficient waste collection prevents these problems that negatively affect people's health and environment [1]. In this aspect, some countries e.g. Argentina have chosen the inclusion of technological solution to the process of waste collection for optimizing trucks' routes, but the problem remains since the there is no monitoring of the capacity of garbage containers [2].

In traditional waste collection systems, trucks collect the garbage periodically using pre-established routes. However, this process cannot be considered an optimal solution since some garbage containers could not be full when trucks are collecting the garbage and other containers could be overflowed, resulting in garbage being left in streets. In this aspect, smart city technologies can contribute to an efficient waste management

© Springer Nature Singapore Pte Ltd. 2021
P. K. Singh et al. (Eds.): FTNCT 2020, CCIS 1396, pp. 228–240, 2021.
https://doi.org/10.1007/978-981-16-1483-5_21

system, because they have revolutionized significantly in the provision of infrastructure and services for citizens through the use of information technologies, with the purpose of generating an intelligent environment that contributes to the improvement of the citizens' life standard [3].

One of the main requirements for an intelligent lifestyle begins with a clean environment, which must start with an effective waste management system [4]; and to reach this objective, it is necessary to use smart waste containers, which can prevent the overflow of waste in the containers by delivering timely notifications when containers are almost full, making it possible for the personnel to plan garbage collection routes in an effectively way.

For the implementation of smart waste management systems, it is essential to talk about the Internet of Things (IoT) since through IoT, objects can connect and communicate themselves [5, 6] allowing the development of different applications in different fields [7]. Additionally, it is important to indicate that one of the interesting things of IoT applications is that most of them require long-range communication and energy efficiency, and the smart waste containers is not the exception. In this situation, the present work has the objective of designing and implementing a smart waste container system considering the long-range communication and energy efficiency factors. To reach this objective, the proposed systems uses the LPWAN technology [8], and among the different LPWAN options (such as Sigfox, NB-IoT and LoraWAN), the LoRaWAN has been chosen since it allows to create totally independent low cost private networks [9–11]; additionally, because LoRaWAN has several advantages over traditional networks such as Wi-Fi and cellular networks in terms of coverage and costs [12].

2 Background

Garbage has become a problem for most of big cities because urbanization is spreading rapidly, leading to a significant increase in waste generation. Nowadays, waste management is a subject of deep analysis since it is common to find public places with overflowing containers which rise the possibility of diseases for the inhabitants [13].

Within the waste management system, the key activities are the garbage collection and its classification, and the traditional way of executing the first activity is the collection of garbage in a pre-established period and route. However, this mechanism is not optimal since the amount of garbage generated in different areas is not a constant but a variable [14]. According to a World Bank's report called "What a Waste 2.0" published in 2018 indicates that the garbage generation per capita and per day is 0.74 kg. The projections towards 2050 indicate that will be an increase of 19% in countries with high income inhabitants and 40% or more in countries with low and middle income inhabitants [15]. In case of Ecuador, where this work is developed, the situation is complex. According to the Instituto Nacional de Estadísticas y Censos, the generation of waste per capita is 0.86 kg per day, being above the world´s average [16]. All these data are reflected in the reality of Ecuadorians, constantly finding containers on the edge of their maximum capacity.

Facing this problem, the best solution is not always the acquisition of more waste collection trucks or installation of larger waste containers, since the problem remains i.e.

the lack of knowledge how full are the garbage containers. In this aspect, maybe one of the best solutions could be smart waste containers equipped with sensors that allow waste management system administrators to know the available capacity of each container. This information could allow administrators to plan more effectively the collection routes of truck.

In the study of the state of art, we have found some proposals of smart waste containers. One of them is a system based on Arduino Uno and Raspberry Pi 2 using ultrasonic and infrared sensors which are used to detect the level of waste in a container. In this solution, the level of waste data is delivered to the collection truck using text messages [17]. Another proposal is an IoT device that includes a GPS module. In this solution, when the waste container is full, it sends a text message with the location of the container [18]. A third proposal is based on the use of wireless sensors which highlights by its versatility, low cost, and communication capacity; three levels are proposed for measuring the level of waste inside container i.e. high, medium and low. This measurement levels allow competent authority to take actions on planning waste collection routes for trucks minimizing the fuel consumption [19]. In a similar way, another solution proposed an intelligent waste container which seeks to control the accumulation of garbage using GSM communication [20]. Other authors propose a solution based on ultrasonic sensors and WeMos, which allows to see the amount of waste a container has in real time using the WiFi network [21].

All the aforementioned solutions try to implement a smart waste container system, but they do not take into account the level of low energy consumption of devices that allow to know how full the waste containers are. Additionally, most of them are not oriented to real implementations since they use low range networks (e.g. WiFi) or use commercial networks such as GSM or GPRS communications which could generate considerable costs. Given this situation, LPWAN networks could be the solution that may be more viable in the development of smart waste containers.

LPWAN networks are rising as an efficient solution for a big number of IoT solutions. The main objective of LPWAN is to provide a wide range networks using low consumption of energy for the connection of smart sensors and gateways. These networks can cover from 10 to 40 km in rural areas and from 1 to 5 km in urban areas. In addition, they are very energy efficient since the batteries of devices can last more than 10 years. Within the different types of LPWAN networks, we have chosen LoRaWAN for our solution because it offers easiness of implementation without requiring a subscription fee for communication as it happens with Sigfox and NB-IoT networks. Additionally, since LoRaWAN is completely open in terms of hardware and software, it provides to researchers the freedom to adjust the solution based on their needs in all aspects and components. LoRaWAN defines the communication protocol and architecture. These networks are based on LoRa; which is a technology that defines the physical layer. LoRa is the first low-cost wide area implementation, because it uses the ISM spectrum. The data transmission rate ranges from 300 bps to 50 kbps depending on bandwidth, and the maximum payload size of a message is 243 bytes [9]. All the aforementioned features allow us to propose a solution to be able to periodically monitor waste containers, taking into account that it is a low-cost solution, so a LoRaWAN network will allow us to meet the objective of this research.

3 Proposed Solution

3.1 Architecture

The proposed architecture provides an alternative solution for waste collection that seeks to reduce the implementation cost by implementing a solution based on LoRaWAN network. Within this architecture, the use of open source hardware and software is contemplated, as well as free services offered by third parties. The architecture has the following components: (1) Data gathering nodes, (2) LoRaWAN gateway, (3) Network server, (4) Application Server, and (5) Web application.

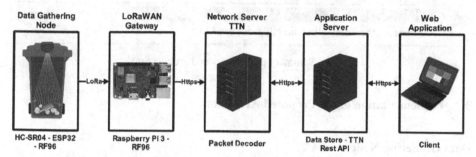

Fig. 1. Proposed architecture

Figure 1 shows the components of the proposed architecture. The architecture starts with the data gathering node, which is responsible for measuring the available capacity of the waste container periodically. The gathered data is sent via LoRa RF communication to the LoRaWAN gateway, which is responsible for forwarding the data to the network server using the HTTP protocol. On the other hand, the network server is responsible for filtering and decoding the received packets and retransmit them to the application server using the HTTP protocol. The application server provides an API which allows users to consume the data through a web application. Regarding the security, the proposed architecture complies with the three encryption keys proposed by the LoRaWAN protocol i.e. application key (AppKey), network session key (NwkSKey) and application session key (AppSkey). It is also important to indicate that the proposed architecture uses open source hardware and software. It also uses network and application servers that are provided by a third parties for free which allow to create a low-cost solution compared to commercial alternatives. As a summary, the Fig. 2 shows a short explanation of each component of the proposed architecture.

The frequency used for LoRa RF communication was 903.9 MHz, since the present work was executed in Latin America and based on the ISM (Industrial, Scientific and Medical) spectrum. Regarding the activation/authentication method between the data gathering node and LoRaWAN gateway, the Activation By Personalization (ABP) was used. This method allows the node to link directly to a specific network without the need for carrying out a join-request negotiation to join the network. Since the present solution uses a single channel for LoRa RF communication and only upload packets to the gateway, the over-the-air activation (OTTA) method was not necessary.

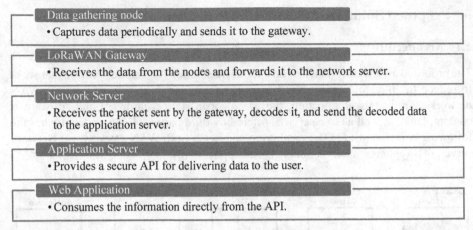

Fig. 2. Summary of the proposed architecture

3.2　Implementation of the Proposed Architecture

Data Gathering Node

This device is responsible for the periodical reading of the amount of waste in the container. The node is equipped with an HC-SR04 ultrasonic sensor, which is used to determine the distance between the sensor and objects [22]. This sensor is connected to an ESP32-DevKitC, which is small development board [23]. The data gathering node also includes a RF96 transmitter, which is a long-range LoRa module providing extended spectrum communication as well as high immunity to interferences while minimizing current consumption [24]. For determining the location of waste containers, a Ublox-Neo-6m-0-001 GPS module was used. In addition, a MOSFET IRFZ44 transistor was used to fulfill the function of a switch to prevent the electrical current flow. This transistor allows all the components of the data gathering node to be energized before a transmission begins, and when this has finished, the transistor turns off the components.

Figure 3 shows how the sensors measure the distance between the roof of the garbage container and the closest object inside it. The present solution uses 3 sensors to cover the entire container, since there may be a case where the waste is accumulated just in one side of the container. The measurement of the sensors is carried out periodically and sequentially, one after the other, to avoid interference between waves of one sensor to another. Once the measurement from the three sensors has been collected, the package is created and sent to the Gateway via LoRa communication.

The packet delivered to the Gateway from the data gathering node has the following format:

ds1%ds2%ds3; latitude; longitude

where ds1, ds2, ds3 are the distance between the sensors and the garbage inside the container. For example, the following message: $15\%13\%12; -0.252132; -75.515544$ represents:

Fig. 3. Smart container

- Sensor 1: 15 cm
- Sensor 2: 13 cm
- Sensor 3: 12 cm
- Latitude: −0.252132
- Longitude: −75.515544

In the present work, we have used 3 sensors to deliver more effectively the level of garbage inside container.

LoRaWAN Gateway: The LoRaWAN gateway is a piece of equipment that has a LoRa concentrator that performs the function of receiving the data transmitted by the data gathering nodes and forwarding it to the network server [25]. For the present work, a Raspberry Pi 3 B+ was used for the development of the LoRaWAN Gateway. The Raspberry Pi 3 B+ was the base board where the RF96 module was connected. The RF96 module provided all the features to have a LoRa-based communication. On the other hand, OpenSource libraries were used to translate the LoRa packets into TCP/IP packets. The LoRaWAN Gateway was connected to a platform called "The Things Network" (TTN) which provides a set of tools to build a low-cost IoT application, guaranteeing security and scalability, as well as allowing to collaborate as a member of the LoRa Alliance [26]. The present work has used Raspberry Pi since it has wired and wireless network interfaces ready to be used and because its operating system i.e. Raspbian can run applications developed in multiple programming languages. In regards of software, the Hallard repository was used, which contains the implementation of a proof of concept for a LoRaWAN gateway [27].

Network Server: For the implementation of the network server, The Things Network (TTN) platform was used, which delivers a platform as a service. To connect to the platform, the transmission frequency and the geographical position of the gateway must be considered. Within TTN platform, both the node and the gateway must be registered. In this component, the packet received from the Gateway is decoded and sent to the application server. Using the TTN platform, it was possible to avoid installation and implementation costs. In addition, since the TTN platform is located on the Internet, it makes possible users to access the data captured by the data gathering node from anywhere in the world.

Application Network: Same as the network server, the application server was deployed on The Things Network (TTN) platform. One of the great advantages of using The Things Network is that it makes possible to integrate with other technologies and protocols, making it an integral option for this work. Among the different integration options, Data Store makes possible to store and deliver data to the user using a REST API. This service can be consumed from any REST client as long as you have the access code generated by the platform.

Web Application (Client): The web application was developed to consume the REST API provided by The Things Network's Data Store service, in order to monitor the level of waste in a container periodically. The NodeJS development environment was used to develop the web application and a NoSQL MongoDB database was used to store the data. The main idea of the client is that the user can see on a map where the container is and its available capacity. To display the aforementioned information on a map, Leaflet was used, which is an open source JavaScript library for displaying interactive maps. It is also compatible with mobile devices and offers all the mapping options [28].

4 Performance Tests

To determine the performance of the proposed solution, different tests were carried out i.e. reach (distance) test, speed test and energy consumption test.

4.1 Reach (Distance) Test

The objective of this test was to determine the maximum transmission distance between the data gathering node and the LoRaWAN gateway. The test consisted of transmission of 25 packages from different geographical locations. The packages went sent using the different components of the proposed architecture and this process was shown in the web client. Within the web client, the latitude and longitude of the data gathering node and the data captured by the ultrasonic sensors to determine the available capacity of the container were visualized. The test was made in Quito, capital city of Ecuador. Table 1 contains all the transmission points and the distance between the point and LoRaWAN gateway.

The results obtained demonstrate that the solution proposed in this research had a maximum coverage of 6.07 km in a straight line between the data gathering node and the gateway. It is also important to indicate that tests were carried out in an urbanized area. The Fig. 4 shows the transmission points visualized on the map. Transmission points are shown in black, and red point represents the LoRaWAN gateway.

Table 1. Transmission points

ID	Latitude	Longitude	Distance
Gateway's location	−0.303971	−78.531911	0 m
1	−0.303228	−78.532085	85 m
2	−0.307596	−78.532721	409 m
3	−0.309522	−78.532957	619 m
4	−0.309302	−78.533926	633 m
5	−0.308285	−78.534078	536 m
6	−0.309757	−78.534507	704 m
7	−0.311298	−78.534148	850 m
8	−0.310375	−78.536488	870 m
9	−0.310328	−78.537645	929 m
10	−0.311026	−78.537569	991 m
11	−0.313141	−78.53733	1.18 km
12	−0.313076	−78.53847	1.24 km
13	−0.312277	−78.54200	1.45 km
14	−0.309056	−78.545111	1.57 km
15	−0.304095	−78.544291	1.39 km
16	−0.30357	−78.546461	1.62 km
17	−0.303332	−78.549089	1.91 km
18	−0.303013	−78.550917	2.12 km
19	−0.301597	−78.555478	2.65 km
20	−0.298808	−78.559807	3.17 km
21	−0.294397	−78.567652	4.42 km
22	−0.292297	−78.574093	4.89 km
23	−0.290781	−78.579182	5.45 km
24	−0.290548	−78.58066	5.62 km
25	−0.288242	−78.583867	6.07 km

4.2 Speed Test

Based on the previous test, the transmission speed was also calculated. The calculation was based on packets' size (i.e. 41 bytes) and airtime provided by The Things Network platform. Table 2 shows the distance, airtime and the transmission speed of delivered packages (Fig. 5).

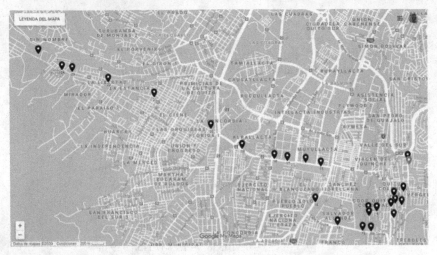

Fig. 4. Transmission points visualized on the map

Table 2. Transmission speed between the gathering node and LoRaWAN gateway

Distance (meters)	Airtime (millisecond)	Speed (kilobyte/second)
85 m	65.12 ms	0.6296
409 m	65.47 ms	0.6262
536 m	65.51 ms	0.6259
619 m	65.55 ms	0.6255
633 m	65.55 ms	0.6255
704 m	65.59 ms	0.6251
850 m	66.01 ms	0.6211
870 m	66.01 ms	0.6211
929 m	66.09 ms	0.6204
991 m	66.11 ms	0.6202
1180 m	66.19 ms	0.6194
1240 m	66.31 ms	0.6183
1390 m	66.31 ms	0.6183
1450 m	66.33 ms	0.6181
1570 m	66.37 ms	0.6177
1620 m	66.38 ms	0.6177
1910 m	66.58 ms	0.6158

(continued)

Table 2. (*continued*)

Distance (meters)	Airtime (millisecond)	Speed (kilobyte/second)
2120 m	66.96 ms	0.6123
2650 m	66.99 ms	0.6120
3170 m	67.20 ms	0.6101
4420 m	67.45 ms	0.6079
4890 m	67.63 ms	0.6062
5450 m	67.87 ms	0.6041
5620 m	67.98 ms	0.6031
6070 m	68.12 ms	0.6019

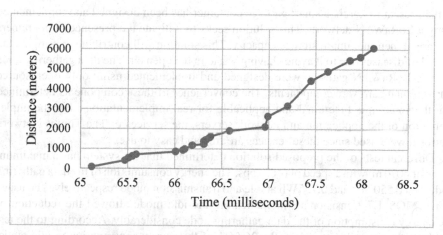

Fig. 5. Distance and delay of packets

4.3 Energy Consumption Test

To determine the energy consumption of the proposed solution, the amperage of the circuit of the data gathering node was measured. An ammeter was used for this measurement and two scenarios were considered: (1) when the node is transmitting data to the LoRaWAN gateway and (2) when the node is in idle mode. The results are shown in Table 3.

Table 3. Data gathering node energy consumption

Scenario	Amperage (mAh)	Power (watt-hour)
Idle mode	110	0.550
Transmission mode	150	0.750

The results indicate that the use of the MOSFET IRFZ44 transistor for creating the idle mode reduces energy consumption by 26.66%. This saving is reached because all the components of the node except the RFM96 module and the ESP32 card are turned off while the device is not transmitting data.

5   Conclusions

In the present research, a smart garbage container has been designed and implemented using a LoRaWAN network. This solution seeks to mitigate the presence of containers that are at their maximum storage capacity. This solution will contribute to mitigate the spread of diseases due to it avoids having waste in the open air. The data gathering node and the LoRaWAN gateway were designed and implemented using only open source software and hardware components. The convergence of these components determined that the solution is functional and applicable for real implementations. For the implementation of the application and network servers, the services of The Things Network platform were used since these services are free and easy to use.

Different tests of the proposed solution determined that the system has a maximum range of 6070 m, with a speed of 6.17 kbps. The energy consumption of the data gathering node was 0.550 Wh and 0.755 Wh at idle and transmission mode respectively. The usage of the MOSFET transistor for implementing the idle mode allowed the reduction of the energy consumption of the data gathering node considerably. According to the test results, it was possible to reduce the 26.66% of the energy consumption in idle mode. The proposed architecture is applicable not only for smart waste containers but for any other solution that requires data gathering functions. The applicability of the present research contributes to the development of similar works, but on different edges.

Acknowledgement. The authors would like to thank to the Corporación Ecuatoriana para el Desarrollo de la Investigación y Academia - CEDIA for the financial support given to the present research, development, and innovation work through its GT program, especially for the IoT and Smart Cities GT fund.

References

1. Zainol, H., Hisham, Z., Soh, C.: Smart waste collection monitoring and alert system via IoT. In: 2019 IEEE 9th Symposium on Computer Applications & Industrial Electronics, pp. 50–54 (2019)

2. Ingrassia, V.: Cómo funciona el primer contenedor de residuos inteligente. https://www.inf obae.com/tendencias/innovacion/2018/07/01/como-funciona-el-primer-contenedor-de-res iduos-inteligente/. Accessed 5 Oct 2019
3. Raut, C.M., Devane, S.R.: Intelligent transportation system for smartcity using VANET. In: Proceedings of the 2017 IEEE International Conference on Communication and Signal Processing, ICCSP 2017, January 2018, pp. 1602–1605 (2018)
4. Kolhatkar, C., Joshi, B., Choudhari, P., Bhuva, D.: Smart E-dustbin. In: 2018 International Conference on Smart City and Emerging Technology, ICSCET 2018, pp. 1–3 (2018)
5. Idwan, S., Zubairi, J.A., Mahmood, I.: Smart solutions for smart cities: using wireless sensor network for smart dumpster management. In: Proceedings of the 2016 International Conference on Collaboration Technologies and Systems, CTS 2016, pp. 493–497 (2016)
6. Yasin, U.D., Ali, T., Khan, J.A., Majid, M., Yasin, S.: A real-time smart dumpsters monitoring and garbage collection system. In: 2017 Fifth International Conference on Aerospace Science & Engineering (ICASE) (2017)
7. Khutsoane, O., Isong, B., Abu-Mahfouz, A.M.: IoT devices and applications based on LoRa/LoRaWAN. In: Proceedings of the IECON 2017 - 43rd Annual Conference of the IEEE Industrial Electronics Society, January 2017, pp. 6107–6112 (2017)
8. Lavric, A., Popa, V.: LoRa^{TM} wide-area networks from an Internet of Things perspective. In: Proceedings of the 9th International Conference on Electronics, Computers and Artificial Intelligence, ECAI 2017, January 2017, pp. 1–4 (2017)
9. González, M.: Estudio de NB - IoT y comparativa con otras tecnologías LPWAN (2019)
10. Andrade, R., Yoo, S.: A comprehensive study of the use of LoRa in the development of smart cities. Appl. Sci. **9**(22), 4753 (2019)
11. Barriga, J., et al.: A smart parking solution architecture based on LoRaWAN and Kubernetes. Appl. Sci. **10**(13), 4674 (2020)
12. Lykov, Y., Bolinova, M., Slobodiuk, V., Lykova, A., Makovetskyi, S.: Investigation of potential opportunities for LoRaWAN technology in conditions of urban construction on the example of Pycom modules. In: Proceedings of the 2018 International Scientific-Practical Conference on Problems of Infocommunications Science and Technology, PIC S and T 2018, pp. 543–547 (2019)
13. Rohit, G.S., Chandra, M.B., Saha, S., Das, D.: Smart dual dustbin model for waste management in smart cities. In: 2018 3rd International Conference for Convergence in Technology (I2CT), pp. 1–5 (2018)
14. Mirchandani, S., Wadhwa, S., Wadhwa, P., Joseph, R.: IoT enabled dustbins. In: 2017 International Conference on Big Data, IoT and Data Science (BID), pp. 73–76 (2017)
15. Kaza, S., Yao, L., Bhada-Tata, P., Van Woerden, F.: What a Waste 2.0: A Global Snapshot of Solid Waste Management to 2050. The World Bank (2018)
16. INEC: Gestión de Residuos Sólidos (2017)
17. Ghadage, S.A., Doshi, M.N.A.: IoT based garbage management (monitor and acknowledgment) system: a review. In: Proceedings of the International Conference on Intelligent Sustainable Systems, ICISS 2017, pp. 642–644 (2018)
18. Draz, U., Ali, T., Khan, J.A., Majid, M., Yasin, S.: A real-time smart dumpsters monitoring and garbage collection system. In: 2017 5th International Conference on Aerospace Science and Engineering, ICASE 2017, pp. 1–8 (2018)
19. Idwan, S., Zubairi, J.A., Mahmood, I.: Smart solutions for smart cities: using wireless sensor network for smart dumpster management. In: 2016 International Conference on Collaboration Technologies and Systems (CTS), pp. 493–497 (2016)
20. Nehete, P., Jangam, D., Barne, N., Bhoite, P., Jadhav, S.: Garbage management using Internet of Things. In: Proceedings of the 2nd International Conference on Electronics, Communication and Aerospace Technology, ICECA 2018, pp. 1454–1458 (2018)

21. Memon, S.K., Shaikh, F.K., Mahoto, N.A., Memon, A.A.: IoT based smart garbage monitoring collection system using WeMos Ultrasonic sensors. In: 2019 2nd International Conference on Computing, Mathematics and Engineering Technologies, iCoMET 2019 (2019)
22. Rush, *Programming the Photon : getting started with the Internet of Things* (2016)
23. Espressif.   https://www.espressif.com/en/products/hardware/esp32-devkitc/overview. Accessed 13 Oct 2019
24. HOPERF, "Rf96/97/98," (2019)
25. The Things Network "Gateways". https://www.thethingsnetwork.org/docs/gateways/. Accessed 16 Oct 2019
26. The Things Network. https://www.thethingsnetwork.org/. Accessed 16 Oct 2019
27. Hallard: Single Channel LoRaWAN Gateway. https://github.com/hallard/single_chan_pkt_fwd. Accessed 19 Oct 2019
28. Leaflet - a JavaScript library for interactive maps. https://leafletjs.com/. Accessed 13 Feb 2020

Simulation of the Semantic Network of Knowledge Representation in Intelligent Assistant Systems Based on Ontological Approach

Victoria V. Bova[✉], Yury A. Kravchenko, Sergey I. Rodzin, and Elmar V. Kuliev

Southern Federal University, Rostov-on-Don, Russia

Abstract. The paper considers the task of building the ontological structure of knowledge in the intelligent assistant systems to reduce the structural and semantic conflicts in the process of searching, accumulation, and processing of information objects in the Internet. The authors develop the semantic net providing the integrated representation of knowledge on user preferences, semantic images of the Internet resource, and search domain in the ontological model. To solve the problem, we propose a method for cluster analysis of the Internet-object structure. This allows us to divide the vector space of the features into semantic clusters with the constraints on the hidden patterns features revealing the content risks. To carry out the experiments on a test set of search queries, we developed a search module for the intelligent assistant system. The estimated relevance coefficient of "query-resource" is 60% higher than manually formed user preferences in popular search systems.

Keywords: Intelligent assistant systems · Ontology · Semantic network · Clustering · Semantic search · Users' preferences

1 Introduction

At present, meeting the information needs of the users is one of the key problems in terms of solving the intelligent assistant systems that provide safety and effectiveness of search and cognitive activity in the Internet [1–3]. The problem of discovering direct knowledge in the distributed educational Internet resources is very important in terms of modeling the scenarios of user interaction. This problem can be considered as semantical and knowledge-based as it is related to the recognition of information objects (queries based on the information needs) connected with the task that the user needs to solve [4–7]. In terms of obtaining the direct knowledge in the semantic search task, challenges can occur due to the volatile character of the users' information needs and uncertain level of their information awareness while forming the search queries.

The paper proposes a method for building the semantic net based on the ontological description of the structure of knowledge in the information space, where we try to carry out the search procedures. The ontological approach allows us to provide an integrated

© Springer Nature Singapore Pte Ltd. 2021
P. K. Singh et al. (Eds.): FTNCT 2020, CCIS 1396, pp. 241–252, 2021.
https://doi.org/10.1007/978-981-16-1483-5_22

representation of the models of information needs, search queries domain, information models of the search images of Internet resources for their future comparison and intelligent processing [4, 8–10]. To increase the accuracy and reduce the structural and semantic conflicts in the information search process, we propose a method for cluster analysis of the structure of volatile Internet objects. Clustering can provide the division of the vector space of Internet objects features into semantic clusters with constraints on the feature of selecting the hidden patterns in the user queries, which indicates the possibility of content risks [11–13]. The suggested approach can improve the effectiveness of the contextual access to the resources in the open information and education environment and provide more accurate user preferences.

2 Problem Statement and Subject Area Analysis

Semantic search is considered as an add-in for the traditional information search, that uses processing of the knowledge on the searched object, users, information resources, search domain, and the possibility to discover knowledge rather than data. The literature analysis of [4, 13–16] has shown that in most existing systems related to semantic search, knowledge bases are used in an implicit way, which leaves the user unable to choose the knowledge important for search. This can lead to the following problems:

1) The users cannot understand the ways of obtaining the results, which can decrease confidence in search systems;
2) Very often these systems cannot find the required knowledge because they are limited to the users' needs and information objects that should be generated in the search results;
3) Discovery of the sources of formalized and structured knowledge;
4) Dynamical update of the knowledge used in the search process.

Besides, the results of the search must contain not abstract but pragmatic information, i.e. useful for the task the user needs to solve.

Generally, the research problem includes the following: to meet the users' information needs effectively, we must obtain the formalized description of the need based on the knowledge about what the user wants to get and in what form. As a rule, the user does not have skills enough to create the formalized descriptions of the problem and search domain (e.g. in the form of a thesaurus). Thus, the mentioned descriptions must be formed automatically. This helps to avoid adding an artificially narrowed and formally described sphere of interests and also provides the means and methods for predicting users' behavior in terms of the proposed model of interaction with the resources of open information and educational environment [1, 4–7]. Also, the model should represent the relationships between information resources and domain, information needs and domain, users' tasks and domain, and users and domain.

To formalize the description of the model elements and provide its automated processing by the intelligent assistant system, it is reasonable to use the ontological representation of the knowledge [7–9]. We propose building the ontological model called *ONT* to describe the information needs, where classes represent the mentioned elements, and relations represent the connections between them.

Let us present a formal problem statement. Assume that U is a set of users, Res is a set of proposed information resources, P is a utility function describing the interest of user $u \in U$ in resource $r' \in Res$ and characterizing the completeness of the searched thematic in the search sampling of a certain size, i.e. $P:U \times Res \rightarrow D$, where D is a parameter of semantic potential (reliability) of the thematical coverage of information resource of the formed information need (thematical query).

$$D_s = \frac{\sum_1^k V_u[k]_{n+1}}{k*(s-k+1)}, s \geq \sum_1^k V_u[k]_{n+1}, \qquad (1)$$

where $\sum_1^k V_u[k]_{n+1}$ is a number of search terms in the user query thesaurus V_u, k is a coefficient of the semantic potential of the query term, free parameter $s = [k;\infty]$ is set by the expert and characterizes the size of the processed search sampling. To optimize the search task, we need to find such information resources $r' \in Res$ for each user $u \in U$ where $P(u,r') = \max\limits_{r' \in Res} d(u, r')$.

3 Method for Ontological Description of the Semantic Net Structure

Ontology can be considered as the basis of the semantic net structure for representing the knowledge on the users' information needs (thematical queries), search images of Internet resources, and domain of terminological search (see Fig. 1) [8, 10].

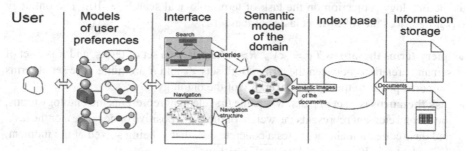

Fig. 1. Semantic search processes in the Internet

Formally, the semantic net can be represented as $SN = <I_C, I_R>$, here $I_C = <I_{C1},...,I_{Cn}>$ is a set of objects, i.e. instances of classes C, defined in the ontology ONT, $I_R = <I_{R1},...,I_{Rm}>$ is a set of instances of relations R, defined in ONT and connecting the objects from I_C. The ontology ONT is composed of thee interconnected ontologies representing the mentioned knowledge components. The ontology of the terminological search domain can be denoted as $O_{SDi} = <V_{SDi}, R_{SDi}, F_{SDi}>, i = \overline{1, n}$. It describes the area of search and cognitive activity of the users. The ontology defines the following:

- $X = \{x_i\}$ is a set of concepts $(i = \overline{1, M})$;
- $V = \{y_u\}$ is a set of terms, thesaurus elements $V_u(u = \overline{1, M})$;

- $R_t = \{r_k\}$ is a set of temporal relations between the concepts defining the relations of semantic potential between the search elements $(k = \overline{1, k})$;
- $d(t) \rightarrow R_{[0;1]}$ is a function of reliability factors of the relations as the moment t, returning the value between $[0;1]$: 0 means 'unknown'; $(0;1)$ means 'reliable in a certain degree'; 1 means 'relations is 100% reliable'.

The relation r_k can thus be defined as: $r_k = <x_i, x_j, v_u, d_k(t)>$, where: x_i, x_j denote the concepts; $d_k(t)$ has a form (1) as a function of reliability factor of the relation r_k between x_i and x_j, defined by the term v_u; $i, j = \overline{1, M}, k = \overline{1, K}$.

$F_t = <F_n, F_s>$ is a set of interpretation functions. F_n is a function of term normalization. At any moment for any term of the ith concept, it returns the number of jth term, which defines the search element with the maximal reliability factor:

$$F_n(N, t) \rightarrow N : \forall i = \overline{1, M}, \forall t \, F_n(i, t) = arg \, max_{v_u = \overline{1, U}} \left(d_{k_{iu}}(t) \right) \qquad (2)$$

where $d_{k_{iu}}(t) \rightarrow R_{[0;1]}$ is the function of the reliability factor of the uth term, defining the ith concept at the moment t.

F_s is a function of terms interpretation. At moment t, it assigns a vector of reliability factor $D = \{d_{k_{iu}}\}$ to the term i^{th} i.e. represents the degree of conformity of uth term to i^{th} concept.

The ontological model of the domain has quite a complex structure, but we can use some part of the knowledge contained in the ontology to meet the user's information needs in terms of solving a specific task of search and cognitive activity. Thus, it is reasonable to use domain thesaurus to model knowledge. Thesaurus can be considered as the ontology projection on the task of terminological search [8–10]. The ontology O_{User} describes the following classes of thesaurus:

- **query terms thesaurus** $T_V = <V_u, R>$, where V_u is a set of terms, and R is a set of semantic relations between the terms. Both sets V_u and R are finite. The set of terms T_V corresponds to the set of concepts X of the ontology O_{SD};
- **task thesaurus** is a set of pairs, where the first element represents the ontology terms, the second element represents the weight of the term (positive or negative) for the task, and their collection characterizes a concrete task that is being solved at the moment, $T_{Sj} = \{ <t_{skj} \in V_{SDi}, w_{kj}>, k = \overline{1, s}\}, j = \overline{1, m}$;
- **query thesaurus** is a set of keywords characterizing one of the users' needs and related to a certain task with previously described task thesaurus T_{Sj}, $T_Q = <\{t_q\}, t_{skj}>, q = \overline{1, u}$;
- **query topic thesaurus** is a set of queries related to the same information need $T_{TH} = <id_{TH}, \{t_q\}>, q = \overline{1, u}$;
- **query result thesaurus** is a set of pairs, where the first element represents the links of information resources, and the second one represents the confidence rating of the information resources assessed by the user $T_{REZ} = <id_u, rel_u>$.

Ontology of the search images of the Internet resources is used to describe the information resources represented in the open information and educational environment [4, 11], that are relevant to the terminological search domain: $O_{RES} = <R_{URL}, \{ <t_{qi},$

$d_{ki}(t)$, $rel>$, $i = \overline{1, n}\}>$. The information model contains the data on the previously found resources in the form of their identifiers, queries by which the resource was found, and the rates of confidence and relevance for the ith user.

4 Method for Cluster Analysis of Models of User Search Queries

Clusters of the Internet objects can be described as models of the user search queries organized as groups by basic intentions of formulating information need [4, 6]. Each information need represents a set of similar behavior indicators introduced in O_{user} and arranged according to the semantic scope of the query t_q.

Clustering can be considered as a task of optimal partitioning of the objects into several groups [16]. Optimization criterion can be defined as the maximization of cluster compactness and minimization of the root-mean-square distance between the center of a cluster and its objects as follows:

$$P_l = \frac{\sum_{i=1}^{nof(U_l^*)} b_{i,l}^2 \times \rho(u_i^*, e_l)^2}{\sum_{i=1}^{nof(U_l^*)} b_{i,l}} \tag{3}$$

where $nof(U_l^*)$ is a number of reliable objects of lth cluster, for which degree of membership is $0 \le b_{i,l} \le 1$; $b_{i,l}$ is a coefficient of membership of the object u_i to the cluster U_l, $0 \le b_{i,l} \le 1$; $\rho(u_i^*, e_l)$ is Euclidean distance between the object $u_i^* \in U_l^*$ and the center e_l of the cluster U_l.

Let us consider clustering as a task of monitoring a set of Internet objects with the n-dimensional feature vector of number features $z_i(t_k) = (z_{i,1}(t_k), ..., z_{i,j}(t_k), ..., z_{i,n}(t_k))$, which coordinates are assigned with the time points t_k, where i corresponds to the number of object $u_i \in U$. The object characteristics are updated at discrete time points t_k. After some time Δt_k, the stability of the cluster structure is verified and corrected if needed (if it is changed dynamically). To consider new Internet objects, we can assume the following dynamical changed in the cluster structure: formation of new clusters, cluster merging, cluster splitting [13, 17].

To avoid affecting by old observations, monitoring of the cluster condition can be organized according to the time slot idea: in the $nof(V_u)$-dimensional space, we only consider those objects, that have been recorded during the time slot last Δt_k.

4.1 Formation of New Clusters

For the set of feature vectors of information needs $U(t_{k+1})$ at the moment $t_{k+1} > t_k$, the formation of the new clusters can be caused by the appearance of new objects or rapid and persistent change of the search activity of the existing objects [17]. In terms of the first case, each new object $u_{nof(U(tk))+p}(t_{k+1}) \in U(t_{k+1})$, $p \ge 1$, represents a single isolated cluster, for which we calculate the Euclidean distance to all other objects $U(t_{k+1})\backslash\{u_{nof(U(tk))+p}(t_{k+1})\}$ and define the object $u_{near}(t_{k+1})$ which would be nearest to $u_{nof(U(tk))+p}(t_{k+1})$:

$$\rho\left(u_{nof(U(tk))+p}(t_{k+1}), u_{near}(t_{k+1})\right) = \min_{1 \le i \le nof(U(t_k))} \rho\left(u_{nof(U(tk))+p}(t_{k+1}), u_i(t_{k+1})\right) \tag{4}$$

The nearest neighbor $u_{near}(t_{k+1})$ helps us to initialize the location of the new object in the cluster structure. Then we continue observing the new user queries u_i at time point Δt_k, which are recorded in the query terms thesaurus V_u. If at t_{k+1} (previous time point) the user $u_i(t_{k+1})$ does not perform any search activity, the increasing V_u will not affect the feature vector. Figure 2 shows the initial cluster structure at time point t_k. If the new objects $u_{nof(U(tk))+p}(t_{k+1}) \in U(t_{k+1}), p \geq 1$ occur during time point Δt_k, new clusters will occur after the repeated clustering (see Fig. 3).

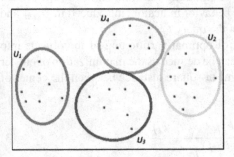 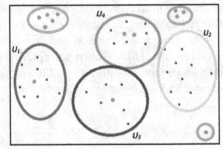

Fig. 2. Clusters at the moment tk **Fig. 3.** Clusters at the moment t_{k+1}

If the user activity changes at the point t_{k+2}, feature vectors, similarity, and distance measures between the objects inside the cluster will be recalculated. The described process leads to the formation of new clusters (see Fig. 4).

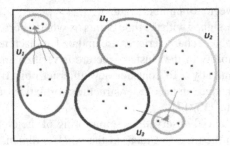

Fig. 4. Rearranging of the objects at the moment $tk+2$

To reveal new clusters, we propose using the membership coefficient of ith object to m^{th} cluster. The membership coefficient $b_{i,m}(t_{k+2})$ of the object $u_i(t_{k+2})$ to the cluster $U_m(t_{k+2})$ from the cluster structure $K(t_{k+2})$ ($U_m(t_{k+2}) \in K(t_{k+2})$) at any moment t_{k+2} can be calculated according to the following formula:

$$b_{i,m}(t_{k+2}) = \frac{1}{\sum_{l=1}^{nof(K(t_{k+2}))} \left(\frac{(\rho_m(t_{k+2}))^2}{(\rho_l(t_{k+2}))^2} \right)} \quad u \sum_{m=1}^{nof(K(t_{k+2}))} b_{i,m}(t_{k+2}) = 1, \quad (5)$$

where $nof(K(t_{k+2}))$ is the number of clusters $K(t_{k+2})$; $\rho_m(t_{k+2})$ is Euclidean distance between the object u_i and center e_m of the mth cluster calculated as follows:

$$\rho_m(t_{k+2}) = \sqrt{\sum_{j=1}^{nof\,(V_u(t_{k+2}))} \left(e_{m,j}(t_{k+2}) - u_{i,j}(t_{k+2})\right)^2}. \tag{6}$$

Revealing a set of new clusters K_{new} starts with defining new objects U^{free} with low membership coefficients to all existing clusters. If the number of these free objects $nof(U^{free})$ is comparable to the cluster size, they will form a compact group of objects with common features [11, 16]. The object compactness is determined by Eq. (3). The possible number of new clusters at t_k is defined by the following formula:

$$nof\left(K^{new}\right) = int\left(\frac{nof\left(U^{free}\right)}{d_1 \times N_{min}}\right), \tag{7}$$

where $nof(U^{free})$ is a number of free objects, which are not assigned to any clusters; d_1 is a threshold between the interval [0,1]; $N_{min} = min\left(nof\left(U_1^*\right), ..., nof\left(U_l^*\right), ..., nof\left(U_{nof(K)}^*\right)\right)$ is the minimal size of a cluster, which considers only reliable objects $U_l^* \in U_l$ with large membership degree, for which the membership coefficient $b_{i,l} \geq d_2$; $nof\left(U_l^*\right)$ is the number of reliable objects of the lth cluster; d_2 is threshold value between [0,1].

4.2 Clusters Merging

Cluster merging includes the formation of new partitioning as $nof(K'') < nof(K')$. Let us consider the case of clusters merging at the time point t_{k+3}. If the search vector changes, some clusters can get closer to each other and merge into a united group (see Fig. 5).

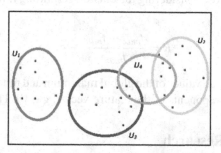

Fig. 5. Merging of the cluster U_4 and rearranging of its objects into clusters U_2 and U_3 в t_{k+3}

The cluster revealing starts with highlighting the objects u_i, that have high membership degree for two clusters simultaneously U_l u U_m: $b_{i,l} \approx b_{i,m} \rightarrow 1$ (Eq. 5). The quantitative criterion for the merging two clusters can be represented as their similarity measure:

$$I_{l,m} = \frac{\sum_{i=1}^{nof\,(U)} min(b_{i,l}, b_{i,m})}{\sum_{i=1}^{nof\,(U)} b_{i,l}}. \tag{8}$$

However, similarity measure $I_{l,m}$ is not symmetrical as $I_{l,m} \neq I_{m,l}$. Thus, we propose using the following measure to reveal the mentioned similarity:

$$Mc_{l,m} = max(I_{i,m}, I_{m,l}).$$ (9)

Clusters are considered as merging if the value of $Mc_{l,m}$ exceeds the threshold $h \in [0, 1]$.

4.3 Cluster Splitting

Cluster splitting can be observed at the moment, say, t_{k+4}, when some clusters become larger due to a lot of new objects. This can lead to the dissimilarity of their internal structure (see Fig. 6).

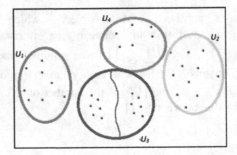

Fig. 6. Splitting of the cluster $U3$ at t_{k+4}

The analysis of multi-extremal feature histograms can be used as a splitting criterion. In [16] the authors propose considering the cluster as splitting if the following condition is satisfied:

$$R = \frac{f_{max} - f_{min}}{f_{max}} \geq g,$$ (10)

where f_{max} and f_{min} are the values of the global maximum and minimum of the histogram of at least one of the components of the feature vector; $g \in [0, 1]$ is a threshold value.

5   Experimental Research

The Software Module for Semantic Search (SMSS) has been developed to estimate the effectiveness of the proposed methods. The experiments were conducted in the semantic net of the previously indexed set of 16,000 of the resources. The test training session was executed in terms of the terminological model of the «Information Technologies» domain. As a search term, we randomly selected the term V_u with the required value of the semantic potential $k = [1...9]$. Pragmatically, the sampling was limited to the hundreds of the discovered information resources. The statistical reliability of the empirical data was provided by the Yandex search system. The experiment was conducted iteratively with more than 300 search procedures, where the user used the set of search terms eliciting the semantic potential of the query term.

The studied parameters to determine the search results include average search time, accuracy – relevance of the results to the query; thematical coverage that includes the search object citation; the number of information resources in the resulting sampling; the number of the search terms to formulate the information need [5]. The numeric results are demonstrated in Figs. 7, 8, 9 and 10.

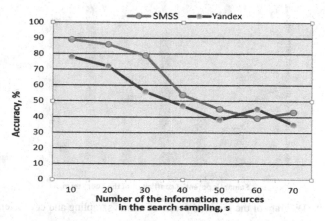

Fig. 7. Diagram of search accuracy and number of information resources

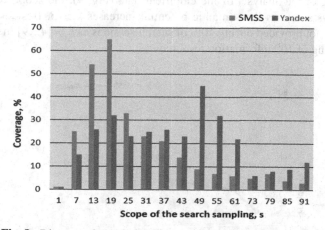

Fig. 8. Diagram of search sampling scope and thematical coverage

The accuracy analysis is represented in Fig. 7. After the first 15 positions, the possibility of finding the information resource, that contains reliable information according to the thematic aspect of the search term, which was not highlighted in the observed sampling, decreases by 40% on average.

The experimental research has shown the empirical relationship between the search sampling scope and semantic coverage of the search term (see Fig. 8). The dependency demonstrates a rapid decrease of thematical coverage in terms of the increasing scope of search sampling.

Increasing thematical complexity of the term can lead to reduced search completeness as the accuracy stays the same. Hence, the percent of the new information decreases during the process of searching in the depth of the sampling and constant search accuracy.

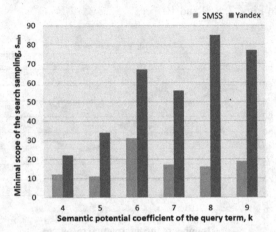

Fig. 9. Diagram of the minimal scope of search sampling and coefficient k

According to the analysis of the empirical data (Fig. 9), the scope of the search sampling stays stable as the semantic potential increases $k > 3$. Besides, thematical coverage was not provided during 40% of search sessions as $k = [4...9]$ in terms of the search sampling of 100 information resources.

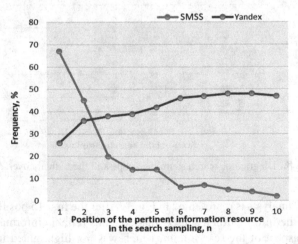

Fig. 10. Diagram of distribution of pertinent resources in the search sampling

The average value of the minimal sampling scope is 19 resources providing the thematical coverage of the search. It is about 3.5 times lower than the standard search in Yandex (68 resources). The distribution of the pertinent pages according to each query V_u (Fig. 10) shows that 97% of the resources that represent the thematical coverage of the search are located in around the first seven positions, and 88% are located in the first four positions.

The results of the analysis allow us to conclude that the time spent for the access to reliable information is decreased by 1,5 times in terms of the information search. The result completeness is increased by 60% as the accuracy of the thematic search results stays the same.

6 Conclusion

In this paper, we proposed a process of forming the semantic net of multi-disciplinary knowledge space based on highlighting the main types of concepts of the users' search activity domain and their information needs. To formalize the semantic net, we developed the ontological structure of the objects, their features, time conditions, and search activity tasks. The mathematical model of the cluster analysis of the Internet objects of dynamic behavior was presented in the paper. The experimental research was carried out with the developed software module and allowed us to define the time and qualitative character-istics of the method working with the real data of test queries on the formulated search thematic. The developed module was compared with the Yandex search system using the user's information needs formulated manually. The comparison criteria included the accuracy and execution time of the methods. The developed module exceeds Yandex by 40% at accuracy and shows the significant time savings in terms of searching the relevant resources. The results have proven the effectiveness of the semantic search module in the intelligent assistant systems that allow us to increase the reliability of the results of search activity, hence, the reliability level of the mentioned systems. Such an approach helps to avoid the possible risks of the digital and educational acumen of the users in terms of search and cognitive activity in the Internet.

Acknowledgment. The reported study was funded by RFBR according to the research project № 18-29-22019.

References

1. Bova, V., Kravchenko, Yu., Rodzin, S., Kuliev, E.: Hybrid method for prediction of users' information behavior in the Internet based on bioinspired search. J. Phys. Conf. Ser. (2019). https://doi.org/10.1088/1742-6596/1333/3/032008
2. Deliang, W., Lingling, X., Chuan, C.H.: Understanding the continuance use of social network sites: a computer self-efficacy perspective. J. Behav. Inf. Technol. **34**, 204–216 (2015)
3. Zhang, Y.: Undergraduate students' mental models of the Web as an information retrieval system. J. Am. Soc. Inform. Sci. Technol. **59**(13), 2087–2098 (2008)

4. Kravchenko, Y.A., Kuliev, E.V., Kursitys, I.O.: Information's semantic search, classification, structuring and integration objectives in the knowledge management context problems. In: 8th IEEE International Conference on Application of Information and Communication Technologies – AICT 2016, Baku, Azerbaijan, pp. 136–141. IEEE Press (2016)

5. Tingting, Z., Chen, L.Y., Liang-Hsien, T.: Understanding user motivation for evaluating online content: a self-determination theory perspective. J. Behav. Inf. Technol. **34**, 479–491 (2015)

6. Jalalirad, A., Tjalkens, T.: Using feature-based models with complexity penalization for selecting features. J. Signal Process. Syst. **90**(2), 201–210 (2018)

7. Kravchenko, Y., Bova, V.: Assessment of ontological structures semantic similarity based on a modified cuckoo search algorithm. In: IOP Conference Series: Materials Science and Engineering, Krasnoyarsk, Russia, p. 12018 (2020)

8. Rogushina, J.: Analysis of automated matching of the semantic wiki resources with elements of domain ontologies. Int. J. Math. Sci. Comput. (IJMSC) **3**(3), 50–58 (2017)

9. Corcho, O., Ruiz-Iniesta, A.: A review of ontologies for describing scholarly and scientific documents. In: 4th Workshop on Semantic Publishing, co-located with the 11th Extended Semantic Web Conference (ESWC 2014), Anissaras, Greece, 12 p. (2014)

10. Rogushina, J., Gladun, A.: Ontology-based competency analyses in new research domains. J. Comput. Inf. Technol. **20**(4), 277–293 (2012)

11. Bova, V.V., Kureichik, V.V., Leshchanov, D.V.: The model of semantic similarity estimation for the problems of big data search and structuring. In: 11th IEEE International Conference on Application of Information and Communication Technologies - AICT 2017, pp. 27–32 (2017)

12. Kravchenko, Yu.A., Markov, V.V., Kursitys, I.O.: Bioinspired algorithm for acquiring new knowledge based on information resource classification. In: Proceedings of IEEE International Russian Automation Conference (RusAutoCon), Sochi, Russia, pp. 1–5 (2019)

13. Dikovitsky, V.V., Nikulina, N. V., Shishaev, M.G.: Architecture and technologies of knowledge-based multi-domain information systems for industrial purposes. In: 5th Computer Science Online Conference (CSOC2016), vol 3. pp. 359–369 (2016)

14. Brandtzaeg, P., Folstad, A.: Trust and distrust in online fact-checking services. J. Commun. ACM **60**(9), 65–71 (2017)

15. Gruber, T.: Collective knowledge systems: where the Social Web meets the Semantic Web. J. Web Semant. **6**(1), 4–13 (2008)

16. Khotilin, M.I. Blagov, A.V.: Visualization and cluster analysis of social networks. In: CEUR Workshop Proceedings, vol. 1638, pp. 843–850 (2016)

17. Kursitys, I., Natskevich, A., Tsyrulnikova, E.: Boosting model of bioinspired algorithms for solving the classification and clustering problems. In: Proceedings of IEEE East-West Design & Test Symposium (EWDTS), Batumi, Georgia, pp. 1–6 (2019)

A Deep Learning Approach for Autonomous Navigation of UAV

Hetvi Shah(✉) ⓘ and Keyur Rana ⓘ

Sarvajanik College of Engineering and Technology, Surat, India
keyur.rana@scet.ac.in

Abstract. Unmanned Aerial Vehicle is an aircraft that operates and flies without a human pilot. It can reach at places where humans may not reach easily, such as search and rescue operations, earthquake mapping and flood mapping. It is additionally valuable for autonomous tasks such as the delivery of any item and target tracking which requires self-governing navigation. Motivated by the mentioned applications, in this paper we present a deep learning model for self-governing navigation of UAV. Our model exploits transfer learning from a well-known network architecture called MobileNet and it is trained on a dataset of images, collected from the various indoor environments. From an image, the model classifies actions such as either to go forward or to stop. Furthermore, after some experiments and results, we infer that among all Convolution Neural Network (CNN) architectures, the MobileNet architecture is ideal and appropriate for our purposed approach.

Keywords: Unmanned Aerial Vehicle (UAV) · Drone · Autonomous navigation · Deep learning approach · Navigation techniques · Deep learning architecture · Convolution Neural Network (CNN) · MobileNet · Inception (GoogleNet)

1 Introduction

Unmanned Aerial Vehicle (UAV) or drone has the ability of sustained and reliable flight without a human pilot [1]. It has few controls like roll, pitch, yaw, throttle, trim, rudder, aileron and elevator [2]. Its types are derived by their weights, wings or rotor, however, among these, quadcopter and hexacopter are best for our purposed approach [3]. It can be applied to various applications such as navigation [4–16], aerial surveillance [11], load delivery [17], agriculture [18], etc. Among these applications, we center around the navigation. The different navigation areas are indoor [11–15], outdoor [11] and it can explore unknown environment such as forest [16]. Among these areas, we focus on indoor navigation where GPS has limited precision.

For autonomous navigation of UAV, various techniques are available such as range sensor [4, 5], SLAM [6, 7], stereo vision [8, 9], vanishing point [10] and deep learning [11–16]. Using sensor based techniques, we need to assemble multiple sensors onboard which consume more power. Whereas our deep learning model can work on a monocular camera for classification of actions such as forward or stop. Because of one camera, it requires low power and low weight. Another limitation of the sensor is, it cannot identify

P. K. Singh et al. (Eds.): FTNCT 2020, CCIS 1396, pp. 253–263, 2021.
https://doi.org/10.1007/978-981-16-1483-5_23

the objects. Thus, it fails in most of the real-time scenarios. However, using one camera, our deep learning model can recognize the environment. Hence, we purpose a model that can travel autonomously in an indoor environment without much computational overhead. Additionally, our methodology is to train a classifier using a deep learning technique that mimics an expert pilot action, either to go forward or to stop for self-sufficient navigation of UAV in indoor corridor scenarios. The contribution of the paper can be identified as follow:

- We purpose a deep learning model using transfer learning for autonomous navigation of UAV.
- We derive that MobileNet is more preferable for our proposed approach.

In Sect. 2, we explain the related work. In Sect. 3, we present the proposed model, dataset and training of a model. In Sect. 4, we assess the experiments and results. At last, Sect. 5 offers the conclusion and future work.

2   Related Work

A wide variety of techniques for drone navigation can be found in the literature. Hence, in this section, we briefly describe related work and their association with our proposed approach.

2.1   UAV Navigation Using Sensors

Navigation of UAV has been a widely studied area motivated by applications in surveillance [11] and transportation [17]. The most prevalent approaches make use of onboard range sensors such as infrared sensors, RGB depth sensors, laser range sensors and ultrasonic sensors to fly autonomously with avoiding obstacles too [4, 5]. However, this is not practically possible for publicly available drones that often have low battery life and low load carrying capacity. Also, we cannot put sensors on it because the publicly available drone is fully assembled. One can also use Simultaneous Localization and Mapping (SLAM) which creates a 3D map of an unknown environment using ranging sensors [6, 7]. However, SLAM is computationally expensive due to 3D construction. On another hand, accurate depth estimation and relative position estimation are possible using a stereo camera for navigation [8, 9]. Nevertheless, an object without a prominent texture makes less reliable for real-time navigation. Also, it's hard to match features in one image to the corresponding feature in the other image. Another solution is, use monocular camera based methods, which uses vanishing point as guidance for flying drone in an indoor environment, yet it still relies on range sensors for collision avoidance [10].

2.2 UAV Navigation Using Deep Learning

To overcome the above mentioned limitations, deep learning can be used. Deep learning model can work on images taken from a monocular camera to navigate autonomously without any 3D map generation. Consequently, it is computationally very efficient and lightweight. Utilizing a camera, the environment is also distinguished. Deep learning methodology can be divided into two main categories: 1) Reinforcement learning based method [13, 19] 2) Supervised learning based method [11, 12, 14, 15, 20].

In [11], a model is proposed that takes an image as an input and produces two outputs which are, a steering angle and collision probability for each single input image. This model was trained on ResNet [21] in outdoor environment and tested in an indoor as well as outdoor environment. In [12], a system has been demonstrated that uses the video feed extracted from the camera of the drone, then passes it to a deep neural network model and decides the next operation. This model was trained on DenseNet [22]. In [13], authors have proposed a model using reinforcement learning. In this, they have collected dataset by crashing a drone 11,500 times and created a big dataset which teaches the drone how not to crash. This model was trained on AlexNet [23]. A CNN is introduced in [14] to estimate the center of a gate robustly. The drone navigates using gates, and it passes 10 gates in 86 s. This model was proposed for drone racing. In [15], a system has been implemented that finds a specific target using only one camera and it stops when the target is found. This model was trained on CaffeNet [24].

Various deep learning architectures are LeNet [25], AlexNet [23], VGGNet [26], ResNet [21], Inception (GoogleNet) [27], MobileNet [28] etc. The generic comparison of these models based on Year of Publication, Dataset [29, 30], Parameters and Accuracy is shown in Table 1. As UAV is one kind of hardware [31], we require a lightweight model that consumes very less memory and power. From the comparison of CNN models, we infer that Inception and MobileNet architecture has very less number of parameters to train among all architectures. Therefore, Inception and MobileNet architectures ideal for our purposed approach. We will see this in detail in Sect. 4.

Table 1. Comparison of CNN architectures.

Sr No.	Model	Year	Dataset	Parameter (in Million)	Accuracy (%)
1	LeNet	1998	MNIST	0.06	99.05
2	AlexNet	2012	ImageNet	60	63.3
3	VGGNet	2014	ImageNet	138	74.4
4	ResNet	2015	ImageNet	60.2	78.57
5	Inception	2015	ImageNet	6.8	69.8
6	MobileNet	2017	ImageNet	4.2	70.6

3 Proposed Model

The objective of our model is the classification of actions to navigate autonomously in an indoor environment. Though we require many actions such as forward, turn left, turn right, up, down, rotate, stop etc., for the navigation, we focus on two actions viz. forward and stop. We have used MobileNet [28], to train our model. Training of the model is done with the supervised learning approach [20]. The model parameters are learned through transfer learning with our custom-made dataset [32]. The input of the model is an image, which goes into a deep neural network model and gives the output as navigation actions. Output is given by the model in the form of probability of two actions.

In this section, we present our proposed approach with dataset, training and model structure.

3.1 Dataset

To train a deep neural network for successful autonomous navigation, our dataset plays an important role to accomplish the objective. Our dataset is composed of images collected from indoor locations. The locations are either a corridor, wall or grill, which are shown in Fig. 1. It shows training images for the forward action and corresponding for the stop action. In both cases, the database consists of 12,027 images. Class wise division of the number of images is shown in Table 2.

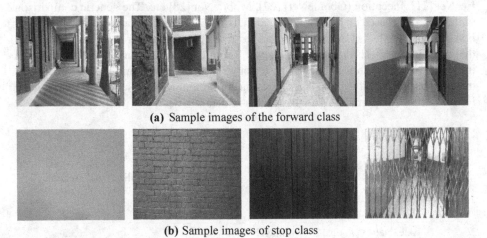

(a) Sample images of the forward class

(b) Sample images of stop class

Fig. 1. Example of captured images for deep neural network raining (a) for forward actions (b) for stop action

Table 2. Dataset division.

Sr No.	Action	Images
1	Forward	5946
2	Stop	6081
	Total images	**12,027**

3.2 Training

We used the MobileNet [28] pretrained model, which is the winner of the ImageNet Large Scale Visual Recognition (ILSVRC) [31, 33] challenge-2017. We trained the model by transfer learning from the MobilcNet architecture [28, 32], which is trained on the ImageNet dataset with 14 Million images. To customize the model for our application, we have trained it on additional 12,027 images. We used a categorical cross-entropy Loss function [34] and Adam optimizer [35] to train our classifier. We have trained our model for 25 epochs with a batch size 12 and 32 both.

3.3 Model Structure

As mentioned before, we carried out a fine-tuning [32] of the MobileNet architecture. Thus, by changing the last layer of the original model, we augmented this model with 2 fully connected (FC) layers followed by the output layer of Softmax [36]. The model structure is depicted in Fig. 2. It takes as an input of size 224 × 224 × 3 (Height × Weight × #Channels) and predicts the probability of two classes. At any instant, the class with the highest probability is followed for UAV navigation [37].

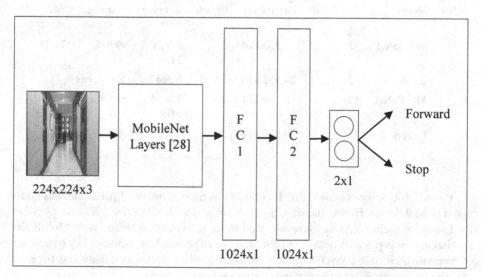

Fig. 2. Proposed deep neural network to classify the actions: forward and stop

4 Experiments and Results

In this section, we brief our Hardware Specification which was used for the proposed model training and testing. Then we compare the results of MobileNet and Inception Architecture to evaluate the performance of our proposed approach.

4.1 Hardware Specification

Our proposed model used the training set consisting of 12,027 images and was trained for 25,052 iterations. The training was conducted on a laptop with an intel i5–8265U CPU 1.60 GHz, 8 GB RAM, and MX250 NVIDIA Graphics on Windows 10, with CUDA 9.0 and CuDNN 7.6.5.

4.2 Results

We have created two models using transfer learning viz. Inception and MobileNet respectively. To check the performance comparison, we have trained and tested both of these models results is shown in Table 3. The Comparison of the model is based on the Batch Size, Training Accuracy, Testing Accuracy, Parameters and Time of training of the Model. The training accuracy is the accuracy of a model on images it was trained on. And the testing accuracy is the accuracy of a model on images it hasn't seen. The computation of training and testing accuracy is the ratio of correct classified images to the total amount of images given for classification.

Table 3. Result analysis of mobilenet and inception architecture.

Sr No	Model	Batch Size	Parameters	Epoch	Training time	Training aaccuracy	Test accuracy
1	MobileNet	32	5,330,114	25	1 h 21 Min	99.98%	71.25%
2	Inception	32	24,952,610	25	Need More Resources		
3	**MobileNet**	**12**	**5,330,114**	**25**	**1 h 44 Min**	**99.99%**	**85.50%**
4	Inception	12	24,952,610	25	3 h 22 Min	99.97%	53.75%

From Table 3, we conclude that Inception has more number of parameters as compared to MobileNet. Hence, the training of the model with batch size 32, is not possible for Inception architecture because we need more resources. Whereas with MobileNet architecture, it is possible because of less number of parameters. Another key parameter of comparison is time taken for training MobileNet outperforms as it takes less time for training and gives better accuracy in training and testing also.

In both, the model structure is equivalent to Fig. 2. Then, we extended the last layers by our layers which are 2 fully connected followed by one Softmax layer. We took 12,027 images for training and 80 images for testing in both models. In testing, MobileNet architecture with batch size 12 has better accuracy which is 85.50%.

We have checked our model performance over all possible locations of the corridor. To test the model, an image goes in the trained CNN classifier, it predicts the probability of two actions, forward and stop. Some example of test image is shown in Fig. 3. It shows the suggested actions in probability along with the image. The highest probability action is followed for Autonomous Navigation of UAV.

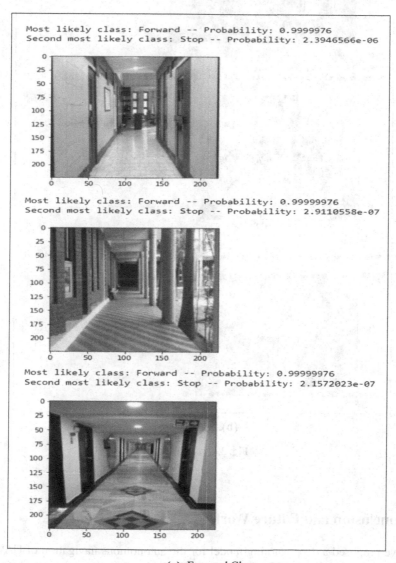

(a). Forward Class

Fig. 3. Example of our proposed model which classify the actions: Forward and Stop

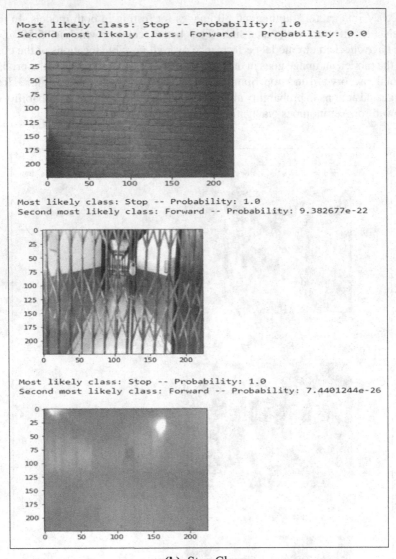

(b). Stop Class

Fig. 3. (*continued*)

5 Conclusion and Future Work

We have proposed a deep learning model for the autonomous navigation of UAV. Our model uses state-of-the-art CNN architecture MobileNet. Training of the model is carried out by the transfer learning concept to classify the actions such as either to go forward or to stop. Additionally, we presented a dataset of images which we have gathered from the various indoor environment. Furthermore, we compared our model with other architectures and, we conclude that MobileNet is best for our proposed approach.

In Future work, we wish to explore the actions from forward and stop to forward, turn left, turn right, up, down and stop using more images from different indoor environments.

References

1. Unmanned aerial vehicle. https://en.wikipedia.org/wiki/Unmanned_aerial_vehicle. Accessed 15 July 2019
2. How to fly a drone, for beginners, using controls, and more. https://skilledflyer.com/how-to-fly-a-drone/. Accessed 19 Sept 2019
3. Types of Drones - Explore the Different Types of UAV's. http://www.circuitstoday.com/types-of-drones. Accessed 19 Oct 2019
4. Bry, A., Bachrach, A., Roy, N.: State estimation for aggressive flight in GPS-denied environments using onboard sensing. In: Proceeding of International Conference on Robotics and Automation, USA, pp. 1–8. IEEE (2012). https://doi.org/10.1109/icra.2012.6225295
5. Roberts, J.F., Stirling, T.S., Zufferey, J., Floreano, D.: In: Quadrotor using minimal sensing for autonomous indoor flight. In: European Micro Air Vehicle Conference and Flight Competition (EMAV), France (2007)
6. Bachrach, A., He, R., Roy, N.: Autonomous flight in unknown indoor environments. Int. J. Micro Air Veh. 1(4), 217–228 (2009). https://doi.org/10.1260/175682909790291492
7. Celik, K., Chung, S., Clausman, M., Somani, A.K.: Monocular vision SLAM for indoor aerial vehicles. In: Proceeding of International Conference on Intelligent Robots and Systems, USA, pp. 205–210. IEEE (2016). https://doi.org/10.1109/iros.2009.5354050
8. Achtelik, M., Bachrach, A., He, R., Prentice, S., Roy, N.: Stereo vision and laser odometry for autonomous helicopters in GPS-denied indoor environments. Proc. SPIE Unmanned Syst. Technol. XI 7332(1), (2009). https://doi.org/10.1117/12.819082
9. Fraundorfer, F., et al.: Vision-based autonomous mapping and exploration using a quadrotor MAV. In: Proceeding of International Conference on Intelligent Robots and Systems, Portugal, pp. 4557–4564. IEEE (2012). https://doi.org/10.1109/iros.2012.6385934
10. Bills, C., Chen, J., Saxena, A.: Autonomous MAV flight in indoor environments using single image perspective cues. In: Proceeding of International Conference on Robotics and Automation, China, pp. 5776–5783. IEEE (2011). https://doi.org/10.1109/icra.2011.598 0136h0
11. Loquercio, A., Maqueda, A.I., Del-Blanco, C.R., Scaramuzza, D.: DroNet: learning to fly by driving. J. Robot. Autom. Lett. 3(2), 1088–1095 (2018)
12. Padhy, R.P., Verma, S., Ahmad, S., Choudhury, S.K., Sa, P.K.: Deep neural network for autonomous UAV navigation in indoor corridor environments. Procedia Comput. Sci. 133, 643–650 (2018). https://doi.org/10.1016/j.procs.2018.07.099
13. Gandhi, D., Pinto, L., Gupta, A.: Learning to fly by crashing. In: Proceeding of International Conference on Intelligent Robots and Systems (IROS), IEEE, Canada (2017). https://doi.org/10.1109/iros.2017.8206247
14. Jung, S., Hwang, S., Shin, H., Shim, D.H.: Perception, guidance, and navigation for indoor autonomous drone racing using deep learning. J. Robot. Autom. Lett. 3(3), 2539–2544 (2018). https://doi.org/10.1109/lra.2018.2808368
15. Kim, D.K., Chen, T.: Deep neural network for real-time autonomous indoor navigation. arXiv: 1511.04668 (2015)

16. Dionisio-Ortega, S., Rojas-Perez, L.O., Martinez-Carranza, J., Cruz-Vega, I.: A deep learning approach towards autonomous flight in forest environments. In: Proceeding of International Autumn Meeting on Power, Electronics and Computing (ROPEC), pp. 139–144 (2018). https://doi.org/10.1109/conielecomp.2018.8327189

17. Clarke, R.: Understanding the drone epidemic. J. Comput. Law Secur. Rev. **30**(3), 230–246 (2014). https://doi.org/10.1016/j.clsr.2014.03.002

18. Ahirwar, S., Swarnkar, R., Bhukya, S., Namwade, G.: Application of drone in agriculture. Int. J. Curr. Microbiol. Appl. Sci. **8**(01), 2500–2505 (2019). https://doi.org/10.20546/ijcmas.2019.801.264

19. Reinforcement Learning. https://www.geeksforgeeks.org/what-is-reinforcement-learning/. Accessed 6 Apr 2020

20. Supervised and Unsupervised Learning. https://www.geeksforgeeks.org/supervised-unsupervised-learning/. Accessed 6 Apr 2020

21. He, K., Zhang, X., Ren, S., Sun, J.: Deep residual learning for image recognition. In: Proceeding of Conference on Computer Vision and Pattern Recognition (CVPR), pp. 770–778. IEEE (2015)

22. Huang, G., Liu, Z., Maaten, L.V.D., Weinberger, K.Q.: Densely connected convolutional networks. CVPR **1**(2), 4700–4708 (2018)

23. Krizhevsky, A., Sutskever, I., Hinton, G.E.: ImageNet classification with deep convolutional neural networks. Commun.. ACM, **60**(6), 84–90 (2012

24. Review: AlexNet, CaffeNet- Winner of ILSVRC 2012 (Image Classification). https://medium.com/coinmonks/paper-review-of-alexnet-caffenet-winner-in-ilsvrc-2012-image-classification-b93598314160. Accessed 23 Mar 2020

25. LeCun, Y., Bottou, L., Yoshua, B., Haffner, P.: Gradient-based learning applied to document recognition. Proc. IEEE **86**(11), 2278–2324 (1998). https://doi.org/10.1109/5.726791

26. Simonyan, K., Zisserman, A.: Very deep convolutional networks for large-scale image recognition. arXiv:1409.1556 (2015)

27. Szegedy, C., et al.: Going deeper with convolutions. In: Proceeding of Conference on Computer Vision and Pattern Recognition (CVPR), pp. 1–9. IEEE (2015)

28. Howard, A.G., et al.: Mobilenets: efficient convolutional neural networks for mobile vision applications. arXiv preprint arXiv:1704.04861 (2017)

29. Deng, L.: The MNIST database of handwritten digit images for machine learning research [best of the web]. Signal Process. Mag. **29**(6), 141–142 (2012). https://doi.org/10.1109/msp.2012.2211477

30. Deng, J., Dong, W., Socher, R., Li, L.J., Li, K., Fei-Fei, L.: Imagenet: a large-scale hierarchical image database. In: Proceeding of Conference on Computer Vision and Pattern Recognition, USA, pp. 248–255. IEEE (2009). https://doi.org/10.1109/cvpr.2009.5206848

31. An Overview Of UAV Hardware Components and Software. https://medium.com/@UAVLance/an-overview-of-uav-hardware-components-and-software-2df983222e31. Accessed 3 Mar 2020

32. Deep Learning for Beginners Using Transfer Learning in Keras. https://towardsdatascience.com/keras-transfer-learning-for-beginners-6c9b8b7143e. Accessed 7 July 2020

33. Large Scale Visual Recognition Challenge (ILSVRC). http://www.image-net.org/challenges/LSVRC/. Accessed 6 Apr 2020

34. Understand Cross Entropy Loss in Minutes. https://medium.com/data-science-bootcamp/understand-cross-entropy-loss-in-minutes-9fb263caee9a. Accessed 6 Apr 2020

35. Gentle Introduction to the Adam Optimization Algorithm for Deep Learning. https://mac hinelearningmastery.com/adam-optimization-algorithm-for-deep-learning/. Accessed 15 Feb 2020
36. Understand the Softmax Function in Minutes. https://medium.com/data-science-bootcamp/understand-the-softmax-function-in-minutes-f3a59641e86d. Accessed 26 July 2019
37. Understanding of Convolutional Neural Network (CNN) - Deep Learning. https://medium.com/@RaghavPrabhu/understandingofconvolutional-neural-network-cnn-deep-learning-99760835f148.s. Accessed 12 July 2019

Framework for Processing Medical Data and Secure Machine Learning in Internet of Medical Things

K. Y. Ponomarev[✉] and A. A. Zaharov

Tyumen State University, Tyumen, Russia

Abstract. The term «Internet of Medical Things» (IoMT) refers to a set of devices and technologies for remote monitoring of patients' health using wearable devices. One primary problem with patient's data is ensuring privacy when it is transmitted over open communication channels and stored in cloud systems. A whole range of different approaches to these issues are available. However, when it comes to millions of IoT devices, technologies that have already become classic for Internet resources are not suitable in many aspects at once. The aim of this work is to develop methods and protocols for secure interaction between portable diagnostic devices and cloud services for the analysis and processing of medical data in the Internet of Medical Things networks. The work considered existing technologies and solutions for ensuring security in IoMT networks and personalized medicine systems; also, it focused on secure machine learning methods. Previous studies have emphasized attribute-based encryption (ABE) as a prospective method for data privacy and security. These algorithms solve many problems for IoMT applications: patient's data confidentiality, flexible key management, fine-grained access control mechanisms, and user control over data. We have proposed a framework for processing patient data from portable diagnostic devices using ABE methods.

Keywords: Internet of things · Data privacy · Attribute-based encryption · Personal health records

1 Introduction

Progress of information and communication technologies is driving the development of personalized healthcare. New healthcare paradigm is characterized by the term 4P, containing four fundamental principles: personalization, predictability, prevention and participation. Although there are no practical realizations of the 4P paradigm, the request from the medical domain has already formed the « Internet of Medical Things » concept. These concepts are based on IoT technologies and denote a set of devices and technologies for remote health monitoring using wearable devices. IoMT systems can be used to combine available medical resources and provide smart health services in the rehabilitation of elderly patients after stroke, as well as to monitor and control the health of patients with chronic diseases, including patients living in remote areas [1, 2].

© Springer Nature Singapore Pte Ltd. 2021
P. K. Singh et al. (Eds.): FTNCT 2020, CCIS 1396, pp. 264–275, 2021.
https://doi.org/10.1007/978-981-16-1483-5_24

To collect data from patients, portable medical devices are used, integrated into a wireless body-area network (WBAN) [3]. Together with the doctor's records and the laboratory tests results, these data form an electronic medical record (EHR). Based on the analysis of EHR, it is possible to identify diagnosis, examine the quality of medical care, etc. Machine learning and Big data technologies are used to extract valid information from unstructured EHR data and identify typical patient categories. Cloud technologies are used to store large volumes of EHR data, control access and provide computing resources. Thus, IoMT is tightly integrated with medical data storages, IoT networks, analytics applications, data services, and other related infrastructure.

User data privacy protection and confidentiality has attracted more attention in the IoMT networks. The key problem with these systems is that data should be secured not only in the sharing over open network process [4, 5], but in the cloud storage too [6, 7]. The study [4] states that the patient has minimal control over his data after it has been transferred to the cloud storage. Also, data is exposed to several privacy threats: malicious insider as an employee of the cloud service provider, data loss, the impact of other virtual environments, and insecure data access interfaces and APIs. The research [6] states that to protect network interactions it is very important to use reliable routing mechanisms, integrity checking methods, and end-to-end cryptography algorithms. It is noted that symmetric encryption algorithms are less resource-intensive and therefore more suitable for low-power IoT devices. However, they are ineffective in terms of key management mechanisms.

New approaches and security models are therefore needed for maintaining user privacy in IoMT systems. The aim of this work is to develop methods and protocols for secure interaction between portable devices and cloud services for the analysis and processing of medical data in the Internet of Medical Things networks.

2 Personalized Healthcare and Personal Health Records

Personal Health Records (PHR) is a main method for storing patient's data in personalized medicine systems. The main idea is that the user stores his own medical records (doctors' reports, test results, etc.) and regulates access to it for medical personnel and institutions. It is assumed that user information is located in a cloud-based secure storage of medical data. The key feature is that the user constantly has access to his medical records and regulates access to it for medical institutions. This is relevant in modern conditions of a large number of medical organizations, each of which maintains its own patient base, and high mobility of citizens (moving within one city or within the entire country). The patient grants permission to his EHR in cloud storage for various medical organizations, clinics and portable diagnostic devices. It can either specify IoMT devices and doctors, or define them using access policies. In the same way, the patient sets up read access for automated analytics services, doctors, insurance or research organizations.

Next list the main security properties of electronic medical record systems.

- Confidentiality: user data must be transmitted over secure channels, and be protected during storage in the cloud storage. It is necessary to protect data from malicious observers in an open network, the cloud provider itself, or attackers who have violated its integrity.

- Patient-centered: the user has full control over their data and grants access by configuring attribute policies. For example, a new patient is able to provide full access to his EHR data, including all the details of the doctors' reports and all previous tests, for a new doctor.
- Delegation and access revocation: the user is able to revoke someone's access to their information or delegate the right to manage their records to someone (for example, relatives). It is also worth noting such a moment as the access of ambulance personnel to user information in emergency situations.

The paper [8] addresses the need for research of EHR storages and healthcare analytic systems since the fact that medical procedures are now shifting from a clinic-oriented system to personal medicine. In this way, patients are treated in different medical centers, so medical information remains shared and distributed across them.

The article [9] presents the results of the design and development of a personal health records storage. The authors note that traditional cryptosystems need to explicitly indicate the recipient of the data (for example, using its public key or certificate), and this is not applicable in the healthcare domain and IoT applications: the patient, when uploading information, may not know specific consumers of information. Thus, modern protection tools based on symmetric and asymmetric cryptosystems are ineffective when working with EHR.

A study [10] presents a cloud storage for electronic medical records, whose specific feature is an ontology graph that contains subject attributes, relationships and data (even each patient visit is stored as graph vertex). System users (doctors, nurses, pharmacists, etc.) create and modify documents that will be encrypted and loaded into the knowledge graph. The authors also note that by shifting all access control into the patient's hands, the system forces them to manually configure access policies for all records. This behavior can lead to additional challenges. Therefore, in the described solution, the one central entity is fully responsible for the access control, distribution and sharing of medical records. User interaction with the data storage is carried out through a specially developed web application.

The majority of prior research has applied attribute-based encryption (*ABE*) algorithms as an effective method for protecting user data, maintaining privacy and confidentiality [11, 12]. *ABE* is an asymmetric cryptosystem, in which a set of attributes of the access subjects is used as a public key. A special attribute authority acts as a key generator service, and is responsible for generating the corresponding private keys. The usage of *ABE* algorithms for EHR systems allows to solve many problems described by the developers and researchers of personalized medicine systems: the confidentiality of patient data in the cloud, simplified cryptographic key management, and patient access control over his data.

3   Attribute-Based Encryption

Attribute-based encryption is a public key cryptosystem. Its genesis can be traced back to Identity-based encryption, proposed by Shamir in 1984 [13]. The main idea is to use any generic public string as a public key such as an email address. To solve this problem a master private-key generator (*PKG*) was proposed that is responsible for providing the decryption keys that are tied to a generic identity. In 2001 Boneh and Franklin [14] proposed an implementation of *IBE* scheme and proved it secure under the chosen-ciphertext attack. Their approach was based on a special form of bilinear mapping - Weil pairings. This mathematical construction provides a method to map a random public string (for example, user's identity) to a cryptographic public key and generate a suitable private key used to decrypt messages encrypted with the corresponding public key. Next Amit Sahai and Brent Waters proposed a *Fuzzy IBE* scheme [15], which became the prototype of ABE.

There are two types of ABE schemes, which differ in the way private keys are mapped to the set of attributes - Key-Policy (*KP-ABE*) and Ciphertext-Policy (*CP-ABE*). In *KP-ABE* schemes, users' private keys are associated with access policies, and ciphertexts are marked with sets of attributes. A user can decrypt a message if and only if the set of message attributes matches the key access structure. In *CP-ABE* schemes, the access structure is included in the ciphertext, and user keys are associated with a set of attributes. Accordingly, a user can decrypt a message if and only if his key set of attributes matches the access structure from the message. *CP-ABE* schemas are more flexible than *KP-ABE* schemas, since, for example, they allow to dynamically define users who have access to data.

Attribute Authority (*AA*) plays a role of *PKG* in *ABE* schemes. It is responsible for generating public and private keys, key management and distribution, verification of attributes received from elements requesting a secret key. Any *CP-ABE* scheme should implement the next functions:

- *Setup() -> (pars, msk)*: AA generates public parameters and secret master key;
- *KeyGeneration(pars, msk, A) -> SK_A*: AA generates new secret key using public parameters, secret master key and attributes of requesting subject;
- *Encrypt(pars, P, M) -> CT*: message sender encrypts message and generates new ciphertext using public parameters, access structure and plaintext;
- *Decrypt(pars, CT, P, SK_A) -> M*: message receiver decrypts message using public parameters, ciphertext, access structure and their own secret key, it's possible only if the attributes of the secret key A satisfy access structure P.

4   Platform for Storage and Processing of Medical Data

Consider an IoMT platform composed of the following core entities:

- Cloud storage of personal health records (*Cloud*): stores patient's medical records and provides an API for accessing data.
- Attribute Authority (*AA*): serves as a registration center for all platform subjects - patients, doctors, IoT devices, various data processing and analysis services. Stores attributes for each of them, generates keys of *ABE* schemes. Patients specify access policies to their data in cloud storage in the form of attribute rules. The Attribute Authority has a shared secret key with each of the registered subjects.

- Portable medical device (*Device*): collects or aggregates medical indicators and vital signs, sends them for further processing to the cloud storage. The patient is able to register his devices in the *Attribute Authority*.
- Token Generation Service (*TGS*): required to verify access to the cloud storage *API*.

Next describe the processes of transferring data - medical indicators of the patient - to the cloud and its processing.

1. The patient performs the registration procedures for himself and his devices in the *Attribute Authority*. As a result, *AA* will know attributes set and shared secret keys for each device. Attributes will be used for generating private keys of the ABE scheme. Shared secret keys will be used for authentication in *Attribute Authority*. With the purpose of attributes verification, there is a possible moderation of patient and devices information by medical personnel.
2. The patient specifies in the *AA* what attribute access structures should be used to access his data through cloud storage *API*. For simplicity, we will assume that only read and write operations are used in cloud storage *API*.
3. The patient configures his portable medical devices: he should set up a shared secret key, created during registration procedure in the first step.
4. In the start the portable device requests the private *ABE* key in the *Attribute Authority*, which will be used for authorization in the cloud storage. *AA* uses the shared secret key specified in the previous step for authentication and authorization.
5. Next *Device* initiates a request to the *Cloud API* with the purpose of transferring patient's data.
6. *Device*, cloud storage, and *TGS* jointly implements the *Attribute Access Control Protocol* to verify *Device's* access to patient's data and *Cloud API*.
7. If the authorization check was successful, the patient's data will be encrypted by *ABE* and recorded to the cloud storage, thus the information will be protected from the cloud provider or from an attacker in case of compromise.

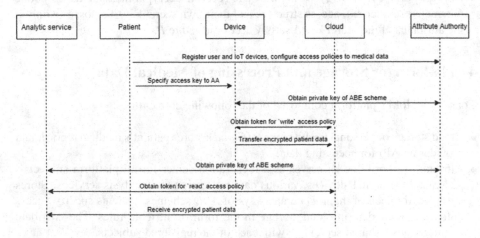

Fig. 1. Sequence diagram in IoMT platform.

8. Analytics and data processing services also receive the private key of the *ABE* scheme from the *Attribute Authority*. They access patient data through *Cloud* API, execute the *Attribute Access Control Protocol* to verify access rights for reading data. It is assumed that these services can detect possible anomalies in patient data, and in critical cases, notify the patient and his hospital.

Based on the described processes, the following requirements for authorization and authentication mechanisms in the IoMT platform can be distinguished. These requirements correspond to the EHR systems properties indicated earlier.

- The patient should specify access policies for operations with his data in the *Cloud API*, for example, for write and read operations. Patient-specified access policies must be used to validate access rights to patient data through the cloud storage *API*.
- The cloud storage knows the owner of the received data, but does not have access to the data itself. We assume that the patient's medical data is encrypted.
- The transmission of information in an open network should go through a secure communication channel.

The implementation of attribute access control methods and *ABE* algorithms increases the efficiency of the security mechanisms of IoMT platforms. Note the following positive aspects of the proposed approach:

- protocols described in the work do not depend on a specific *ABE* algorithm and can use practically any *CP-ABE* scheme;
- attribute-based access model is the most suitable for modern dynamic networks of the Internet of Things and allows the use of flexible and fine-grained access policies;
- *ABE* is used both for checking access rights and for protecting information during its transmission over an open network and storage in the cloud;
- due to the use of *ABE*, the mechanism of Single Sign-On is implemented, when the private key received from the *Attribute Authority* can be used to access various cloud resources and *APIs*;
- key management mechanisms are simplified by using *ABE*, the sender and recipient do not need to follow the pre-key exchange procedures.

5 Attribute Access Control Protocol

In this part, we will describe an Attribute Access Control Protocol - a mechanism for reading and writing patient data to the cloud using attribute-based access control and ABE algorithms for authorizing and protecting data during storage. Notations are presented in Table 1.

Next, we describe some initial assumptions. The patient registered his portable medical devices in the *AA*, therefore they are able to obtain the secret key of the attribute-based encryption scheme by requesting *Attribute Authority* API. The patient indicates the attribute access structures to his data through the cloud storage API. This information is available not only to the *Attribute Authority* itself, but also *TGS* knows it. Note that

Table 1. Notations

Symbol	Notation
TGS	Identificator of Token Generation Service
D	Identificator of patient's portable device
C	Identificator of Cloud Storage
$attr_D$	Attributes denoting portable device
$attr_{TGS}$	Attributes denoting Token Generation Service
$attr_{AS}$	Attributes denoting access structure to the patient's data in the cloud storage
$ID_{SESSION}$	Identificator of session between cloud and device
K_{TC}	Shared secret key of TGS and cloud storage
CT	Ciphertext of attribute-based encryption scheme
E^{ABE}	Encryption procedure of attribute-based encryption scheme
E	Symmetric encryption algorithm
H	Hash function

specific methods and mechanisms for key distribution are not discussed in this article. We will also assume that *Cloud* and *TGS* have a shared secret symmetric key K_{TC}.

$$D \rightarrow C : D \tag{1}$$

Patient's portable medical device initiates data transfer to the storage and execution of the protocol by sending its identifier.

$$C \rightarrow D : C, Z = E_{K_{TC}}(R_0 || D) \tag{2}$$

In response, the cloud storage sends a special access code, which will later be used to verify the protocol session: the response from *TGS* came exactly within this session, and was not forged or repeated by the attacker.

$$D \rightarrow TGS : D, C, Z, CT_1 = E_{attr_{TGS}}^{ABE}(R_1) \tag{3}$$

The *Device* sends a request to the *TGS* in order to check the access to the cloud storage *API*, in addition, the token generation service is authenticated through an attribute-based handshake.

$$TGS \rightarrow D : CT_2 = E_{attr_{AS}}^{ABE}(R_2), \ H(R_1 || R_2 || D) \tag{4}$$

In turn, the *TGS* checks the *Device's* access to the cloud storage API through the attribute-based handshake using an access structure specified by the patient at step 1. Using a hash from all nonces, the token generation service finished an authentication procedure to the portable medical device: only the one with the private key for $attr_{TGS}$ attributes could recognize R_1.

$$D \rightarrow TGS : H(R_1 || R_2 || TGS) \tag{5}$$

The portable medical device authenticates to the *TGS* by sending a hash value from all nonces. Only the one with a private key for $attr_{AS}$ attributes could recognize R_2.

$$TGS : JWE = \{attr_D, \; timestamp, \; E_{K_{TC}}(K)\}$$

TGS generates a session key K for interaction between the cloud and the portable device. In addition to it, *TGS* applies the timestamp.

$$TGS \to D : E_{attr_D}^{ABE}(K), \; JWE, \; Z' = H(Z||K_{TC}||K) \tag{6}$$

TGS sends to the *Device* a new generated session key and session information for the cloud storage. Using the previously received access code, the token generation service generates a new access code to authenticate himself. Only the one who knows K_{TC} and generates K could form a Z' value.

Further, the patient's portable medical device sends a request to the cloud, including to it all the tokens received from the TGS. They then use the new session key to authenticate messages during the session.

$$D \to C : request, \; JWE, \; Z', \; H(request||K) \tag{7}$$

$$C \to D : ID_{SESSION}, \; response, \; H(response||K) \tag{8}$$

The presented model of attribute-based access control has the following characteristics that correspond to the previously mentioned security requirements for IoMT platforms:

- the patient determines the attribute access structures to his data in the *Attribute Authority*, with the help of these access structures authorization occurs when requesting the cloud storage API;
- using attribute-based encryption it is possible to transfer and store encrypted data in the cloud;
- as a result of the implementation of the presented protocol a shared session key is generated for the portable device and the cloud, with the help of which it is possible to create a secure communication channel.

For the security overview we will use the Dolev-Yao model, according to which all transmitted messages can be viewed and intercepted by an intruder. The operation attribute-based handshake protocol, which is part of the presented algorithm, was analyzed using the AVISPA software for automatic verification of cryptographic protocols in order to verify the mutual authentication of the parties. Consider the following possible attacks.

Device impersonation attack: *Device* is checked for the presence of attributes corresponding to the requested access structure in steps 4–5, so it is not possible to impersonate an authorized device in communication with *TGS*. An attacker will not be able to forge a response to the cloud at step 7, since the Z' value is associated with the access code generated at the first step.

TGS impersonate attack: an attacker cannot impersonate a *TGS*, since at steps 3–4 service is checked for the presence of attributes of the *Token Generation Service*, in this way the *Device* knows that it is interacting with the *TGS*. In its turn *Cloud* knows that *Device* interacted with the one who owns the shared key - K_{TC}, since only it could generate an access code at step 6 of the protocol.

Cloud impersonate attack: the cloud storage has implicit authentication procedure - if the attacker impersonates the *Cloud*, then it will not be able to decrypt the session key received in step 6, therefore it will not be able to further interact with the *Device*.

Repeat message attack: repeating step 2 of the protocol in order to impersonate the *Cloud* will be useless for the attacker, since as mentioned above, the attacker will not be able to decrypt the session key. Repeating step 3 in order to impersonate a *Device* will be useless for the attacker, since it will not be able to generate a hash for step 5. Repeating step 6 in order to impersonate a *Device* will be useless for the attacker, since it will not be able to access the session key.

Token substitution attack: an attacker couldn't generate a token with a session key by himself, since it does not know the shared K_{TC} key. Sending a token from previous sessions is impossible, since the access code is associated with the value generated by the *Cloud* itself in the first step.

Parallel sessions attack: using messages from one parallel protocol session is useless, since the protocol steps are linked to each other with nonces.

6 Attribute-Based Access Control in FIWARE Platform

The open platform FIWARE is widely used as a tool for building IoT systems in the literature and industry. Technically, FIWARE is a platform of production-ready interconnected components called Generic Enablers that provide a simple and powerful set of services and APIs. This approach, together with a free software license, allows developers of IoT systems to use the FIWARE platform as the basis for their applications, without wasting time creating complex subsystems. Community-developed, open specifications simplify and standardize interoperability between different software systems.

The security and data privacy within FIWARE are the goal of a lot of research. For example, study [16] discusses authentication methods for clouds in IoT systems based on FIWARE technology. The presented methods allow IoT-devices to join the clouds, transfer data, and users to gain access to the system depending on their privileges. In research [17], it is stated that FIWARE lacks methods of distributed confidentiality and data control.

The methods and protocols presented in this paper could improve the mechanisms of sharing information and data confidentiality within the platform, in particular within communication between *IoT* devices and platform services. As well they are able to improve API's security, access control mechanisms and protect data in the cloud storage from malicious insiders. More specifically, the benefits of integrating presented models into the FIWARE platform are given below:

- Flexible and fine-grained attribute-based access control, allowing detailed description of access policies.

- Loose coupling between services, IoT devices and user applications: in fact, the interaction interfaces need to know only the attributes of the other side and be able to interact with the *Attribute Authority*.
- The interacting sides do not need to pre-exchange cryptographic keys to create a secure communication channel.
- Patient's data are kept in encrypted form inside a cloud storage in order to protect it from a cloud provider itself or malicious insiders, it may be relevant for systems operating personal or other confidential data.

Next, we will briefly introduce how to integrate the previously presented attribute-based access control mechanisms into the *FIWARE* platform.

Attribute Authority can be implemented as a backend service, access to which will be protected by standard services in FIWARE - the *Keyrock Identity Management* authentication service and the *Wilma PEP* proxy service. Patients and their IoT devices are registered in *IdM*, then using the *OAuth2* protocol they can authenticate in *Attribute Authority* API. Thus, *Keyrock IdM* acts as the authentication provider for the *Attribute Authority* service. *PEP Proxy* provides integration with *IdM*: it checks *OAuth2* tokens in *IdM* and redirects traffic to the protected service. Using *OAuth2*, patients and their portable devices perform all the previously described functions in the *Attribute Authority*: specifying data access structures, obtaining secret keys of attribute-based encryption scheme. Note that the *Token Generation Service* must have access to the data of the *Attribute Authority*, however, it is not necessary to block access to it using *Wilma PEP Proxy*, since it participates in the work of the *Attribute Access Control Protocol*.

The main component of the *FIWARE* platform - *Orion Context Broker*, it is a storage of context information for IoT devices based on *MongoDB* database. *Context Broker* can act as a cloud storage for patient's data. Access to it will be regulated through a special service - *IoT Agent*, which, on the one side will interact with IoT devices and *TGS* using attribute-based protocols, and on the other side, transfer data to the *Context Broker*. This agent approach is a standard solution within the *FIWARE* platform, it allows interaction with devices operating on different network protocols. For example, there are IoTAs communicating over the following protocols: *HTTP, MQTT, CoAP*. The developers of the *FIWARE* platform provide a template for developing your own implementations of the *IoT Agent*, which makes it possible to develop an *IoTA* service based on the *Attribute Access Control Protocol*.

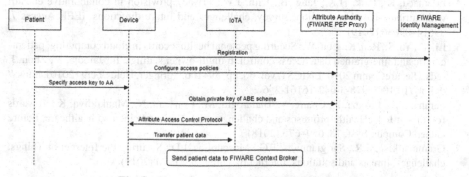

Fig. 2. Sequence diagram in FIWARE platform.

7 Conclusion

The development of new mechanisms and security models for personalized healthcare systems and IoT networks is an actual research subject. In this work, we considered a model of attribute-based access control to patient data for IoT systems. We presented: a secure communication model for the Internet of Medical Things platforms, an attribute-based access control protocol, a method for integrating the described models into the FIWARE platform. In the future we will focus on the next questions:

- multi-authority attribute-based encryption schemes in IoT platforms and their applications in IoMT systems;
- development of methods to integrate attribute access control models into existing platforms and solutions, in particular, further study of methods of working with the FIWARE platform;
- studying the possibilities of further effective work and data confidentiality in case of compromise of the *Attribute Authority*;
- methods and protocols for revoking attributes and secret keys in attribute-based encryption schemes.

Acknowledgments. The reported study was funded by Russian Ministry of Science (information security).

References

1. Li, X., Lu, R., Liang, X., Shen, X., Chen, J., Lin, X.: Smart community: an internet of things application. IEEE Commun. Mag. **49**(11), 68–75 (2011)
2. Masood, I., Wang, Y., Daud, A., Aljohani, N.R., Dawood, H.: Towards smart healthcare: patient data privacy and security in sensor-cloud infrastructure. Wireless Commun. Mob. Comput. (2018)
3. Kołodziej, J., Grzonka, D., Widłak, A., Kisielewicz, P.: Ultra wide band body area networks: design and integration with computational clouds. In: Kołodziej, J., González-Vélez, H. (eds.) High-Performance Modelling and Simulation for Big Data Applications. LNCS, vol. 11400, pp. 279–306. Springer, Cham (2019). https://doi.org/10.1007/978-3-030-16272-6_10
4. Edemacu, K., Park, H.K., Jang, B., Kim, J.W.: Privacy provision in collaborative ehealth with attribute-based encryption: survey, challenges and future directions. IEEE Access **7**, 89614–89636 (2019)
5. Li, M., Yu, S., Ren, K., Lou, W.: Securing personal health records in cloud computing: patient-centric and fine-grained data access control in multi-owner settings. In: Jajodia, S., Zhou, J. (eds.) SecureComm 2010. LNICST, vol. 50, pp. 89–106. Springer, Heidelberg (2010). https://doi.org/10.1007/978-3-642-16161-2_6
6. Farahani, B., Firouzi, F., Chang, V., Badaroglu, M., Constant, N., Mankodiya, K.: Towards fog-driven IoT eHealth: promises and challenges of IoT in medicine and healthcare. Future Gener. Comput. Syst. **78**, 659–676 (2018)
7. Grammatikis, P.I.R., Sarigiannidis, P.G., Moscholios, I.D.: Securing the Internet of Things: challenges, threats and solutions. Internet of Things **5**, 41–70 (2019)

8. Romero, J., López, P., Noguera, J.L.V., Cappo, C., Pinto-Roa, D.P., Villalba, C.: Integrated, reliable and cloud-based personal health record: a scoping review. arXiv preprint arXiv:1609. 03615 (2016)

9. Wang, C., Liu, X., Li, W.: Implementing a personal health record cloud platform using ciphertext-policy attribute-based encryption. In: 2012 Fourth International Conference on Intelligent Networking and Collaborative Systems, pp. 8–14. IEEE, September 2012

10. Joshi, M., Joshi, K., Finin, T.: Attribute based encryption for secure access to cloud based EHR systems. In: 2018 IEEE 11th International Conference on Cloud Computing (CLOUD), pp. 932–935. IEEE, July 2018

11. Narayan, S., Gagné, M., Safavi-Naini, R.: Privacy preserving EHR system using attribute-based infrastructure. In: Proceedings of the 2010 ACM Workshop on Cloud Computing Security Workshop, pp. 47–52, October 2010

12. Qureshi, B.: An affordable hybrid cloud based cluster for secure health informatics research. Int. J. Cloud Appl. Comput. (IJCAC) **8**(2), 27–46 (2018)

13. Shamir, A.: Identity-based cryptosystems and signature schemes. In: Blakley, G.R., Chaum, D. (eds.) CRYPTO 1984. LNCS, vol. 196, pp. 47–53. Springer, Heidelberg (1985). https:// doi.org/10.1007/3-540-39568-7_5

14. Boneh, D., Franklin, M.: Identity-based encryption from the weil pairing. In: Kilian, J. (ed.) CRYPTO 2001. LNCS, vol. 2139, pp. 213–229. Springer, Heidelberg (2001). https://doi.org/ 10.1007/3-540-44647-8_13

15. Sahai, A., Waters, B.: Fuzzy identity-based encryption. In: Cramer, R. (ed.) EUROCRYPT 2005. LNCS, vol. 3494, pp. 457–473. Springer, Heidelberg (2005). https://doi.org/10.1007/ 11426639_27

16. Sotiriadis, S., Vakanas, L., Petrakis, E., Zampognaro, P., Bessis, N.: Automatic migration and deployment of cloud services for healthcare application development in FIWARE. In: 2016 30th International Conference on Advanced Information Networking and Applications Workshops (WAINA), pp. 416–419. IEEE, March 2016

17. Barreto, L., Celesti, A., Villari, M., Fazio, M., Puliafito, A.: Identity management in iot clouds: a fiware case of study. In: 2015 IEEE Conference on Communications and Network Security (CNS), pp. 680–684. IEEE, September 2015

18. Cirillo, F., Solmaz, G., Berz, E.L., Bauer, M., Cheng, B., Kovacs, E.: A standard-based open source IoT platform: Fiware. IEEE Internet of Things Mag. **2**(3), 12–18 (2019)

Path Planning for Autonomous Robot Navigation: Present Approaches

Shagun Verma[1](✉) and Neerendra Kumar[2]

[1] Department of Computer Science, IT Central University of Jammu, Jammu 181143, India
shagunverma1994@gmail.com
[2] Doctoral School of Applied Informatics and Applied Mathematics, Óbuda University, Budapest, Hungary
neerendra.kumar@phd.uni-obuda.hu

Abstract. An intelligent autonomous robot is in demand for robotic operations in the fields such as industry, medical, bionics, military. For any machine, designed to follow a precise sequence of instructions, self-positioning, path framing, map architecture, and obstacle prevention are the prerequisites of navigation. This paper presents a survey about the key navigation approaches explored by various authors in the last decade. The survey has a brief insight into the various approaches used for robot navigation concerning to the variable and invariable nature of the vicinity and the obstacle. The comprehensive look-over presented in this paper provides an in-depth analysis and assessment of the discrete classical and heuristic approaches used by the researchers. The research assessment is finally concluded by aggregating the complete knowledge of the various path planning techniques by reviewing the literature.

Keywords: Path Planning · Autonomous navigation algorithms · Mobile robot

1 Introduction

The major application of portable robot covers the field of giant industries such as mining, space research, nuclear industry, landmine detection without any human intervention [1]. The essential constraints of the precise and optimal path design are the accessibility of environmental and odometric information [2]. Nowadays smart devices are indulged in every activity of humans to increase the convenience in living [3]. The self-directed mobile robot should define its locus in its frame of orientation by knowing its local coordinates. The mode of plotting navigation entails four main stages [4] as follows:

i. Observation.
ii. Localization/Plotting.
iii. Cognizance/Preparation.
iv. Kinetics control.

© Springer Nature Singapore Pte Ltd. 2021
P. K. Singh et al. (Eds.): FTNCT 2020, CCIS 1396, pp. 276–286, 2021.
https://doi.org/10.1007/978-981-16-1483-5_25

In the observation or perception phase, the robot collects the surroundings data with the support of actual sensors. The formation of a local coordinate designates the location of the robot and it acquires the information of the vicinity. Therefore, to know the robot's position and orientation is called Localization or Plotting. After localization, the robot must plan how to steer to the goal by deciding the path from the source to destination. It is personified as Cognition or preparation of path planning. In the fourth juncture, the robot controls the movement to accomplish the desired trajectory. The preferred route forecasting strategy for mobile robot course-plotting is articulated. This deliberately is proficient in discovering an ideal collision evasion path from the inceptive location of the robot to a terminal position in the ambiguous surroundings as detailed in [5]. The wheel equipped mobile robots are usually seen in industries where mechanical labour is required to do some needful task [6]. The different approaches to solve the problem of triangulation in familiar and unfamiliar surroundings are given in [7]. The two accessions of path planning methodologies [8] are as follows:

i.   Global path planning or offline path planning approach.
ii. Local path planning or online path planning approach.

In global path planning methods, the statistics about the location is past perceptive, that is, different variables like the position, size, shape of the obstacle are already provided, whereas, in local path planning methods, no information is provided to the robot about the environment [9]. The mobile robot fetches facts about the location through the sensors throughout its passage [10]. In [2], the doctrine of global path planning methods such as Cell decomposition, Roadmap, Subgoal network, artificial potential field, and Voronoi diagram are not applicable for on-line enactment. Therefore, local path planning approaches such as Neural Network (NN), Genetic Algorithm (GA), Fuzzy Logic (FL) etc. are reliable and have been advised for the operational execution of mobile robot exploration [11, 12].

2   Traditional Procedures Executed for Mobile Robot Navigation

Navigation became the core of research and many intellectuals have conferred a survey paper on the analysis based on the research done [13, 14]. The statistics gathered through the assessment does not provide in-depth sight on the various navigation techniques. The navigational policies have been broadly categorized into two types as classical and heuristic approaches [15].

2.1   Classical Approaches

Cell Decomposition Approach: The cell decomposition strategy dissociates the domain area into a non-concurring network. The derived unit forms the effective cells and they achieve the subsequent path from the initial grid to the final grid while the corrupted cells further split into more pure cells and now these cells form the basis to form a new path [16]. The area that is decomposed into smaller units constructs a connectivity graph according to the association between the cells The process is bifurcated into two arrangements: Exact cell decomposition and Approximate cell decomposition [17]. The interpretation of exact cell decomposition gives a brief notion about the motion of a robot. The region is divided into smaller units. And the path is found through the mid-points of the intersection of the adjacent cells. The derived expanse after the arrangement of these units is the same as the initial free space in every aspect. In approximate cell decomposition, the entire framework is in pre-resolute architecture. When the region is intercepted then it is further divided into four smaller cells of the same shape [18] and this repeats itself until it touches the resultant boundaries. The arrangement forms a quadtree (as shown in Fig. 1) which is generally called a cell [19].

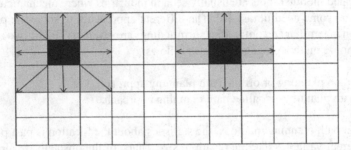

Fig. 1. Approximate cell decomposition (8-connected and 4-connected grids) [15].

Roadmap Approach: The roadmap approach is a union of curves such that all initial and goal points can be associated to form a path. It is called a roadmap approach [20]. The two main graphs that are entitled to determine the continuous path are the Voronoi graph and Visibility graphs. Both of them are used to generate the roadmap. Figure 2 depicts the visibility graph in which the colored area represents the obstacle and line showcase different paths which connect the edges of the obstacles and the final configuration is as shown in the highlighted line [21]. The Voronoi diagram [22] is a planner of the roadmap procedure used in a configuration area for determining the path. In this method parabolic curves are formed which are equidistant points from the two obstacles [23]. This enables the robot to navigate in a hassle-free path. Figure 3 shows how Voronoi curves are formed. Many approaches are been developed combining the two graphs and potential field methods [24] to get more precise outcomes.

Artificial Potential Field Approach: The potential field method is a simple and effective motion planning approach in which potential fields are created to regulate the robot in a certain space [25]. An imaginary force develops between the goal and destination which leads robots to the destination without any hassle as shown in Fig. 4. This method is usually praised by several intellectuals because of its efficiency for effective path scheduling [26]. The charged surfaces create a potent force on the robot and therefore it moves. To enhance the execution of the artificial potential field path planner, numerous techniques such as the genetic Algorithm [27], particle swarm optimization [28] are used.

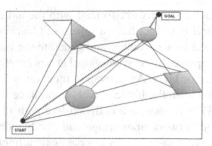

Fig. 2. Visibility graph [15].

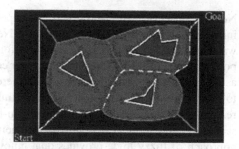

Fig. 3. Voronoi graph [15].

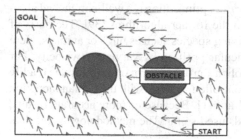

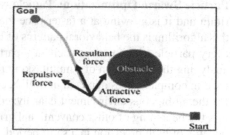

Fig. 4. Artificial potential field approach [15].

2.2 Heuristic Approaches

Fuzzy Logic: The conception of fuzzy provide valuable flexibility for reasoning [29] and is used in almost all spheres of innovation and advancement, based on human observation and inference, fuzzy rationality systems are stimulated by gained knowledge. On top, a certain set of input values collaborate to transform into a fuzzy set of interpretation rules throughout the fuzzification step. The fuzzification is followed by the defuzzification process where the generated results get altered into another set of values via membership function [30]. Lately, fuzzy logic is being used in collaboration with further navigation techniques [31] to enhance the learning of proximity surroundings. Many researchers are using data-driven approaches to get a more precise result in a dynamic environment. Mamdani used a fuzzy logic regulator deliberately for an automated mobile robot in [32]. To maintain the diversification and to avoid untimely union, fuzzy logic was epitomized in [33] in ant colony optimization. A portable self-balancing robot is used in [34] which provides dedicated feedback mechanism and aims at providing inclusive knowledge of fuzzy concepts and its enactment in the embedded system. In [35] the research aims at providing a hybrid approach in real life situations by improvising fuzzy logic with artificial neural network by reducing the issues of ambiguity, scalability, time complexity etc. The classical gaps are reduced and produce the results that meet the client expectations.

Neural Network: The neural network approach is a network formed with the aid of interconnected neurons linked artificially. Neural networks have a supervised learning way in which the input nodes can alter information accordingly and generate the best possible outcome [36]. The network further comprises of three individual layers entitled as the input layer, the hidden layer, and the output layer. An activation function is fed to the input layers. The output layers are linked with the hidden layers to produce the results. Two neural networks were used in [37] to generate a collision-free path in a relatively unidentified environment. The neural network upon usage with the blended approach of fuzzy logic provides dual innovative benefits in an unsystematic ailment [38].

Particle Swarm Optimization: Particle swarm optimization is a well-entrenched algorithm and it is growing at a faster pace than the former algorithms [39]. The basis of this algorithm is the behavioral patterns of living species such as birds or animals. Here every particle tries to adapt itself in a particular position by varying its velocity. For analyzing the navigation of a multitasking robot, Particle swarm optimization is readily used in complex cases depicted in [40]. A controlled strategy with the human inception for the ambiguous environment is analyzed in [41]. Because of more accurate results, it is the becoming of other conventional grids used so far. The methodology gives dual benefits of high precision in a short period.

Ant Colony Optimization: Ant colony optimization (ACO) is swarm intelligence centered algorithm used to find paths through graphs [42]. Ant colony mimics the behavioral patterns of ants as they reach the destination from the shortest path avoiding collisions. The population produced method is used here to find the favorable trail for movement. The usage in dynamic path planning is reproduced in [43]. Also to enhance the conduct of the present approach in a static environment few contributions are proposed in [44]. The proposal for mobile robot navigation using ant colony optimization in an anonymous predictable ambiance is suggested by [45]. Ant colony optimization has engrossed itself in three dimensional fronts for underwater automobiles where the main agenda is to filter the best suitable concussion free path from source to destination [46]. A new fuzzy approach emphasizes diversity control in Ant Colony Optimization where the main notion is to evade or undermine complete convergence through the dynamic discrepancy of a specific factor [47].

Genetic Algorithm: Genetic algorithms are constructed on an analogy with genetic composition [48] formulated on the assumption of the "survival of the fittest" theory [49]. Being a metaheuristic algorithm it symbolizes to be a dominant tool for escalation of problems of varied forms. In [50], an adaptive evolutionary planner is used as a novel approach for pathfinding. Multiple mobile robot machines are induced in [51] to navigate in real scenarios. Various operators are involved in [52] such as real coding, fitness functions, and definite genetic operators for mobile steering in an indefinite situation. Conduct of missile control, endowed with the amalgam of the Genetic algorithm method and fuzzy judgment, has been validated in [53]. Genetic algorithm has also inclined its application into the military operations for the decision making of appropriate unmanned aerial vehicles [54]. Genetic algorithm has proven to be a blessing in the research area as described in [55] where the variable length of chromosomes is introduced in genetic algorithm to improve the adaptability of path planning.

3 Discussion

The manifesting literature review on itinerant robot navigation is grounded on the nature of the environment. On drawing comparison, it has been analyzed that the enactment of heuristic methods is comparatively more accurate and preferred than classical methods. The limitations of classical methods involve deceiving in local minima and time complexity in elevated magnitudes. The pie chart in Fig. 5 depicts the percentage area of conventional and Artificial intelligence approaches applied in various fields. Also, Fig. 6 shows the percentage variation of classical approaches and the heuristic approaches being used in years from 1970 to date. In today's era there is a substantial development made in the field of robot perceiving and navigating their surroundings. For instance in the self-driven coaches, mapping and navigation can endure to further progress but upcoming robots should have a profound understanding in the unexplored and less presumed locations. Some upcoming scope improvements that might be considered may include:

- To significantly connect and distinguish properties of sights.
- Improved information of the graphical representation for healthier facts of the vicinity.
- To determine new entity and hindrance in the location through the live sensors.
- In an environment where transmission of information in robot swarms is done, it would be complex for a robot to traverse. In such case, a robot should be capable of not only traversing but should be able to perceive the environment to avoid collisions with other robots in the swarm (Table 1).

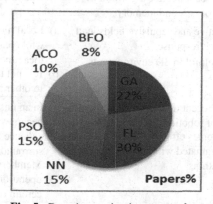

Fig. 5. Reactive navigation approaches.

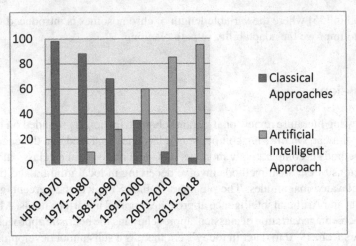

Fig. 6. Development of mobile robot navigation approaches [4].

Table 1. Advantages and disadvantages of various navigation methods.

Navigation method	Advantages	Disadvantages
Cell Decomposition	a) The cells can spread easily and often faster than the roadmap technique b) Easy algorithm to learn	a) Initial and final points should be known b) Less useful in unknown environments
Roadmap Approach	a) Visibility and Voronoi graphs provide generalized view of the number of paths b) It is a cost effective algorithm in terms of cost and memory	a) Close proximity to the obstacles which may cause collisions b) Multiple goals can sometimes lead to confusion
Artificial Potential Field	a) Attractive and repulsive fields lead to quick responses b) It is helpful in 3D environments	a) Local minima problem can occur while reaching at the target location b) It is not that useful as compared to other algorithms
Fuzzy Logic	a) It is a recent development in the field of robotics b) It becomes effective when amalgamated with other navigation algorithms	a) In an unstructured environment it becomes sometimes difficult to enhance the patterns of the surroundings b) Membership function can be less operational sometimes due to certain rules

(*continued*)

Table 1. (*continued*)

Navigation method	Advantages	Disadvantages
Neural Network	a) It can give a generalized view due to an intelligent interconnected system b) Massive parallelism can be done using two or more neural networks	a) Multiple layers mainly responsible for navigation failures b) Complexity in terms of computation due to higher number of layers
Particle Swarm Optimization	a) It traverses the path which the best particle follows b) Understandable topology structure	a) Parameters has to be adjusted prior the navigation b) Difficult in case of linear continuous function
Ant Colony Optimization	a) A simple and less complex algorithm b) Performs good in vigorous environments	a) Difficulty in acquiring the theoretical knowledge
Genetic Algorithm	a) Modifications can be easily done in different parameters b) Coding of this method is less complex than other	a) In changing environments, it becomes arduous to yield efficient outcome b) Optimal solutions are not guaranteed

4 Conclusion

This study provided a review of the approaches in path planning and generation of the shortest path from start to destination. The review elucidated distinct methods in path planning. As per the literature suggested, classical approaches are not well-grounded in terms of reliability and authenticity because of their incompatibility with the precedent surroundings. On the other side, heuristic methods find compatibility with the dynamic and unpredictable nature of the environment. Heuristic methods are resourceful in terms of time computation and are more proficient in terms of memory. However, classical approaches can be enhanced additionally to accomplish elevated results when used in fusion with the heuristic methods. After evaluating the whole assessment of the literature, the following viewpoints have come up and are stated as below:

- Mobile robot navigation is magnificently executed by various Local and Global based methodologies.
- The AI grounded methods are more feasible as it provides results in dynamic situations with more precision than the nature inspired methods.
- The study on mobile robot navigation by employing the nature inspired algorithm is very restricted for path design in convoluted and anonymous ambience.

References

1. Truong, X., Ngo, T.D.: Toward socially aware robot navigation in dynamic and crowded environments. IEEE Trans. Autom. Sci. Eng. **14**, 18 (2017)
2. Goyal, J.K.: A new approach of path planning for mobile robots, pp. 863–867 (2014)
3. Sharma, R., Sharma, A.: A review on interoperability and integration in smart homes. In: Singh, P.K., Sood, S., Kumar, Y., Paprzycki, M., Pljonkin, A., Hong, W.-C. (eds.) FTNCT 2019. CCIS, vol. 1206, pp. 116–128. Springer, Singapore (2020). https://doi.org/10.1007/978-981-15-4451-4_11
4. Thoa, T., Copot, C., Trung, D., De Keyser, R.: Heuristic approaches in robot path planning: a survey. Rob. Auton. Syst. **86**, 13–28 (2016)
5. Kavraki, L.E., LaValle, S.M.: Motion planning. In: Siciliano, B., Khatib, O. (eds.) Springer Handbook of Robotics, pp. 109–131. Springer, Heidelberg (2008). https://doi.org/10.1007/978-3-540-30301-5_6
6. Papachristos, C., et al.: Autonomous exploration and inspection path planning for aerial robots using the robot operating system. In: Koubaa, A. (ed.) Robot Operating System (ROS). SCI, vol. 778, pp. 67–111. Springer, Cham (2019). https://doi.org/10.1007/978-3-319-91590-6_3
7. Zhang, H., Lin, W., Chen, A.: Path planning for the mobile robot: a review. Symmetry (Basel) **10**(10), 450 (2018)
8. Sai, A., Haran, H.: A survey of autonomous mobile robot path planning approaches, pp. 27–29 (2017)
9. Raja, P.: Optimal path planning of mobile robots: a review. Int. J. Phys. Sci. **7**(9), 1314–1320 (2012)
10. Goerzen, C., Kong, Z., Mettler, B.: A survey of motion planning algorithms from the perspective of autonomous UAV guidance. J. Intell. Robot. Syst. Theory Appl. **57**(1–4), 65–100 (2010)
11. Wang, L.C., Yong, L.S., Ang, M.H.: Hybrid of global path planning and local navigation implemented on a mobile robot in indoor environment. In: IEEE International Symposium on Intelligent Control - Proceedings, pp. 821–826 (2002)
12. Atyabi, A., Powers, D.M.W.: Review of classical and heuristic-based navigation and path planning approaches. Int. J. Adv. Comput. Technol. **5**, 1 (2013)
13. Yang, L., Qi, J., Song, D., Xiao, J., Han, J., Xia, Y.: Survey of robot 3D path planning algorithms. J. Control Sci. Eng. (2016). https://www.hindawi.com/journals/jcse/2016/7426913/. Accessed 27 June 2020
14. Hoy, M., Matveev, A.S., Savkin, A.V.: Algorithms for collision free navigation of mobile robots in complex cluttered environments: a survey. Robotica (2015). https://www.scopus.com/inward/record.uri/. Accessed 27 June 2020
15. Patle, B.K., Babu L, G., Pandey, A., Parhi, D.R.K., Jagadeesh, A.: A review: on path planning strategies for navigation of mobile robot. Def. Technol. **15**(4), 582–606 (2019)
16. Milos, S.: Roadmap methods vs. cell decomposition in robot motion planning. WSEAS (2007). https://www.semanticscholar.org/paper/Roadmap-methods-vs.-cell-decomposition-in-robot-Seda/. Accessed 27 June 2020
17. Regli, W.: Robot Lab: robot path planning. Lecture notes of department of computer science. Drexel University. https://www.google.com/search?q=Regli+W."RobotLabArobotpath planning/. Accessed 27 June 2020
18. Schwartz, J.T., Sharir, M.: On the 'piano movers' problem I". The case of a two-dimensional rigid polygonal body moving amidst polygonal barriers. Commun. Pure Appl. Math. **36**(3), 345–398 (1983)
19. Ajani, S.N., Amdani, S.Y.: Path planning techniques for navigation of mobile robot: a survey. IOSR J. Eng. **09**(5), 77–84 (2019)

20. Latombe, J.-C.: Roadmap methods. In: Robot Motion Planning, pp. 153–199. Springer, Boston (1991). https://doi.org/10.1007/978-1-4615-4022-9_4
21. Siméon, T., Laumond, J.-P., Nissoux, C.: Visibility-based probabilistic roadmaps for motion planning. Adv. Robot. **14**(6), 477–493 (2000)
22. Choset, H., et al.: Kavraki Lab | Principles of Robot Motion: Theory, Algorithms, and Implementation. MIT Press, Cambridge (2005). https://www.kavrakilab.org/publications/choset-burgard2005principles-of-robot.html. Accessed 06 July 2020
23. Kim, J.: Workspace exploration and protection with multiple robots assisted by sensor networks. Int. J. Adv. Robot. Syst. **15**(4) (2018)
24. Masehian, E., Amin-Naseri, M.R.: A Voronoi diagram-visibility graph-potencial field compound algorithm for robot path planning. J. Robot. Syst. **21**(6), 275–300 (2004)
25. Khatib, O.: Real-time obstacle avoidance for manipulators and mobile robots. Int. J. Rob. Res. **5**(1), 90–98 (1986). https://doi.org/10.1177/027836498600500106
26. Hwang, Y.K., Ahuja, N.: A potential field approach to path planning. IEEE Trans. Robot. Autom. **8**(1), 23–32 (1992). https://doi.org/10.1109/70.127236
27. Raja, R., Dutta, A., Venkatesh, K.S.: New potential field method for rough terrain path planning using genetic algorithm for a 6-wheel rover. Rob. Auton. Syst. **72**, 295–306 (2015)
28. Kuo, P.H., Li, T.H.S., Chen, G.Y., Ho, Y.F., Lin, C.J.: Migrant-inspired path planning algorithm for obstacle run using particle swarm optimization, potential field navigation, and fuzzy logic controller. Knowl. Eng. Rev. (2016). https://www.cambridge.org/core/journals/knowledge-engineering-review? Accessed 27 June 2020
29. Zadeh, L.A.: Fuzzy sets. Inf. Control **8**(3), 338–353 (1965)
30. Gul, F., et al.: A comprehensive study for robot navigation techniques. Cogent Eng. **6**(1) (2019). Electrical & Electronic Engineering | Review Article
31. Carelli, R., Freire, E.O.: Corridor navigation and wall-following stable control for sonar-based mobile robots. Rob. Auton. Syst. **45**(3–4), 235–247 (2003)
32. Nazari Maryam Abadi, D., Khooban, M.H.: Design of optimal Mamdani-type fuzzy controller for nonholonomic wheeled mobile robots. J. King Saud Univ. Eng. Sci. **27**(1), 92–100 (2015)
33. Castillo, O., Neyoy, H., Soria, J., García, M., Valdez, F.: Dynamic fuzzy logic parameter tuning for ACO and its application in the fuzzy logic control of an autonomous mobile robot. Int. J. Adv. Robot. Syst. **10**(1) (2013)
34. Odry, Á., Fullér, R., Rudas, I.J., Odry, P.: Fuzzy control of self-balancing robots: a control laboratory project. Comput. Appl. Eng. Educ. **28**(3), 512–535 (2020). https://doi.org/10.1002/cae.22219
35. Singh, Y.V., Kumar, B., Chand, S., Sharma, D.: A hybrid approach for requirements prioritization using logarithmic fuzzy trapezoidal approach (LFTA) and artificial neural network (ANN). In: Singh, P.K., Paprzycki, M., Bhargava, B., Chhabra, J.K., Kaushal, N.C., Kumar, Y. (eds.) FTNCT 2018. CCIS, vol. 958, pp. 350–364. Springer, Singapore (2019). https://doi.org/10.1007/978-981-13-3804-5_26
36. Chen, J.: Neural Network Definition. Investopedia (2020)
37. Janglova, D.: Neural Networks in Mobile Robot Motion, December 2004
38. Pothal, J.K., Parhi, D.R.: Navigation of multiple mobile robots in a highly clutter terrains using adaptive neuro-fuzzy inference system. Rob. Auton. Syst. **72**, 48–58 (2015)
39. Eberhart, R., Kennedy, J.: New optimizer using particle swarm theory. In: Proceedings of the International Symposium on Micro Machine and Human Science, pp. 39–43 (1995)
40. Tang, Q., Eberhard, P.: Cooperative motion of swarm mobile robots based on particle swarm optimization and multibody system dynamics. Mechanics Based Design of Structures and Machines **39**(2), 179–193 (2011)
41. Chen, Y.L., Cheng, J., Lin, C., Wu, X., Ou, Y., Xu, Y.: Classification-based learning by particle swarm optimization for wall-following robot navigation. Neurocomputing **113**, 27–35 (2013)

42. Dorigo, M., Gambardella, L.M.: Ant colony system: a cooperative learning approach to the traveling salesman problem. IEEE Trans. Evol. Comput. **1**(1), 53–66 (1997)
43. Tan, G.Z., He, H., Sloman, A.: Ant colony system algorithm for real-time globally optimal path planning of mobile robots. Zidonghua Xuebao/Acta Autom. Sin. **33**(3), 279–285 (2007)
44. Liu, J., Yang, J., Liu, H., Tian, X., Gao, M.: An improved ant colony algorithm for robot path planning. Soft. Comput. **21**(19), 5829–5839 (2016). https://doi.org/10.1007/s00500-016-2161-7
45. Purian, F.K., Sadeghian, E.: Mobile robots path planning using ant colony optimization and Fuzzy Logic algorithms in unknown dynamic environments. In: CARE 2013 - 2013 IEEE International Conference on Control, Automation, Robotics and Embedded Systems, Proceedings (2013)
46. Liu, L.Q.: Path planning of underwater vehicle in 3D space based on ant colony algorithm (2008). https://www.researchgate.net/publication/291078044. Accessed 06 July 2020
47. Castillo, O., Neyoy, H., Soria, J., Melin, P., Valdez, F.: A new approach for dynamic fuzzy logic parameter tuning in Ant Colony Optimization and its application in fuzzy control of a mobile robot. Appl. Soft Comput. J. **28**, 150–159 (2015)
48. Bremermann, H.: The evolution of intelligence: the nervous system as a model of its environment. Department of Mathematics, University of Washington, Seattle, Washington (1958)
49. Holland, J.: Adaptation in Natural and Artificial Systems: An Introductory Analysis with Applications to Biology, Control, and Artificial Intelligence. MIT Press, Cambridge (1992). https://ieeexplore.ieee.org/book/6267401. Accessed 06 July 2020
50. Xiao, J., Michalewicz, Z., Zhang, L., Trojanowski, K.: Adaptive evolutionary planner/navigator for mobile robots. IEEE Trans. Evol. Comput. **1**(1), 18–28 (1997)
51. Kala, R.: Coordination in navigation of multiple mobile robots. Cybern. Syst. **45**(1), 1–24 (2014)
52. Shi, P., Cui, Y.: Dynamic path planning for mobile robot based on genetic algorithm in unknown environment. In: 2010 Chinese Control and Decision Conference, CCDC 2010, pp. 4325–4329 (2010)
53. Creaser, P.A., Stacey, B.A., White, B.A.: Evolutionary generation of fuzzy guidance laws. In: IEE Conference Publication, no. 455, pp. 883–888, February 1998
54. Lin, K.P., Hung, K.C.: An efficient fuzzy weighted average algorithm for the military UAV selecting under group decision-making. Knowl. Based Syst. **24**(6), 877–889 (2011)
55. Ni, J., Wang, K., Huang, H., Wu, L., Luo, C.: Robot path planning based on an improved genetic algorithm with variable length chromosome. In: 2016 12th International Conference on Natural Computation, Fuzzy Systems and Knowledge Discovery (ICNC-FSKD), pp. 145–149, August 2016

Development of a Routing Protocol Based on Clustering in MANET

Said Muratchaev(✉) and Alexey Volkov

National Research University of Electronic Technology, Bld. 1, Shokin Square, 124498 Moscow, Russia

Abstract. Wireless self-organizing networks are becoming more popular than usual networks. With the help of this type of network, it is possible to implement special purpose systems of varying complexity and focus, from search missions to automated production in the IIoT systems. One of the main problems in this class of networks is the problem of routing. This paper presents clustering methods for further implementation as part of zone-based protocols. This work will help automate and organize devices into groups with the subsequent automation of routing configuration processes.

Keywords: Routing protocol · Ad hoc networks · Clustering

1 Introduction

Wireless network MANET (Mobile Ad hoc NETwork) is an autonomous self-organizing wireless network consisting of a collection of autonomous nodes or terminals that communicate with each other, forming a multi radio system. Self-organizing network MANET is a wireless advertising network. This technology does not have a strictly configured structure, because wireless transmission protocols are used in the MANET structure, such as Wi-Fi, Bluetooth, WiMAX, same like in other cellular and satellite data transmission.

MANET is widely used in a fixed network infrastructure, as well as base stations and reference nodes. Thanks to the use of wireless data transmission protocols, the deployment of the MANET network is applicable in a ground installation and in a ground-air installation, as well as zero gravity conditions. Due to the possibility of self-organization, the need for its administration disappears, hence it becomes possible to quickly replace devices, as well as add new network nodes. MANET is widely used in military services, emergency rescue operations, industrial and commercial applications in the Smart Home system, and in the organization of satellite communications.

The disadvantage of such networks is the complexity of scaling, which increases in proportion to the speed and uneven movement of nodes within the network. Well-known routing algorithms partially solve the problem of reducing service traffic within one

The research was supported financially by Russian Foundation for Basic Research (Project No. 19-37-90095).

MANET network segment. The transition to a two-tier representation in one MANET network segment allows to apply different routing algorithms within each of the layers, which will reduce the amount of overhead traffic.

This concept is supposed to organize nodes into clusters using clustering for communication with small coverage, where there is no need for high power consumption. To scale huge networks, usually, specific ideas are applied: the optimal ratio of nodes within clusters, followed by frequency control and signal transmission power. This is achieved by controlling the number of cluster nodes, and frequency of distribution using cluster heads. In turn, the head of the cluster has two active interfaces: the first for communication within the cluster, and the second for communication between other clusters. Any information generated by cluster nodes is passed through the cluster head nodes.

Clustering has been used in networks for a long time, but nothing concrete has been achieved. This work [1] presents one of the options for assessing the effectiveness of clustering in mobile transport networks. The criteria by which the performance of various networks is assessed is one of the important problems in the development of new generation networks.

One of the main tasks solved by clustering is to maintain routing stability. Clustering can group devices so that they work most efficiently in local groups. The article [2] provides examples of the use of clustering to maintain the stability of routes in MANET networks. The main principle on how to optimize clusters is to control the number of nodes in clusters, in order to increase the stability of communication. Such methods of using clustering increase the stability of the route by an average of 10–20%.

A large number of routing protocols have been developed using clustering algorithms. One of the options for using clustering is presented in the form of a two-rank protocol architecture [3]. The development is based on Multihop routing using clustering. The main benefit is achieved in balancing traffic within the network. The result is increased lifetime of the network by complicating the existing structure of the protocol.

Sometimes the problems caused by the optimal choice of clusters are solved with the help of mathematics, for example, game theory [4]. A lot of research has been done on the application of game theory to the problem of cluster selection and routing. The mathematical calculations of the implementation of algorithms for solving clustering problems and the results of the developed solution are presented. In the conclusion, ideas are presented for the implementation of a neural network with the help of which the optimal method of grouping nodes into clusters will be achieved.

2   Methodology

2.1   Two-Rank Architecture

This work is based on the concept of implementing a two-rank MANET network, where nodes are independently organized into clusters, and selected to be a route between clusters. Based on numerous studies of the nature of proactive and reactive routing protocols [5–7], AODV and OLSR were selected. The organization of routing within the cluster is arranged using the AODV protocol, due to the chaotic movement of the nodes. The OLSR protocol is used between the clusters, because of the slow dynamic of changing the network topology. In turn, communication between nodes within the cluster is carried out by using wi-fi physics 5 GHz, since these frequencies are more critical to the communication range. Communication between the clusters is arranged using 2.4 GHz wi-fi technology, due to the signal propagation range and wider signal coverage. The concept of using this kind of network architecture is shown in Fig. 1.

One of the main problems with this concept is the selection and clustering of nodes along the most optimal path. Grouping devices is a rather difficult task, since there are many criteria by which grouping occurs. In the article [8] a classification of routing protocols based on clustering is carried out. The main goals of using clustering in routing are: scalability, energy efficiency, and lifetime maximization of the system. In machine learning, there is a wide variety of clustering algorithms, but not all of them are applicable specifically to MANET networks due to the fact that clustering must first of all take into account the physical location of devices relative to each other. This fact increases the likelihood of the correct distribution of nodes across clusters. To determine the algorithms for cluster analysis, the basic clustering models used in practice were studied and considered.

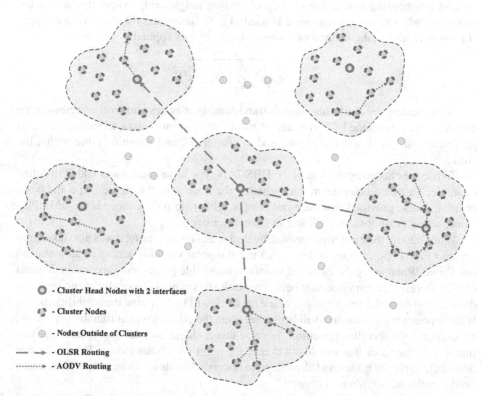

Fig. 1. Two-rank MANET network topology

The considered models included the following attributes: connectivity model, centroid model, distribution model, and density model. To determine the applicable clustering models in the MANET network, it is necessary to find the radius of visibility and the number of objects in its range. These conditions are used in connectivity models and density models. As with the analyzed clustering methods [9], the following algorithms were selected: clustering algorithm by connectivity components and DBSCAN [10].

The main measures of distances were considered for the possibility of applying clustering algorithms. They are needed to determine the similarity of objects, followed by combining into clusters. There are four basic distance measures that are used to determine the similarity of objects: Euclidean distance, Euclidean distance squared, city block distance (Manhattan distance) and Chebyshev distance. The analysis showed that the most suitable metric for finding "similar" points in the MANET network is the Euclidean distance metric. The results of the current analysis will be taken into account when introducing clustering algorithms into the reactive routing protocol of the MANET ZRP network.

2.2 Finding Neighboring Nodes

To find neighboring nodes, the method of finding neighboring points that are in the visibility radius of the current node is used (1). To determine the distance and apply clustering methods, the method of finding a measure was applied.

$$R_{vision} \geq \sqrt{\sum_{i=1}^{k} \left(x_i - x_i' \right)^2} \tag{1}$$

To implement the clustering algorithm and combine devices into groups, a clustertype container was developed for convenient use of the common data space inside it. Its parameters included: a list of cluster nodes, cluster ID, and a routing table within the cluster.

To use the clustering method of the DBSCAN type, a parameter was added to define the node. This parameter determines whether the node is of the "Core" type and has a positive result, provided that the number of neighboring points exceeds the «MinPts» value, which is an obvious indicator of cluster density.

When adding the clustering method, by the type of connectivity, it was also taken into account for its application: nodes cannot use the point visibility radius as an inclusion condition. When using the radius of visibility, all visible points will be combined into a cluster, therefore, communication between the clusters cannot physically occur, since the distance between the border nodes of the network will be less than the visibility radius. If these points are within the visibility radius, then the clusters will automatically merge, according to the specified condition. To solve this problem, an additional parameter was introduced, the value that should not exceed the point's visibility radius. This parameter allows clustering of nodes, and also allows to observe the rule of communication between border nodes of neighboring clusters.

In order to define a transmission node, a complete overview of the group's routing table is required. To fill in the routing table and to find the minimum path, distance vector routing protocols are used, as well as routing protocols based on the state of channels based on the construction of the shortest routes - graphs. Distance vector routing protocols are based on the Bellm-on-Ford algorithm. To determine the shortest distance, a minimum number of steps is considered, for the possibility of sending a message to the required node, by filling the route output table, using the iterative calculation method. Channel state routing protocols are based on Dijkstra's algorithm, for its calculation, parameters are used according to the channel state to find the total minimum shortest path.

As an algorithm for determining the routing table, Dijkstra's algorithm was chosen to find the shortest routes for a zone. This algorithm constructs the shortest route, using the number of transitions between points as parameters for constructing the shortest metric.

To solve the problem of finding the central node of a cluster, it is necessary to apply methods for solving problems using graph theory. To find the main node of the graph, it is necessary to find the shortest path from the node to each vertex of the graph, and determine its eccentricity (2). Let ν be an arbitrary vertex of the graph $G = (V, E)$, then, the eccentricity of the vertex ν is defined as: where L is the minimum path length from the vertex ω to the vertex ν. The point with the lowest eccentricity will be the center point of the node.

$$\max\{\min\{L\}\} \atop \varpi \in V$$

(2)

2.3 Routing Within Clusters

When building a routing map, the shortest distances were identified between each node of the cluster. To find the central node of the cluster, it is necessary to find the eccentricity of each node, to compare them and find the central point of the node.

Using the routing table also allows the algorithm to find the edge nodes of the cluster. To do this, it is necessary to define the central point of the cluster and its routing table. When displaying the routing table in the form of pairs of points through which the minimum route of the remaining tree passes, the algorithm can notice that if the point is internal, then the number of its entries in the routing table will exceed the value of one. Therefore, it is necessary to search for points, the occurrence of which will have a single value, and indicate their role as a boundary point of the cluster.

Figure 2 shows a method for dividing nodes into clusters, each color corresponds to a specific cluster. This parameter was tuned to achieve optimal ratios of nodes within the cluster so that the loss in data packets within the cluster does not exceed 80%. All simulations were carried out in the NS-3 environment, and the results were processed using programming languages. The simulation model is written in C++ and embedded in the NS-3 simulator structure. The main difficulty was the integration of the clustering algorithm into the structure of the existing routing protocols AODV and OLSR. Difficulties were also observed in integrating various protocols into one model.

3 Results

After starting the model in the NS-3 environment, the process of generating a file with the «. flowmon» extension is started. It is an XML-like document that contains a lot of information about modeling. For models in the NS-3 environment, the file is saved in the root folder of the project being developed. The file includes the following data:

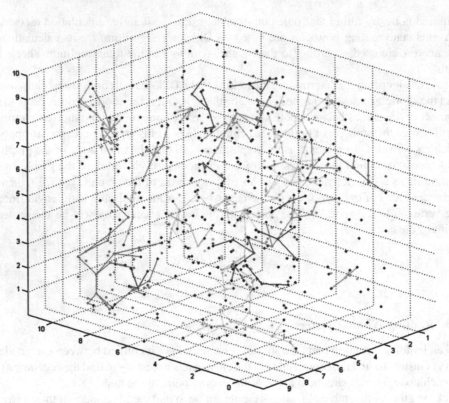

Fig. 2. Image of the process of splitting nodes into clusters.

- timeFirstTxPacket - transmission time of the first packet by the end node in the stream;
- timeFirstRxPacket - time of delivery of the first packet by the end node in the stream;
- timeLastTxPacket - time of transmission of the last packet by the end node in the stream;
- timeLastRxPacket - time of delivery of the last packet by the end node in the stream;
- delaySum - total delay time for all received packets of the stream;
- jitterSum - total route establishment time for all received packets of the stream;
- lastDelay - last measured packet delay;
- txPackets - total number of transmitted packets for the stream;
- rxPackets - total number of packets received;
- txBytes - total number of bytes sent;
- rxBytes - the total number of bytes received;
- lostPackets - the total number of lost packets;
- timesForwarded - total number of redirects.

All characteristics are provided in the file in the form of an array. Based on the statistical data graphs of the delay and the packet delivery rate were built. To compare the efficiency of the proposed two-rank architecture, it was decided to use the ZRP protocol instead of the one-rank topology. This routing protocol [11] is endowed with all the advantages of grouping devices into zones. This will allow us to compare the effectiveness of the two-rank architecture and clustering in comparison with the one-rank protocol.

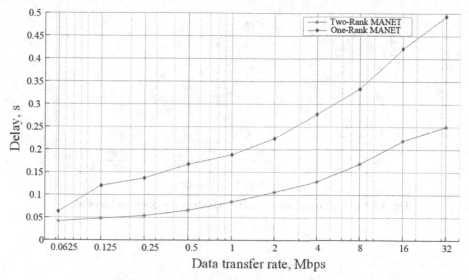

Fig. 3. Graph of average route delay across the entire network.

Figure 3 shows that the latency increases with an increase in the data transfer rate and for a ZRP protocol it is higher. At the minimum value, within the framework of the simulation, the data transfer delay for both networks is about 0.05 s. However, in a ZRP protocol, the average latency grows faster, and for a data rate of 32 Mbps, the difference between the average network latency is 0.25 s.

According to Fig. 4, the packet delivery rate decreases with increasing nodes. For a two-peer network, it is significantly higher than a ZRP protocol, however, with a small number of nodes, the difference is quite large - 12%, but with the growth of nodes in the network, the difference between them decreases to 7%. The gap between a two-rank and ZRP protocol is obvious, and the percentage of received packets is higher for a transport telecommunication network based on a two-rank model.

Based on the simulation results, a three-dimensional dependence of the average network delay, data transmission coefficient on the number of nodes in the network was built. To build this dependence, it was necessary to carry out additional simulations with a variable data rate. That is, the data transfer rate range was taken from 64 kbps to 4 Mbps, and for each value, simulations were carried out with a variable number of nodes from 10 to 100 units. Thus, a matrix of values was obtained, on the basis of which this dependence was built, presented in Fig. 5.

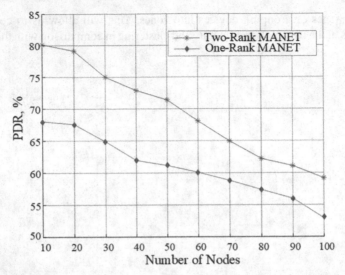

Fig. 4. Packet delivery rate versus the number of nodes in the network.

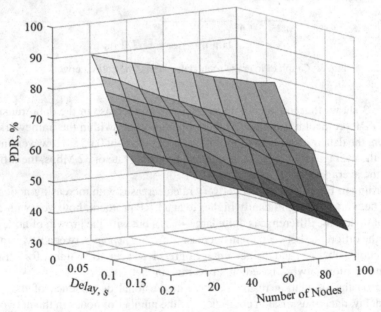

Fig. 5. Average latency and packet delivery rate from the number of nodes for a tworank MANET network.

The best network performance is observed in the yellow and orange areas on the graph, that is, the value of the packet delivery rate does not fall below 80–70%, and the average delay is not higher than 0.15 s. Thus, the limiting value for the stable functioning of the network is the number of nodes up to 60 units and the data transfer rate of about 256 kbps.

4   Conclusion

Based on the results obtained, it was possible to achieve a gain in latency and PDR parameters, which directly affects the network lifetime. The developed solution was compared with the ZRP protocol, which is one of the popular protocols based on grouping of nodes. The proposed two-rank architecture works more efficiently, gaining 0.2 s in average latency and 11% in PDR.

In the future, it is planned to introduce algorithms for finding a route based on multicriteria optimization with a choice in terms of network life parameters, energy efficiency, speed and traffic prioritization. Furthermore, one of the most likely ways of developing this system may be the introduction of neural network algorithms to solve the problem of finding a route and organizing clusters.

References

1. Kaur, N., Kad, S.: Cluster connectivity selection criteria in vehicular ad hoc networks. In: 2016 2nd International Conference on Contemporary Computing and Informatics (IC3I), Noida, pp. 381–385 (2016). https://doi.org/10.1109/IC3I.2016.7917993.
2. Shakarami, M., Movaghar, A.: A clustering algorithm to improve routing stability in mobile ad-hoc networks. In: 2009 14th International CSI Computer Conference, Tehran, pp. 83-88 (2009). https://doi.org/10.1109/CSICC.2009.5349360
3. Wang, K., Shi, Y.: A two-layered clustering-based multihop routing protocol. In: 2014 5th International Conference on Intelligent Systems, Modelling and Simulation, Langkawi, pp. 573–578 (2014). https://doi.org/10.1109/ISMS.2014.105
4. Tran, T.N., Nguyen, T., Shim, K., An, B.: A game theory based clustering protocol to support multicast routing in cognitive radio mobile ad hoc networks. IEEE Access **8**, 141310–141330 (2020). https://doi.org/10.1109/ACCESS.2020.3013644
5. Bai, Y.M., Wang, N.: Performance comparison and evaluation of the proactive and reactive routing protocols for MANETs. In: 2017 Wireless Telecommunications Symposium (WTS), Chicago, IL, pp. 1–5 (2017). https://doi.org/10.1109/WTS.2017.7943538
6. Mbarushimana, C., Shahrabi, A.: Comparative study of reactive and proactive routing protocols performance in mobile ad hoc networks. In: 21st International Conference on Advanced Information Networking and Applications Workshops (AINAW 2007), Niagara Falls, Ontario, pp. 679–684 (2007). https://doi.org/10.1109/AINAW.2007.123
7. Er-Rouidi, M., Moudni, H., Mouncif, H., Merbouha, A.: An energy consumption evaluation of reactive and proactive routing protocols in mobile ad-hoc network. In: 2016 13th International Conference on Computer Graphics, Imaging and Visualization (CGiV), Beni Mellal, pp. 437–441 (2016). https://doi.org/10.1109/CGiV.2016.90
8. Singh, S.P., Sharma, S.C.: A survey on cluster based routing protocols in wireless sensor networks. Procedia Comput. Sci. **45**, 687–695 (2015)
9. Muratchaev, S.S., Volkov, A.S., Martynov, V.S., Zhuravlev, I.A.: Application of clustering methods in MANET. In: 2020 IEEE Conference of Russian Young Researchers in Electrical and Electronic Engineering (EIConRus), St. Petersburg and Moscow, Russia, pp. 1711-1714 (2020). https://doi.org/10.1109/EIConRus49466.2020.9039143
10. Shen, J., Hao, X., Liang, Z., Liu, Y., Wang, W., Shao, L.: Real-time superpixel segmentation by DBSCAN clustering algorithm. IEEE Trans. Image Process. **25**(12), 5933–5942 (2016). https://doi.org/10.1109/TIP.2016.2616302
11. Xijie, Z., Chunxiu, X., Jiaqi, X.: Hierarchical ZRP's performance vs ZRP's performance in MANET. In: 2015 IEEE International Conference on Communication Software and Networks (ICCSN), Chengdu, pp. 423–426 (2015)

Threat Model for Trusted Sensory Information Collection and Processing Platform

Tatiana Kosachenko[1]([envelope]), Danil Dudkin[1], Anton Konev[1], and Alexander Sharamok[2]

[1] Tomsk State University of Control, Systems and Radioelectronics, Tomsk, Russian Federation
{734_kts,725_ddg}@fb.tusur.ru, kaal@keva.tusur.ru
[2] National Research University of Electronic Technology (MIET), Moscow, Russian Federation

Abstract. The number of systems responsible for the processing and transmission of sensory information is steadily growing, which naturally gives rise to the need for a scalable trusted Platform that provides the formation of end-to-end processes in various priority sectors of the economy and social sphere and is an automated information control system for collecting and processing sensory information.

When designing such a system, it is important to pay sufficient attention to the elaboration of the information security issue, which inevitably is based on the development of a threat model.

The proposed Platform is subdivided into 6 subsystems: micromodule subsystem, end device subsystem, border gateway subsystem, cloud service subsystem, operating system subsystem, and user application subsystem.

This article proposes a threat model for each subsystem of the Platform, as well as lists of threats to the Platform's subsystems and their operating environments.

Keywords: Information security · Sensory information · Threat model · IoT · Cloud service · Security threat

1 Introduction

Wireless sensor networks are a type of IoT system that is used to wirelessly transmit data from a source to a user, using sensors as a link.

Sensors are part of end sensor devices with low processing power. End devices are mobile and distributed over a large area. This type of network is self-configured, which allows new connected terminal devices to be recognized and registered in the network. These types of endpoints are susceptible to cyber attacks on network nodes. The authors of articles [1, 2] raise the issue of information security of wireless sensor networks, especially for networks used in medical institutions [3, 4].

As for the protection of information of this type of networks, in the scientific literature some authors suggest using data encryption methods [5], various protocols [6–8] and attack detection methods [9–11]. For example, paper [12] describes an energy efficient distributed deterministic key management scheme for wireless sensor networks with limited resources. The main feature of this system is that attention is focused on the creation and maintenance of pair keys, as well as local cluster keys. Using an elliptic

© Springer Nature Singapore Pte Ltd. 2021
P. K. Singh et al. (Eds.): FTNCT 2020, CCIS 1396, pp. 296–304, 2021.
https://doi.org/10.1007/978-981-16-1483-5_27

curve digital signature algorithm in the proposed system, sensors can safely join the sensor network. As an alternative, the authors of [13] suggest using the convolutional method that generates security bits using convolutional codes to prevent malicious node attacks on wireless sensor networks.

2 Literature Review

Wireless sensor networks can be used to automate various processes in industrial facilities, in residential buildings and even in urban infrastructure [14], as well as to monitor various indications and characteristics in the environment or in agriculture [15]. In addition, such networks are widely used in medicine in the field of monitoring vital indications of patients [16–18].

The paper [19] states that the IoT has its own protocol stack, which differs from the OSI reference network model and TCP/IP protocol stacks. The protocol stack of the IoT model includes the following layers: application layer (Message Queue Telemetry Transport MQTT protocols, Constrained Application Protocol CAOP, Advanced Message Queuing Protocol AMOP, Web-Socket), Internet layer (6LowPAN, IPv4/IPv6 and RPL protocols) and physical/link layer (protocols (IEEE). 802.11 series) and (BLE, LTE). In addition, this article discusses in more detail the data transfer protocols involved in various IoT applications, such as MQTT, CAOP, AMQP and WebSocket.

IoT devices form a computing network, but these networks can face threats that are often referred to as "zero-day vulnerabilities" or 0-day (transformation of those threats into a network attack is called "zero attack"). The paper [20] proposes a framework for countering zero-day attacks in IoT networks. The proposed approach uses the contextual behavior of IoT devices as a discovery mechanism, followed by alert messaging and critical communication protocols for reliable communications while countering zero-day attacks.

The article [21] discusses the threat information management platform in the IoT environment. It consists of a device information collection system, a vulnerability information analysis system, and a threat information exchange system. This platform works according to the following principle. The data collection system checks devices connected to the Internet and collects detailed information about them. The analysis system then collates and analyzes the vulnerability information about the scanned devices received from the collection system.

The authors of [22] propose a system model that provides a secure end-to-end connection between low-power IoT devices and unmanned aerial vehicles used to solve the problem of collecting and processing information in heterogeneous wireless sensor networks.

3 Threat Model for a Trusted Platform for Collecting and Processing Sensory Information

The main goal of any information security protection system is to ensure the stable operation of the protected object, as well as to prevent security threats directed at this object.

Our object of protection was the Platform, which is an automated information-controlled system for collecting and processing sensory information, which ensures the formation of end-to-end processes in various priority sectors of the economy and social sphere.

The studied architecture of the Platform for the collection and processing of sensory information (see Fig. 1) consists of 4 levels:

– device level;
– data exchange level;
– cloud services level;
– application level.

In addition, the Platform was decomposed into subsystems that require close attention when developing lists of security threats:

– end devices subsystem;
– border gateway subsystem;
– cloud services subsystem;
– user services subsystem.

The subsystem of end devices is a collection of end devices that allow receiving and processing information from various types of sensors. The end device provides conversion of information received from various types of sensors, its primary processing (including verification and event generation) and transmission to the border gateway. At the device level, end devices collect information from sensors, which is sent to the border gateway for further processing and sending to the cloud service.

The border gateway subsystem is a collection of border gateways. The number of gateways in a system is determined by the platform architecture, as well as the number of endpoints and the maximum number of endpoints supported by one edge gateway. Each border gateway includes - a processor element, a communication module, an operating system and firmware. At the level of data exchange, the received data is transmitted and concentrated.

The cloud services subsystem is a collection of redundant servers, operating systems, databases and a set of specialized programs for managing network elements, processing events, and basic analytics. The cloud service layer allows processing, collecting statistics and transmitting control signals to sensor devices.

The subsystem of user services is a collection of workstations and special software that interacts with the subsystem of cloud services in order to ensure the functioning of services of the consumer. The application layer aims to provide information to users who can receive data selectively, depending on the model of interaction with the system (for example, data from individual components or full analytics that are formed in the cloud).

Threat model construction based on the approaches [23, 24] splitted into three stages:

– building a system model;
– compiling a list of threats to information security;
– determination of the list of threats for each subsystem.

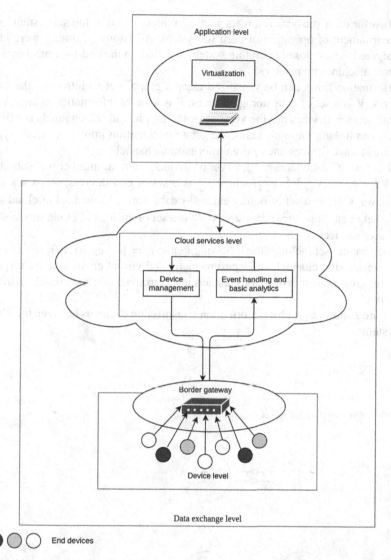

Fig. 1. Architecture of the Platform for the collection and processing of sensory information

At the first stage of forming the threat model, 217 threats to information security were selected and 74 threats that were not applicable to this system were excluded. 79 actual threats to information security were identified. Actual threats are determined according to the method described in the regulatory documents of the Russian Federation. Since this stage is outside the scope of this article, it is not considered in more detail.

At the second stage, threats from the list obtained at the first stage are updated by means of an expert assessment of the degree of possible damage from the implementation of a threat to information security and calculation of the possibility of realizing a security threat. As a result, 66 irrelevant threats were excluded at this stage.

Then for each subsystem threats were identified aimed at the subsystem itself and the environment of operation of each subsystem. Additionally, threats were identified that targeted the supposed operating system installed on the end-user machines and the end-user machines themselves.

Information flows can be visualized using a graph. Let us introduce the following concepts: V is a set of data storage devices, E is a set of information channels. In fact, the data storage devices are the vertices of the graph, and the channels are the edges. Thus, when linking these elements, we get an information flow $g = (v_i, e_l, v_j)$, where v_i, v_j are storage devices and e_l is an information channel.

The set of data storage devices is divided into a number of subsets: $V = \{V_2^1, V_2^2, V_3^1, V_3^2, V_3^2, V_2^4, V_2^5\}$, where V_2^1 is a set of end devices, V_2^2 is a set of border gateways, V_3^1 is a set of border gateways data stores, V_2^3 is a set of cloud services, V_3^2 is a set of cloud services data stores, V_2^4 is a set of utilities of cloud services, V_2^5 is a set of user services.

The channel set includes the following items: $E = \{e_1, e_2, e_3, e_4\}$, where e_1, e_2 are local transmission channels in electromagnetic and virtual environments, respectively, and e_3, e_4 are remote transmission channels in electromagnetic and virtual environments, respectively.

Figure 2 shows a graph of information transmission channels between the Platform's subsystems.

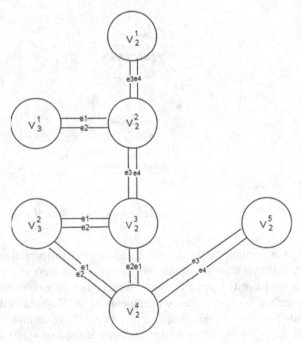

Fig. 2. Model of information flows of the Platform

This article will clearly analyze the process of forming a threat model exclusively for the subsystems of the end devices and the border gateway, since for the remaining subsystems and information flows between them, the model is built in a similar way. Thus, subsets of data storage devices will be considered V_2^1, V_2^2, V_3^1, as well as channels of information transfer between them.

Considering all of the above, the set of all streams will be as follows: $G = \{g_1, g_2, g_3, g_4\}$, where $g_1 = \{V_2^1, e_3, V_2^2\}, g_2 = \{V_2^1, e_4, V_2^2\}, g_3 = \{V_3^1, e_1, V_2^2\}, g_4 = \{V_3^1, e_2, V_2^2\}$.

Threats to confidentiality, integrity, and availability are considered to create a threat model. As an example, this article discusses threats to confidentiality of information.

Let us designate the set of possible typical threats to the information confidentiality:

$$p = \{p_1, p_2, p_3, p_4\},$$

where p_1, p_2, p_3, p_4 are typical privacy threats, namely p_1 is unauthorized sending of data to the first element of a pair, p_2 is unauthorized sending of data to the second element of a pair, p_3 is data interception, p_4 is data transmission using an unauthorized protocol.

Since each of the threats is applicable to each flow, a new set can be obtained, consisting of combinations of flows and their threats, which is in fact the cartesian product of the original sets. The cardinality of such a result set in our case will be equal to:

$$|G * P| = |G| * |P| = 4 * 4 = 16$$

All selected typical threats are presented in Tables 1, 2, 3, 4.

Table 1. Typical threats to the flow $g_1 = \left(V_2^1, e_3, V_2^2\right)$

	Threat description	Threat implementation	Item name
p_1	Sending data from an authorized end device to an unauthorized border gateway	Spoofing an edge gateway in a network	$g_1 p_1$
p_2	Sending data from an authorized border gateway to an unauthorized end device	Spoofing an end device in a network	$g_1 p_2$
p_3	Interception and analysis of traffic between the border gateway and the end device during transmission in the electromagnetic environment	Connecting a sniffer in the communication channel and hardware redirection of a copy of traffic to the sniffer through incidental electromagnetic radiation	$g_1 p_3$
p_4	Use of unauthorized data transfer protocol between the end device and the border gateway	Enabling an unauthorized data transfer protocol using physical access to the device	$g_1 p_4$

Table 2. Typical threats to the flow $g_2 = \left(V_2^1, e_4, V_2^2 \right)$

	Threat description	Threat implementation	Item name
p_1	Sending data from an authorized end device to an unauthorized border gateway	Adding an unauthorized border gateway to the network using the Evil Twin principle	g_2p_1
p_2	Sending data from an authorized border gateway to an unauthorized end device	Changing the whitelist of ip addresses by elevating user account rights	g_2p_2
p_3	Interception and analysis of traffic between the border gateway and the end device during transmission in the virtual environment	Interception of traffic using a sniffer	g_2p_3
p_4	Use of unauthorized data transfer protocol between the end device and the border gateway	Change network settings	g_2p_4

Table 3. Typical threats to the flow $g_3 = \left(V_3^1, e_1, V_2^2 \right)$

	Threat description	Threat implementation	Item name
p_1	Reading information from ROM by unauthorized software	Physical access to device ROM and full copying to unauthorized data storage device	g_3p_1
p_2	Writing data to a public ROM area	Adding an unauthorized hard drive to the device configuration	g_3p_2
p_3	Data recovery from ROM	Data recovery from device ROM using unauthorized hardware connection	g_3p_3
p_4	Writing data to ROM using an unauthorized driver	Including an unauthorized driver in the border gateway configuration using physical access to the device	g_3p_4

Thus, as an example, a list of 16 typical threats to the information confidentiality was compiled for 4 information flows between subsystems V_2^1, V_2^2, V_3^1. In total, the proposed model of information flows contains 14 information flows, as a result, 168 typical threats to confidentiality, integrity and availability for the Platform were identified.

All of the above types of security threats are considered in the proposed threat model. At the same time, the model developed by us includes a detailed description of threats concerning each individual subsystem of the system for collecting and processing sensory information, which indicates that the proposed model considers the types of

Table 4. Typical threats to the flow $g_4 = \left(V_3^1, e_2, V_2^2 \right)$

	Threat description	Threat implementation	Item name
p_1	Reading information from ROM by unauthorized software	Search for system vulnerabilities using specialized software	$g_4 p_1$
p_2	Writing data to a public ROM area	Flashing the device and changing the settings for recording confidential information	$g_4 p_2$
p_3	Data recovery from ROM	Recovering data from device ROM using an unauthorized device	$g_4 p_3$
p_4	Writing data to ROM using an unauthorized driver	Changing data transfer settings due to vulnerabilities in the current driver	$g_4 p_4$

threats in more detail, and also provides additional information that may be useful, for example, in the further formation of information security requirements for the system under consideration.

4 Conclusion

In this paper, the process of modeling threats to confidentiality of information for the transfer of data between the border gateway and the end device in the sensor system was considered in detail. 56 typical threats to confidentiality of information were identified. Also, 79 relevant types of threats for the IoT system for collecting and processing sensory information were selected.

The results of the work can be used to formulate information security requirements in wireless sensor networks, as well as to organize a set of security measures at the organizational and software-technical levels aimed at protecting the information resources of the system from information security threats.

Acknowledgments. The article was prepared as part of the implementation of the Leading Research Center (LRC) program "Trusted sensory systems" (Agreement № 009/20 dated 04/10/2020).

References

1. Araujo, A., Blesa, J., Romero, E., Villanueva, D.: Security in cognitive wireless sensor networks. Challenges and open problems. EURASIP J. Wirel. Commun. Networking **48**, 1–18(2012)
2. Pei, C., Xiao, Y., Liang, W., Han, X.: Trade-off of security and performance of lightweight block ciphers in industrial wireless sensor networks. EURASIP J. Wirel. Commun. Networking **117**, 1–18 (2018)

3. Ng, H.S., Sim, M.L., Tan, C.M.: Security issues of wireless sensor networks in healthcare applications. BT Technol. J. **24**, 138–144 (2006)
4. Al Ameen, M., Liu, J., Kwak, K.: J. Med. Syst. **36**, 93–101 (2012)
5. Alotaibi, M.: Security to wireless sensor networks against malicious attacks using Hamming residue method. EURASIP J. Wirel. Commun. Networking **8**, 1–18(2019)
6. Gupta, S., Verma, H.K., Sangal, A.L.: Efficient security mechanism to counter the malicious attack in wireless sensor networks. CSI Trans. ICT **2**, 35–41(2014)
7. Messai, M.L., Aliouat, M., Seba, H.: Tree based protocol for key management in wireless sensor networks. EURASIP J. Wirel. Commun. Networking **2010**, 910695 (2010)
8. Shelupanov, A., Konev, A., Kosachenko, T., Dudkin, D.: Threat model for IoT systems on the example of OpenUNB protocol. Int. J. Eng. Res. **7**, 9 (2019)
9. Lai, G.-H.: Detection of wormhole attacks on IPv6 mobility-based wireless sensor network. EURASIP J. Wirel. Commun. Networking **2016**, 274 (2016)
10. Ganeshkumar, P., Vijayakumar, K.P., Anandaraj, M.: A novel jammer detection framework for cluster-based wireless sensor networks. EURASIP J. Wirel. Commun. Networking **2016**, 35 (2016)
11. Nikiforov, D.S., Konev, A.A., Antonov, M.M., Shelupanov, A.A.: Structure of information security subsystem in the systems of commercial energy resources accounting. J. Phys. Conf. Ser. **1145** (2019). https://doi.org/10.1088/1742-6596/1145/1/012018
12. Zhang, X., He, J., Wei, Q.: EDDK: energy-efficient distributed deterministic key management for wireless sensor networks. EURASIP J. Wirel. Commun. and Networking **2011**, (2011)
13. Turki Ali Alghamdi: Convolutional technique for enhancing security in wireless sensor networks against malicious nodes. Hum. Centric Comput. Inf. Sci. **9**, 38 (2019)
14. Batalla, J.M., Gonciarz, F.: Deployment of smart home management system at the edge: mechanisms and protocols. Neural Comput. Appl. **31**, 1301–1315 (2019)
15. Ibrahim, H., et al.: A layered IoT architecture for greenhouse monitoring and remote control. SN Appl. Sci. **1**, 223 (2019)
16. Al-khafajiy, M., Kolivand, H., Baker, T., Tully, D., Waraich, A.: Smart hospital emergency system. Multimedia Tools Appl. **78**, 20087–20111 (2019)
17. Al-khafajiy, M., et al.: Remote health monitoring of elderly through wearable sensors. Multimedia Tools Appl. **78**, 24681–24706 (2019)
18. El-Sappagh, S., Ali, F., Hendawi, A., Jang, J.-H., Kwak, K.-S.: A mobile health monitoring-and-treatment system based on integration of the SSN sensor ontology and the HL7 FHIR standard. BMC Med. Inform. Decis. Mak. **19**, 97 (2019)
19. Bahashwan, A.A.O., Manickam, S.: A brief review of messaging protocol standards for Internet of Things (IoT). J. Cyber Secur. Mobility **8**, 1–14
20. Sharma, V., Lee, K., Kwon, S., Kim, J., Park, H., Yim, K., Lee, S.-Y.: A consensus framework for reliability and mitigation of zero-day attacks in IoT. Secur. Commun. Networks (2017). https://doi.org/10.1155/2017/4749085
21. Ko, E., Kim, T., Kim, H.: Management platform of threats information in IoT environment. J. Ambient Intell. Hum. Comput. (2017). https://doi.org/10.1007/s12652-017-0581-6
22. Rajakaruna, A., Manzoor, A., Porambage, P., Liyanage, M., Ylianttila, M., Gurtovy, A.: Enabling end-to-end secure connectivity for low-power IoT devices with UAVs. In: 2nd Workshop on Intelligent Computing and Caching at the Network Edge at 2019 IEEE Wireless Communications and Networking Conference (WCNC), Marrakech, Morocco (2019). https://doi.org/10.1109/WCNCW.2019.8902746
23. Novokhrestov, A., Konev, A., Shelupanov, A.: Model of threats to computer network software. Symmetry **11**(12), 1506 (2019)
24. Shelupanov, A., Evsyutin, O., Konev, A., Kostyuchenko, E., Kruchinin, D., Nikiforov, D.: Information security methods-modern research directions. Symmetry **11**(2), 150 (2019)

Autonomous Navigation of Mobile Robot with Obstacle Avoidance: A Review

Mahvish Bijli[1(✉)] and Neerendra Kumar[2]

[1] Department of Computer Science & IT, Central University of Jammu, Jammu, India
[2] Doctoral School of Applied Informatics & Applied Mathematics, Obuda University, Budapest, Hungary
neerendra.kumar@phd.uni-obuda.hu

Abstract. Navigation of mobile robot with obstacle avoidance is a successful research area owing to its comprehensive applications. Secure and smooth mobile robot navigation through different (static and dynamic) environments for single and multiple robot system to attain its goal with following secure path and producing a most fulfilling end result is the principal purpose of navigation. Many techniques are developed for mobile robot navigation. This paper proposes the soft computing techniques used in mobile robot navigation namely fuzzy logic, neural network and neuro-fuzzy. This paper concludes with strength, limitations, efficiency and tabular data of each methods.

Keywords: Autonomous navigation · Mobile robot · Obstacle avoidance · Robot path planning · Fuzzy logic · Neural network

1 Introduction

Mobile robots are type of robots that can move, sense, and read in the given environment and can perform navigation and tasks without human intercession [1]. Autonomous robot navigation and obstacle avoidance are crucial problems in robotics. Mobile robot navigation is the ability to find feasible path in a stated environment from initial position to goal position with obstacle avoidance competence. The navigation environment can be categorized as known environment and an unknown or partially known environment.

Obstacle avoidance is one of the most significant necessities identified with the navigation of mobile robots. Obstacle avoidance can be categorized into two sub stages: obstacle detection and collision avoidance [2]. Different algorithms use different sensors for obstacle detection such as ultrasonic sensors, laser range finders, touch sensors, infrared sensors, and so on. Sensor data is analyzed and the controller sends end-effector signals so as to stop obstacles.

Navigation strategy for mobile robots can be grouped into three types: global navigation, local navigation and personal navigation [3]. In global navigation, robot possess complete prior information like map of environment, position, shape, orientation. It produces the globally optimal path and deals with a completely known environment. Different techniques are produced for the global navigation, viz. Artificial potential

© Springer Nature Singapore Pte Ltd. 2021
P. K. Singh et al. (Eds.): FTNCT 2020, CCIS 1396, pp. 305–316, 2021.
https://doi.org/10.1007/978-981-16-1483-5_28

method [4], Cell decomposition method [5], Dijkstra algorithm [6], Visibility graph [7], Voronoi diagram [8], and many more. In local navigation instead of priory information, the robot can determine its motion and orientation using sensors placed on robot for recognizing environment. Therefore, local navigation approach deals with the partially known or unknown environment Numerous strategies are utilized by researchers to effectively tackle the local navigation issue such as Genetic algorithm (GA) [9], Firefly algorithm (FA) [10], Fuzzy logic (FL) [11], Particle swarm optimization (PSO) algorithm [12], Neural network (NN) [13], Neuro-fuzzy [14], Simulated annealing (SA) [15], Ant colony optimization (ACO) algorithm [16], Bee colony optimization (BCO) [17] algorithm, etc. Personal Navigation is dealing with different environmental factors relative to one another by examining their position The fundamental steps needed for navigating mobile robot [18] are illustrated in Fig. 1.

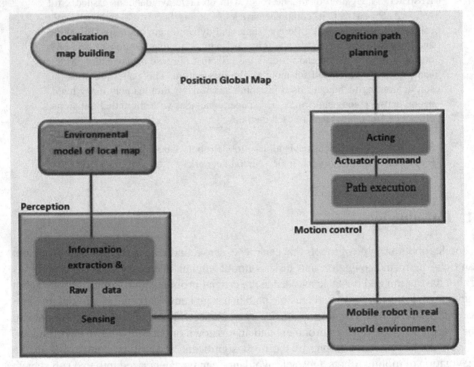

Fig. 1. Flowchart for robot navigation system [18].

Paper presents literature review of soft computing techniques for navigation of robot based on

- Fuzzy Logic (FL)
- Neural Network (NN)
- Neuro-fuzzy

The rest part of the paper is structured as follows: Sect. 2. Deals with the study of Literature review for various methodologies for mobile robot navigation. Section 3. Provides discussion of literature review followed by conclusion in Sect. 4.

2 Techniques for Navigation of Mobile Robot

From past few years, many strategies have been proposed by researchers for navigation of robot in different environments with capability of avoiding obstacles. The following are different approaches used to navigate mobile robot both in static and dynamic environment (Fig. 2).

2.1 Fuzzy Logic (FL) Approach for Navigation

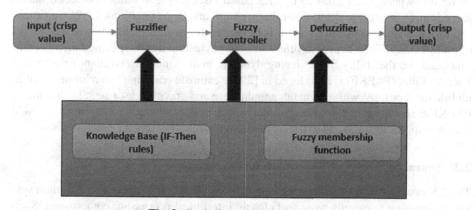

Fig. 2. Basic fuzzy logic system [3].

The concept of Fuzzy was first presented in [19]. In fuzzy logic, input as crisp values accumulates and together convert into fuzzy set along with a number of inference rules in the process of fuzzification. Afterwards the result produced by defuzzification step is converted by a membership function (MFs) to crisp values. The fuzzy logic system mimics human reasoning that function based on perception. In [20], the fuzzy logic controller with Mamdani-type and Sugeno-type fuzzy inference systems avoid the obstacles in path of mobile robot and pure pursuit algorithm finds straight route from start to next target position. However, fuzzy controllers in [21, 20] are biased towards right turns for obstacles occurring in center of the laser scans. In [22], authors have proposed two obstacle avoidance algorithms: one using fuzzy logic, another hybrid algorithm based on line, wall following algorithm, and tangent bug. Furthermore, each algorithms is executed for the bicycle vehicle version of a mobile robot for avoiding obstacles. In [23], the combinatorial algorithm based on fuzzy and ant colony optimization (FACO) is presented to reduce the repetitive ACO learning error by utilizing fuzzy logic control. ACO algorithm discovers shortest path, ultrasonic transducers detect any barrier in front of robot and for avoiding any obstacle steering angle of mobile robot is modified. In

[24], the multiple robot navigation issue is resolved by utilizing fuzzy controller (fc) and Petri net. Fuzzy rules help robot to navigate within working area as per the distribution of obstacles and location of targets. Each Mobile robot controllers empowers to avoid obstacles in cluttered environment and maintain a strategic distance from other mobile robots. In [25], authors presented a model based on fuzzy inference (fis) for solving the path planning problems of mobile robots. The current speed and obstacle/goal locations of the robot are recognized from sensors in an unknown dynamic environment. Three vital navigation goals: target seeking, obstacle avoidance, and movement of rotation are incorporated in cost function of that model for searching the effective heading angle. In [26], author examined Autonomous navigation of a mobile robot in presence of obstacles within an unknown environment. Their methodology, takes target, distance and direction among the robot and the obstacle under consideration. The user-adaptive navigation framework based on fuzzy for navigating autonomous mobile robots in an unknown environment is presented in [27]. The authors tested the framework in mobile robot and on robotic wheelchair, furnished by PLS based laser sensor in order to detect obstacle and odometry sensors to determine robot location and target positions. In [28], a simple and efficient fuzzy controller system is presented for avoiding obstacles in navigation of mobile robot. Their approach offers smooth navigation due to specified membership functions and the ability for achieving dynamic goal. A new fuzzy adaptive extended Kalman Filter (FAEKF) is introduced in [29] to estimate real-time behavior of versatile mobile devices fitted with magnetic, angular rate and gravity sensor sets. Furthermore, FAEKF are being applicable to every other mobile system where an estimation of attitude is important for location and extrinsic disruption strongly affect the filter precision.

2.2 Neural Network (NN) Approach for Navigation

The NN system attempts to shape the human brain's biological function. It is a smart system comprising numerous basic and closely interlinked processing components. Such components transmit information to external inputs via their dynamic state feedback capability. Learning biological system requires adaptation to strongly integrated synaptic neural connections, they adjust to the given data set. The application of neural networks in a partially unknown environment for navigation of wheeled mobile robot is proposed in [30]. The author developed a collision free path based on two neural network mechanisms: The first one searches free space with the help of data received from sensors and next, neural network mechanism avoids closest obstacle by finding a safe path. A dynamic approach to mobile robot navigation with trajectory planning based on Artificial Neural Network has been presented in [31]. Authors developed mobile robot motion solution on the basis of extended back-propagation using time based algorithm that avoids obstacles by employing potential fields. Furthermore, presented method possess obstacle avoidance capability, with no need of specific robot framework. In [32], authors introduced neural network and reinforcement based automation learning strategy. Their research is distinguished by the fact that, depending on the complexities of the environment, neural network (NN) changes the addition and removal of new secret layers without human intervention during training to perform the navigation task. A novel hybrid solution by integrating FL and NN for navigation of mobile robot has been proposed in [33]. NN efficiently determines optimal amount of activation rules in real-time

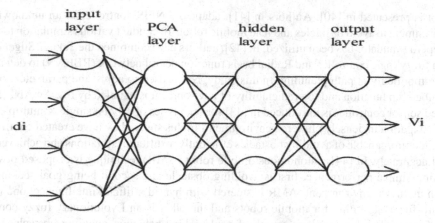

Fig. 3. Topology of PCA network [30].

to minimize evaluation of applications. In [34], authors presented obstacle avoidance and goal reaching behavior by incorporating NN and reinforcement learning to permit mobile robot to understand created environment all alone. An adaptive NN controller for the formation navigation of multiple robots is introduced in [35]. The algorithm relies on the Lyapunov function, PSO algorithm, and graph theory. Initially, the approach produces a successive route as per the current perceived obstacle for leader robot. The subsequent (follower) robot then utilizes this information for executing its navigation efficiently. A hybrid controller based on reactive navigation for non-holonomic robot is proposed in [36]. Control system is designed using a NEAT algorithm (Neuro evolution of Augmented Topologies) and prepared with designed simulation that incorporates various knowledge fields like discrete-time simulation, system modeling, and control. A multilayer feed-forward NN has been created in [37] that controls heading angle of mobile robots by oneself both in a static environment as well as in dynamic environment. Input of NN comprises of obstacle distance (LEFT, RIGHT, & FRONT), the angle present between robot & target, and output is heading angle (Fig. 3).

2.3 Neuro Fuzzy Approach for Navigation

In [38], an approach PAFARTNA (Prune-able fuzzy adaptive resonance theory neural network architecture) is followed. Because of its global path planning capability, the mobile robot can automatically navigate in a complex environment with a degree of optimality, by applying dynamically trained and updated world model online. In [39], authors proposed a five-layer adaptive neuro-fuzzy model comprising of a training system and fuzzy logic controller having 48 fuzzy rules. The two training algorithms were created for fine-tuning membership function parameters. Therefore automatically reducing the issue of repetitive fuzzy rules. Furthermore, a trajectory between dynamic obstacles and goals is created in a dynamic environment for the mobile robot. Good results demonstrate the algorithm's effectiveness. However, the suggested method needs significant efforts for tuning the parameters. An obstacle avoidance approach using IT2FNN (Interval type-2 fuzzy neural network) controller for stabilizing the orientation of the mobile robot is presented in [40]. Authors in [41], adapted ANFIS controller in an unknown environment to avoid obstacles and lead mobile robot. To conduct various simulation test Khepera Simulator has been utilized. In [42], authors have combined the Takagi-Sugeno type fuzzy logic controller and Radial basis function neural network (RBFNN) to determine mobile robot path planning. In this study, NN is used to adjust the parameters of membership function and unpredictability of environment is handled by FL. An ANFIS based sensor controller is introduced in [43] for both types of robots (single & multiple) for navigation in densely cluttered environment. In this study, they have created control architecture, capable of avoiding obstacles efficiently in different situations and achieved goal accurately. In [44], autonomous mobile robot (AMR) technique is proposed possessing simple performance, first is avoiding obstacle and second being goal-seeking in an unknown environment. AMR is steered with hybrid artificial intelligence, one is Neuro-fuzzy algorithm for mobile robots and the other is an Evolutionary fuzzy control for mobile robots. This approach of goal-seeking behavior, avoiding obstacles at each occurrence enhances the performance of mobile robot in navigation approach. An integrated strategy based on Logarithmic Fuzzy Trapezoidal Approach and ANN for requirements prioritization (RP) is presented in [45] to address problems related to RP and provide customers satisfaction with all the technological features.

3 Discussion

From last 15 years, considerable development has been made towards the mobile robots navigation. Throughout this study, 46 papers covering appropriate scope of work related to mobile robot navigation and obstacle avoidance were reviewed. An analysis of most prominent robot navigation techniques consisting of fuzzy logic (FL), neural network (NN), and neuro-fuzzy were carried out [46]. Application of reviewed studies are summarized in Table 1 and Table 2. Each technique has certain benefits and limitations. Pros and Cons of each soft computing methods are discussed below as well as outlined in Table 3. Followed by efficiency of each method in Table 4. The NN has indeed been extensively used, in navigation of robot due to its nonlinear mapping, parallel processing, and learning ability. However, it typically takes time because it has a wide range of parameters that need to be modified. Additionally, it also needs a sufficient assortment of training databases with potentially high learning costs. One more limitation of neural network is the functionality cannot be interpreted as it is a black box. It is also challenging to assess the number of neurons and layers. Fuzzy logic has the ability to stimulate human thought through if-then laws and linguistic variables, however, FL finds it difficult to choose better appropriate rule and membership functions. One way to build a FL system would be, attempt to mimic an action of experts. It is thought to generate good performance. A good feature about Fuzzy law is that it is presented in simple and straight forward linguistic variables. Neuro-fuzzy a hybrid technique based on neural network and fuzzy logic offers far better outcome than discrete method. Typically, the hybrid approaches generally suffer from time utilization issue.

Table 1. Applications of mobile robot navigation techniques.

Author	Year	Approach	Type of obstacle	Target type	Kinematic model
N.Kumar [20]	2017	FL	D	D	N
N.Kumar [21]	2018	FL	S/D	D	N
R.Singh [22]	2018	FL	S	S	Y
C.T.Yen [23]	2013	FL/ACO	S	S/D	N
V.M.Puri [24]	2005	FL	S/D	S	N
H.Chang [25]	2018	FL	S	S	Y
G.Mester [26]	2008	FL	S	S	N
M.A.O.Mendez [27]	2007	FL	S	S	N
I.Hassanzadeh [28]	2008	FL	S	S	N
D.Janglova [30]	2004	NN	S	S	Y
I.Engedy [31]	2009	NN	S/D	S	Y
J.Qiao [32]	2009	NN	S	S	N
A.Abubakar [33]	2012	NN	S	S	Y
O.Motlagh [34]	2014	NN	S	D	N
X.Chen [35]	2006	NN/PSO	S/D	S/D	Y
C.Caceres [36]	2017	NN	S	S	Y
M.K.Singh [37]	2011	NN	S	S	Y
R.Araujo [38]	2006	PAFARTNA	S/D	S	Y
A.Zhu [39]	2009	Neuro-Fuzzy	S	S	N
C.J.Kim [40]	2015	IT2FNN	S	S	Y
M.Algabri [41]	2014	Neuro-Fuzzy	S	S	N
J.Godjevac [42]	1999	Neuro-Fuzzy	S	S	N
J.K.Pothal [43]	2015	Neuro-Fuzzy	S/D	S	N
A.M.Rao [44]	2017	Neuro-Fuzzy	S	S	Y

Here S stands for "Static", D stands for "Dynamic", Y stands for "Yes", and N stands for "No".

Table 2. Table 1 (continue).

Author	Obstacle Shape	Simulation Output	Real time System	Navigation Environment
N.Kumar [20]	Arbitrary	Yes	Yes	Un
N.Kumar [21]	Arbitrary	Yes	Yes	Un
R.Singh [22]	Circle	Yes	No	S
C.T.Yen [23]	Various	Yes	No	Un
V.M.Puri [24]	Arbitrary	Yes	Yes	Cluttered
H.Chang [25]	Corridor	Yes	Yes	Un
G.Mester [26]	Arbitrary	Yes	Yes	Un
M.A.O.Mendez [27]	Various	Yes	Yes	Un
I.Hassanzadeh [28]	Rectangle	Yes	Yes	D
D.Janglova [30]	Arbitrary	Yes	Yes	Un/D
I.Engedy [31]	Arbitrary	Yes	Yes	Un
J.Qiao [32]	Arbitrary	Yes	Yes	Un
A.Abubakar [33]	L-Shaped	Yes	No	Un
O.Motlagh [34]	Various	Yes	No	Un
X.Chen [35]	Circle	Yes	Yes	Un
C.Caceres [36]	Points	Yes	No	Un
M.K.Singh [37]	Arbitrary	Yes	Yes	D
R.Araujo [38]	Arbitrary	Yes	Yes	D
A.Zhu [39]	Arbitrary	Yes	Yes	Un
C.J.Kim [40]	Asterisk	Yes	Yes	Un
M.Algabri [41]	Rectangle	Yes	Yes	Un
J.Godjevac [42]	S-Shaped	Yes	Yes	Un
J.K.Pothal [43]	Arbitrary	Yes	Yes	Cluttered
A.M.Rao [44]	Arbitrary	Yes	Yes	Un

Here S stands for "Static", D stands for "Dynamic", Un stands for "Unknown".

Table 3. Pros and Cons of soft computing techniques in navigation of mobile robot.

Approach	Pros	Cons
Fuzzy logic (FL)	1) Continuous responsiveness includes the integration of professional expertise into system operation. 2) Efficient if incorporated with distinctive algorithms.	1) Difficult to develop fuzzy rules in an unknown environment for MFs. 2) High cost of computation containing more inputs and outputs.
Neural Network (NN)	1) Contributes in furnishing learning skills and generalization. 2) Provides considerable support in controlling MFs. 3) Simulation along with real-time testing can be performed.	1) Convergence speed is slow. 2) Computational cost escalates with increase in amount of layers. 3) Difficult to manage amount of layers embedded in the neuron structure.
Neuro-Fuzzy	1) Owns potential to take out Fl rules and membership function automatically.	1) Needs intricate training in firm hardware with minimal execution.

Table 4. Efficiency of methods involved in navigation of mobile robots.

Method	Robustness	Computational cost	Time complexity	Responsive	Flexibility
Fuzzy	Moderate	High cost	High complexity	Moderate	Moderate
Neural	High	High cost	High complexity	Moderate	High
Neuro-Fuzzy	High	Low cost	Low complexity	High	High

4 Conclusion

The paper presents literature review of different soft computing methods used for mobile robot navigation with obstacle avoidance competence. The key points are listed below.

1. From the literature review, majority of researchers have employed these techniques (fuzzy logic, neural network, neuro-fuzzy) for navigation of mobile robot and obstacle avoidance purpose only in static environment. Few researchers, nevertheless, addressed mobile robot navigation in dynamic environments.
2. According to the literature survey, most papers demonstrate only computer simulation. Papers on real-time implementation are fewer.
3. Review Papers on hybrid algorithms are few compared with those on a single algorithm.
4. To date, most published research papers deal with the static environment as compared to the unknown dynamic environment.
5. Few research papers are present based on robot navigation in dynamic environment with a dynamic target problem rather than problem of dynamic obstacle.

In future, there is an incredible breadth in integrating soft computing methods with recently developed biological inspired algorithms such as ACO, PSO, GA, FA, and BCO. They would offer a viable solution in navigating robot in unknown turbulent environments in the case of extreme uncertainty. Moreover, they can be used to develop new forms of hybrid strategies which can reduce the cost of computing, the complexity of time, increase accuracy and performance by using these strategies to their full benefit and limiting drawbacks. Such methods for future study are strongly recommended.

References

1. Goris, K.: Autonomous Mobile Robot Mechanical Design (2005)
2. Vayeda Anshav Bhavesh: Comparison of various obstacle avoidance algorithms. Int. J. Eng. Res. **V4**(12), 629–632 (2015)
3. Patle, B.K., Babu, G., Pandey, L.A., Parhi, D.R.K., Jagadeesh, A.: A review: on path planning strategies for navigation of mobile robot. Def. Technol. **15**(4), 582–606 (2019). https://doi.org/10.1016/j.dt.2019.04.011
4. Khatib, O.: Real-time obstacle avoidance for manipulators and mobile robots. In: IEEE International Conference on Robotics and Automation, St. Louis, pp. 500–505 (1985)
5. Park, K.H., Kim, Y.J., Kim, J.H.: Modular Q-learning based multi-agent cooperation for robot soccer. Rob. Auton. Syst. **35**(2), 109–122 (2001). https://doi.org/10.1016/S0921-8890(01)00114-2
6. Wang, H., Yu, Y., Yuan, Q.: Application of Dijkstra algorithm in robot path-planning. In: 2011 2nd International Conference on Mechanical Automation Control Engineering MACE 2011 - Proceedings, no. 2010011004, pp. 1067–1069 (2011). https://doi.org/10.1109/mace.2011.5987118
7. Piaggio, M., Zaccaria, R.: Using roadmaps to classify regions of space for autonomous robot navigation. Rob. Auton. Syst. **25**(3–4), 209–217 (1998). https://doi.org/10.1016/S0921-8890(98)00050-5
8. Takahashi, O., Schilling, R.J.: Motion planning in a plane using generalized voronoi diagrams. IEEE Trans. Robot. Autom. **5**(2), 143–150 (1989). https://doi.org/10.1109/70.88035
9. Choueiry, S., Owayjan, M., Diab, H., Achkar, R.: Mobile robot path planning using genetic algorithm in a static environment. In: 2019 4th International Conference on Advances Computing Tools Engineering Applications ACTEA 2019, pp. 1–6 (2019). https://doi.org/10.1109/actea.2019.8851100
10. Yang, X.S.: Firefly algorithm, stochastic test functions and design optimization. Int. J. Bio-Inspired Comput. **2**(2), 78–84 (2010). https://doi.org/10.1504/IJBIC.2010.032124
11. Sai, T., Nakhaeinia, D., Karasfi, B.: Application of fuzzy logic in mobile robot navigation. Fuzzy Log. Control. Concepts, Theor. Appl. (2012). https://doi.org/10.5772/36358
12. Algabri, M.M.: S.C. Techniques and U Environment, Comparison of Soft Computing Techniques for mobile robot navigation in Unstructured Environment, pp. 1–21 (2012)
13. Kung, S.Y., Hwang, J.N.: Neural network architectures for robotic applications. IEEE Trans. Robot. Autom. **5**(5), 641–657 (1989). https://doi.org/10.1109/70.88082
14. Zhu, A., Yang, S.X.: Neurofuzzy-based approach to mobile robot navigation in unknown environments. IEEE Trans. Syst. Man Cybern. Part C Appl. Rev. **37**(4), 610–621 (2007). https://doi.org/10.1109/tsmcc.2007.897499
15. Van Laarhoven, P.J.M., Reidel, D.: Simulated Annealing: Theory and Applications, vol. 12, pp. 108–111 (1988)

16. Garcia, M.A.P., Montiel, O., Castillo, O., Sepúlveda, R., Melin, P.: Path planning for autonomous mobile robot navigation with ant colony optimization and fuzzy cost function evaluation. Appl. Soft Comput. J. **9**(3), 1102–1110 (2009). https://doi.org/10.1016/j.asoc.2009.02.014

17. Teodorovíc, D., Selmíc, M., Davidovíc, T.: Bee colony optimization part II: the application survey. Yugosl. J. Oper. Res. **25**(2), 185–219 (2015). https://doi.org/10.2298/YJOR13102 9020T

18. Ichikawa, Y., Ozaki, N.: Auton. Mobile Robot. **2**(1) (1985)

19. Zadeh, L.A.: Fuzzy sets. Inf. Control **8**, 338–353 (1965). https://doi.org/10.1016/S0019-995 8(65)90241-X

20. Kumar, N., Vámossy, Z.: Robot navigation with obstacle avoidance in unknown environment. Int. J. Eng. Technol. **7**(4), 2410–2417 (2018). https://doi.org/10.14419/ijet.v7i4.14767

21. Kumar, N., Takács, M., Vámossy, Z.: Robot navigation in unknown environment using fuzzy logic. In: SAMI 2017 - IEEE 15th International Symposium on Applied Machine Intelligence Informatics, Proceedings, pp. 279–284 (2017). https://doi.org/10.1109/sami.2017.7880317

22. Singh, R., Bera, T.K.: Obstacle avoidance of mobile robot using fuzzy logic and hybrid obstacle avoidance algorithm. In: IOP Conference on Series Materials Science Engineering, vol. 517, no. 1 (2019). https://doi.org/10.1088/1757-899x/517/1/012009

23. Yen, C.T., Cheng, M.F.: A study of fuzzy control with ant colony algorithm used in mobile robot for shortest path planning and obstacle avoidance. Microsyst. Technol. **24**(1), 125–135 (2018). https://doi.org/10.1007/s00542-016-3192-9

24. Pen, V.M., Simon, D.: Logic Control, pp. 337–342 (2005)

25. Chang, H., Jin, T.: Command fusion based fuzzy controller design for moving obstacle avoidance of mobile robot. Lecture Notes in Electrcal Engineering. LNEE, vol. 235, pp. 905–913 (2013). https://doi.org/10.1007/978-94-007-6516-0_99

26. Mester, G.: Obstacle avoidance and velocity control of mobile robots. In: SISY 2008 - 6th International Symposium on Intelligent Systems Informatics (2008). https://doi.org/10.1109/SISY.2008.4664918

27. Méndez, M.Á.O., Madrigal, J.A.F.: Fuzzy logic user adaptive navigation control system for mobile robots in unknown environments. In: 2007 IEEE International Symposium on Intelligence Signal Processing WISP, 2007. https://doi.org/10.1109/wisp.2007.4447633

28. Hassanzadeh, I., Ghadiri, H., Dalayimilan, R.: Design and implemention of a simple fuzzy algorithm for obstacle avoidance navigation of a mobile robot in dynamic environment. In: Proceeding 5th International Symposium Mechatronics its Application ISMA 2008, pp. 25–30 (2008). https://doi.org/10.1109/ISMA.2008.4648863

29. Odry, Á., Kecskes, I., Sarcevic, P., Vizvari, Z., Toth, A., Odry, P.: A novel fuzzy-adaptive extended kalman filter for real-time attitude estimation of mobile robots. Sensors (Switzerland) **20**(3), 1–29 (2020). https://doi.org/10.3390/s20030803

30. Janglová, D.: Neural networks in mobile robot motion. Int. J. Adv. Robot. Syst. **1**(1), 15–22 (2004). https://doi.org/10.5772/5615

31. Engedy, I., Horváth, G.: Artificial neural network based mobile robot navigation. In: WISP 2009 - 6th IEEE International Symposium Intelligening Signal Processing - Proceedings, pp. 241–246 (2009). https://doi.org/10.1109/wisp.2009.5286ing557

32. Qiao, J., Fan, R., Han, H., Ruan, X.: Q-learning based on dynamical structure neural network for robot navigation in unknown environment. In: Yu, W., He, H., Zhang, N. (eds.) ISNN 2009. LNCS, vol. 5553, pp. 188–196. Springer, Heidelberg (2009). https://doi.org/10.1007/978-3-642-01513-7_21

33. AbuBaker, A.: A novel mobile robot navigation system using neuro-fuzzy rule-based optimization technique. Res. J. Appl. Sci. Eng. Technol. **4**(15), 2577–2583 (2012)

34. Motlagh, O., Nakhaeinia, D., Tang, S.H., Karasfi, B., Khaksar, W.: Automatic navigation of mobile robots in unknown environments. Neural Comput. Appl. **24**(7–8), 1569–1581 (2014). https://doi.org/10.1007/s00521-013-1393-z

35. Chen, X., Li, Y.: Smooth formation navigation of multiple mobile robots for avoiding moving obstacles. Int. J. Control Autom. Syst. **4**(4), 466–479 (2006)

36. Caceres, C., Rosario, J.M., Amaya, D.: Approach of kinematic control for a nonholonomic wheeled robot using artificial neural networks and genetic algorithms. In: 2017 International Work Conference Bio-Inspired Intelligence Systems Biodiversity Conservation IWOBI 2017 - Proceedings (2017). https://doi.org/10.1109/iwobi.2017.7985533

37. Singh, M.K., Parhi, D.R.: Path optimisation of a mobile robot using an artificial neural network controller. Int. J. Syst. Sci. **42**(1), 107–120 (2011). https://doi.org/10.1080/002077209034 70155

38. Araújo, R.: Prune-able fuzzy ART neural architecture for robot map learning and navigation in dynamic environments. IEEE Trans. Neural Networks **17**(5), 1235–1249 (2006). https://doi.org/10.1109/TNN.2006.877534

39. Zhu, A., Yang, S.X.: An adaptive neuro-fuzzy controller for robot navigation. Recent Adv. Intell. Control Syst. 277–307 (2009). https://doi.org/10.1007/978-1-84882-548-2_12

40. Kim, C.J., Chwa, D.: Obstacle avoidance method for wheeled mobile robots using interval type-2 fuzzy neural network. IEEE Trans. Fuzzy Syst. **23**(3), 677–687 (2015). https://doi.org/10.1109/TFUZZ.2014.2321771

41. Algabri, M., Mathkour, H., Ramdane, H.: Mobile robot navigation and obstacle-avoidance using ANFIS in unknown environment. Int. J. Comput. Appl. **91**(14), 36–41 (2014). https://doi.org/10.5120/15952-5400

42. Godjevac, J., Steele, N.: Neuro-fuzzy control of a mobile robot. Neurocomputing **28**(1–3), 127–143 (1999). https://doi.org/10.1016/S0925-2312(98)00119-2

43. Pothal, J.K., Parhi, D.R.: Navigation of multiple mobile robots in a highly clutter terrains using adaptive neuro-fuzzy inference system. Rob. Auton. Syst. **72**, 48–58 (2015). https://doi.org/10.1016/j.robot.2015.04.007

44. Rao, A.M., Ramji, K., Sundara, B.S.K., Rao, S., Vasu, V., Puneeth, C.: Navigation of nonholonomic mobile robot using neuro-fuzzy logic with integrated safe boundary algorithm. Int. J. Autom. Comput. **14**(3), 285–294 (2017). https://doi.org/10.1007/s11633-016-1042-y

45. Singh, Y.V., Kumar, B., Chand, S., Sharma, D.: A hybrid approach for requirements prioritization using logarithmic fuzzy trapezoidal approach (LFTA) and artificial neural network (ANN). In: Singh, P.K., Paprzycki, M., Bhargava, B., Chhabra, J.K., Kaushal, N.C., Kumar, Y. (eds.) FTNCT 2018. CCIS, vol. 958, pp. 350–364. Springer, Singapore (2019). https://doi.org/10.1007/978-981-13-3804-5_26

46. Nayak, N., Nath, V., Singhal, N.: Futuristic Trends in Network and Communication Technologies, vol. 958 (2019)

Design of a Distributed Debit Management Network of Operating Wells of Deposits of the CMW Region

Ivan M. Pershin[1,2], Anatol V. Malkov[3], and Irina S. Pomelyayko[3(✉)]

[1] Department of Control Systems and Information Technologies, North Caucasus Federal University, ISTD, Pyatigorsk, Russian Federation
[2] Department of Automation and Control Processes, Saint Petersburg Electrotechnical University "LETI", Saint Petersburg, Russian Federation
[3] "Narzan-Hydroresources", Kislovodsk, Russian Federation

Abstract. The article considers a system for monitoring the state of hydrolytospheric processes in the region. The results of pilot filtration work (PFW) at the field under consideration are presented. Based on PFW, a methodology for determining the parameters of a link approximating the static coefficients of mutual influence of producing wells is shown. Using the obtained link, the procedure for determining the optimal number of producing wells located on a given size section is shown. Using the results of PFW, the parameters of the discrete mathematical model of the hydrolyte-sphere processes of the field were verified. The technique of designing a distributed network for controlling the flow rate of producing wells of a given field is shown. Using a verified mathematical model of the hydrolyte-sphere process, the operation of a closed control system was simulated.

Keywords: Control network · Distribution systems · Hydrolithospheric processes · Distributed regulator · Experimental filtration studies

1 Introduction

The region of Caucasian Mineral Waters (CMW) occupies a special place among the resort regions of Russia due to the variety of valuable mineral waters and healing mud, landscape and climatic conditions. The most important sources of mineral water known outside of Russia are the deposits of Kislovodsk (mineral water Narzan), Essentuki (mineral water Essentuki № 4, Essentuki № 17), Zheleznovodsk (mineral water Slavyanovskaya, Smirnovskaya)

The analysis over the past two decades allows us to conclude that:

- the volume of mineral water production more than doubled, which significantly changed the overall picture of the distribution of natural vertical hydraulic gradients in the upper part of the hydrolyte sphere. The result of such an impact - a decrease in the quality indicators of the groundwater mineral composition began to be observed at many deposits;

© Springer Nature Singapore Pte Ltd. 2021
P. K. Singh et al. (Eds.): FTNCT 2020, CCIS 1396, pp. 317–328, 2021.
https://doi.org/10.1007/978-981-16-1483-5_29

- there is a change in the natural vertical hydraulic gradients in the opposite direction, which is associated with the influx of ground and surface water polluted by municipal wastewater into the working aquifers.

The current state of research in this area is characterized by an increase in scale, and in many cases, studies need to be considered on a regional scale, since the hydrolyte sphere is a multicomponent system and in its structure has complex relationships.

The developed system and technology for the synthesis of distributed controllers and the modeling of hydrolytospheric processes, in their entirety, form a new methodological and experimental-design base for monitoring, managing and predicting the development of hydrolytospheric processes in the CMW.

The resulting system and technology can be used in other regions. The developed system (Fig. 1), containing effective modeling complexes, for the first time will allow solving a number of important problems related to the conservation, control and rational use of the unique hydromineral base of the CMW region.

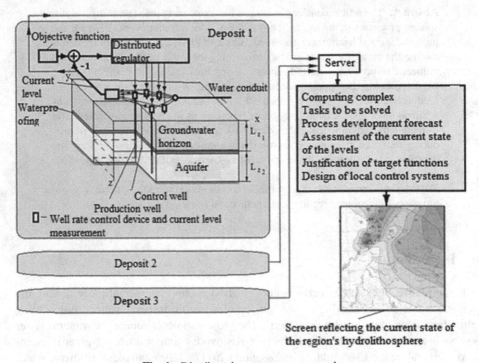

Fig. 1. Distributed management network.

2 Materials and Methods

Experimental filtration studies. Pilot and filtration studies were carried out on well cluster № 107 D (disturbing) and two observational: № 87 on the Lower Valanginian aquifer subhorizon, and № 107 on the upper aquifer subhorizon, 180 m from the disturbing well № 107-D (Fig. 2). The results of the PFW are presented in Table 1. The total duration of the PFW was 10 days. The flow rate of the well had a range of changes from 497 m³/day up to 527 m³/day. Interpretation of PFW data (see Table 1) was carried out using the graphoanalytical method. Parameters taken from the schedule of temporary tracking by well № 87, the following: $A_2 = 0.0024$; $C_2 = 0.00125$; $km_2 = 146.4$ m²/day; $a * 2 = 1.2 * 10^6$ m²/day; $\mu * = 0.00012$ of the input impact. The average flow rate of the disturbing well № 107D (the average flow rate is 508 m³/day) serves as the input impact on the considered object. The output function is to change the level of wells № 107D and № 87. The distance between the wells is $r_2 = 190$ m. Static transmission coefficients: K_1 = (lowering of the level in the well № 107 D/average flow rate) = $(12.5-1.11)/508 = 0.0224$; K_2 = (lowering the level in well № 87/average flow rate) = $(8.2-7)/508 = 0.00236$.

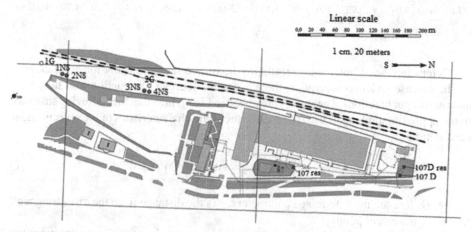

Fig. 2. The layout of the wells of the Northern flank of the Kislovodsk mineral water deposit

Table 1. Results of PFW for wells of the Northern flank of the Central section.

Date, hour, min	T, day	lgt, day	Well № 107 D			Well № 107			Well № 87		
			Q, m³/day	H, m	S, m	H, m	S, m	S/Q	H, m	S, m	S/Q
17.07.04 10:00	0		0	12,5	0	8,4	0,00		8,20	0,00	
17.07.04 10:20	0,01	−1,857	507	1,25	11,25						
17.07.04 10:40	0,03	−1,556	530	1,25	11,25	8,1	0,30	0,00057	7,73	0,47	0,00089
17.07.2004 11:00	0,04	−1,38	527	1,25	11,25						
17.07.04 11:20	0,06	−1,255	526	1,23	11,27	7,93	0,47	0,00089	7,60	0,60	0,00114

(continued)

Table 1. (*continued*)

Date, hour, min	T, day	lg$t$, day	Well № 107 D			Well № 107			Well № 87		
			Q, m³/day	H, m	S, m	H, m	S, m	S/Q	H, m	S, m	S/Q
17.07.04 11:40	0,07	−1,158	524	1,23	11,27						
26.07.04 9:00	8,96	0,952	500	1,08	11,42	7,4	1,00	0,00200	6,99	1,21	0,00242
26.07.04 12:45	9,11	0,96	499	1,1	11,4	7,4	1,00	0,00200	6,99	1,21	0,00242
26.07.04 17:00	9,29	0,968	499	1,1	11,4	7,4	1,00	0,00200	7,00	1,20	0,00240
27.07.04 8:28	9,94	0,997	500	1,11	11,39	7,35	1,05	0,00210	7,00	1,20	0,00240

Determination of link parameters approximating a static transmission coefficient.

In the case under consideration, there is one input effect (production well flow rate) and two output functions. The studies presented in [1–3] show that the following structure of the approximating link is used to describe the static characteristics of the objects under consideration:

$$W_a = \frac{K}{\beta} \cdot \exp(-\beta \cdot r); \beta = (D)^{1/2}, \tag{1}$$

where: D, K, a are the determined parameters, r is the distance from the disturbing well to the measurement point.

The considered procedure for determining the parameters of the approximating link is divided into the following stages:

Stage 1. Equating the static gains of the approximating link to the value of K_1 and K_2, we obtain:

$$\begin{cases} K_1 = \frac{K}{\beta} \cdot \exp(-\beta \cdot r_0) \\ K_2 = \frac{K}{\beta} \cdot \exp(-\beta \cdot r_2), \beta = (D)^{1/2} \end{cases} \tag{2}$$

Substituting the source data: $K_1 = 0.0224$; $K_2 = 0.00236$; $r_0 = 0.2$; $r_2 = 180$ and solving the system of Eq. (2), we obtain K = 0.00028106; D = 0.00015665. The static transmission coefficient of the object in question is written as:

$$W_a = \frac{0.00028106}{\beta} \cdot \exp(-\beta \cdot r), \beta = (0.00015665)^{1/2}, r_0 \le r. \tag{3}$$

Figure 3 shows a graph of the change in the static coefficient of transfer with r.

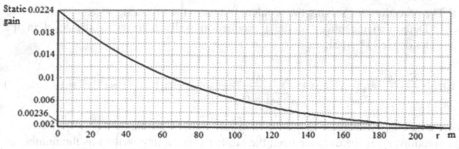

Fig. 3. Static gear ratio graph

Determination of the optimal number of producing wells.

The scheme of the considered field is shown in Fig. 4. The statement of the problem of optimizing the number of producing wells. For a field whose static transmission coefficient has the form (3), it is necessary to determine the number of producing wells (n) that provide the maximum profit for ten years of field operation. At the same time, we will assume: the extraction of hydromineral raw materials is carried out within 3650 days; $r_{0,i} = 0.2$ m; N-cost of 1 m^3 of hydromineral raw materials is 300/1000000 million rubles; C_p-costs for the arrangement and maintenance of one well for 10 years are 6 million rubles; subsoil use tax 7.5%; expenses for the maintenance of buildings and equipment and personnel for ten years of operation is 87 million rubles; the location of production wells is shown in Fig. 4 ($L_{sk} = 150$ m); the predetermined decrease in the level in the wells is 12 m.

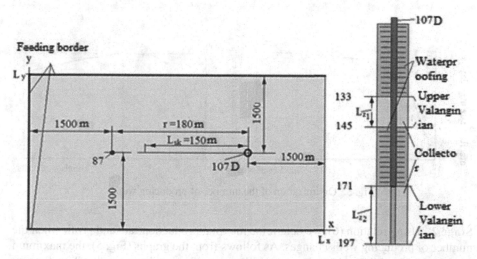

Fig. 4. Well layout

The procedure for solving the problem falls into the following stages:

1. Determine the effect of the j production well on lowering the level in the i-production well [1, 4, 5]:

$$\Delta H_i = \frac{K_i \cdot Q_i}{\beta} \cdot \exp(-\beta(r_{0,i})) + \sum_{j=1, j \neq 1}^{n} \frac{K_i \cdot Q_j}{\beta} \cdot \exp(-\beta(r_{i,j})), \beta = (G_1)^{1/2}, i = 1, \ldots n, \quad (4)$$

where: ΔH_i is the decrease in level in the i well under consideration ($i = 1 \ldots n$); $r_{0,j}$– given radius; $r_{i,j}$ is the distance from the i to the j interacting wells; n is the number of wells; Q_i is the flow rate of the i well; Q_j is the flow rate of the j well.

$$C_i = \frac{K_i}{\beta} \cdot \exp(-\beta \cdot (r_{0,i})), C_{i,j} = \frac{K_i}{\beta} \cdot \exp(-\beta \cdot (r_{i,j})), \beta = (G_1)^{1/2}, \quad (5)$$

Assuming (5) and transforming, we obtain the matrix equation for determining the production rates of production wells

$$\begin{bmatrix} Q_1 \\ Q_2 \\ \cdots \\ Q_n \end{bmatrix} = \begin{bmatrix} C_1, C_{1,2}, \ldots, C_{1,n} \\ C_{2,1}, C_2, \ldots, C_{2,n} \\ \cdots \\ C_{n,1}, C_{n,2}, \ldots, C_n \end{bmatrix}^{-1} \cdot \begin{bmatrix} \Delta H_1 \\ \Delta H_2 \\ \cdots \\ \Delta H_n \end{bmatrix} \quad (6)$$

The total flow rate (Q) can be determined from the ratio: $Q = \sum_{j=1}^{n} Q_j$.

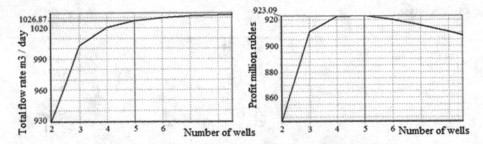

Fig. 5. Optimization of the number of producing wells

Stage 2. Using relation (6), we determine the total production rate and profit when the number of producing wells changes. As follows from the graphs (Fig. 5), the maximum profit (923.09 million rubles) is achieved by using five producing wells. The distance between producing wells is 37.5 m.

3 Results and Discussion

The mathematical model of the control object. The mathematical model of the hydrolytospheric processes of the field (Fig. 4) has the form [1, 6, 7]:

Upper Valanginian

$$\frac{\partial H_1(x,y,z,\tau)}{\partial \tau} = \frac{1}{\eta_1}\left(k_{1,x}\frac{\partial^2 H_1(x,y,z,\tau)}{\partial x^2} + k_{1,y}\frac{\partial^2 H_1(x,y,z,\tau)}{\partial y^2} + k_{1,z}\frac{\partial^2 H_1(x,y,z,\tau)}{\partial z_1^2}\right);$$

$$0 < x < L_x; 0 < y < L_y; 0 < z < L_{z_1}.$$

$$\frac{\partial H_2(x,y,z,\tau)}{\partial \tau} = \frac{1}{\eta_2}\left(k_{2,x}\frac{\partial^2 H_2(x,y,z,\tau)}{\partial x^2} + k_{2,y}\frac{\partial^2 H_2(x,y,z,\tau)}{\partial y^2} + k_{2,z}\frac{\partial^2 H_2(x,y,z,\tau)}{\partial z_2^2}\right)$$

$$+ V \cdot \delta(x_0, y_0); 0 < x < L_x; 0 < y < L_y; 0 < z < L_{z_2}$$

Lower Valanginian

where: H_ξ - head in the studied ξ aquifer ($\xi = 1,2$); $k_{\xi,x}$, $k_{\xi,y}$, $k_{\xi,z}$ - filtration coefficients according to the spatial coordinates of the ξ formation; η_ξ- elastic capacity of the ξ formation ($\xi = 1,2$); $V = Q \cdot K_f$ - the impact of the producing well on the head (Q-flow rate of the producing well, K_f-given coefficient); $\delta(x_0, y_0)$ is a function equal to unity if $x = x_0$, $y = y_0$ and equal to zero in other cases (in the well 107D under consideration, perfect water intake is performed); x, y, z - spatial coordinates; τ time.

The boundary conditions between the layers are set in the form:

$$H_1(x, y, L_{z_1}, \tau) = H_1(x, y, L_{z_1}, \tau) + b_1 \cdot (H_2(x, y, 0, \tau) - H_1(x, y, L_{z_1}, \tau)),$$

$$H_2(x, y, 0, \tau) = H_2(x, y, 0, \tau) - b_1 \cdot (H_2(x, y, 0, \tau) - H_1(x, y, L_{z_1}, \tau))$$

where b_1 is the overflow parameter.

The upper boundary of the upper layer: $\partial H_1(x, y, 0, \tau)/\partial z = 0$

Lower boundary of the lower layer: $\partial H_2(x, y, L_{z_2}, \tau)/\partial z = 0$

Side faces.

$$H_1(0, y, z, \tau) = H_{1,0}; H_2(0, y, z, \tau) = H_{2,0},$$

$$\partial H_1(L_x, y, z, \tau)/\partial x = 0; \partial H_2(L_x, y, z, \tau)/\partial x = 0.$$

When forming boundary conditions along the y coordinate, we assume that the thickness of the layers is such that disturbances from the intake wells do not affect the state of the formation at the boundary points:

$$H_\xi(x, 0, z, \tau) = H_\xi(x, L_y, z, \tau) = H_\xi(x, y, z, \tau), \xi = 1, 2.$$

where: $H_{1,0}$, $H_{2,0}$ - initial states of unperturbed groundwater and strata, which are given in the form:

$$H_{1,0}(x, 0, z, \tau) = 193 - 50 \cdot x/L_x, 0 < x < L_x, 0 < y < L_y, 0 < z < L_{z_1},$$

$$H_{2,0}(x, 0, z, \tau) = 193 - 50 \cdot x/L_x, 0 < x < L_x, 0 < y < L_y, 0 < z < L_{z_2}.$$

A feature of the field under consideration is the presence of an upper low-permeable layer (water resistance). Geometrical parameters of the field (see Fig. 4). $L_x = 3180$ m, $L_y = 3000$ m, $L_{z1} = 12$ m, $L_{z2} = 26$ m.

According to geological exploration data, the numerical values of the physical parameters used to model the control object were determined (see Table 2).

Table 2. Object parameter values.

Values of physical parameters of an object		Values of adjusted parameters of an object	
Upper layer	Lower layer	Upper layer	Lower layer
$k_{x1} = 148.4/86400$	$k_{x2} = 148.4/86400$	$k_{x1} = 148.4/86400$	$k_{x2} = 148.4/86400$
$k_{y1} = 24.64/86400$	$k_{y2} = 24.64/86400$	$k_{y1} = 14.64/86400$	$k_{y2} = 7.34/86400$
$k_{z1} = 14.64/86400$	$k_{z2} = 14.64/86400$	$k_{z1} = 14.64/86400$	$k_{z2} = 3.95/86400$
$\eta_1 = 0.00012$	$\eta_2 = 0.00012$	$\eta_1 = 0.000128$	$\eta_2 = 0.0008$
	$b_1 = 0.00128/86400$		$b_1 = 0.000012/86400$

Verification of the parameters of the mathematical model.

Distributed objects have the feature [1, 2, 4], the dynamic and static characteristics of a continuous model (described by partial differential equations) and a discrete model (described by discrete relationships) are significantly different. By verifying the discrete model, we will assume that the proximity of the static and dynamic characteristics obtained by the results of the PFW for the wells of the Northern flank of the Central section and the static and dynamic characteristics of the discrete model are achieved. The static characteristics obtained experimentally (PFW) are as follows: transmission coefficients $K_1 = 0.0224$; $K_2 = 0.00236$. As a result of experimental studies, it was found that the net retardation of disturbance from production well № 107 D to control well № 87 is 28 min. We will adjust the parameters of the discrete model to achieve the closeness of the static and dynamic characteristics obtained as a result of the PFW.

The adjusted object parameters are given in Table 2. The adjusted value of $K_f = 20.51747163$.

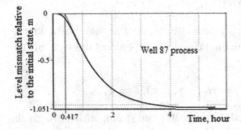 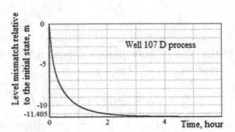

Fig. 6. Transients in the adjusted model

The transmission coefficients of the adjusted model (Fig. 6): $K_1 = 11.405/508 = 0.02245$; $K_2 = 1.051/508 = 0.002069$; the delay time of the disturbance from the production well 107D to the control well 87 is 0.417 h (25 min). The obtained parameter values are close to the values obtained as a result of the PFW.

Designing a distributed production flow control system for producing wells.

The design technique of a distributed control system for hydrolyte-sphere processes consists of the following steps [1]:

1. Selection of Spatial Modes

As is known [1], in determining the static and dynamic characteristics of a distributed object, spatial modes are used (eigenvectors are functions of the operator of the object). Field experiments show that at a distance of 150 m from the disturbing well (the static transmission coefficient is 0.00343, which is $0.00343/0.0224 = 0.15$ part of the static coefficient of the disturbing well.). Equating to zero the disturbance at a distance of 150 m from the disturbing well, we form the spatial modes of the input action in the form: $\sin(\psi_i \cdot x)$, $0 \le x \le L_m$, where $\psi_i = \pi \cdot i/L_m$, $L_m = 450$ m (see Fig. 7).

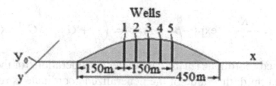

Fig. 7. Formation of input impact mode

2. Determination of the Static and Dynamic Characteristics of the Object

Figure 7 shows the formation of the first mode ($i = 1$) of the input action. The input action for the selected spatial mode (function (V) represents a discrete function along the x coordinate:

$$V_\mu(x_\mu, y_0, \tau) = -KQ \cdot \sin(\psi_i \cdot x) \cdot \delta(x_\mu, y_{0,}, \tau), \mu = 1, \ldots 5,$$

where: x_μ, y_0-coordinates of the producing wells; (the "−" sign indicates that hydro-mineral raw materials are being taken from the working well).

When modeling the hydrolithosphere process, it is necessary to take into account that the flow rate of each well is distributed over the entire thickness of the formation used (perfect water intake has been implemented). As the output functions, we choose the change in the level of the hydrolytosphere process in the zones of production wells at points $z = 0.5 * z_2$. Figure 8 shows graphs of the object's reactions to the first spatial and second modes, under static action ($Q = 100$ m^3/day, or 0.001157 m^3/s) and to the first mode under dynamic action ($Q = 100 * \sin(\omega * \tau)$).

$K_{m1} = 5355.1$, $K_{m2} = 2063.9$.

Determination of the static and dynamic characteristics of the object.

Figure 7 shows the formation of the first mode ($i = 1$) of the input action. The input for the selected spatial mode (function (V), represents a discrete function along the x coordinate.

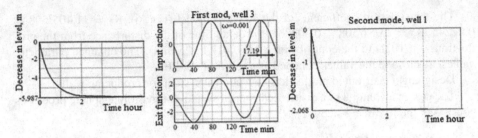

Fig. 8. Graph of level changes in the area of the third production well.

Period $T = 2 * \pi/\omega = 2 * \pi/0.001 = 6283.18$ s $= 104.72$ m. The phase shift of the output function relative to the input action $\Delta \varphi 1 = 2\pi * (-17.19)/104.72 = -1.0314$ rad.

3. Approximation of the Static and Dynamic Characteristics of the Object

To describe the dynamic characteristics of the objects under consideration, the following structure of approximating links can be used [1, 2]:

$$W_a(s, G) = \frac{K}{\beta + 1} \cdot \exp(-\beta \cdot \Delta r), \beta = \left(\frac{s}{a} + G\right)^{1/2}, G_1 \leq G \leq \infty. \tag{7}$$

where: G-generalized coordinate (in the case under consideration, for the selected spatial modes, the first and third, the value of the generalized coordinate is respectively equal to: $G_1 = (\pi * 1/L_m)^2$; $G_3 = (\pi * 3/L_m)^2$; Δr, K and a are the determined parameters.

Writing down (7), for $s = j\omega = 0$, for the selected spatial modes, we obtain

$$\begin{cases} K_{M1} = \frac{K}{\beta_1 + 1} \cdot \exp(-\beta_1 \cdot \Delta r) \\ K_{M2} = \frac{K}{\beta_2 + 1} \cdot \exp(-\beta_2 \cdot \Delta r), \end{cases} \beta_v = (G_v)^{1/2}, v = 1, 2.$$

Substituting the initial data (K_{m1}, K_{m2}, G_1, G_2) into the equation system and solving, we arrive at the following result: K $= 13895.2829$; $\Delta r = 135.582$; a $= 6.44169$.

Assuming $s = j\omega$ ($\omega = \omega_1$) in (7), we write the relation for determining the phase of the approximating link:

$$\Delta f_1 = -Im(\beta_1) \cdot \Delta x - \arctan (Im(\beta_1)) \big/ (Re(\beta_1) + 1), \beta_1 = (j\omega_1/a + G_1)^2$$

Setting in $\Delta f_1 = \Delta \varphi m_1 = -1.0314$, $\omega_1 = 0.001$ and solving by the numerical method, we get a $= 6.441693$.

The transfer function of the approximating link is written as:

$$W_a(s, G) = \frac{13895.5}{\beta + 1} \cdot \exp(-\beta \cdot 135.58); \beta = \left(\frac{s}{6.44} + G\right)^{1/2}, G_1 \leq G \leq \infty. \tag{8}$$

4. Synthesis of a Distributed Controller

Statement of the synthesis problem: for a control system for a distributed object, the transfer function of which is described in the form (8), synthesize a distributed controller, while the stability margins and the parameter Δ are subject to the following restrictions:

phase stability margin $\Delta\varphi \geq \pi/6$; stability margin modulo $\Delta L \geq 10$ dB; parameter Δ $= 1.7$.

The method for the synthesis of distributed controllers is described in a number of books and articles [1, 2, 4]. The transfer function of the most commonly used distributed controller is:

$$W(x,s) = E_1 \cdot \left[\frac{n_1 - 1}{n_1} - \frac{1}{n_1}\nabla^2 \right] + E_4 \cdot \left[\frac{n_4 - 1}{n_4} - \frac{1}{n_4}\nabla^2 \right] + E_2 \cdot \left[\frac{n_2 - 1}{n_2} - \frac{1}{n_2}\nabla^2 \right] \cdot s, \tag{9}$$

where E_i are the given numbers ($i = 1,2,4$); x - spatial coordinate; Laplacian; s is the Laplace operator; n_i - weight coefficients ($i = 1, 2, 4$), ($n_1 \geq 1$).

The synthesis technique is implemented in the software product of the Department of Control Systems and Engineering Technologies of the North Caucasus Federal University. As a result of the calculation, the following values of the parameters of the distributed controller were determined:

$$n_1 = 1.0, \ E_1 = 7.7568, \ n_4 = 1.0, \ E_4 = 0.011606, \ n_2 = \infty, \ E_2 = 0.14142.$$

Using a verified mathematical model of the hydrolithospheric process, the closed-loop control system was simulated. The synthesized distributed controller is written as:

$$W(x,s) = 7.7568 \cdot \left[-\nabla^2 \right] + 0.011606 \cdot \left[-\nabla^2 \right] \cdot \frac{1}{s} + 0.14142 \cdot s, X_{0,1} \leq x \leq X_{0,5}.$$

Figure 9 shows the graphs of the transient process in the first and third production wells. Similar plots were obtained for other wells.

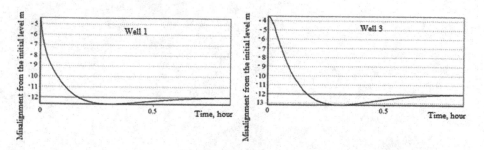

Fig. 9. Transient graphs.

4 Conclusions

1. The proposed structure of the approximating link allows to solve the problem of determining the interaction of wells distributed over the area of the field.
2. The procedure for determining the parameters of the approximating link does not require lengthy, expensive experimental filtration work.

3. Using the proposed structure, a distributed control network has been designed and it has been shown that it is quite effective to manage the operating modes of a set of interacting wells.

The considered distributed control network rather effectively controls the hydrolithospheric process in the area of the well cluster.

References

1. Malkov, A.V., Pershin, I.M., Pomelyayko, I.S.: Kislovodsk Deposit of Carbonic Mineral Waters: System Analysis, Diagnostics, Forecast, Management. Science, Moscow, p. 283 (2015)
2. Pershin, I.M., Malkov, A.V., Pomelyayko, I.S.: Designing a control system for underground water intakes. In: International Science and Technology Conference "Earth Science". IOP Conference Series: Earth and Environmental Science, vol. 272, p. 022026. IOP Publishing (2019). https://doi.org/10.1088/1755-1315/272/2/022026
3. Bogomyakov, G.P., Nudner, V.A.: Calculation of a rational system of deep groundwater intake. J. Explor. Protection Mineral Resour. 5, 15–21 (1964)
4. Malkov, A.V., Pershin, I.M., Pomelyayko, I.S.: 2015 Problems of ecological safety of the hydromineral base of the resort of Kislovodsk. In: National Scientific Forum "NARZAN-2015" "Actual Problems of the Hydrolithosphere (Diagnostics, Forecast, Control, Optimization and Automation", pp. 92–116 (2019)
5. Borevsky, B.V., Samsonov, B.G., Yazvin, L.S.: Methods for Determining the Parameters of Aqui-Fers Based on Pumping Data. Nedra, Moscow, p. 302 (1973)
6. Bochever, F.M.: Theory and Practical Methods of Hydrogeological Calculations of Operational Re-Serves of Groundwater. Nedra, Moscow, p. 325 (1968)
7. Bochever, F.M., Lapshin, N.N.: On the Issue of Hydrogeological Calculations of Wells in Layered Strata. VODGEO, Moscow, p. 145 (1968)

Analysis of Complex Natural Processes Activation with Catastrophic Consequences Using Bayesian Belief Network

Victoria N. Taran(✉) [iD]

V.I. Vernadsky Crimean Federal University, Simferopol, Russian Federation
victoriya_yalta@ukr.net

Abstract. The article presents an analysis of factors on which the activation of complex natural processes with catastrophic consequences depends. The model for forecasting catastrophic consequences of natural processes using the Bayesian belief network is proposed. The tops of the Bayesian network have been singled out, the expert estimation of possible values of indicators and training of the Bayesian network based on expert estimations has been carried out. The factor "Investments" was proposed as a managing influence on the network. Modeling and forecasting of possible development scenarios of complex natural processes and their catastrophic consequences were carried out. It is proposed to use Bayesian networks in building a decision support system for forecasting and assessment of risks of catastrophic consequences from damage caused by hazardous natural processes.

Keywords: Bayesian belief networks · Complex natural processes · Modeling of natural processes · Catastrophic consequences · Forecasting and prediction of activation of natural processes · Scenario analysis · Risk assessment · Decision support system

1 Introduction

At the beginning of the XXI century there is a sharp jump in the number of natural and man-made disasters. Particularly affected by natural phenomena are the coastal areas, where an increased level of urbanization is observed. The density of buildings, roads, and communications represents increased risks and is subject to destruction in the first place. Human activities are related to water resources (reservoirs, rivers, and seas), so special attention should be focused on coastal areas and especially the mountainous areas around them. Thus, there is a problem of assessing the risks of damage from natural and anthropogenic hazards, which can have a significant impact on economic activity.

The scientific study of natural phenomena and processes, as stated by the author [1] consists of creating a model of relationships and interrelationships that occur within these processes, and if the model is "good", it can help us understand, predict, or even control the behavior of a complex system that demonstrates this phenomenon.

P. K. Singh et al. (Eds.): FTNCT 2020, CCIS 1396, pp. 329–338, 2021.
https://doi.org/10.1007/978-981-16-1483-5_30

Thus, the reliability of the test results and the ability to predict trends [2] of activation and course of complex natural processes, as well as catastrophic consequences depending on changes in the external environment, i.e., endogenous and exogenous factors, directly depend on the effectiveness of the applied modeling methods and the corresponding numerical methods of data processing.

The decision-makers connected with the prevention of an increase in costs and damages of buildings and constructions, and also to avoid fatal cases at that, need suitable methods of risk assessment of dangerous events and natural processes [3].

Complex natural systems not only consist of a large number of components but also depend on their interaction with each other and with the environment, i.e. they react to the transfer of information, transmit and receive it both inside the system and in exchange with external sources. The informational exchange during a dynamic interaction is usually non-linear, while self-relationships are possible. In other words, the reaction to the influence is time delayed, i.e. there is a lag za-dependence or autocorrelation. In this case, the previous value of the external environment may activate the process or, conversely, contain it, the connection may be positive (intensifying the activation) and negative (deterring it). In such a system, information is transmitted only with the "neighbor", while the general state of the system may not change when some components are changed or affected. It means that each part of the system is not aware of the behavior of the system as a whole.

Natural systems are open complex systems due to their interaction with the external environment, which means that their state is not in equilibrium, although they aspire to it. The excitatory effects of external factors activate these processes, and human technogenic activity is mostly aimed at containing destructive natural processes, but sometimes it happens and vice versa. Undue human activity destroys sustainable natural ecosystems, which leads to irreparable consequences and disasters.

Thus, as a result of the destructive perturbation of the external environment, the author [4] identifies two main tasks in the analysis of complex natural phenomena: first, to detect the fact of perturbation and, perhaps, changes in the natural process; second, to determine the optimal (stable) in a certain sense, the organization of behavior of the natural system and possible managing (stabilizing) impacts and the adoption of appropriate decisions.

The complexity of natural systems is also due to the high level of uncertainty. It is sometimes difficult to identify the most significant factors if they have an accumulative effect, i.e. they change insignificantly, but having reached a certain value, they cause a sharp change and activation of the natural phenomenon, while the factor itself still changes insignificantly. Also, to observe and monitor a complex natural phenomenon requires reference points, special devices that can be successfully installed on uninhabited terrain (in the field, in the forest, on a slope, in the sea, etc.), and in a city where everything is built up and cast in concrete, it is very problematic.

Nevertheless, there is a wide range of observations, many parameters characterizing natural processes with possibly catastrophic consequences are recorded, but there is a question of processing these data, finding connections between them. Sometimes, the expert with great experience trusts his intuition and visual perception more, but it is not enough to make convincing forecasts and plan measures to prevent the destruction as a result of the activation of natural processes.

Complex natural processes have a long history, their past is the reason for their present state and behavior, so any analysis must be done over a long period, on large observation data, and use modern methods of analysis and simulation of complex systems.

Thus, the task is to combine the experience of professionals and mathematical methods of modeling, information computer technology to develop forecasts and make decisions on planning and implementation of measures aimed at counteracting the destruction due to natural disasters.

The use of Bayesian belief networks provides powerful tools for modeling complex stochastic processes, analyzing the structure and dependencies between components, using algorithms of numerical methods to analyze retrospective, current period, and predict the probability of activation of new destructive natural processes based on new and historical data.

The purpose of this article is to analyze factors and relationships for building the Bayesian Belief Network to model and predict the activation of complex natural phenomena and to make decisions about measures to prevent catastrophic destruction.

2 Bayesian Belief Networks as a Tool for Modeling Stochastic Processes

Bayesian networks are an effective tool for modeling stochastic processes occurring in time in various industries and spheres of activity [5]. They can be used to solve a wide range of tasks, including detection of anomalies, justification, diagnostics, time series forecasting, automatic understanding, and decision-making under conditions of uncertainty [6]. The Bayes Belief networks combine the processing of statistical data, time series, as well as interval estimates and expert evaluation for further analysis of the peculiarities of functioning and identification of causal relationships between the variables, forecasting of behavior and further development of the system, recognition of images and situations [7].

A model based on the Bayesian belief network allows combining both statistical data and expert judgment on the nature of behavior and relationships between elements [8]. In particular, the experts' knowledge and their assessments are used at various stages of model construction, as well as in selecting methods of model construction or its full description, including the model structure and parameters.

Bayesian belief networks can make a significant contribution to the study and modeling of complex systems of different natures through high transparency, the ability to combine empirical data with expert knowledge, and their apparent relevance to uncertainty [9].

At the present stage, Bayesian belief networks are used in information systems of analysis and represent a convenient probabilistic toolkit for a description of dynamics and statics of processes of different nature to analyze their functioning [7]. Formally, Bayesian networks are a pair: (G; P), where G = <X, E> - an acyclic directional graph on the finite set of X (vertexes), bound together by a set of oriented edges E, and P - a set of conditional probability distributions. Thus, Bayesian belief networks are a fairly accurate tool for describing very complex processes and events with uncertainties [10–13]. The Bayesian network theory is based on the Bayesian formula and the rule of constructing and calculating the network, which is a generalization of the rule of probability multiplication by calculating the joint probability distribution of random dependent events. Each vertex is a priori associated with numerical characteristics corresponding to the law of distribution of random variables [14].

The procedure for analysis of natural hazards carrying possible catastrophic destruction using Bayesian networks is as follows:

- identification of factors that have a direct impact on the activation of the natural process;
- identification of targets of the natural process, which have a destructive effect;
- assessment of the level of destruction, specification of qualitative and quantitative characteristics;
- identification of management impacts that can stabilize the natural phenomenon or reduce (minimize) the consequences of destruction;
- building the structure of the Bayes network, by distributing the identified factors and indicators by network levels and establishing dependencies between them;
- defining probability distributions for nodes (marginal distributions) and arcs (conditional distributions);
- calculation of a priori distribution of a target variable (e.g., damage from a natural hazard or possible timing of this phenomenon);
- compute a posteriori distributions for specific situations or scenarios by replacing a priori distributions of some variables with specific values observed in the situation.

The explicit consideration of uncertainties in Bayesian belief networks allows for the preparation of informed risk assessments for decision-makers [3].

3 Definition of the Bayesian Network Structure for the Assessment of Damage Risks from Natural Phenomena

To design a system for modeling the response of complex natural ecological systems to various changes and impacts we will build the Bayes network [15–19]. To determine the structure of the network, we identify the factors that primarily affect the activation of a natural process or phenomenon that can produce destructive actions.

First, we should take into account solar activity. It has long been established that the 11-year cycle of solar activity directly affects quantitative indicators in all spheres, namely, the number of natural disasters, social unrest, and the intensification of hostilities, fertility, and mortality, etc.

Secondly, it is necessary to analyze the process of the phenomenon itself, its speed and direction, to take into account whether there was an increase or decrease inactivation during the previous observed period.

Third, we will consider the factor that directly affects the activation of a complex natural phenomenon. For example, precipitation, seismic activity, sharp temperature changes, geological or geomorphological structure, etc. Professional experts determine these factors depending on the process or phenomenon for which the Bayesian network model will be built.

The next step is to consider the resulting indicators, such as the activation of a natural phenomenon, the level of destruction and disasters, the time left before the activation of the process. The latter indicator plays an important role as it allows us to take into account how much time is available for decision making and implementation of activities aimed at preventing or minimizing catastrophic consequences.

The study of natural and man-made disasters reveals the prospect of their formal description using three main variables: time, place, and power of a disaster or a stymie-disaster [20].

In addition to the above-mentioned indicators of activation of complex natural phenomena or processes, we propose to take into account a generalized indicator - the amount of money spent on preventive measures and rehabilitation after destruction.

All we have to offer is a controlling factor, which helps to counteract the activation of natural processes or minimize the level of destruction. The factor Investment in measures for the prevention of negative consequences to some extent satisfies the property of management of natural processes.

Each of the considered values takes "Yes" or "No", and the "Destruction Level" value will take "Low", "Medium" and "Catastrophic" values.

The graph of the Bayes belief network is constructed as a "tree" (see Fig. 1). The variables discussed above take on the values: *Yes* or *No*, and the variable *"Damage_Level"* takes on the values: *Min, Overage,* and *Catastrophic (Max).* We place the input factors *"Solar_Activity", "Past_Period_Activation", "Significant factor"* and the controlling *"Investments"* on the upper level, the three resulting indicators *"Activation_Risk",* and under *"Damage_Level", "Time_Risk"* on the next level, and the generalizing indicator *"Total_Costs"* on the lower level.

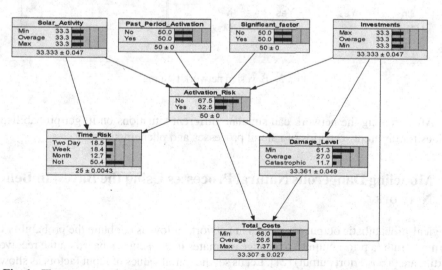

Fig. 1. The structure of the Bayesian network for modeling natural hazards and processes

The Bayesian network training is carried out by filling in tables of conditional probabilities for variables of the middle and lower levels and unconditional probabilities for input factors lying at the upper level (based on observation results). The tables are filled in with the help of expert assessments given by experts [12]. Modeling, construction, and training of a Bayesian network are carried out in the shareware program Netica. The training of the Bayesian belief network is shown in Fig. 2.

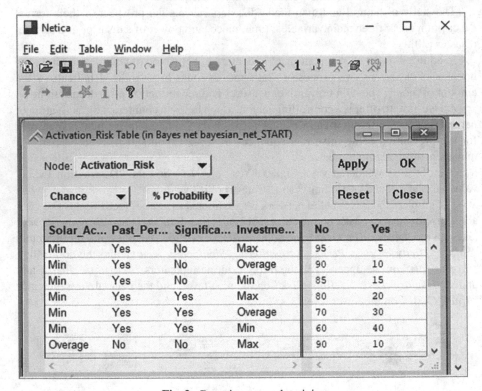

Fig. 2. Bayesian network training

After training the network can simulate different situations on it, get probabilistic values for different scenarios of natural processes and phenomena.

4 Modeling Dangerous Natural Processes Using the Bayesian Belief Network

Logical-probabilistic output operations in networks allow us to obtain the probability of formula truth (a priori output), to change estimates in the network based on the received certificate (a posteriori output) [21]. Let us set the initial values of input factors as shown in Fig. 3.

We see an encouraging picture with unfavorable values of factors. The activation of natural processes will occur with a probability of 75%, but the level of destruction will reach a catastrophic value with a probability of 7.75% (and the minimum - 60%). While the Total Costs will reach the maximum value with a probability of 6%, and the minimum value - 66% (at the expense of funds previously invested in preventive measures).

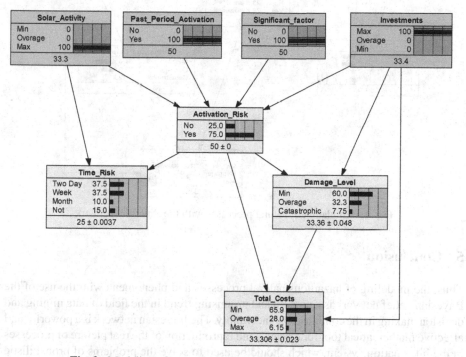

Fig. 3. Modeling of natural processes using the Bayesian network

Bayesian networks also allow modeling the situation from bottom to top, when you set the values of the resulting indicators and determine what the input factors should be to get the desired value for the result. For example, let's calculate what probabilities should be followed so that the Total Cost takes the minimum value (Fig. 4).

The result of the simulation shows that the distribution of the Investments is as follows: Max - 44%, Average - 34%, and Minimum - 22%, we get that the minimum level of costs is achieved, with the activation of natural processes about 76%, but no damage or they are minimal with a probability of 55% and will occur either within a week or the next two days - 38% each.

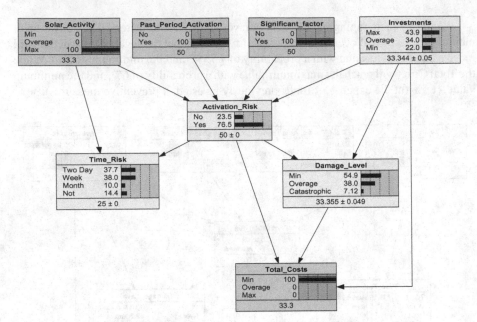

Fig. 4. Simulation of natural processes with the Bayesian network

5   Conclusion

Thus, the modeling of hazardous natural processes and phenomena with the use of the Bayesian belief network is a modern and promising trend in the field of data mining and decision making in the conditions of uncertainty. The Bayesian network is a powerful and effective mathematical tool for research and reproduction of the real picture of processes in the information system, which should be used to solve the problems of probabilistic forecasting and risk assessment [8].

The effectiveness of applied modeling methods and corresponding numerical methods of data processing directly depends on the reliability of test results and the ability to predict trends in the activation of hazardous natural processes and phenomena by changes in the environment. Bayesian networks provide rather powerful functional capabilities for modeling the structure of stochastic processes and algorithms of numerical methods of analysis of retrospective, current period, and forecasting of probabilities [2] of scenarios of natural processes, subsequent destructions, and the level of costs for the reconstruction of objects and territories.

Stochastic graphical models have long been used for the analysis of complex systems in various areas of research, for example, a typical structure of an auto-compensation system [22]; the synchronization process is analyzed, which consists of detecting a time interval with an optical pulse [23]; an analytical expression for the correct detection probability calculation of the photon impulse receipt in the algorithm proposed for the sync initialization of the QKDS [24].

The proposed Bayesian belief network model is interesting for modeling and forecasting the activation of complex natural systems with catastrophic consequences and the level of costs for the reconstruction of objects and territories.

References

1. Cilliers, P., et al.: Complexity, modeling, and natural resource management. Ecol. Soc. **18**(3) (2013). https://doi.org/10.5751/ES-05382-180301
2. Azarnova, T.V., Asnina, N.G., Proskurin, D.K., Polukhin, P.V.: Bayesian network structure formation of information systems reliability testing process. Bull. Voronezh State Tech. Univ. **13**(6), 45–51 (2017)
3. Kulygin, V.V.: Joint use of Bayesian networks and GIS for assessing the risks of storm races in delta R. Don. Bull. SGUGiT **23**(2), 92–107 (2018)
4. Petrenko, S.A., Vorobieva, D.E.: A method of ensuring cyber resilience of digital platforms based on the theory of catastrophes. In: IEEE: International Conference on Soft Computing and Measurements, vol. 1, pp. 148–152 (2019)
5. Polukhin, P.V.: Tools for improving the efficiency of numerical algorithms for learning the structure of dynamic Bayesian networks. Voronezh State Univ. Bull. Ser. Syst. Anal. Inf. Technol. **4**, 132–140 (2019)
6. Suvorova, A.V., Tulupiev, A.L.: Synthesis of Bayesian trust network structures for assessing the characteristics of risky behavior. Inf. Control Syst. **1**, 116–122 (2019). https://doi.org/10.15217/issnl684-8853.2018.1.116
7. Trukhan, S.V., Bidyuk, P.I.: Application of Bayesian networks to the construction of actuarial process risk assessment models. ScienceRise **8** (2(25)), 6–14 (2016) https://doi.org/10.15587/2313-8416.2016.74962
8. Suvorova, A.V.: Models for respondents behavior rate estimate: bayesian network structure synthesis. In: 2017: Proceedings of 2017 XX IEEE International Conference on Soft Computing and Measurements (SCM), pp. 87–89 (2017). https://doi.org/10.1109/SCM.2017.7970503
9. Skvortsov, Yu.S.: Development of an information subsystem to support decision-making based on a Bayesian network for an agro-industrial enterprise. Modeling Optim. Inf. Technol. Sci. J. **4**(19) (2017). https://moit.vivt.ru/
10. Taran, V.N.: Modeling of natural catastrophic processes of the southern coast of crimea with the help of the Bayes network. Auditorium **3**(11), 47–54 (2016)
11. Taran, V.N.: Bayesian networks for modeling complex systems. In: 2017 IEEE II International Conference on Control in Technical Systems (CTS), pp. 240–243 (2017). https://doi.org/10.1109/CTSYS.2017.8109535
12. Taran, V.N.: Modeling complex (hazardous) natural processes using the Bayesian trust network. Caspian J. Manag. High Technol. **2**(46), 90–100 (2019). https://doi.org/10.21672/2074-1707.2019.46.2.090-100
13. Terentyev, A.N., Korshevnyuk, L.A., Bidyuk, P.I.: Bayesian network as instrument of intelligent data analysis. J. Autom. Inf. Sci. **39**(8), 28–38 (2007). https://doi.org/10.1615/JAutomatInfScien.v39.i8.40
14. Skvortsov, Yu.S.: Development of an information subsystem of decision support based on a Bayesian network for an agro-industrial enterprise. Modeling Optim. Inf. Technol. Sci. J. **4**(19) (2017). https://moit.vivt.ru/
15. Maiyar, L.M., Tiwari, M.K., Cho, K., Kiritsis, D., Thoben, K.-D.: Optimising online review inspired product attribute classification using the self-learning particle swarm-based bayesian learning approach. Int. J. Prod. Res. **57**(10), 3099–3120 (2019). https://doi.org/10.1080/00207543.2018.1535724

16. Tang, J., Li, C., Zeng, L., Zhang, C., Ran, H., Zhou, Z.: How to optimize ecosystem services based on a Bayesian model: a case study of Jinghe river basin. Sustainability **11**(15), 4149 (2019)
17. Lehikoinen, A.J., et al.: Evaluating complex relationships between ecological indicators and environmental factors in the baltic sea: a machine learning approach. Ecol. Indicators **101**, 117–125 (2019). https://doi.org/10.1016/j.ecolind.2018.12.053
18. Zolotin, A.A., Tulupyev, A.L.: Matrix-vector algorithms for global a posteriori output in algebraic Bayesian networks. In: 2017 IEEE Proceedings of the XXI International Conference on Soft Computing and Measurements SCM 2018, pp. 45–48 (2018). https://doi.org/10.1109/SCM.2017.7970483
19. Marcot, B.G., Penman, T.D.: Advances in Bayesian network modeling: integration of modeling technologies. Environ. Model. Softw. **111**, 386–393 (2019). https://doi.org/10.1016/j.envsoft.2018.09.016
20. Akimov, V.A., Didenko, S.L.: Algebraic foundations of the elementary theory of catastrophes for the study of emergency situations. Civ. Secur. Technol. **16**(4(62)), 4–8 (2019)
21. Kharitonov, N.A., Tulupyev, A.L.: Algebraic Bayesian networks: isolated fusion of fragments of knowledge in conditions of information scarcity. Sci. Tech. Bull. Inf. Technol. Mech. Optics **19**(4), 641–649 (2019). https://doi.org/10.17586/2226-1494-2019-19-4-641-649
22. Pljonkin, A.P.: Vulnerability of the synchronization process in the quantum key distribution system. Int. J. Cloud Appl. Comput. **9**(1) (2019). https://doi.org/10.4018/IJCAC.2019010104
23. Pljonkin, A., Singh, P.K.: The review of the commercial quantum key distribution system. In: 2018 Fifth International Conference on Parallel, Distributed and Grid Computing. IEEE (2018). https://doi.org/10.1109/PDGC.2018.8745822
24. Pljonkin, A., Rumyantsev, K.: Single-photon synchronization mode of quantum key distribution system. In: International Conference on Computational Techniques in Information and Communication Technologies, pp. 531–534 (2019). https://doi.org/10.1109/ICCTICT.2016.7514637

Author Index

Printed in the United States
by Baker & Taylor Publisher Services

Printed in the United States
by Baker & Taylor Publisher Services